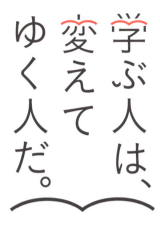

学ぶ人は、
変えて
ゆく人だ。

目の前にある問題はもちろん、
人生の問いや、
社会の課題を自ら見つけ、
挑み続けるために、人は学ぶ。
「学び」で、
少しずつ世界は変えてゆける。
いつでも、どこでも、誰でも、
学ぶことができる世の中へ。

旺文社

JN249257

2023年度版

※ 英検®には複数の方式があります（p.11参照）。本書に収録されている問題は、「従来型」の過去問のうち、公益財団法人 日本英語検定協会から提供を受けたもののみです。準会場・海外受験などの問題とは一致しない場合があります。英検S-CBTの過去問は公表されていませんが、問題形式・内容は従来型と変わりませんので、受験準備のためには本書収録の過去問がご利用いただけます。

※ このコンテンツは、公益財団法人 日本英語検定協会の承認や推奨、その他の検討を受けたものではありません。

英検®は、公益財団法人 日本英語検定協会の登録商標です。　旺文社

2022年度 第2回
二次試験・A日程
(2022.11.6 実施)

問題カード

この問題カードは切り取って、本番の面接の練習用にしてください。質問は本文p.41にありますので、参考にしてください。

You have **one minute** to prepare.

This is a story about a couple that wanted to save money.

You have **two minutes** to narrate the story.

Your story should begin with the following sentence:
One day, a woman was talking with her husband.

2022年度 第2回
二次試験・C日程
(2022.11.23 実施)

問題カード

この問題カードは切り取って、本番の面接の練習用にしてください。
質問は本文p.43にありますので、参考にしてください。

You have **one minute** to prepare.

This is a story about a couple who lived near the ocean.

You have **two minutes** to narrate the story.

Your story should begin with the following sentence:
One day, a couple was taking a walk by the beach.

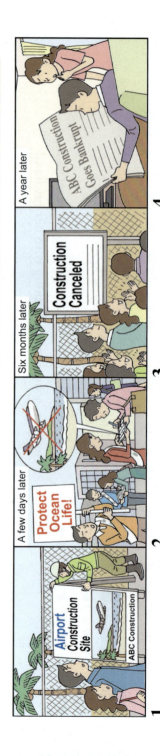

2022年度 第1回 二次試験・A日程
(2022.7.3 実施)

問題カード

この問題カードは切り取って、本番の面接の練習用にしてください。質問は本文p.69にありますので、参考にしてください。

You have **one minute** to prepare.

This is a story about a mayor who wanted to help her town.

You have **two minutes** to narrate the story.

Your story should begin with the following sentence:
One day, a mayor was having a meeting.

2021年度 第3回
二次試験・A日程
(2022.2.20 実施)

問題カード

この問題カードは切り取って、本番の面接の練習用にしてください。質問は本文p.97にありますので、参考にしてください。

You have **one minute** to prepare.

This is a story about a couple that wanted to be involved with their community.

You have **two minutes** to narrate the story.

Your story should begin with the following sentence:
One day, a husband and wife were going on a walk together.

2021年度 第3回
二次試験・C日程
(2022.3.6 実施)

問題カード

この問題カードは切り取って、本番の面接の練習用にしてください。質問は本文p.99にありますので、参考にしてください。

You have **one minute** to prepare.

This is a story about a woman who wanted to go on a trip.

You have **two minutes** to narrate the story.

Your story should begin with the following sentence:
One day, a woman was talking with her friend.

2022年度第2回　英検準1級　解答用紙

[注意事項]
① 解答にはHBの黒鉛筆（シャープペンシルも可）を使用し、解答を訂正する場合には消しゴムで完全に消してください。
② 解答用紙は絶対に汚したり折り曲げたり、所定以外のところへの記入はしないでください。
③ マーク例

良い例	悪い例
●	◐ ✗ ◖

 これ以下の濃さのマークは読めません。

筆記解答欄 1

問題番号	1	2	3	4
(1)	①	②	③	④
(2)	①	②	③	④
(3)	①	②	③	④
(4)	①	②	③	④
(5)	①	②	③	④
(6)	①	②	③	④
(7)	①	②	③	④
(8)	①	②	③	④
(9)	①	②	③	④
(10)	①	②	③	④
(11)	①	②	③	④
(12)	①	②	③	④
(13)	①	②	③	④
(14)	①	②	③	④
(15)	①	②	③	④
(16)	①	②	③	④
(17)	①	②	③	④
(18)	①	②	③	④
(19)	①	②	③	④
(20)	①	②	③	④
(21)	①	②	③	④
(22)	①	②	③	④
(23)	①	②	③	④
(24)	①	②	③	④
(25)	①	②	③	④

筆記解答欄 2

問題番号	1	2	3	4
(26)	①	②	③	④
(27)	①	②	③	④
(28)	①	②	③	④
(29)	①	②	③	④
(30)	①	②	③	④
(31)	①	②	③	④

筆記解答欄 3

問題番号	1	2	3	4
(32)	①	②	③	④
(33)	①	②	③	④
(34)	①	②	③	④
(35)	①	②	③	④
(36)	①	②	③	④
(37)	①	②	③	④
(38)	①	②	③	④
(39)	①	②	③	④
(40)	①	②	③	④
(41)	①	②	③	④

※筆記4の解答欄はこの裏にあります。

リスニング解答欄

	問題番号	1	2	3	4
	No.1	①	②	③	④
	No.2	①	②	③	④
	No.3	①	②	③	④
	No.4	①	②	③	④
	No.5	①	②	③	④
Part 1	No.6	①	②	③	④
	No.7	①	②	③	④
	No.8	①	②	③	④
	No.9	①	②	③	④
	No.10	①	②	③	④
	No.11	①	②	③	④
	No.12	①	②	③	④
A	No.13	①	②	③	④
	No.14	①	②	③	④
B	No.15	①	②	③	④
	No.16	①	②	③	④
C	No.17	①	②	③	④
Part 2	No.18	①	②	③	④
D	No.19	①	②	③	④
	No.20	①	②	③	④
E	No.21	①	②	③	④
	No.22	①	②	③	④
F	No.23	①	②	③	④
	No.24	①	②	③	④
G	No.25	①	②	③	④
H	No.26	①	②	③	④
Part 3 I	No.27	①	②	③	④
J	No.28	①	②	③	④
K	No.29	①	②	③	④

2022年度第2回　Web特典「自動採点サービス」対応 オンラインマークシート

※検定の回によって2次元コードが違います。
※筆記1〜3、リスニングの採点ができます。
※PCからも利用できます（本書 p.8 参照）。

※実際の解答用紙に似せていますが、デザイン・サイズは異なります。

・指示事項を守り、文字は、はっきり分かりやすく書いてください。
・太枠に囲まれた部分のみが採点の対象です。

4 English Composition

Write your English Composition in the space below.

2022年度第1回　英検準1級　解答用紙

【注意事項】
① 解答にはHBの黒鉛筆（シャープペンシルも可）を使用し、解答を訂正する場合には消しゴムで完全に消してください。
② 解答用紙は絶対に汚したり折り曲げたり、所定以外のところへの記入はしないでください。

③ マーク例

良い例	悪い例
●	◐ ✗ ◖

これ以下の濃さのマークは読めません。

筆記解答欄

問題番号	1	2	3	4
(1)	①	②	③	④
(2)	①	②	③	④
(3)	①	②	③	④
(4)	①	②	③	④
(5)	①	②	③	④
(6)	①	②	③	④
(7)	①	②	③	④
(8)	①	②	③	④
(9)	①	②	③	④
(10)	①	②	③	④
(11)	①	②	③	④
(12)	①	②	③	④
(13)	①	②	③	④
(14)	①	②	③	④
(15)	①	②	③	④
(16)	①	②	③	④
(17)	①	②	③	④
(18)	①	②	③	④
(19)	①	②	③	④
(20)	①	②	③	④
(21)	①	②	③	④
(22)	①	②	③	④
(23)	①	②	③	④
(24)	①	②	③	④
(25)	①	②	③	④

(1欄)

筆記解答欄

問題番号	1	2	3	4
(26)	①	②	③	④
(27)	①	②	③	④
(28)	①	②	③	④
(29)	①	②	③	④
(30)	①	②	③	④
(31)	①	②	③	④

(2欄)

筆記解答欄

問題番号	1	2	3	4
(32)	①	②	③	④
(33)	①	②	③	④
(34)	①	②	③	④
(35)	①	②	③	④
(36)	①	②	③	④
(37)	①	②	③	④
(38)	①	②	③	④
(39)	①	②	③	④
(40)	①	②	③	④
(41)	①	②	③	④

(3欄)

※筆記4の解答欄はこの裏にあります。

リスニング解答欄

問題番号	1	2	3	4
Part 1 No.1	①	②	③	④
No.2	①	②	③	④
No.3	①	②	③	④
No.4	①	②	③	④
No.5	①	②	③	④
No.6	①	②	③	④
No.7	①	②	③	④
No.8	①	②	③	④
No.9	①	②	③	④
No.10	①	②	③	④
No.11	①	②	③	④
No.12	①	②	③	④
Part 2 A No.13	①	②	③	④
No.14	①	②	③	④
B No.15	①	②	③	④
No.16	①	②	③	④
C No.17	①	②	③	④
No.18	①	②	③	④
D No.19	①	②	③	④
No.20	①	②	③	④
E No.21	①	②	③	④
No.22	①	②	③	④
F No.23	①	②	③	④
No.24	①	②	③	④
Part 3 G No.25	①	②	③	④
H No.26	①	②	③	④
I No.27	①	②	③	④
J No.28	①	②	③	④
K No.29	①	②	③	④

2022年度第1回
Web特典「自動採点サービス」対応
オンラインマークシート

※検定の回によって2次元コードが違います。
※筆記1〜3、リスニングの採点ができます。
※PCからも利用できます（本書 p.8 参照）。

※実際の解答用紙に似せていますが、デザイン・サイズは異なります。

切り取り線

・指示事項を守り、文字は、はっきり分かりやすく書いてください。
・太枠に囲まれた部分のみが採点の対象です。

4 English Composition

Write your English Composition in the space below.

2021年度第3回　英検準1級　解答用紙

【注意事項】
① 解答にはHBの黒鉛筆（シャープペンシルも可）を使用し、解答を訂正する場合には消しゴムで完全に消してください。
② 解答用紙は絶対に汚したり折り曲げたり、所定以外のところへの記入はしないでください。
③ マーク例

良い例	悪い例
●	

これ以下の濃さのマークは読めません。

筆記解答欄

問題番号	1	2	3	4
(1)	①	②	③	④
(2)	①	②	③	④
(3)	①	②	③	④
(4)	①	②	③	④
(5)	①	②	③	④
(6)	①	②	③	④
(7)	①	②	③	④
(8)	①	②	③	④
(9)	①	②	③	④
(10)	①	②	③	④
(11)	①	②	③	④
(12)	①	②	③	④
(13)	①	②	③	④
(14)	①	②	③	④
(15)	①	②	③	④
(16)	①	②	③	④
(17)	①	②	③	④
(18)	①	②	③	④
(19)	①	②	③	④
(20)	①	②	③	④
(21)	①	②	③	④
(22)	①	②	③	④
(23)	①	②	③	④
(24)	①	②	③	④
(25)	①	②	③	④

（1）

筆記解答欄

問題番号	1	2	3	4
(26)	①	②	③	④
(27)	①	②	③	④
(28)	①	②	③	④
(29)	①	②	③	④
(30)	①	②	③	④
(31)	①	②	③	④

（2）

筆記解答欄

問題番号	1	2	3	4
(32)	①	②	③	④
(33)	①	②	③	④
(34)	①	②	③	④
(35)	①	②	③	④
(36)	①	②	③	④
(37)	①	②	③	④
(38)	①	②	③	④
(39)	①	②	③	④
(40)	①	②	③	④
(41)	①	②	③	④

（3）

※筆記4の解答欄はこの裏にあります。

リスニング解答欄

問題番号	1	2	3	4
Part 1 No.1	①	②	③	④
No.2	①	②	③	④
No.3	①	②	③	④
No.4	①	②	③	④
No.5	①	②	③	④
No.6	①	②	③	④
No.7	①	②	③	④
No.8	①	②	③	④
No.9	①	②	③	④
No.10	①	②	③	④
No.11	①	②	③	④
No.12	①	②	③	④
Part 2 A No.13	①	②	③	④
No.14	①	②	③	④
B No.15	①	②	③	④
No.16	①	②	③	④
C No.17	①	②	③	④
No.18	①	②	③	④
D No.19	①	②	③	④
No.20	①	②	③	④
E No.21	①	②	③	④
No.22	①	②	③	④
F No.23	①	②	③	④
No.24	①	②	③	④
Part 3 G No.25	①	②	③	④
H No.26	①	②	③	④
I No.27	①	②	③	④
J No.28	①	②	③	④
K No.29	①	②	③	④

2021年度第3回
Web特典「自動採点サービス」対応
オンラインマークシート

※検定の回によって2次元コードが違います。
※筆記1～3，リスニングの採点ができます。
※PCからも利用できます（本書 p.8 参照）。

※実際の解答用紙に似せていますが、デザイン・サイズは異なります。

切り取り線

・指示事項を守り、文字は、はっきり分かりやすく書いてください。
・太枠に囲まれた部分のみが採点の対象です。

4 English Composition

Write your English Composition in the space below.

2021年度第2回　英検準1級　解答用紙

[注意事項]
① 解答にはHBの黒鉛筆(シャープペンシルも可)を使用し、解答を訂正する場合には消しゴムで完全に消してください。
② 解答用紙は絶対に汚したり折り曲げたり、所定以外のところへの記入はしないでください。
③ マーク例

良い例	悪い例
●	◯ ✕ ◉

 これ以下の濃さのマークは読めません。

筆記解答欄 1

問題番号	1	2	3	4
(1)	①	②	③	④
(2)	①	②	③	④
(3)	①	②	③	④
(4)	①	②	③	④
(5)	①	②	③	④
(6)	①	②	③	④
(7)	①	②	③	④
(8)	①	②	③	④
(9)	①	②	③	④
(10)	①	②	③	④
(11)	①	②	③	④
(12)	①	②	③	④
(13)	①	②	③	④
(14)	①	②	③	④
(15)	①	②	③	④
(16)	①	②	③	④
(17)	①	②	③	④
(18)	①	②	③	④
(19)	①	②	③	④
(20)	①	②	③	④
(21)	①	②	③	④
(22)	①	②	③	④
(23)	①	②	③	④
(24)	①	②	③	④
(25)	①	②	③	④

筆記解答欄 2

問題番号	1	2	3	4
(26)	①	②	③	④
(27)	①	②	③	④
(28)	①	②	③	④
(29)	①	②	③	④
(30)	①	②	③	④
(31)	①	②	③	④

筆記解答欄 3

問題番号	1	2	3	4
(32)	①	②	③	④
(33)	①	②	③	④
(34)	①	②	③	④
(35)	①	②	③	④
(36)	①	②	③	④
(37)	①	②	③	④
(38)	①	②	③	④
(39)	①	②	③	④
(40)	①	②	③	④
(41)	①	②	③	④

※筆記4の解答欄はこの裏にあります。

リスニング解答欄

問題番号	1	2	3	4
Part 1 No.1	①	②	③	④
No.2	①	②	③	④
No.3	①	②	③	④
No.4	①	②	③	④
No.5	①	②	③	④
No.6	①	②	③	④
No.7	①	②	③	④
No.8	①	②	③	④
No.9	①	②	③	④
No.10	①	②	③	④
No.11	①	②	③	④
No.12	①	②	③	④
Part 2 A No.13	①	②	③	④
No.14	①	②	③	④
B No.15	①	②	③	④
No.16	①	②	③	④
C No.17	①	②	③	④
No.18	①	②	③	④
D No.19	①	②	③	④
No.20	①	②	③	④
E No.21	①	②	③	④
No.22	①	②	③	④
F No.23	①	②	③	④
No.24	①	②	③	④
Part 3 G No.25	①	②	③	④
H No.26	①	②	③	④
I No.27	①	②	③	④
J No.28	①	②	③	④
K No.29	①	②	③	④

2021年度第2回 Web特典「自動採点サービス」対応 オンラインマークシート
※検定の回によって2次元コードが違います。
※筆記1〜3、リスニングの採点ができます。
※PCからも利用できます(本書 p.8 参照)。

※実際の解答用紙に似せていますが、デザイン・サイズは異なります。

・指示事項を守り、文字は、はっきり分かりやすく書いてください。
・太枠に囲まれた部分のみが採点の対象です。

4 English Composition

Write your English Composition in the space below.

2021年度第1回　英検準1級　解答用紙

【注意事項】
① 解答にはHBの黒鉛筆（シャープペンシルも可）を使用し、解答を訂正する場合には消しゴムで完全に消してください。
② 解答用紙は絶対に汚したり折り曲げたり、所定以外のところへの記入はしないでください。

③ マーク例

良い例	悪い例
●	◐ ✗ ◓

これ以下の濃さのマークは読めません。

筆記解答欄

問題番号	1	2	3	4
(1)	①	②	③	④
(2)	①	②	③	④
(3)	①	②	③	④
(4)	①	②	③	④
(5)	①	②	③	④
(6)	①	②	③	④
(7)	①	②	③	④
(8)	①	②	③	④
(9)	①	②	③	④
(10)	①	②	③	④
(11)	①	②	③	④
(12)	①	②	③	④
(13)	①	②	③	④
(14)	①	②	③	④
(15)	①	②	③	④
(16)	①	②	③	④
(17)	①	②	③	④
(18)	①	②	③	④
(19)	①	②	③	④
(20)	①	②	③	④
(21)	①	②	③	④
(22)	①	②	③	④
(23)	①	②	③	④
(24)	①	②	③	④
(25)	①	②	③	④

（1）

筆記解答欄

問題番号	1	2	3	4
(26)	①	②	③	④
(27)	①	②	③	④
(28)	①	②	③	④
(29)	①	②	③	④
(30)	①	②	③	④
(31)	①	②	③	④

（2）

筆記解答欄

問題番号	1	2	3	4
(32)	①	②	③	④
(33)	①	②	③	④
(34)	①	②	③	④
(35)	①	②	③	④
(36)	①	②	③	④
(37)	①	②	③	④
(38)	①	②	③	④
(39)	①	②	③	④
(40)	①	②	③	④
(41)	①	②	③	④

（3）

※筆記4の解答欄はこの裏にあります。

リスニング解答欄

問題番号	1	2	3	4
Part 1 No.1	①	②	③	④
No.2	①	②	③	④
No.3	①	②	③	④
No.4	①	②	③	④
No.5	①	②	③	④
No.6	①	②	③	④
No.7	①	②	③	④
No.8	①	②	③	④
No.9	①	②	③	④
No.10	①	②	③	④
No.11	①	②	③	④
No.12	①	②	③	④
Part 2　A No.13	①	②	③	④
No.14	①	②	③	④
B No.15	①	②	③	④
No.16	①	②	③	④
C No.17	①	②	③	④
No.18	①	②	③	④
D No.19	①	②	③	④
No.20	①	②	③	④
E No.21	①	②	③	④
No.22	①	②	③	④
F No.23	①	②	③	④
No.24	①	②	③	④
Part 3　G No.25	①	②	③	④
H No.26	①	②	③	④
I No.27	①	②	③	④
J No.28	①	②	③	④
K No.29	①	②	③	④

2021年度第1回
Web特典「自動採点サービス」対応　オンラインマークシート

※検定の回によって2次元コードが違います。
※筆記1～3、リスニングの採点ができます。
※PCからも利用できます（本書 p.8 参照）。

※実際の解答用紙に似せていますが、デザイン・サイズは異なります。

切り取り線

・指示事項を守り、文字は、はっきり分かりやすく書いてください。
・太枠に囲まれた部分のみが採点の対象です。

4 English Composition

Write your English Composition in the space below.

2020年度第3回　英検準1級　解答用紙

【注意事項】
① 解答にはHBの黒鉛筆（シャープペンシルも可）を使用し、解答を訂正する場合には消しゴムで完全に消してください。
② 解答用紙は絶対に汚したり折り曲げたり、所定以外のところへの記入はしないでください。

③ マーク例

良い例	悪い例
●	◐ ✗ ◖

これ以下の濃さのマークは読めません。

筆記解答欄

問題番号	1	2	3	4
(1)	①	②	③	④
(2)	①	②	③	④
(3)	①	②	③	④
(4)	①	②	③	④
(5)	①	②	③	④
(6)	①	②	③	④
(7)	①	②	③	④
(8)	①	②	③	④
(9)	①	②	③	④
(10)	①	②	③	④
(11)	①	②	③	④
(12)	①	②	③	④
(13)	①	②	③	④
(14)	①	②	③	④
(15)	①	②	③	④
(16)	①	②	③	④
(17)	①	②	③	④
(18)	①	②	③	④
(19)	①	②	③	④
(20)	①	②	③	④
(21)	①	②	③	④
(22)	①	②	③	④
(23)	①	②	③	④
(24)	①	②	③	④
(25)	①	②	③	④

（大問番号 1）

筆記解答欄

問題番号	1	2	3	4
(26)	①	②	③	④
(27)	①	②	③	④
(28)	①	②	③	④
(29)	①	②	③	④
(30)	①	②	③	④
(31)	①	②	③	④

（大問番号 2）

筆記解答欄

問題番号	1	2	3	4
(32)	①	②	③	④
(33)	①	②	③	④
(34)	①	②	③	④
(35)	①	②	③	④
(36)	①	②	③	④
(37)	①	②	③	④
(38)	①	②	③	④
(39)	①	②	③	④
(40)	①	②	③	④
(41)	①	②	③	④

（大問番号 3）

※筆記4の解答欄はこの裏にあります。

リスニング解答欄

問題番号	1	2	3	4
Part 1　No.1	①	②	③	④
No.2	①	②	③	④
No.3	①	②	③	④
No.4	①	②	③	④
No.5	①	②	③	④
No.6	①	②	③	④
No.7	①	②	③	④
No.8	①	②	③	④
No.9	①	②	③	④
No.10	①	②	③	④
No.11	①	②	③	④
No.12	①	②	③	④
Part 2　A　No.13	①	②	③	④
No.14	①	②	③	④
B　No.15	①	②	③	④
No.16	①	②	③	④
C　No.17	①	②	③	④
No.18	①	②	③	④
D　No.19	①	②	③	④
No.20	①	②	③	④
E　No.21	①	②	③	④
No.22	①	②	③	④
F　No.23	①	②	③	④
No.24	①	②	③	④
Part 3　G　No.25	①	②	③	④
H　No.26	①	②	③	④
I　No.27	①	②	③	④
J　No.28	①	②	③	④
K　No.29	①	②	③	④

2020年度第3回
Web特典「自動採点サービス」対応 オンラインマークシート
※検定の回によって2次元コードが違います。
※筆記1～3，リスニングの採点ができます。
※PCからも利用できます（本書 p.8 参照）。

※実際の解答用紙に似せていますが、デザイン・サイズは異なります。

切り取り線

・指示事項を守り、文字は、はっきり分かりやすく書いてください。
・太枠に囲まれた部分のみが採点の対象です。

4 English Composition

Write your English Composition in the space below.

Introduction

はじめに

実用英語技能検定（英検®）は，年間受験者数410万人（英検IBA，英検 Jr.との総数）の小学生から社会人まで，幅広い層が受験する国内最大級の資格試験で，1963年の第１回検定からの累計では１億人を超える人々が受験しています。英検®は，コミュニケーションに欠かすことのできない４技能をバランスよく測定することを目的としており，英検®の受験によってご自身の英語力を把握できるだけでなく，進学・就職・留学などの場面で多くのチャンスを手に入れることにつながります。

この『全問題集シリーズ』は，英語を学ぶ皆さまを応援する気持ちを込めて刊行しました。本書は，2022年度第２回検定を含む６回分の過去問を，皆さまの理解が深まるよう，日本語訳や詳しい解説を加えて収録しています。また，正答率が高かった設問の解説には 正答率 ★75%以上 マーク（別冊p.3参照）がついているので，特におさえておきたい問題を簡単にチェックできます。

本書が皆さまの英検合格の足がかりとなり，さらには国際社会で活躍できるような生きた英語を身につけるきっかけとなることを願っています。

最後に，本書を刊行するにあたり，多大なご尽力をいただきました入江 泉先生に深く感謝の意を表します。

2023年　春

もくじ

Contents

本書の使い方 ……………………………………… 3

音声について ……………………………………… 4

Web特典について ………………………………… 7

自動採点サービスの利用方法 …………………… 8

英検インフォメーション ………………………… 10
試験内容／英検の種類／合否判定方法／英検（従来型）受験情報—2023年
度試験日程・申込方法

2022年度の傾向と攻略ポイント ……………… 14

二次試験・面接の流れ …………………………… 16

2022年度　第2回検定（筆記・リスニング・面接）…… 17

第1回検定（筆記・リスニング・面接）…… 45

2021年度　第3回検定（筆記・リスニング・面接）…… 73

第2回検定（筆記・リスニング・面接）… 101

第1回検定（筆記・リスニング・面接）… 129

2020年度　第3回検定（筆記・リスニング・面接）… 157

執　　筆：入江 泉，斉藤 敦
編集協力：日本アイアール株式会社，株式会社鷗来堂，久島智津子
録　　音：ユニバ合同会社
デザイン：林 慎一郎（及川真咲デザイン事務所）
組版・データ作成協力：幸和印刷株式会社

本書の使い方

ここでは，本書の過去問および特典についての活用法の一例を紹介します。

本書の内容

過去問 6回分	英検 インフォ メーション (p.10-13)	2022年度の 傾向と 攻略ポイント (p.14-15)	二次試験・ 面接の流れ (p.16)	Web特典 (p.7-9)

本書の使い方

一次試験対策

情報収集・傾向把握
- ・英検インフォメーション
- ・2022年度の傾向と攻略ポイント

過去問にチャレンジ
- ・2022年度第2回一次試験
- ・2022年度第1回一次試験
- ・2021年度第3回一次試験
- ・2021年度第2回一次試験
- ・2021年度第1回一次試験
- ・2020年度第3回一次試験
  - ※【Web特典】自動採点サービスの活用

二次試験対策

情報収集・傾向把握
- ・二次試験・面接の流れ
- ・【Web特典】
  面接シミュレーション／面接模範例

過去問にチャレンジ
- ・2022年度第2回二次試験
- ・2022年度第1回二次試験
- ・2021年度第3回二次試験
- ・2021年度第2回二次試験
- ・2021年度第1回二次試験
- ・2020年度第3回二次試験

過去問の取り組み方

1セット目

【本番モード】
本番の試験と同じように，制限時間を設けて取り組みましょう。どの問題形式に時間がかかりすぎているか，正答率が低いかなど，今のあなたの実力を把握しましょう。
「自動採点サービス」を活用して，答え合わせをスムーズに行いましょう。

2～5セット目

【学習モード】
制限時間をなくし，解けるまで取り組みましょう。
リスニングは音声を繰り返し聞いて解答を導き出してもかまいません。すべての問題に正解できるまで見直します。

6セット目

【仕上げモード】
試験直前の仕上げに利用しましょう。
時間を計って本番のつもりで取り組みます。
これまでに取り組んだ6セットの過去問で間違えた問題の解説を本番試験の前にもう一度見直しましょう。

音声について

一次試験・リスニングと二次試験・面接の音声を聞くことができます。本書とともに使い，効果的なリスニング・面接対策をしましょう。

収録内容と特長

 一次試験・リスニング

本番の試験の音声を収録	➡	スピードをつかめる！
解答時間は本番通り10秒間	➡	解答時間に慣れる！
収録されている英文は，別冊解答に掲載	➡	聞き取れない箇所を確認できる！

 二次試験・面接（スピーキング）

| 実際の流れ通りに収録 | ➡ | 本番の雰囲気を味わえる！ |

・ナレーションの準備（本番と同じ1分間）
・ナレーション（ナレーション例を収録）
・質問（練習用に10秒の解答時間）

| 各質問のModel Answerも収録 | ➡ | 模範解答が確認できる！ |
| Model Answerは，別冊解答に掲載 | ➡ | 聞き取れない箇所を確認できる！ |

3つの方法で音声が聞けます！

音声再生サービスご利用可能期間

2023年2月24日～2024年8月31日

※ご利用期間内にアプリやPCにダウンロードしていただいた音声は，期間終了後も引き続きお聞きいただけます。

※これらのサービスは予告なく変更，終了することがあります。

① 公式アプリ「英語の友」(iOS/Android) でお手軽再生

リスニング力を強化する機能満載

- 再生速度変換（0.5～2.0倍速）
- お気に入り機能（絞込み学習）
- オフライン再生
- バックグラウンド再生
- 試験日カウントダウン

※画像はイメージです。

[ご利用方法]

1 「英語の友」公式サイトより，アプリをインストール

https://eigonotomo.com/ [英語の友 🔍]

（右の2次元コードから読み込めます）

2 アプリ内のライブラリよりご購入いただいた書籍を選び，「追加」ボタンを押してください

3 パスワードを入力すると，音声がダウンロードできます
[パスワード：hzvbtu]　※すべて半角アルファベット小文字

※本アプリの機能の一部は有料ですが，本書の音声は無料でお聞きいただけます。
※詳しいご利用方法は「英語の友」公式サイト，あるいはアプリ内ヘルプをご参照ください。

② パソコンで音声データダウンロード（MP3）

［ご利用方法］

1　Web特典にアクセス　　詳細は，p.7をご覧ください。

2　「一次試験［二次試験］音声データダウンロード」から
　　聞きたい検定の回を選択してダウンロード

※音声ファイルはzip形式にまとめられた形でダウンロードされます。
※音声の再生にはMP3を再生できる機器などが必要です。ご使用機器，音声再生ソフト等に関する技術的なご質問は，ハードメーカーもしくはソフトメーカーにお願いいたします。

③ スマートフォン・タブレットで ストリーミング再生

［ご利用方法］

1　自動採点サービスにアクセス　　詳細は，p.8をご覧ください。
　　（右の2次元コードから読み込めます）

2　聞きたい検定の回を選び，
　　リスニングテストの音声再生ボタンを押す

※自動採点サービスは一次試験に対応していますので，一次試験・リスニングの音声のみお聞きいただけます。（二次試験・面接の音声をお聞きになりたい方は，①リスニングアプリ「英語の友」，②音声データダウンロードをご利用ください）
※音声再生中に音声を止めたい場合は，停止ボタンを押してください。
※個別に問題を再生したい場合は，問題番号を選んでから再生ボタンを押してください。
※音声の再生には多くの通信量が必要となりますので，Wi-Fi環境でのご利用をおすすめいたします。

CDをご希望の方は，別売「2023年度版英検準1級過去6回全問題集CD」
（本体価格2,100円+税）をご利用ください。

持ち運びに便利な小冊子とCD4枚付き。　※本書では，収録箇所をCD 1 **1**～**14**のように表示。

Web特典について

購入者限定の「Web特典」を，みなさんの英検合格にお役立てください。

ご利用可能期間	2023年2月24日〜2024年8月31日 ※本サービスは予告なく変更，終了することがあります。	
アクセス方法	スマートフォン タブレット	右の2次元コードを読み込むと， パスワードなしでアクセスできます！
	PC スマートフォン タブレット 共通	1. Web特典（以下のURL）にアクセスします。 　https://eiken.obunsha.co.jp/p1q/ 2. 本書を選択し，以下のパスワードを入力します。 　hzvbtu　※すべて半角アルファベット小文字

〈特典内容〉

(1)自動採点サービス

リーディング（筆記1〜3），リスニング（Part1〜3）の自動採点ができます。詳細はp.8を参照してください。

(2)解答用紙

本番にそっくりの解答用紙が印刷できるので，何度でも過去問にチャレンジすることができます。

(3)音声データのダウンロード

一次試験リスニング・二次試験面接の音声データ（MP3）を無料でダウンロードできます。
※スマートフォン・タブレットの方は，アプリ「英語の友」（p.5）をご利用ください。

(4)準1級面接対策

【面接シミュレーション】入室から退室までの面接の流れが体験できます。本番の面接と同じ手順で練習ができるので，実際に声に出して練習してみましょう。

【面接模範例】入室から退室までの模範応答例を見ることができます。各チェックポイントで，受験上の注意点やアドバイスを確認しておきましょう。

【問題カード】面接シミュレーションで使用している問題カードです。印刷して，実際の面接の練習に使ってください。

自動採点サービスの利用方法

正答率や合格ラインとの距離，間違えた問題などの確認ができるサービスです。

ご利用可能期間	2023年2月24日～2024年8月31日		
	※本サービスは予告なく変更，終了することがあります。		
アクセス方法	スマートフォン タブレット	右の2次元コードを読み込んでアクセスし，採点する検定の回を選択してください。	
	PC スマートフォン タブレット 共通	p.7の手順で「Web特典」にアクセスし，「自動採点サービスを使う」を選択してご利用ください。	

［ご利用方法］

1. **オンラインマークシートにアクセスします**
   Web特典の「自動採点サービスを使う」から，採点したい検定回を選択するか，各回のマークシートおよび問題編の各回とびらの2次元コードからアクセスします。

2. **「問題をはじめる」ボタンを押して筆記試験を始めます**
   ボタンを押すとタイマーが動き出します。制限時間内に解答できるよう，解答時間を意識して取り組みましょう。

3 筆記試験を解答し終わったら，タイマーボタン  を押して
タイマーをストップさせます

4 リスニングテストは画面下にある音声再生ボタンを押して
音声を再生し，問題に取り組みましょう
　　一度再生ボタンを押したら，最後の問題まで自動的に
　　進んでいきます。

5 リスニングテストが終了したら，
「答え合わせ」ボタンを押して答え合わせをします

採点結果の見方

タブの選択で【あなたの成績】と【問題ごとの正誤】が切り替えられます。

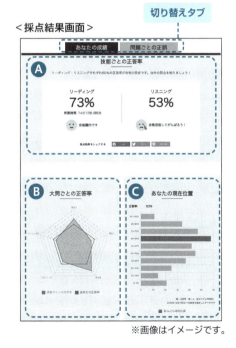

【あなたの成績】
Ⓐ 技能ごとの正答率が表示されます。準1級の合格の目安，正答率70%を目指しましょう。
Ⓑ 大問ごとの正答率が表示されます。合格ラインを下回る大問は，対策に力を入れましょう。
Ⓒ 採点サービス利用者の中でのあなたの現在位置が示されます。

【問題ごとの正誤】
各問題のあなたの解答と正解が表示されます。間違っている問題については色で示されますので，別冊解答の解説を見直しましょう。

※画像はイメージです。

英検®Information インフォメーション

出典：英検ウェブサイト

英検準1級について

準1級では，「社会生活で求められる英語を十分理解し，また使用できる」ことが求められます。
転職や就職，単位認定，教員採用試験・海外留学や入試など，多方面で幅広く活用される資格です。
目安としては「大学中級程度」です。

試験内容

一次試験 筆記・リスニング

主な場面・状況	家庭・学校・職場・地域（各種店舗・公共施設を含む）・電話・アナウンス・講義など
主な話題	社会生活一般・芸術・文化・歴史・教育・科学・自然・環境・医療・テクノロジー・ビジネス・政治など

✏ 筆記試験 ⏱90分

問題	形式・課題詳細	問題数	満点スコア
1	文脈に合う適切な語句を補う。	25問	
2	パッセージの空所に文脈に合う適切な語句を補う。	6問	750
3	パッセージの内容に関する質問に答える。	10問	
4	指定されたトピックについての英作文を書く。（120〜150語）	1問	750

🔊 リスニング ⏱約30分 放送回数／1回

問題	形式・課題詳細	問題数	満点スコア
Part 1	会話の内容に関する質問に答える。	12問	
Part 2	パッセージの内容に関する質問に答える。	12問	750
Part 3	Real-Life形式の放送内容に関する質問に答える。	5問	

2022年12月現在の情報を掲載しています。試験に関する情報は変更になる可能性がありますので，受験の際は必ず英検ウェブサイトをご確認ください。

二次試験　面接形式のスピーキングテスト

主な場面・題材	社会性の高い分野の話題
過去の出題例	在宅勤務・レストランでの喫煙・チャイルドシート・住民運動・キャッチセールス・護身術 など

スピーキング　約8分

面接の構成	形式・課題詳細	満点スコア
自由会話	面接委員と簡単な日常会話を行う。	750
ナレーション	4コマのイラストの展開を説明する。(2分間)	
No.1	イラストに関連した質問に答える。	
No.2 / No.3	カードのトピックに関連した内容についての質問に答える。	
No.4	カードのトピックにやや関連した，社会性のある内容についての質問に答える。	

英検®の種類

英検には，実施方式が異なる複数の試験があります。実施時期や受験上の配慮など，自分に合った方式を選択しましょう。なお，従来型の英検とその他の英検は問題形式，難易度，級認定，合格証明書発行，英検CSEスコア取得等はすべて同じです。

▶英検®(従来型)
紙の問題冊子を見て解答用紙に解答。二次試験を受験するためには，一次試験に合格する必要があります。

▶英検S-CBT
コンピュータを使って受験，1日で4技能を受験することができ，申込時に会場・日程・ライティングの解答方式が選べます。原則，毎週土日に実施されています（級や地域により毎週実施でない場合があります）。ほかの実施方式で取得した一次試験免除の資格も申請可能です。

▶英検S-Interview
点字や吃音等，CBT方式では対応が難しい受験上の配慮が必要な方のみが受験可能。

受験する級によって選択できる方式が異なります。各方式の詳細および最新情報は英検ウェブサイト（https://www.eiken.or.jp/eiken/）をご確認ください。

合否判定方法

統計的に算出される英検CSEスコアに基づいて合否判定されます。Reading，Writing，Listening，Speakingの4技能が均等に評価され，合格基準スコアは固定されています。

▶▶ 技能別にスコアが算出される！

技能	試験形式	満点スコア	合格基準スコア
Reading（読む）	一次試験（筆記1〜3）	750	1792
Writing（書く）	一次試験（筆記4）	750	
Listening（聞く）	一次試験（リスニング）	750	
Speaking（話す）	二次試験（面接）	750	512

● 一次試験の合否は，Reading，Writing，Listeningの技能別にスコアが算出され，それを合算して判定されます。
● 二次試験の合否は，Speakingのみで判定されます。

▶▶ 合格するためには，技能のバランスが重要！

英検CSEスコアでは，技能ごとに問題数は異なりますが，スコアを均等に配分しているため，各技能のバランスが重要となります。なお，正答数の目安を提示することはできませんが，2016年度第1回一次試験では，1級，準1級は各技能での正答率が7割程度，2級以下は各技能6割程度の正答率の受験者の多くが合格されています。

▶▶ 英検CSEスコアは国際標準規格CEFRにも対応している！

CEFRとは，Common European Framework of Reference for Languages の略。語学のコミュニケーション能力別のレベルを示す国際標準規格。欧米で幅広く導入され，6つのレベルが設定されています。
4技能の英検CSEスコアの合計「4技能総合スコア」と級ごとのCEFR算出範囲に基づいた「4技能総合CEFR」が成績表に表示されます。また，技能別の「CEFRレベル」も表示されます。

CEFR	英検CSEスコア	実用英語技能検定　各級の合格基準スコア
C2	4000・3300	CEFR算出範囲　　　　　　　　　　　　B2扱い　　C1扱い　1級 満点3400
C1	3299・2600	2級 満点2600　準1級 満点3000　3299 合格スコア 2630
B2	2599・2300	準2級 満点2400　B1扱い　合格スコア 2304　2599 2304
B1	2299・1950	3級 満点2200　A2扱い　2299 合格スコア 1980 1980
A2	1949・1700	A1扱い　合格スコア 1728　1949 合格スコア 1980　1728 CEFR算出範囲外
A1	1699・1400	合格スコア 1456　1699　1400 CEFR算出範囲外　CEFR算出範囲外
	1399・0	CEFR算出範囲外　CEFR算出範囲外

※ 4級・5級は4技能を測定していないため「4技能総合CEFR」の対象外。
※ 詳しくは英検ウェブサイトをご覧ください。

英検®(従来型) 受験情報

※「従来型・本会場」以外の実施方式については，試験日程・申込方法が異なりますので，英検ウェブサイトをご覧ください。
※ 受験情報は変更になる場合があります。

◉ 2023年度 試験日程

	第 1 回	第 2 回	第 3 回
申込受付	3月31日 ▶ 5月2日	8月1日 ▶ 9月8日	11月1日 ▶ 12月14日
一次試験	6月 4日(日)	10月 8日(日)	1月21日(日) 2024年
二次試験	A 7月 2日(日) C 7月16日(日)	A 11月 5日(日) C 11月23日(木祝)	A 2月18日(日) 2024年 C 3月 3日(日) 2024年

※ 一次試験は上記以外の日程でも準会場で受験できる可能性があります。
※ 二次試験にはA日程，B日程(2〜3級)，C日程(1級，準1級)があり，受験級などの条件により指定されます。
※ 詳しくは英検ウェブサイトをご覧ください。

◉ 申込方法

団体受験	▶	学校や塾などで申し込みをする団体受験もあります。詳しくは先生にお尋ねください。
個人受験	▶	インターネット申込・コンビニ申込・英検特約書店申込のいずれかの方法で申し込みができます。詳しくは英検ウェブサイトをご覧ください。

お問い合わせ先

英検サービスセンター	英検ウェブサイト
TEL.03-3266-8311	www.eiken.or.jp/eiken/
(月)〜(金)9：30〜17：00 (祝日・年末年始を除く)	試験についての詳しい情報を見たり，入試等で英検を活用している学校の検索をすることができます。

2022年度の傾向と攻略ポイント

2022年度第1回検定と第2回検定を分析し，出題傾向と攻略ポイントをまとめました。準1級の合格に必要な正答率は7割程度と予測されます。正答率が7割を切った大問は苦手な分野だと考えましょう。

一次試験　筆記（90分）

1　短文の語句空所補充
文脈に合う適切な語句を補う。

問題数 **25**問　めやす **15**分

傾向　第1回・第2回とも，例年通り25問のうち単語の意味を問うものが21問，句動詞の意味を問うものが4問出題された。出題される品詞のバランスは回により異なる。

攻略ポイント　語彙力を増やすには英字新聞などを通じて多くの英文に触れることが必要なのはもちろんだが，1つ新しい単語を覚えたら，同時にその単語の派生語（違う品詞の形）を調べて覚えるようにすると，語彙力を効率よく強化できる。

2　長文の語句空所補充
パッセージの空所に文脈に合う適切な語句を補う。

問題数 **6**問　めやす **15**分

傾向　約250語の2つの長文にそれぞれ空所が3つあり，適切な選択肢を選ぶという形式は例年と変わらない。今年度も，接続表現を問う問題が毎回出題された。

攻略ポイント　空所の前後を重点的に読み解くのが基本だが，それだけでは容易に正解が導けない場合もある。そのときは，長文全体の文脈の流れに視野を広げて読み解こう。

3　長文の内容一致選択
パッセージの内容に関する質問に答える。

問題数 **10**問　めやす **35**分

傾向　3つの長文は約300語，約400語，約500語の順で出題され，前半2つの長文に設問が3つ，最後の長文に設問が4つという形式は例年と変わらない。

攻略ポイント　設問の順序は長文の流れと基本的に一致しているので，解答につながる箇所を見つけるのは難しくはないが，設問を先に読んでから関連する情報を探しながら読む「スキャニング」と呼ばれる速読法が時間の節約に役立つ。

4　英作文
指定されたトピックについての英作文を書く。

問題数 **1**問　めやす **25**分

傾向　指定されたトピックについて，与えられた4つのポイントのうち2つを用いて，120～150語でエッセイを書くことが求められる。

攻略ポイント　トピックの意味を正確に把握することを心がけよう。また，必ずしも自分の意見を正直に書く必要はなく，与えられたポイントから書きやすいものを選べばよい。過去問に挑戦することでパターンを身につけ，不安なく使える表現を増やそう。

一次試験 リスニング（約30分）

Part 1　会話の内容一致選択
会話の内容に関する質問に答える。　問題数 **12問**

傾向　100語前後の男女間の会話とそれに関する質問を聞き，問題用紙の選択肢の中から答えを選ぶという形式に変化はない。会話が行われる状況は，家庭，職場，学校，街中など多岐にわたっており，男女の人間関係もさまざまである。

攻略ポイント　それぞれの話者の意図，合意・決定したこと，一方がもう一方に提案していることなどに注意しながら聞くことが大切である。

Part 2　文の内容一致選択
パッセージの内容に関する質問に答える。　問題数 **12問**

傾向　150語前後のパッセージを聞き，続いて放送される2つの質問の答えを選択肢から選ぶ形式に変化はない。6つのパッセージのトピックは，環境，社会，健康，自然科学，文化など多岐にわたり，内容や使用される語彙も高度である。

攻略ポイント　2つの質問のうち，基本的に1つ目のものはパッセージの前半部分，2つ目は後半部分に関するものとなっている。しかし，中には「〜について何が分かるか」のように，全体の内容から判断しなければならないものもあるので，選択肢を先に読んで質問をある程度予測して聞くというテクニックも必要である。

Part 3　Real-Life形式の内容一致選択
Real-Life形式の放送内容に関する質問に答える。　問題数 **5問**

傾向　問題用紙に印刷された状況と質問を10秒間で読んでから，電話の音声メッセージ，施設内アナウンスなど，日常生活で実際にあり得る100語前後のパッセージを聞き，選択肢の中から答えを選ぶ形式に変化はない。質問は基本的に全て「あなたは何をすべきか」などの適切な行動を問うものである。

攻略ポイント　あらかじめ状況設定と質問を理解してからリスニングを始めることができるので，必要な情報に注意を集中させて聞くことができる。しかしそのためには10秒で状況と質問（できれば選択肢まで）を読み切るだけの速読力も必要。

二次試験 面接（約8分）

4コマのイラストがついたカードが渡される。1分の黙読の後，そのイラストのストーリーを2分間で説明するよう指示される。それから，4つの質問がされる。

最初の質問はイラストの4コマ目の特定の人物について「あなたがこの人物だったらどう思うか」というもの，残りの3つはイラストのトピックに関連した，あるいは一般的な社会問題について自分の意見を問うもの。意見には明快な理由や説明が伴わなければならない。

二次試験・面接の流れ

(1) 入室とあいさつ

係員の指示に従い，面接室に入ります。あいさつをしてから，面接委員に面接カードを手渡し，指示に従って，着席しましょう。

(2) 名前と受験級の確認

面接委員があなたの名前と受験する級の確認をします。その後，簡単な会話をしてから試験開始です。

(3) ナレーションの考慮時間

問題カードを手渡されます。指示文を黙読し，4コマのイラストについてナレーションの準備をします。時間は1分間です。

※問題カードには複数の種類があり，面接委員によっていずれか1枚が手渡されます。本書では英検協会から提供を受けたもののみ掲載しています。

(4) ナレーション

ナレーションをするよう指示されるので，問題カードで指定された言い出し部分から始めます。時間は2分間です。超過しないよう時間配分に注意しましょう。

(5) 4つの質問

面接委員の4つの質問に答えます。1つ目の質問に答える際には問題カードを見てもかまいませんが，2つ目以降は問題カードを裏返して答えます。また，自然な聞き返しであれば減点の対象になりません。積極的に自分の意見を話しましょう。

(6) カード返却と退室

試験が終了したら，問題カードを面接委員に返却し，あいさつをして退室しましょう。

2022-2

一次試験　2022.10.9実施
二次試験　A日程　2022.11.6実施
　　　　　C日程　2022.11.23実施

Grade Pre-1

試験時間

筆記：90分
リスニング：約30分

一次試験・筆記　　　　　p.18〜33
一次試験・リスニング　　p.34〜39
二次試験・面接　　　　　p.40〜43

＊解答・解説は別冊p.5〜48にあります。
＊面接の流れは本書p.16にあります。

2022年度第2回　**Web特典「自動採点サービス」対応**
　　　　　　　オンラインマークシート
　　　　　　　※検定の回によって2次元コードが違います。
　　　　　　　※筆記1〜3，リスニングの採点ができます。
　　　　　　　※PCからも利用できます（本書p.8参照）。

一次試験
筆 記

1 To complete each item, choose the best word or phrase from among the four choices. Then, on your answer sheet, find the number of the question and mark your answer.

(1) *A:* Mom, can you make hamburgers for dinner tonight?
B: Yes, but I'll have to take the meat out of the freezer and let it
( ) first.
1 reckon **2** thaw **3** stray **4** shatter

(2) Jocelyn always reminded her son not to tell lies. She believed it was important to ( ) a strong sense of honesty in him.
1 remodel **2** stumble **3** overlap **4** instill

(3) Zara was very angry with her boyfriend, but she forgave him after hearing his ( ) apology. She was sure that he really was sorry.
1 detectable **2** earnest **3** cumulative **4** underlying

(4) At first, the Smiths enjoyed their backyard swimming pool, but keeping it clean became such a ( ) that they left it covered most of the time.
1 bureau **2** nuisance **3** sequel **4** metaphor

(5) Throughout the course of history, many great thinkers were at first ( ) for their ideas before eventually being taken seriously.
1 saturated **2** flattered **3** ingested **4** ridiculed

(6) At first, the little girl felt ( ) in front of the large audience at the speech contest, but after about a minute she began to feel more confident.
1 mortal **2** bashful **3** pious **4** concise

18

(7) Typewriters are a (   ) of the past. They remind us how far technology has advanced since they were common in offices and homes.

1 jumble   **2** relic   **3** fraud   **4** treaty

(8) When the man approached the tiger's cage, the huge animal (   ) deeply. The man stepped back in fear at the terrifying sound.

1 sparkled   **2** leered   **3** disproved   **4** growled

(9) Police officers must promise to (   ) the law. This includes, of course, following the law themselves.

1 gravitate   **2** detach   **3** uphold   **4** eradicate

(10) All employees have a (   ) medical checkup every year. Companies are required by law to make sure all their workers do it.

1 gloomy   **2** compulsory **3** reminiscent **4** muddled

(11) Biology students must learn how cell (   ) works, as this process of a single cell splitting into two is commonly found in nature.

1 division   **2** appliance   **3** imposition   **4** longitude

(12) After the two companies (   ), several senior employees became unnecessary and lost their jobs.

1 merged   **2** posed   **3** conformed   **4** flocked

(13) In order to avoid becoming (   ) while exercising, one should always drink enough water. The longer the workout, the more water is necessary.

1 dehydrated **2** eternal   **3** punctuated   **4** cautious

19

(14) Ken was always well behaved at home, so his mother was shocked when his teacher said he was one of the most (　　) students in his class.
1 momentary　**2** miniature　**3** disobedient　**4** invincible

(15) The police questioned (　　) at the scene of the crime, hoping someone who had been nearby had seen what happened.
1 bystanders　**2** reformers　**3** mourners　**4** pioneers

(16) Several generals attempted to (　　) the country's prime minister. However, they were unsuccessful, and he remains in power.
1 irrigate　**2** harmonize　**3** outpace　**4** overthrow

(17) Caleb finished a draft of his proposal, so he asked his manager to (　　) it. Unfortunately, she thought it still needed a lot of improvement.
1 scrub　**2** enchant　**3** prune　**4** evaluate

(18) American presidents Thomas Jefferson and John Adams exchanged letters with each other for over 50 years. This (　　) is an important part of American history.
1 matrimony　　　　　　　**2** federation
3 horizon　　　　　　　　**4** correspondence

(19) During the riot, the town was in a state of (　　). People were out in the streets fighting and breaking windows, and many stores were robbed.
1 disclosure　**2** admittance　**3** attainment　**4** anarchy

(20) The flowers of some plants are actually (　　) and can be used to make salads both more delicious and more visually attractive.
1 stationary　**2** candid　**3** edible　**4** hideous

(21) No one was surprised when the famous scientist made many mistakes during his speech. He is (   ) for his poor speaking skills.

1 treacherous   **2** momentous   **3** flirtatious   **4** notorious

(22) All of Brad's hard work and long hours (   ) when his boss gave him a promotion last month.

1 paid off   **2** wrote back   **3** chopped up   **4** made over

(23) Since the CEO's speech was so vague, it took Gina a while to (   ) to the fact that the company was in serious financial trouble.

1 fill in   **2** duck out   **3** catch on   **4** give up

(24) Each member of the team has a job to do for the new project, but the responsibility for coordinating all of their efforts (   ) the manager.

1 falls on   **2** squares with
3 drops by   **4** stacks up

(25) The employee tried to (   ) his theft from the company by destroying files and other evidence that proved his guilt.

1 tuck away   **2** latch onto   **3** cover up   **4** doze off

2 Read each passage and choose the best word or phrase from among the four choices for each blank. Then, on your answer sheet, find the number of the question and mark your answer.

Nabta Playa's Stone Circle

Many prehistoric societies constructed stone circles. These were created for various reasons, such as tracking the sun's movement. The oldest such circle known to scientists can be found at Nabta Playa in Egypt. At around 7,000 years old, this circle predates England's Stonehenge — probably the world's best-known prehistoric stone circle — by more than 1,000 years. Nabta Playa's climate is extremely dry today, but this was not always the case. (**26**), heavy seasonal rainfall during the period when the circle was built led to the formation of temporary lakes, and these attracted cattle-grazing tribes to the area.

Nabta Playa's first settlers arrived around 10,000 years ago. Archaeologists have uncovered evidence that these settlers created a system of deep wells that gave them access to water year-round, and that they arranged their homes in straight rows and equipped them with storage spaces. They also practiced a religion that focused on the worship of cattle, which were central to their lives. These discoveries are evidence that the settlers (**27**).

Research findings show that some of the circle's stones would have lined up with the sun on the longest day of the year around 7,000 years ago. This suggests the circle was used as a calendar. One astrophysicist, however, believes the circle (**28**). He points out that the positions of other stones match those of stars in the constellation Orion at the time the circle was built. Because of this, he proposes that the circle was an astrological map showing the positions of stars in the night sky.

22

(26) 1 On the other hand
2 In fact
3 Despite this
4 Similarly

(27) 1 questioned religious ideas
2 lost interest in raising cattle
3 experienced serious internal conflicts
4 developed a sophisticated society

(28) 1 also had another purpose
2 was created much earlier
3 was originally built elsewhere
4 caused people to avoid the area

The Good Roads Movement

Beginning in the late nineteenth century, the Good Roads Movement transformed America's landscape, helping to create the nation's system of roads and highways. This movement (**29**   ). While most people today assume that the road system was first developed in response to the needs of automobile drivers, this is a myth. Actually, the demand started mainly with cyclists. The invention of the modern bicycle led to a cycling craze in the 1890s, and millions of Americans wanted better, safer roads to cycle on.

Cyclists began pressuring local governments to improve the quality of roads, which were often poorly maintained and dangerous. At first, the movement was resisted by farmers, who did not want their tax dollars to be spent supporting the leisure activities of cyclists from cities. Gradually, however, farmers (**30**   ). One reason for this was an influential pamphlet called *The Gospel of Good Roads: A Letter to the American Farmer*. It convinced many farmers by emphasizing the benefits of roads, such as making it easier for them to transport their crops to markets.

As automobiles became common, the movement quickly gained momentum. (**31**   ), the invention of the Ford Model T in the early 1900s led to many new drivers, who were also eager for better roads. Millions of these affordable cars were sold, and the increase in drivers put pressure on governments to build more roads and improve the quality of existing ones.

24

(29) **1** was started by car manufacturers
   2 had a surprising origin
   3 created disagreement among drivers
   4 angered many cyclists

(30) **1** increased their protests
   2 started using different roads
   3 began to change their minds
   4 turned against cyclists

(31) **1** By contrast
   2 In particular
   3 Nonetheless
   4 Therefore

3 *Read each passage and choose the best answer from among the four choices for each question. Then, on your answer sheet, find the number of the question and mark your answer.*

Recognizing Faces

Humans are generally very good at recognizing faces and quickly interpreting their expressions. This is achieved by having specific areas of the brain that specialize in processing facial features. The development of this ability makes sense in terms of evolution, since early humans would have needed to judge, for example, whether those around them were angry and therefore potentially dangerous. One unintended consequence, however, is that people often think they see faces on objects in their environment. People perceive these so-called false faces on a variety of objects, from clouds and tree trunks to pieces of food and electric sockets.

Researchers in Australia recently performed a study to learn more about how the brain processes false faces. Previous studies have revealed that for real faces, people's judgment of what emotion a face is expressing is affected by the faces they have just seen. Seeing a series of happy faces, for example, tends to make people assess the face they next see as expressing happiness. In the Australian study, the researchers showed participants a series of false faces that expressed a particular emotion. They found that, as with real faces, the participants' judgments of the emotions expressed by the false faces were affected by the ones they had just been shown. Based on this finding, the researchers concluded that the brain processes false faces in a way similar to how it processes real ones.

The researchers also noted that any object with features that even loosely resemble the layout of a human face — two eyes and a nose above a mouth — can trigger the brain to assess those features for emotional expression. In other words, the brain's criteria for recognizing a face are general rather than specific. The researchers say this is one reason the brain can assess facial expressions so quickly.

26

(32) In the first paragraph, why does the author of the passage mention objects such as clouds?

1 To support the idea that people's surroundings can affect how well they are able to judge the emotions of others.
2 To describe how people who cannot identify faces also have trouble identifying certain other objects.
3 To help explain that our reactions to everyday objects in our environment are controlled by different areas of the brain.
4 To provide examples of everyday things on which people imagine they can see faces.

(33) Previous studies have shown that

1 people's judgments about what emotions real faces are expressing are influenced by other real faces they have seen immediately before.
2 people attach emotional meaning to false faces more quickly than they do to real faces.
3 people tend to judge the emotions expressed by false faces as happier and more positive than those expressed by real faces.
4 people take longer to distinguish false faces when the faces are not expressing any emotions.

(34) What do the researchers in Australia say about the brain's ability to assess the emotions expressed by faces?

1 The ability will likely disappear over time as it no longer provides an advantage to humans in terms of survival.
2 The fact that the brain uses loose criteria to identify faces allows people to quickly judge the emotions faces express.
3 The brain is only able to accurately identify the emotions faces express if those faces have very specific features.
4 The evolution of this ability occurred even though it created disadvantages as well as benefits for humans in the past.

Durians and Giant Fruit Bats

The football-sized durian fruit is well known for its unpleasant smell and creamy, sweet flesh. Known as the "king of fruits," durians are believed to have originated in Borneo, but they are now cultivated more widely, with over half of all durians consumed worldwide being grown in Thailand. Durians have long been popular throughout Southeast Asia, but their popularity is now spreading to other parts of the world. There are hundreds of kinds of durians, but the Musang King variety, which is grown almost exclusively in Malaysia, is one of the most highly valued. Durians contain high levels of vitamins, so they are often promoted for their health benefits, which has led to rising exports. In fact, experts predict there will be a 50 percent increase in shipments from Malaysia to China alone during the next decade. In order to take advantage of this situation, many Malaysian farmers have stopped producing crops such as palm oil in favor of producing durians.

Durian trees are not easy to grow, however. They require regular watering and feeding with fertilizer, and they are highly sensitive to temperature. Furthermore, they do not naturally grow in groves, but rather thrive when grown among other trees and shrubs, so growing them in an orchard as a single crop presents a challenge. Ensuring sufficient pollination of the flowers for the trees to produce a good harvest of fruit is a further difficulty for farmers. One characteristic of durian trees is that their flowers only release pollen at night, so insects such as honeybees that feed during the day do not pollinate them. Animals that are active at night take over the role of pollination, but only about 25 percent of a durian tree's flowers ever get pollinated naturally. Because of this, many farmers resort to the labor-intensive practice of pollinating by hand.

Studies have shown that giant fruit bats are the main natural pollinators of durian flowers. However, these bats are chased away or killed by many farmers, who simply see them as pests because they cause damage and reduce profits by feeding on the fruit. The bats are also threatened as a result of being hunted and sold as food, since there is a belief in some Southeast Asian cultures that eating the bats' meat helps to cure breathing problems. Without educating people about the benefits of giant fruit bats, the bats' numbers may decline further, which could have serious consequences for durian farming.

(35) According to the first paragraph, what is true about durian production?

1 Durians are now mainly grown in Malaysia because there is no longer enough land available to cultivate them in other Southeast Asian countries.

2 Although durians have been selling well in places where they were traditionally grown, they have yet to gain popularity in other countries.

3 Premium varieties of durians have been criticized by consumers because they have no more nutritional value than cheaper varieties.

4 Because of the increasing demand for durians, Malaysian farmers are switching from growing other crops to growing durians.

(36) One factor that durian farmers need to consider is that

1 although durian trees can be grown in almost any warm climate, they do best in areas where there are few other plants growing.

2 the tendency of durian trees to push out other plants is causing a sharp decline in the number of native plants.

3 durian trees should be grown in a location where they can be easily found by honeybees and other daytime pollinators.

4 if durian trees are left alone to be pollinated naturally, the trees are unlikely to produce a large amount of fruit.

(37) What is one thing the author of the passage says regarding giant fruit bats?

1 Durian production might suffer if awareness is not raised about the important role giant fruit bats play in durian flower pollination.

2 Many people in Southeast Asia have become ill as a result of eating bat meat that was sold illegally at some markets.

3 Some durian farmers deliberately attract giant fruit bats to their orchards so that they can catch them and sell their meat.

29

4 There has been a significant drop in natural pollinators of durian flowers because many giant fruit bats have died from breathing problems.

The Long Range Desert Group

During World War II, the British fought against Germany and Italy in the deserts of North Africa. Desert warfare was characterized by small battles between troops that were widely spread out, and there was a need to move quickly and at night to avoid both detection and the dangerous daytime heat. The area's vast size and sandy terrain made transporting supplies difficult, and the lack of water severely limited operations.

However, for one British army officer, Major Ralph Bagnold, these harsh conditions presented a strategic opportunity. Having spent years exploring the North African desert before the war, Bagnold knew the terrain well, and he was convinced that a small, highly mobile motorized unit that could observe and track enemy forces would be invaluable. At first, British commanders rejected his proposal to form such a unit, believing airplanes were better suited for such long-range intelligence gathering. Bagnold insisted, however, that gathering information on the ground would be advantageous, and his persistence led to the formation of the Long Range Desert Group (LRDG), with Bagnold as commander, in June 1940.

The LRDG was an unconventional unit from the outset. Usual distinctions between ranks did not apply; officers and regular soldiers were on first-name terms, and they were all expected to perform the same tasks. Rather than seeking men who would fight bravely on the battlefield, Bagnold wanted individuals with great stamina, resourcefulness, and mental toughness — men who could, for example, remain motivated and alert for extended periods despite limited access to drinking water. With specialized trucks adapted to desert conditions, the LRDG's patrols were equipped to operate independently for around three weeks and over a range of more than 1,600 kilometers. All necessary items, such as fuel, ammunition, and food, were carried by the unit, so careful supply planning was extremely important.

The LRDG's work mainly involved traveling deep behind enemy lines to observe their movements. The unit had access to a range of weaponry, and while the men were primarily trained to gather intelligence, they also planted mines and launched attacks against enemy airfields and fuel depots. When the Special Air Service (SAS) — a British army unit formed in 1941 to conduct raids behind enemy lines — suffered heavy casualties after parachuting into enemy territory on its first mission, the LRDG was tasked with bringing back the survivors. The rescue mission was a success, and because of its men's extensive knowledge of the desert, the LRDG was given the responsibility of bringing the SAS to and from all future targets by land, providing both transportation and navigation. This almost certainly helped the SAS accomplish its raids with greater success and fewer casualties.

The LRDG's greatest achievement came in 1943, when the unit found a route that enabled British forces to get around heavily defended enemy lines without being detected, allowing them to attack at weaker points in the defenses. This was a crucial turning point in the campaign in North Africa and contributed greatly to the British victory there. The LRDG went on to make significant contributions to the war effort in Europe until 1945.

(38) Major Ralph Bagnold was able to convince British army commanders that

    1 their soldiers were having limited success on missions in the desert because they were not being supplied with the right resources.

    2 the airplanes being used to fly over enemy territory and make observations in the desert were in need of major improvements.

    3 he could lead a unit of men on missions in the desert despite the fact that he had little experience in such an environment.

    4 using a ground-based unit to gather information about enemy activities in the desert would be an effective strategy.

(39) What is true regarding the Long Range Desert Group (LRDG)?

    1 The characteristics of the men chosen for it and the way it operated were different from those of traditional military units.

    2 Because of its limited budget, it had to manage with fewer resources and older weapons than other units.

3 There were a large number of men in its patrols, so the officers had to have special training in management techniques.

4 The success of its missions was heavily dependent on the group having supplies sent to it behind enemy lines on a regular basis.

(40) Which of the following best describes the relationship between the LRDG and the Special Air Service (SAS)?

1 The two units were combined so that land and air raids could be performed at the same time.

2 The similar nature of their operations led to competition between the two units and their unwillingness to assist each other.

3 The LRDG used its knowledge of the desert to help the SAS improve both the effectiveness and safety of its missions.

4 The involvement of the SAS in LRDG missions made it more difficult for the LRDG to stay behind enemy lines for long periods of time.

(41) According to the author of the passage, what happened in 1943?

1 A mistake made by the LRDG allowed enemy forces to strengthen their hold on territory that the British hoped to gain.

2 The transfer of the LRDG to Europe meant the SAS had no choice but to attack enemy forces in a heavily defended area without LRDG support.

3 The activities of the LRDG made it possible for the British army to gain a significant advantage that led to it defeating enemy forces in the area.

4 British commanders decided the LRDG would be better put to use defending British-held territory than observing enemy activities.

4
- *Write an essay on the given TOPIC.*
- *Use TWO of the POINTS below to support your answer.*
- *Structure: introduction, main body, and conclusion*
- *Suggested length: 120–150 words*
- *Write your essay in the space provided on Side B of your answer sheet.*

Any writing outside the space will not be graded.

TOPIC

Should people trust information on the Internet?

POINTS

- Learning
- News
- Online shopping
- Social media

一次試験
リスニング

──────── **Listening Test** ────────

There are three parts to this listening test.

Part 1	Dialogues: 1 question each	Multiple-choice
Part 2	Passages: 2 questions each	Multiple-choice
Part 3	Real-Life: 1 question each	Multiple-choice

※ Listen carefully to the instructions.

Part 1   ▶MP3 ▶アプリ ▶CD 1 **1**～**14**

No. 1
1 Get a blood test today.
2 Try to eat less for breakfast.
3 Go to lunch with Noah.
4 Have a medical checkup next week.

No. 2
1 She needs to take more time off.
2 She should be less concerned about money.
3 She is not ready for so much responsibility.
4 She deserves more pay.

No. 3
1 He needs to undergo further tests.
2 He will not be able to play in the game.
3 He needs to find a different form of exercise.
4 He has to stay at the hospital.

No. 4
1 Contact the new employee.
2 Speak to the manager.
3 Work the shift herself.
4 Change shifts with him.

No. 5
1 Contact the hotel about Internet access.
2 Confirm the meeting schedule.
3 Finish preparing the presentation.
4 Buy a ticket for the flight.

No. 6	1 Take a taxi home.
	2 Order more wine.
	3 Catch the last train home.
	4 Walk to the closest bus stop.

No. 7	1 Pick up the children from school.
	2 Cook dinner for his family.
	3 Buy the ingredients for tonight's dinner.
	4 Order food from a new restaurant.

No. 8	1 He has to pay an unexpected fee.
	2 He canceled his insurance policy.
	3 He is late for a meeting.
	4 The company cannot find his policy number.

No. 9	1 The man should not change his major.
	2 A career in communications might suit the man better.
	3 Graphic design is a good choice for the man.
	4 The man is not doing well in class.

No. 10	1 Find another online chat tool.
	2 Prepare a request for a software upgrade.
	3 Get more people to join online meetings.
	4 Ask to increase the company's budget.

No. 11	1 Go to the plant.
	2 Study Spanish.
	3 Meet with Barbara.
	4 Look for an interpreter.

No. 12	1 Radio for an ambulance.
	2 Move the woman's car for her.
	3 Give the woman a parking ticket.
	4 Wait in his police car.

Part 2 ◀)) ▶MP3 ▶アプリ ▶CD 1 **15**〜**21**

(A)

No. 13
1 It could not fly high enough.
2 It was too small and light.
3 It could only fly short distances.
4 It used a rare kind of fuel.

No. 14
1 It was tougher than other planes.
2 It had a new kind of weapon.
3 It could land very quickly.
4 It could drop bombs accurately.

(B)

No. 15
1 Water supplies decreased.
2 The air became less polluted.
3 Many people had to leave the island.
4 The number of trees increased.

No. 16
1 How to classify the new ecosystem.
2 What to use the water supply for.
3 Whether native plants should be protected.
4 Where agriculture should be allowed.

(C)

No. 17
1 She carried her camera everywhere.
2 She made friends with emergency workers.
3 She lent her camera to the children she took care of.
4 She went to many places as a tourist.

No. 18
1 She became famous early in her career.
2 She mainly took photos at auctions.
3 She held very large exhibitions.
4 She did not show people her photos.

36

(D)

No. 19
1 It does not require the use of fresh water.
2 It can only be done in certain climates.
3 It produces a large amount of gas.
4 It uses less meat than it did in the past.

No. 20
1 The machines it uses are very expensive.
2 It is damaging to wide areas of land.
3 It releases chemicals into nearby farmland.
4 It is frequently dangerous for workers.

(E)

No. 21
1 Young people's changing interests.
2 Young people's increasing need for exercise.
3 Young people's economic situation.
4 Young people's passion for nature.

No. 22
1 They are unlikely to survive long.
2 They do not do well outside of cities.
3 They rarely employ local people.
4 They take up too much space.

(F)

No. 23
1 Alligators have efficient jaws.
2 Alligators are related to dinosaurs.
3 Alligators have muscles in unusual places.
4 Alligators evolved at the same time as *T. rex*.

No. 24
1 To help with food digestion.
2 To sense other animals.
3 To create new blood vessels.
4 To control their body temperature.

||||| Part 3 ||||||||||||||||||||||||||||||||||||||||||| ◀» ▶MP3 ▶アプリ ▶CD 1 **22**～**27**

(G)

No. 25

Situation: You are on a plane that has just landed, and you need to catch your connecting flight. A flight attendant is making an announcement.

Question: What should you do first after getting off the plane?

1 Collect your luggage.
2 Take a bus to another terminal.
3 Find a gate agent.
4 Get a new boarding pass printed.

(H)

No. 26

Situation: You want to buy some stick-type incense to burn to help you relax. A store clerk tells you the following.

Question: Which incense brand should you buy?

1 Bouquet Himalaya.
2 Magnolia's Sanctuary.
3 Akebono.
4 Shirley's Gift.

(I)

No. 27

Situation: It is Monday, and you receive a voice mail from a representative at your new Internet provider. You have to work this Thursday from noon to 8 p.m.

Question: What should you do?

1 Reschedule for this weekend.
2 Reschedule for a weekday next week.
3 Reschedule for this Thursday morning.
4 Reschedule for this Friday after 6 p.m.

(J)

No. 28

Situation: You are applying to a college to study psychology. An admissions officer is talking to you about your application.

Question: What should you do?

1 Pay your application fee.
2 Go to a campus event next week.
3 Get a letter of recommendation.
4 Submit your high school records.

(K)

No. 29

Situation: You are on a trip abroad and want to take a free local tour. You get carsick easily. You are told the following at your hotel's information desk.

Question: Which tour is the best for you?

1 The one from 1 p.m.
2 The one from 2:30 p.m.
3 The one from 3 p.m.
4 The one from 5 p.m.

二次試験
面　接

問題カード（A日程）　　▶MP3　▶アプリ　▶CD4 **1**～**5**

You have **one minute** to prepare.

This is a story about a couple that wanted to save money.
You have **two minutes** to narrate the story.

Your story should begin with the following sentence:
One day, a woman was talking with her husband.

Questions

No. 1   Please look at the fourth picture. If you were the woman, what would you be thinking?

No. 2   Do you think it is better to buy a home than to rent a place to live?

No. 3   Should Japan increase the amount of green space in its cities?

No. 4   Do people these days maintain a good balance between their private lives and their careers?

問題カード（C日程）　　　▶MP3　▶アプリ　▶CD 4 6〜9

You have **one minute** to prepare.

This is a story about a couple who lived near the ocean.
You have **two minutes** to narrate the story.

Your story should begin with the following sentence:
One day, a couple was taking a walk by the beach.

Questions

No. 1   Please look at the fourth picture. If you were the husband, what would you be thinking?

No. 2   Do you think Japanese people should express their political opinions more?

No. 3   Do you think companies should do more to help society?

No. 4   Is it possible for the actions of individuals to help reduce global warming?

2022-1

一次試験　2022.6.5実施
二次試験　A日程　2022.7.3実施
　　　　　C日程　2022.7.17実施

Grade Pre-1

試験時間

筆記：**90分**
リスニング：**約30分**

一次試験・筆記　　　　　p.46〜61
一次試験・リスニング　　p.62〜67
二次試験・面接　　　　　p.68〜71

＊解答・解説は別冊p.49〜92にあります。
＊面接の流れは本書p.16にあります。

2022年度第1回　**Web特典「自動採点サービス」対応　オンラインマークシート**
※検定の回によって2次元コードが違います。
※筆記1〜3，リスニングの採点ができます。
※ PC からも利用できます（本書 p.8 参照）。

筆 記

1 To complete each item, choose the best word or phrase from among the four choices. Then, on your answer sheet, find the number of the question and mark your answer.

(1) After considering the case, the judge decided to show (   ) and only gave the man a warning. She said that he was clearly very sorry for his crime.
1 disgrace **2** closure **3** mercy **4** seclusion

(2) Lisa looks exactly like her twin sister, but she has a completely different (   ). She is very calm and rarely gets angry, unlike her sister.
1 temperament **2** accumulation
3 veneer **4** glossary

(3) *A:* Annabel, don't just (   ) your shoulders when I ask you if you've finished your homework. Give me a clear answer.
B: Sorry, Mom. I'm almost done with it.
1 echo **2** bow **3** dump **4** shrug

(4) When there is a big business convention in town, it is almost impossible to find a hotel with a (   ). Most hotels quickly get fully booked.
1 sprain **2** segment **3** transition **4** vacancy

(5) The detective (   ) the gang member for hours, but he would not say who had helped him commit the crime. Eventually, the detective stopped trying to get information from him.
1 discharged **2** converted
3 interrogated **4** affiliated

(6) To treat an injured ankle, doctors recommend (   ). This can be done by wrapping a bandage tightly around the injury.

1 depression   **2** progression   **3** compression   **4** suspicion

(7) *A:* It suddenly started raining heavily on my way home, and I got completely wet.

B: You should have (   ) my advice and taken an umbrella with you.

1 molded   **2** heeded   **3** twisted   **4** yielded

(8) As a way of attracting more (   ) customers, the perfume company began advertising its products in magazines read mainly by wealthy people.

1 theatrical   **2** brutal   **3** frantic   **4** affluent

(9) The teacher said that, apart from a few (   ) errors, the student's essay was perfect. He gave it the highest score possible.

1 trivial   **2** conclusive   **3** palatial   **4** offensive

(10) The injured soccer player watched (   ) as his replacement played in the final game. He had really wanted to continue playing.

1 substantially **2** previously   **3** enviously   **4** relevantly

(11) The new hotel in front of Abraham's apartment building is not tall enough to (   ) his view of the mountains beyond the city. He can still see them clearly.

1 obstruct   **2** delegate   **3** entangle   **4** boost

(12) Having spilled red wine on the white carpet, Martha tried to remove the (   ) with soap and water. However, she could not remove it completely.

1 stain   **2** slit   **3** bump   **4** blaze

(13) The war continued for a year, but neither side could (   ). With victory seemingly impossible, the two countries agreed to stop fighting.

1 devise　　　**2** prevail　　　**3** evolve　　　**4** reconstruct

(14) The leader used the political instability in his country as a (   ) for introducing strict new laws aimed at preventing any opposition to his rule.

1 trance　　　**2** downfall　　　**3** rampage　　　**4** pretext

(15) The suspect continued to (   ) his innocence to the police. He told them repeatedly he had been nowhere near the place where the crime had occurred.

1 conceal　　　**2** counter　　　**3** expire　　　**4** assert

(16) Good writers make every effort to (   ) mistakes from their work, but occasionally they miss some errors and have to make corrections later.

1 eliminate　　　**2** expend　　　**3** stabilize　　　**4** oppress

(17) After the kidnappers returned the child to its parents in exchange for a large (   ), they tried to escape with the money. Police soon caught them, however, and returned the money to the couple.

1 ransom　　　**2** applause　　　**3** monopoly　　　**4** prank

(18) Gaspar applied to go to a (   ) university. Unfortunately, his grades were not good enough, so he had to go to a lesser-known one.

1 prestigious　　　**2** spontaneous　　　**3** cordial　　　**4** petty

(19) The spies (   ) themselves as army officers in an attempt to enter the military base without being noticed.

1 chronicled　　　**2** disguised　　　**3** rendered　　　**4** revitalized

48

(20) Timothy is a very ( ) employee. He is reliable and eager to help, and he always shows loyalty to his company and coworkers.

1 grotesque   **2** defiant   **3** devoted   **4** feeble

(21) To help Paul lose weight, his doctor recommended that he ( ) his diet. Specifically, she suggested that he eat fewer fatty foods and more fiber.

1 modify   **2** pluck   **3** exclaim   **4** distill

(22) *A:* I've been so busy at work, and now I have to ( ) training our newest employee.

    B: That's too much. You should ask your boss if someone else can do it instead.

1 turn over   **2** contend with
3 prop up   **4** count off

(23) The young boy tried to blame his dog for the broken vase. However, his mother did not ( ) the lie and sent him to his room.

1 fall for   **2** hang on   **3** see out   **4** flag down

(24) In his speech, the CEO ( ) his plan for the company's development over the next five years. He hoped this would help guide everyone's work as the company grew.

1 mapped out   **2** leaped in   **3** racked up   **4** spaced out

(25) Last year, Harold spent all his money buying shares in various companies. He was ( ) the stock market performing well over the next few years.

1 casting away   **2** putting down
3 stepping up   **4** betting on

2

Read each passage and choose the best word or phrase from among the four choices for each blank. Then, on your answer sheet, find the number of the question and mark your answer.

The Peter Principle

A theory known as the Peter Principle may explain why there are many people in managerial positions who (**26**). According to the theory, employees who perform well in lower-level positions will eventually rise to positions they are not prepared for. The reason for this is that employees generally get promoted based on how well they perform in their current positions. Although this kind of promotion policy may seem logical, failing to fully consider employees' strengths and weaknesses results in them eventually reaching positions for which their abilities are unsuited.

One study examined the careers of salespeople who were promoted to managerial positions. As expected, the study found that the best salespeople were the most likely to receive promotions, but it also found that they performed the worst in managerial roles. The study showed that promoting employees based solely on current performance (**27**). Not only do companies end up with poor managers but they also lose their best workers in lower-level positions.

The researchers who carried out the study say that one problem is that companies make the mistake of simply assuming that high-performing employees will naturally be good managers. In most companies, new employees receive specialized training in how to do their jobs. (**28**), new managers are often given little or no training. This seems to suggest that one way to lessen the effects of the Peter Principle is to provide proper training for new managers.

(26) 1 earn lower-than-average salaries
2 love their jobs
3 have worked for several companies
4 perform poorly

(27) 1 has two disadvantages
2 cannot be avoided
3 is a gamble worth taking
4 prevents creative thinking

(28) 1 Of course
2 On the other hand
3 What is more
4 For a similar reason

Nearsightedness

Nearsightedness has been increasing around the world at a rapid rate. People with this condition can see objects that are close to them clearly, but objects that are far away appear blurry. Many people blame this trend on the use of digital screens. They claim that using devices such as computers and smartphones leads to eyestrain, and that blue light, which is produced by digital screens, damages light-sensitive cells in the back of the eye. However, there is no clear evidence that digital screens (29   ).

In fact, the rise in nearsightedness began before digital screens became widely used. Some research suggests that the real issue is that people (30   ). This results in a lack of exposure to natural light. Nearsightedness is caused by the stretching of the lens in the eye, which reduces its ability to focus light. However, the release of dopamine, a chemical produced by the brain, can prevent this from occurring, and exposure to natural light leads to greater dopamine production.

Some experts say that being outdoors for about three hours a day can help prevent nearsightedness. For many people, however, doing this is impossible due to school and work schedules. (31   ), it may be more practical for people to change the kind of lighting they use in their homes. There is already lighting available that provides some of the benefits of natural light, and it is hoped that research will provide more alternatives in the future.

(29) **1** have long-term effects on eyesight
      2 can help solve the problem
      3 can be used on all devices
      4 will improve in the future

(30) **1** sit too close to their screens
      2 rely too much on vision
      3 spend too much time indoors
      4 fail to do enough physical exercise

(31) **1** In the same way
      2 For example
      3 Despite this
      4 Instead

3 Read each passage and choose the best answer from among the four choices for each question. Then, on your answer sheet, find the number of the question and mark your answer.

Honey Fungus

The largest living organism on Earth is not a whale or other large animal. Rather, it belongs to the group of organisms which includes mushrooms and toadstools. It is a type of fungus commonly known as honey fungus, and its rootlike filaments spread underground throughout a huge area of forest in the US state of Oregon. DNA testing has confirmed that all the honey fungus in the area is from the same organism, and, based on its annual rate of growth, scientists estimate it could be over 8,000 years old. They also calculate that it would weigh around 35,000 tons if it were all gathered together.

As impressive as this honey fungus is, it poses a problem for many trees in the forest. The fungus infects the trees and absorbs nutrients from their roots and trunks, often eventually killing them. Unfortunately, affected trees are usually difficult to spot, as the fungus hides under their bark, and its filaments are only visible if the bark is removed. In the late fall, the fruiting bodies of the fungus appear on the outside of the trees, but only for a few weeks before winter. Although the trees attempt to resist the fungus, they usually lose the battle in the end because the fungus damages their roots, preventing water and nutrients from reaching their upper parts.

Full removal of the honey fungus in Oregon has been considered, but it would prove to be too costly and time-consuming. Another solution currently being researched is the planting of tree species that can resist the fungus. Some experts have suggested, however, that a change of perspective may be necessary. Rather than viewing the effects of the honey fungus in a negative light, people should consider it an example of nature taking its course. Dead trees will ultimately be recycled back into the soil, benefiting the area's ecosystem.

(32) According to the passage, what is one thing that is true about the honey fungus in Oregon?

1 It is a combination of different mushroom species that started to grow together over time.

2 It grew slowly at first, but it has been expanding more rapidly in the last thousand years.

3 It shares the nutrients it collects with the trees and other types of plant life that it grows on.

4 It is a single organism that has spread throughout a wide area by growing and feeding on trees.

(33) Honey fungus is difficult to find because

1 the mushrooms it produces change color depending on the type of tree that it grows on.

2 it is generally not visible, except when it produces fruiting bodies for a short time each year.

3 not only does it grow underground, but it also has an appearance that is like that of tree roots.

4 it is only able to survive in areas that have the specific weather conditions it needs to grow.

(34) What do some experts think?

1 People should regard the honey fungus's effects on trees as a natural and beneficial process.

2 The only practical way to deal with the honey fungus is to invest more time and money in attempts to remove it.

3 Trees that have been infected by the honey fungus can be used to prevent it from spreading further.

4 The honey fungus can be harvested to provide people with an excellent source of nutrients.

Intentional Communities

For hundreds of years, people have formed self-sustaining communities, often referred to as intentional communities, which are characterized by shared ideals, collective ownership, and common use of property. The first known intentional community was established in the sixth century BC by a Greek philosopher. Over the following centuries, a number of such communities were created by religious groups wishing to live outside mainstream society. Some of these, such as Christian monasteries and the collective farms called kibbutzim in Israel, remained successful for generations, while others lasted only a few years.

In the twentieth century, philosophical idealism, as seen in the back-to-the-land movement of the 1960s and 1970s, also motivated people to form intentional communities. By the early 1970s, it has been estimated that there were thousands of such communities in the United States alone, though many of those later disbanded. The Foundation for Intentional Communities now lists fewer than 800 communities in the United States and just under 250 in the rest of the world. Intentional communities that failed generally faced a similar challenge. Some people who came to stay were committed to ideals of shared work, growing their own food, and living collectively, but others were less serious. A cofounder of one community recalled, "We had an impractical but noble vision that was constantly undermined by people who came just to play."

Not all intentional communities are destined to fall apart, however. The ongoing success of Damanhur, a spiritual and artistic collective near Turin, Italy, is attributed to open communication and a practical approach. Damanhur organizes its members into family-like groups of 15 to 20 people. The community has found that creating intimacy becomes difficult if a "family" has more than 25 people. In contrast, when there are too few people in the "family," there is not enough collective knowledge to allow for effective decision-making. Damanhur's ideals, which are outlined in its constitution, are upheld by elected leaders, and tensions in the community are handled by holding playful mock battles where people fight with paint-filled toy guns.

It seems that all successful intentional communities share a common trait: the ability to constantly think ahead. As one Damanhur member put it, "You should change things when they work—not when they don't work." This strategy of making changes before problems occur has worked well for Damanhur and other successful communities, which suggests it is an effective way for intentional communities to fulfill the needs of their members in the long term.

(35) A common issue faced by intentional communities that failed was that

1 a majority of the community was in favor of someone joining, but a small number of individuals opposed it.
2 people joined the community with genuine interest, but they lacked the skills or knowledge to contribute effectively.
3 some members worked hard to follow the community's ideals, while others took a more casual approach to communal living.
4 the community set out to complete an ambitious project, but it could not complete it because of a lack of knowledge and financial resources.

(36) What is true of the social structure at Damanhur?

1 "Families" are free to create their own rules and do not necessarily have to follow the rules contained in the community's constitution.
2 The number of people in a "family" is controlled to create the best conditions for resolving group issues and maintaining good relationships.
3 The mock battles that are intended to solve disagreements sometimes become serious and result in some members leaving their "families."
4 The community contains "families" of different sizes so that members can choose whether to live in a large or a small group setting.

(37) According to the passage, how is Damanhur similar to other successful intentional communities?

1 Members of the community are allowed to exchange their responsibilities from time to time to prevent them from becoming exhausted.

2 The type of work the community does to earn income changes periodically so that members can learn new skills.

3 Members of the community take turns carrying out maintenance on the buildings and equipment that are owned collectively.

4 The community continually finds ways to satisfy the needs of its members rather than simply reacting to problems when they arise.

The British in India

Established in 1600, the British-owned East India Company was one of the world's largest corporations for more than two centuries. By trading overseas with various countries, such as India and China, it was able to import luxury items from these countries into Britain. The British government received a portion of the company's vast profits, so it was more than willing to provide political support. Due to its size, power, and resources, which included a private army of hundreds of thousands of Indian soldiers, the company pressured India into accepting trade contracts that, in general, were only of benefit to the company. After winning a battle against a local ruler in the 1750s, the company seized control of one of the wealthiest provinces in India. As a result, the East India Company was no longer solely acting as a business but also as a political institution, and it began forcing Indian citizens to pay it taxes.

The East India Company gained a reputation among the countries it did business with for being untrustworthy. It also started to lose popularity within the British Parliament because the company's dishonest trading habits damaged foreign relations with China. Then, in the 1850s, angered by the way they were being treated, a group of soldiers in the East India Company's army rebelled. They marched to Delhi to restore the Indian emperor to power, and their actions caused rebellion against the British to spread

58

to other parts of India. The rebellion was eventually brought under control after about two years, but it triggered the end of the East India Company. The British government, which blamed the East India Company for allowing the rebellion to happen, took control of India, and an era of direct British rule began. The British closed down the East India Company, removed the Indian emperor from power, and proceeded to rule India for almost a century.

While some claim that India benefited from British rule, typically using the construction of railways as an example, many historians argue that the country was negatively affected. In an effort to reinforce notions that British culture was superior, Indians were educated to have the same opinions, morals, and social preferences as the British. The British also implemented a policy known as "divide and rule," which turned Indians from different religious backgrounds against each other. The British government used this strategy to maintain its control over India, as members of these religions had joined forces during the earlier rebellion. However, nationalist feelings among Indians increased from the early 1900s, and India eventually gained its independence in the late 1940s.

Although the East India Company stopped operating more than a century ago, it has had a lasting influence. Some experts say it pioneered the concept of multinational corporations and ultimately led to the economic system of capitalism that is widespread today. Moreover, the connection between the British government and the East India Company set a precedent for using political power to help achieve business objectives.

(38) What was one result of India doing business with the East India Company?

1 India could afford to increase the size of its military because it was able to make trade deals with other countries.

2 India had little choice but to agree to business agreements that were unfavorable to it.

3 The Indian government needed to raise taxes in order to pay for losses from failed trade contracts.

4 The Indian government's relationship with China became worse, which almost resulted in a break in trade between the two countries.

(39) What led to the British government taking control of India?

1 The British government held the East India Company responsible for an uprising that occurred.

2 The Indian people voted for British rule after losing confidence in the Indian emperor's ability to rule the country effectively.

3 The Indian people asked for the help of the British in preventing a war between India and China.

4 The Indian emperor decided to join forces with the British as a political strategy to maintain control of India.

(40) One effect that British rule had on India was that

1 Indians were able to take part in the process of building a government that reflected their economic and social needs.

2 schools made an effort to educate their students to have an awareness of both Indian and British cultures.

3 divisions were created between different groups of Indians to prevent them from challenging British rule.

4 many of the railroads and other transportation systems built by the Indian government were destroyed.

(41) What does the author of the passage say about the East India Company?

1 The company prevented the British government from achieving its aim of expanding its rule to other countries in Asia.

2 While the company may have been successful during its time, its business model would not be effective in today's economy.

3 Although the company no longer exists, it has had a large impact on the present-day global economic landscape.

4 If the company had never been established, another one would likely have ended up having similar political and economic influence.

4
- *Write an essay on the given TOPIC.*
- *Use TWO of the POINTS below to support your answer.*
- *Structure: introduction, main body, and conclusion*
- *Suggested length: 120–150 words*
- *Write your essay in the space provided on Side B of your answer sheet.*

Any writing outside the space will not be graded.

TOPIC
Should people's salaries be based on their job performance?

POINTS
- Age
- Company profits
- Motivation
- Skills

リスニング

---- Listening Test ----

There are three parts to this listening test.

Part 1	Dialogues: 1 question each	Multiple-choice
Part 2	Passages: 2 questions each	Multiple-choice
Part 3	Real-Life: 1 question each	Multiple-choice

※**Listen carefully to the instructions.**

Part 1　　　▶MP3　▶アプリ　▶CD 1 28〜41

No. 1
1　He no longer drives to work.
2　His car is being repaired.
3　He cannot afford to buy gas.
4　His new bicycle was stolen.

No. 2
1　He wants to move out.
2　He likes to have parties.
3　He is not very open.
4　He is very messy.

No. 3
1　The other candidates were more qualified.
2　He forgot to call the manager yesterday.
3　The manager did not like him.
4　He missed the interview.

No. 4
1　The woman needs to pass it to graduate.
2　It does not match the woman's goals.
3　It is too advanced for the woman.
4　Passing it could help the woman find a job.

No. 5
1　The woman should take a break from school.
2　Working as a server is physically demanding.
3　Restaurant workers do not make much money.
4　Students should not get part-time jobs.

62

| No. 6 | 1 Buy a gift from the list.
2 Decline the wedding invitation.
3 Speak to Carla and Antonio.
4 Return the silver dining set. |

| No. 7 | 1 It has large portions.
2 It is a short drive from home.
3 It is cheaper than other places.
4 It has a good reputation. |

| No. 8 | 1 Spend time hiking.
2 Go fishing at a lake.
3 Take a ski trip.
4 Go sightseeing. |

| No. 9 | 1 Some customers complained about it.
2 One of the posts needs to be revised.
3 Kenneth should not edit the latest post.
4 It should be updated more frequently. |

| No. 10 | 1 Her wallet is missing.
2 Her train pass expired.
3 She missed her train.
4 She wasted her money. |

| No. 11 | 1 She did not like the pianist's playing.
2 She arrived at the concert late.
3 She could not focus on the concert.
4 She was unable to find her ticket. |

| No. 12 | 1 Call him back in the evening.
2 Give him new delivery instructions.
3 Change her delivery option online.
4 Tell him what time she will be home. |

Part 2 ◀)) ▶MP3 ▶アプリ ▶CD 1 42～48

(A)

No. 13
1 Water levels have decreased in many of them.
2 Laws to protect them need to be stricter.
3 Countries sharing them usually have the same usage rights.
4 They often make it difficult to protect borders.

No. 14
1 To suggest a solution to a border problem.
2 To suggest that poor nations need rivers for electricity.
3 To show that dams are often too costly.
4 To show how river usage rights can be complicated.

(B)

No. 15
1 It could be used as a poison.
2 It was tested on snakes.
3 It was difficult to make.
4 It was the first medical drug.

No. 16
1 It took many days to make.
2 Only small amounts could be made daily.
3 Production was very loosely regulated.
4 People there could watch it being made.

(C)

No. 17
1 They hunted only spirit bears with black fur.
2 They tried to keep spirit bears a secret.
3 They thought spirit bears were dangerous.
4 They believed spirit bears protected them.

No. 18
1 It is easier for them to catch food.
2 They are less sensitive to the sun.
3 It is harder for hunters to find them.
4 Their habitats are all well-protected.

64

(D)

No. 19
1 They generate power near where the power is used.
2 They are preferred by small businesses.
3 They do not use solar energy.
4 They are very expensive to maintain.

No. 20
1 Governments generally oppose its development.
2 Energy companies usually do not profit from it.
3 It can negatively affect property values.
4 It often pollutes community water sources.

(E)

No. 21
1 Caring for them costs too much money.
2 They are too difficult to capture.
3 They suffer from serious diseases.
4 They rarely live long after being caught.

No. 22
1 Zoos need to learn how to breed them.
2 Governments must make sure laws are followed.
3 They must be moved to new habitats.
4 Protecting them in the wild is not possible.

(F)

No. 23
1 They are more numerous than is typical.
2 They are similar to those of a distant area.
3 They are the largest in the region.
4 They include images of Europeans.

No. 24
1 To indicate certain times of the year.
2 To warn enemies to stay away.
3 To show the way to another settlement.
4 To provide a source of light.

Part 3 ◀» ▶MP3 ▶アプリ ▶CD1 49~54

(G)

No. 25

Situation: You want to feed your parrot, Toby, but cannot find his pet food. You check your cell phone and find a voice mail from your wife.

Question: Where should you go to find Toby's food?

1 To the kitchen.
2 To the living room.
3 To the front door.
4 To the garage.

(H)

No. 26

Situation: You want to read a book written by the author Greta Bakken. You want to read her most popular book. A bookstore clerk tells you the following.

Question: Which book should you buy?

1 *The Moon in Budapest.*
2 *Along That Tree-Lined Road.*
3 *Mixed Metaphors.*
4 *Trishaws.*

(I)

No. 27

Situation: Your company's president is making an announcement about a change in office procedures. You want to take time off next week.

Question: What should you do?

1 Speak to your manager.
2 Submit a request on the new website.
3 E-mail the members of your department.
4 Contact ABC Resource Systems.

(J)

No. 28

Situation: Your professor is showing your class a course website. You want to get extra credit to improve your grade.

Question: What should you do?

1 Submit an extra research paper through the website.
2 Complete additional reading assignments.
3 Create an online resource for the class.
4 Sign up for a lecture via the news section.

(K)

No. 29

Situation: You are a writer for a newspaper. You arrive home at 8:30 p.m. and hear the following voice mail from your editor. You need two more days to finish your column.

Question: What should you do?

1 Send the file to Bill.
2 Send the file to Paula.
3 Call Bill's office phone.
4 Call Bill on his smartphone.

問題カード（A日程）   ▶MP3 ▶アプリ ▶CD 4 10〜14

You have **one minute** to prepare.

This is a story about a mayor who wanted to help her town.
You have **two minutes** to narrate the story.

Your story should begin with the following sentence:
One day, a mayor was having a meeting.

Questions

No. 1   Please look at the fourth picture. If you were the mayor, what would you be thinking?

No. 2   Do you think people should spend more time outdoors to learn about nature?

No. 3   Should companies provide workers with more vacation days?

No. 4   Should the government do more to protect endangered animals?

問題カード（C日程） ▶MP3 ▶アプリ ▶CD 4 15～18

You have **one minute** to prepare.

This is a story about a woman who wanted to advance her career.
You have **two minutes** to narrate the story.

Your story should begin with the following sentence:
One day, a woman was talking with her company's CEO in the office.

Questions

No. 1 Please look at the fourth picture. If you were the woman, what would you be thinking?

No. 2 Are parents too protective of their children these days?

No. 3 Does the fast pace of modern life have a negative effect on people?

No. 4 Do you think the birth rate in Japan will stop decreasing in the future?

2021-3

一次試験　2022.1.23実施
二次試験　A日程　2022.2.20実施
　　　　　C日程　2022.3.6実施

Grade Pre-1

試験時間

筆記：90分
リスニング：約30分

一次試験・筆記　　　　p.74〜89
一次試験・リスニング　p.90〜95
二次試験・面接　　　　p.96〜99

＊解答・解説は別冊p.93〜136にあります。
＊面接の流れは本書p.16にあります。

2021年度第3回　**Web特典「自動採点サービス」対応 オンラインマークシート**
※検定の回によって2次元コードが違います。
※筆記1〜3，リスニングの採点ができます。
※PCからも利用できます（本書p.8参照）。

一次試験
筆　記

1 To complete each item, choose the best word or phrase from among the four choices. Then, on your answer sheet, find the number of the question and mark your answer.

(1) Roberto was a true (　　　　), so he immediately volunteered to join the army when his country was attacked by its neighbor.
1 villain　　　**2** patriot　　　**3** spectator　　　**4** beggar

(2) "Let's take a break now," said the chairperson. "We'll (　　　　) the meeting in about 15 minutes to talk about the next item on the agenda."
1 parody　　　**2** resume　　　**3** impede　　　**4** erect

(3) The first time Dan tried skiing, he found it difficult, but on each (　　　　) ski trip, he got better. Now he is an expert skier.
1 sufficient　　　**2** arrogant　　　**3** subsequent　　　**4** prominent

(4) The professor is an expert in his field but his (　　　　) behavior is a source of embarrassment to his colleagues. "He's always doing or saying strange things," said one.
1 secular　　　**2** eccentric　　　**3** vigilant　　　**4** apparent

(5) Because the vegetable stand was unable to (　　　　) that the vegetables it sold were organic, Eddie refused to buy them. It was his strict policy to eat only organic foods.
1 diverge　　　**2** certify　　　**3** evade　　　**4** glorify

(6) As a school guidance counselor, Ms. Pereira specializes in helping students find their (　　　　). She believes people should have careers that fit their personality and skills.
1 boredom　　　**2** vocation　　　**3** insult　　　**4** publicity

74

(7) The marathon runner was so thirsty after the race that she drank a large sports drink in just a few (   ) and then quickly asked for another one.

1 herds   **2** lumps   **3** gulps   **4** sacks

(8) The sleeping baby was (   ) by the loud music coming from her brother's room. She woke up crying, and it took a long time before she fell asleep again.

1 startled   **2** improvised   **3** prolonged   **4** tolerated

(9) *A:* I've been living in this apartment for a year now, and the (   ) is about to end. I have to decide if I should stay or move.

    B: If your rent will be the same, I recommend renewing your contract and staying.

1 token   **2** lease   **3** vicinity   **4** dialect

(10) The presidential candidate blamed the (   ) economy on the current president. He promised he would improve it if he were elected.

1 bulky   **2** functional   **3** ethnic   **4** sluggish

(11) *A:* Annie, how have you been? Did you enjoy your trip to Italy last year?

    B: I did, Pablo. Actually, I loved it so much that I've been (   ) moving there. I'd have to wait until my son graduates from high school, though.

1 contemplating   **2** emphasizing
3 vandalizing   **4** illustrating

(12) All the senators said they supported the new law, so it was no surprise when they voted for it (   ).

1 unanimously   **2** abnormally
3 mockingly   **4** savagely

(13) *A:* Did you go to Professor Markham's lecture?
   B: I did, but it was so boring I could only (   ) it for 15 minutes. After that, I left and went to a café.
   1 execute   **2** discern   **3** endure   **4** relay

(14) Houses built in cold regions can be surprisingly (   ) during the winter. Fireplaces, wood furniture, and nice carpets give the homes a warm, comfortable feeling.
   1 rigid   **2** rash   **3** cozy   **4** clumsy

(15) Mrs. Wilson was angry when her son broke the window, but she was more disappointed that he tried to (   ) her by telling her that someone else had done it.
   1 pinpoint   **2** suppress   **3** reroute   **4** deceive

(16) After Wanda was late for the third time in one month, her manager had a long talk with her about the importance of (   ).
   1 congestion   **2** drainage   **3** optimism   **4** punctuality

(17) The young author decided not to follow (   ) storytelling rules and wrote his novel in a unique style.
   1 vulnerable   **2** clueless   **3** conventional **4** phonetic

(18) The items in the box were packaged carefully because they were (   ), but some of them were still damaged when they were being delivered.
   1 coarse   **2** fragile   **3** immovable   **4** glossy

(19) The queen (   ) her adviser to the palace, but she became extremely angry when he took a long time to arrive.
   1 summoned   **2** hammered   **3** mingled   **4** trembled

(20) The general knew his troops were losing the battle, so he ordered them to (   ). Once they were safely away from the battlefield, he worked on a new plan to defeat the enemy.

1 entrust   **2** discard   **3** strangle   **4** retreat

(21) After Bill began university, he quickly realized that he did not have the (   ) to study advanced math, so he changed his major to geography.

1 capacity   **2** novelty   **3** bait   **4** chunk

(22) The police officer was shocked when his partner suggested they (   ) a suspect in order to force him to admit he had stolen money. Using violence in this way was not allowed.

1 rough up   **2** give out   **3** break up   **4** take over

(23) Julius was lucky to see a rare eagle on his first day of bird-watching. However, 20 years (   ) before he saw another one.

1 held out   **2** went by   **3** laid off   **4** cut off

(24) *A:* Are you going to cancel your weekend beach trip? There's a typhoon coming.

    B: We haven't (   ) going yet. It depends on which direction the typhoon moves in.

1 ruled out   **2** stood down
3 dragged into   **4** scooped up

(25) Jun always saved as much money as possible so he would have something to (   ) if he lost his job.

1 look up to   **2** fall back on
3 come down with   **4** do away with

2

Read each passage and choose the best word or phrase from among the four choices for each blank. Then, on your answer sheet, find the number of the question and mark your answer.

Donor Premiums

In recent years, it has become common for charities to give donor premiums — small gifts such as coffee mugs — to people who donate money to them. Many charities offer them, and it is widely believed that people give more when they receive donor premiums. However, researchers say that donor premiums tend to (**26**). Most people initially give money because they want to make the world a better place or help those who are less fortunate. When they receive gifts, though, people can start to become motivated by selfishness and desire. In fact, they may become less likely to donate in the future.

There may, however, be ways to avoid this problem. Research has shown that telling people they will receive gifts after making donations is not the best way to ensure they will contribute in the future. In one study, donors responded better to receiving gifts when they did not expect them. (**27**), future donations from such people increased by up to 75 percent. On the other hand, donors who knew that they would receive a gift after their donation did not value the gift highly, regardless of what it was.

Donor premiums may also have indirect benefits. Experts say gifts can (**28**). Items such as fancy shopping bags with charity logos, for example, signal that a donor is part of an exclusive group. Such gifts not only keep donors satisfied but also increase the general public's awareness of charities.

(26) 1 use up charities' resources
2 change donors' attitudes
3 encourage people to donate more
4 improve the public's image of charities

(27) 1 Instead
2 Nevertheless
3 In contrast
4 Furthermore

(28) 1 help promote charities
2 easily be copied
3 have undesirable effects
4 cause confusion among donors

Government Policy and Road Safety

Traffic-related deaths have declined in the United States due to the introduction of safety measures such as seat belts. Many critics of government policy claim, however, that fatalities could be further reduced with stricter government regulation. In fact, some say current government policies regarding speed limits may (**29**   ). This is because speed limits are often set using the "operating speed method." With this method, speed limits are decided based on the speeds at which vehicles that use the road actually travel, and little attention is paid to road features that could increase danger. Unfortunately, this means limits are sometimes set at unsafe levels.

Critics also point out that the United States is behind other nations when it comes to vehicle-safety regulations. In the United States, safety regulations are (**30**   ). Although some vehicles have become larger and their shape has changed, laws have not changed to reflect the increased danger they pose to pedestrians. Critics say that regulating only the safety of vehicle occupants is irresponsible, and that pedestrian deaths have increased even though there are simple measures that could be taken to help prevent them.

One measure for improving road safety is the use of cameras at traffic signals to detect drivers who fail to stop for red lights. Many such cameras were installed in the 1990s and have been shown to save lives. (**31**   ), the number of such cameras has declined in recent years. One reason for this is that there is often public opposition to them due to privacy concerns.

(29) 1 further support this trend
2 reduce seat-belt use
3 encourage dangerous driving
4 provide an alternative solution

(30) 1 designed to protect those inside vehicles
2 opposed by many drivers
3 actually being decreased
4 stricter for large vehicles

(31) 1 For instance
2 Likewise
3 Despite this
4 Consequently

3 Read each passage and choose the best answer from among the four choices for each question. Then, on your answer sheet, find the number of the question and mark your answer.

Caligula

The Roman emperor Caligula, also known as the "mad emperor," became so infamous that it is difficult to separate fact from legend regarding his life. During his reign, Caligula suffered what has been described as a "brain fever." It has often been said that this illness caused him to go insane, a claim that is supported by his seemingly irrational behavior following his illness. Today, however, some historians argue that his actions may have been a deliberate part of a clever, and horribly violent, political strategy.

After his illness, Caligula began torturing and putting to death huge numbers of citizens for even minor offenses. He also claimed to be a living god. These actions may suggest mental instability, but another explanation is that they were intended to secure his position. While Caligula was ill, plans were made to replace him, since he had not been expected to survive, and he likely felt betrayed and threatened as a result. Similarly, while claiming to be a god certainly sounds like a symptom of insanity, many Roman emperors were considered to become gods upon dying, and Caligula may have made the claim to discourage his enemies from assassinating him.

The story of how Caligula supposedly tried to appoint his horse Incitatus to a powerful government position is also sometimes given as evidence of his mental illness. However, Caligula is said to have frequently humiliated members of the Roman Senate, making them do things such as wearing uncomfortable clothing and running in front of his chariot. Elevating his horse to a position higher than theirs would have been another way to make the Senate members feel worthless. Eventually, though, Caligula's behavior went too far, and he was murdered. Efforts were made to erase him from history, leaving few reliable sources for modern historians to study. As a result, it may never be known whether he truly was the mad emperor.

(32) Some modern historians argue that

1 Caligula's seemingly crazy actions may actually have been part of a carefully thought-out plan.

2 the "brain fever" that Caligula suffered was more serious than it was originally believed to be.

3 Caligula should not be judged based on the period when he was suffering from a mental illness.

4 many of the violent acts that Caligula is reported to have carried out were performed by other Roman emperors.

(33) What may have been one result of Caligula's illness?

1 The fact that he almost died caused him to stop being interested in anything except gods and religion.

2 He felt that he could no longer trust anyone, leading him to change the way he governed.

3 Roman citizens thought he was still likely to die, so he attempted to show them that the gods would protect him.

4 He began to doubt old beliefs about Roman emperors, which led to serious conflicts with other members of the government.

(34) According to the passage, how did Caligula feel about the members of the Roman Senate?

1 He felt the people should respect them more, since they would do anything to protect him from his enemies.

2 He wanted to show his power over them, so he often found ways to make them feel they had no value.

3 He disliked them because he felt that they were physically weak and had poor fashion sense.

4 He was grateful for their support, so he held events such as chariot races in order to honor them.

The Friends of Eddie Coyle

In 1970, American writer George V. Higgins published his first novel, *The Friends of Eddie Coyle*. This crime novel was inspired by the time Higgins spent working as a lawyer, during which he examined hours of police surveillance tapes and transcripts in connection with the cases he was involved in. What he heard and read was the everyday speech of ordinary criminals, which sounded nothing like the scripted lines of TV crime dramas at the time. Higgins learned how real criminals spoke, and their unique, often messy patterns of language provided the basis for *The Friends of Eddie Coyle*. The novel's gritty realism was far removed from the polished crime stories that dominated the bestseller lists at the time. Higgins neither glamorized the lives of his criminal characters nor portrayed the police or federal agents in a heroic light.

One aspect that distinguishes *The Friends of Eddie Coyle* from other crime novels is that it is written almost entirely in dialogue. Given the crime genre's reliance on carefully plotted stories that build suspense, this was a highly original approach. Important events are not described directly, instead being introduced through conversations between characters in the novel. Thus, readers are given the sense that they are secretly listening in on Eddie Coyle and his criminal associates. Even action scenes are depicted in dialogue, and where narration is necessary, Higgins writes sparingly, providing only as much information as is required for readers to follow the plot. The focus is primarily on the characters, the world they inhabit, and the codes of conduct they follow.

Although Higgins's first novel was an immediate hit, not all readers liked the author's writing style, which he also used in his following books. Many complained that his later novels lacked clear plots and contained too little action. Yet Higgins remained committed to his belief that the most engaging way to tell a story is through the conversations of its characters, as this compels the reader to pay close attention to what is being said. Despite writing many novels, Higgins was never able to replicate the success of his debut work. Toward the end of his life, he became disappointed and frustrated by the lack of attention and appreciation his books received. Nevertheless, *The Friends of Eddie Coyle* is now considered by many to be one of the greatest crime novels ever written.

(35) According to the passage, George V. Higgins wrote *The Friends of Eddie Coyle*

1 because he believed that the novel would become a bestseller and enable him to quit the law profession to write full time.

2 after becoming frustrated about the lack of awareness among ordinary Americans regarding the extent of criminal activity in the United States.

3 because he wanted to show readers how hard lawyers worked in order to protect the victims of crime.

4 after being inspired by what he found during the investigations he carried out while he was a lawyer.

(36) In the second paragraph, what do we learn about *The Friends of Eddie Coyle*?

1 Higgins wanted to produce a novel which proved that the traditional rules of crime fiction still held true in modern times.

2 The novel is unusual because Higgins tells the story through interactions between the characters rather than by describing specific events in detail.

3 Higgins relied heavily on dialogue throughout the novel because he lacked the confidence to write long passages of narration.

4 Although the novel provides an authentic description of the criminal world, Higgins did not consider it to be a true crime novel.

(37) Which of the following statements would the author of the passage most likely agree with?

1 Despite the possibility that Higgins could have attracted a wider readership by altering his writing style, he remained true to his creative vision.

2 The first book Higgins produced was poorly written, but the quality of his work steadily increased in the years that followed.

85

3 It is inevitable that writers of crime novels will never gain the same level of prestige and acclaim as writers of other genres.
4 It is unrealistic for writers of crime novels to expect their work to appeal to readers decades after it was first published.

Mummy Brown

Thousands of years ago, ancient Egyptians began practicing mummification — the process of drying out the bodies of the dead, treating them with various substances, and wrapping them to preserve them. It was believed this helped the dead person's spirit enter the afterlife. Beginning in the twelfth century, however, many ancient mummies met a strange fate, as a market arose in Europe for medicines made using parts of mummies. People assumed the mummies' black color was because they had been treated with bitumen — a black, petroleum-based substance that occurs naturally in the Middle East and was used by ancient societies to treat illnesses. However, while ancient Egyptians did sometimes preserve mummies by coating them with bitumen, this method had not been used on many of the mummies that were taken to Europe. Furthermore, an incorrect translation of Arabic texts resulted in the mistaken belief that the bitumen used to treat mummies actually entered their bodies.

By the eighteenth century, advances in medical knowledge had led Europeans to stop using mummy-based medicines. Nevertheless, the European public's fascination with mummies reached new heights when French leader Napoleon Bonaparte led a military campaign in Egypt, which also included a major scientific expedition that resulted in significant archaeological discoveries and the documentation of ancient artifacts. Wealthy tourists even visited Egypt to obtain ancient artifacts for their private collections. In fact, the unwrapping and displaying of mummies at private parties became a popular activity. Mummies were also used in various other ways, such as being turned into crop fertilizer and fuel for railway engines.

One particularly unusual use of mummies was as a pigment for creating brown paint. Made using ground-up mummies, the pigment, which came to be known as mummy brown, was used as early as the sixteenth century, though demand for it grew around the time of

Napoleon's Egyptian campaign. Its color was praised by some European artists, who used it in artworks that can be seen in museums today. Still, the pigment had more critics than fans. Many artists complained about its poor drying ability and other negative qualities. Moreover, painting with a pigment made from deceased people increasingly came to be thought of as disrespectful — one well-known British painter who used mummy brown immediately buried his tube of the paint in the ground when he learned that real mummies had been used to produce it.

Even artists who had no objection to mummy brown could not always be certain its origin was genuine, as parts of dead animals were sometimes sold as mummy parts. Also, the fact that different manufacturers used different parts of mummies to produce the pigment meant there was little consistency among the various versions on the market. Additionally, the mummification process itself, including the substances used to preserve the bodies, underwent changes over time. These same factors make it almost impossible for researchers today to detect the presence of mummy brown in specific paintings. Given the pigment's controversial origins, however, perhaps art lovers would be shocked if they discovered that it was used in any of the paintings they admire.

(38) According to the author of the passage, why were ancient Egyptian mummies used to make medicines in Europe?

1 Disease was widespread in Europe at the time, so Europeans were willing to try anything to create effective medicines.

2 Because the mummies had not turned black in spite of their age, Europeans assumed they could provide health benefits.

3 Europeans mistakenly believed that a substance which was thought to have medical benefits was present in all mummies.

4 The fact that the mummies had religious significance to ancient Egyptians caused Europeans to believe they had special powers.

(39) What is one thing we learn about Napoleon Bonaparte's military campaign in Egypt?

1 A number of leaders saw it as a reason to also invade Egypt,

87

which led to the destruction of many ancient artifacts.

2 It revealed information about ancient Egyptian culture that led Europeans to change their opinion of medicines made from mummies.

3 It was opposed by wealthy Europeans, who thought it would result in their collections of ancient artifacts being destroyed.

4 It led to an increased interest in mummies and inspired Europeans to use them for a number of purposes.

(40) The author of the passage mentions the British painter in order to

1 provide an example of how the use of mummy brown was opposed by some people because it showed a lack of respect for the dead.

2 explain why mummy brown remained popular among well-known artists in spite of its poor technical performance.

3 give support for the theory that mummy brown was superior to other paint pigments because of its unique ingredients.

4 describe one reason why some artists developed a positive view of mummy brown after initially refusing to use it.

(41) What is one thing that makes it difficult to determine whether a painting contains mummy brown?

1 The substances that were added to the pigment to improve its color destroyed any biological evidence that tests could have detected.

2 The way that ancient Egyptians prepared mummies changed, so the contents of the pigment were not consistent.

3 Artists mixed the pigment with other types of paint before applying it to paintings, so it would only be present in very small amounts.

4 The art industry has tried to prevent researchers from conducting tests on paintings because of concerns that the results could affect their value.

4
- *Write an essay on the given TOPIC.*
- *Use TWO of the POINTS below to support your answer.*
- *Structure: introduction, main body, and conclusion*
- *Suggested length: 120–150 words*
- *Write your essay in the space provided on Side B of your answer sheet.*

Any writing outside the space will not be graded.

TOPIC
Should people stop using goods that are made from animals?

POINTS
- Animal rights
- Endangered species
- Product quality
- Tradition

リスニング

―― Listening Test ――

There are three parts to this listening test.

Part 1	Dialogues: 1 question each	Multiple-choice
Part 2	Passages: 2 questions each	Multiple-choice
Part 3	Real-Life: 1 question each	Multiple-choice

※**Listen carefully to the instructions.**

Part 1　　　　　　　🔊　▶MP3　▶アプリ　▶CD 2 **1**〜**14**

No. 1
1　His recent test scores.
2　Having to drop the class.
3　Finding a job.
4　Staying awake in class.

No. 2
1　The man could lose his job.
2　The man forgot his mother's birthday.
3　The man did not reply to her e-mail.
4　The man is not liked by the CEO.

No. 3
1　They take turns driving.
2　They were in a serious accident.
3　They work in a car repair shop.
4　Neither of them can drive next week.

No. 4
1　He cannot use his credit card.
2　He forgot to contact his card issuer.
3　He is short of cash today.
4　He lost his debit card.

No. 5
1　He is not suited to the call-center job.
2　He is learning the wrong interview techniques.
3　He should go to the interview he has been offered.
4　He should prioritize finding his dream job.

90

No. 6	1 Have the man take some tests.
	2 Encourage the man to exercise more.
	3 Give the man advice about work-related stress.
	4 Recommend the man to a specialist.

No. 7	1 He will take his vacation later in the year.
	2 He will meet with the personnel manager.
	3 He will do what his manager asks him to do.
	4 He will ask the woman to help him.

No. 8	1 It needs brighter colors.
	2 It fits the company's image.
	3 It is too similar to the current one.
	4 It needs to be redesigned.

No. 9	1 He has not read Alice's book yet.
	2 He cannot attend Alice's party.
	3 He is no longer friends with Alice.
	4 He was disappointed with Alice's book.

No. 10	1 Make sure she catches an earlier train.
	2 Use a different train line.
	3 Ride her bicycle to the office.
	4 Go into the office on weekends.

No. 11	1 Garbage collection has become less frequent.
	2 Garbage bags will become more expensive.
	3 Local taxes are likely to rise soon.
	4 The newspaper delivery schedule has changed.

No. 12	1 Try using some earplugs.
	2 Have Ranjit talk to her neighbors.
	3 Complain about her landlord.
	4 Write a message to her neighbors.

21年度第3回 リスニング

Part 2 ◀» ▶MP3 ▶アプリ ▶CD 2 15～21

(A)

No. 13
1 There are too many food choices available.
2 Schools often prepare uninteresting food.
3 They copy their parents' eating habits.
4 They have a desire to lose weight.

No. 14
1 Getting children to help make their own meals.
2 Encouraging children to play more sports.
3 Sometimes letting children eat unhealthy foods.
4 Rewarding children for eating vegetables.

(B)

No. 15
1 Ching Shih's pirates gained a number of ships.
2 Many pirate commanders were captured.
3 Most of the pirates were killed.
4 Ching Shih agreed to help the Chinese navy.

No. 16
1 She left China to escape punishment.
2 She gave away her wealth.
3 She formed a new pirate organization.
4 She agreed to stop her pirate operations.

(C)

No. 17
1 Their numbers increase at certain times.
2 They are being hunted by humans.
3 Their habitats have become smaller recently.
4 They have been eating fewer snowshoe hares.

No. 18
1 They only travel when looking for food.
2 They sometimes travel long distances.
3 They live much longer than other wildcats.
4 They always return to their original territories.

(D)

No. 19
1 Modern burial places are based on their design.
2 They were used for religious purposes.
3 They were only used by non-Christians.
4 The entrances were only found recently.

No. 20
1 Women used to be priests long ago.
2 The tunnels were not used as churches.
3 Few early Christians were women.
4 Priests used to create paintings.

(E)

No. 21
1 They often have successful family members.
2 They often have low levels of stress.
3 They may miss chances to enjoy simple pleasures.
4 They may make people around them happy.

No. 22
1 They do not need family support to stay happy.
2 Their incomes are not likely to be high.
3 Their positive moods make them more active.
4 They are more intelligent than unhappy people.

(F)

No. 23
1 They are becoming better at fighting disease.
2 Their numbers are lower than they once were.
3 Many of them are not harvested for food.
4 The waters they live in are becoming cleaner.

No. 24
1 Native American harvesting practices helped oysters grow.
2 Native American harvesting methods included dredging.
3 Native Americans still harvest oysters.
4 Native Americans only harvested young oysters.

93

Part 3 ◀» ▶MP3 ▶アプリ ▶CD 2 22~27

No. 25

(G)

Situation: You are about to take a tour bus around a town in Italy. You want to join the guided walking tour. You hear the following announcement.

Question: Which bus stop should you get off at?

1 Stop 4.
2 Stop 7.
3 Stop 9.
4 Stop 13.

No. 26

(H)

Situation: You are abroad on a working-holiday program. You call the immigration office about renewing your visa and are told the following.

Question: What should you do first?

1 Fill out an application online.
2 Request salary statements from your employer.
3 Show evidence of your savings.
4 Obtain a medical examination certificate.

No. 27

(I)

Situation: You are a supermarket manager. You want to reduce losses caused by theft. A security analyst tells you the following.

Question: What should you do first?

1 Give some staff members more training.
2 Install more security cameras.
3 Review customer receipts at the exit.
4 Clearly mark prices for fruit.

(J)

No. 28

Situation: You want a new washing machine. You currently own a Duplanne washing machine. You visit an electronics store in July and hear the following announcement.

Question: What should you do to save the most money?

1 Download the store's smartphone app.
2 Apply for the cash-back deal.
3 Exchange your washing machine this month.
4 Buy a new Duplanne washing machine in August.

(K)

No. 29

Situation: You see a suit you want in a local store, but it does not have one in your size. You do not want to travel out of town. A clerk tells you the following.

Question: What should you do?

1 Wait until the store gets some new stock.
2 Have the clerk check the other store.
3 Order the suit from the online store.
4 Have the suit delivered to your home.

二次試験
面　接

問題カード（A日程）　　◀))　▶MP3　▶アプリ　▶CD 4 19～23

You have **one minute** to prepare.

This is a story about a couple that wanted to be involved with their community.
You have **two minutes** to narrate the story.

Your story should begin with the following sentence:
One day, a husband and wife were going on a walk together.

Questions

No. 1   Please look at the fourth picture. If you were the wife, what would you be thinking?

No. 2   Do you think parents should participate in school events such as sports festivals?

No. 3   Do public libraries still play an important role in communities?

No. 4   Should more companies offer their employees flexible work schedules?

問題カード（C日程）　　　🔊　▶MP3　▶アプリ　▶CD 4 **24**〜**27**

You have **one minute** to prepare.

This is a story about a woman who wanted to go on a trip.
You have **two minutes** to narrate the story.

Your story should begin with the following sentence:
One day, a woman was talking with her friend.

Questions

No. 1 Please look at the fourth picture. If you were the woman, what would you be thinking?

No. 2 Do you think it is good for university students to have part-time jobs?

No. 3 Do you think it is safe to give personal information to online businesses?

No. 4 Should the government do more to increase the employment rate in Japan?

2021-2

一次試験　2021.10.10 実施
二次試験　A日程　2021.11.7 実施
　　　　　C日程　2021.11.23 実施

Grade Pre-1

試験時間

筆記：90分
リスニング：約30分

一次試験・筆記　　　　p.102～117
一次試験・リスニング p.118～123
二次試験・面接　　　　p.124～127

＊解答・解説は別冊p.137～180にあります。
＊面接の流れは本書p.16にあります。

2021年度第2回　**Web特典「自動採点サービス」対応 オンラインマークシート**
※検定の回によって2次元コードが違います。
※筆記1～3，リスニングの採点ができます。
※ PC からも利用できます (本書 p.8 参照)。

筆記

1 To complete each item, choose the best word or phrase from among the four choices. Then, on your answer sheet, find the number of the question and mark your answer.

(1) Kevin's boss believes the need for safety (　　) the time savings that come with taking risks. He would rather deal with delays in construction projects than with careless accidents.
  1 grasps　　**2** outweighs　　**3** declares　　**4** captivates

(2) *A:* Why do you want to move? Your apartment is so nice.
  B: I need somewhere more (　　). This place is too small for all my possessions.
  1 tragic　　**2** legible　　**3** tentative　　**4** spacious

(3) The publishers of *Nature Lover* magazine are worried about its (　　). The number of readers has declined from over 40,000 five years ago to 15,000 today.
  1 aviation　　　　　　**2** circulation
  3 commencement　　**4** imprisonment

(4) The young politician has a small but (　　) following. His supporters are extremely enthusiastic at his campaign events, and they travel long distances just to hear him speak.
  1 holistic　　**2** fanatical　　**3** mellow　　**4** illogical

(5) A (　　) built shelf would have supported Salma's heavy books, but the cheap one she decided to use broke under the weight.
  1 loyally　　**2** fondly　　**3** sturdily　　**4** vastly

(6) The ambassador worked hard to (　　) a close relationship between the two countries so that they would never go to war again.
  1 tickle　　**2** swallow　　**3** litter　　**4** nurture

(7) The climate expert said that vehicle (　　　) were a major cause of global warming. He presented data showing how much CO_2 cars released into the environment each year.

1 withdrawals　　　　　**2** collisions
3 settlements　　　　　**4** emissions

(8) Robert lives in a log cabin in a very (　　　) area. The nearest village is more than 90 minutes away by car.

1 remote　　**2** virtual　　**3** blunt　　**4** swift

(9) Yesterday, Rhett (　　　) while working in the garden. When he woke up, his wife and children were standing around him with worried faces.

1 diluted　　**2** fainted　　**3** persisted　　**4** corrected

(10) The writer edited his essay for (　　　), making an extra effort to improve the parts where his writing was difficult to understand.

1 clarity　　**2** appetite　　**3** shelter　　**4** preference

(11) The company had a (　　　) in sales last year, so it has launched a more aggressive advertising campaign to regain customers.

1 suite　　**2** coma　　**3** dip　　**4** ramp

(12) Randy was known for his (　　　) lying, so no one believed his stories about his incredible trip even though they were true.

1 miserly　　**2** sacred　　**3** habitual　　**4** stale

(13) As a young man, Stephano was extremely (　　　). He was so concerned about his appearance that he spent nearly all his salary on clothes, shoes, and skin products.

1 crafty　　　　　**2** inopportune
3 unsound　　　　**4** vain

103

(14) Although Suzanne was puzzled by the bright blue lights in the night sky, as a scientist, she knew there had to be a (   ) explanation for them.

1 steep   **2** lawless   **3** rational   **4** downcast

(15) The (   ) members at the college have a great reputation, and young people come from across the country to be taught by them.

1 custody   **2** faculty   **3** retainer   **4** seizure

(16) When Bert and Eva were asked how they have been able to (   ) their relationship for 40 years, they said the key is to always communicate honestly with each other.

1 dispatch   **2** mistrust   **3** impair   **4** sustain

(17) At the newspaper, the editors work on (   ) shifts. For one month, some of them work early shifts and some work late shifts. The following month, they switch.

1 rotating   **2** dissolving   **3** devoting   **4** exerting

(18) Nora did not enjoy watching the horror movie. Every time something frightening happened, she had to resist the (   ) to scream.

1 pessimism   **2** pitch   **3** impulse   **4** vacuum

(19) The man's hike through the forest was cut short when he was arrested for (   ). He had no idea that he had accidentally entered land owned by the government.

1 trespassing   **2** endorsing   **3** swaying   **4** convening

(20) Leo played well in the final game of the chess tournament, but he was unable to (   ) his opponent. She was just too good.

1 outsmart   **2** inflame   **3** update   **4** shepherd

(21) Martin had spent four hours cleaning up his yard. When he realized that he was only half finished, he suddenly felt very ( ).

1 steady   **2** hasty   **3** weary   **4** sly

(22) When the man saw a young girl fall off the boat, he immediately ( ) the sea and swam to rescue her.

1 wheeled out   **2** whipped up
3 plunged into   **4** tucked in

(23) *A:* This wind is perfect for flying our kite.
B: Yeah, you're right. We should head to the park before it ( ).

1 dies down   **2** acts up   **3** falls apart   **4** peels away

(24) *A:* Honey, we may have to ( ) the family picnic this week. The weather forecast is predicting rain.
B: In that case, we can just have a pizza party at home instead.

1 get by   **2** opt for   **3** call off   **4** play up

(25) Greg enjoyed his part-time job at the café, but he found he could not ( ) the salary he was getting, so he started looking for a full-time job.

1 roll around   **2** rip up
3 wash down   **4** live on

2 Read each passage and choose the best word or phrase from among the four choices for each blank. Then, on your answer sheet, find the number of the question and mark your answer.

The Hanging Gardens of Babylon

In the fifth century BC, lists of the world's most impressive works of art and architecture began appearing in Greek texts. The most famous such list describes seven particularly amazing sites. Only one of these "Seven Wonders of the Ancient World" — the Pyramids of Giza, in Egypt — survives today. (　**26**　), historians and archaeologists have discovered sufficient evidence to confirm that five more actually existed. The seventh, however, remains a mystery: the Hanging Gardens of Babylon.

The gardens were long thought to have been constructed by King Nebuchadnezzar II in the city of Babylon, in present-day Iraq. Written records from the time of Nebuchadnezzar's rule, however, (　**27**　). The gardens have been mentioned in various ancient texts, which describe a tall, multileveled structure lined with vegetation, but these were all produced centuries after the gardens were said to have been built. Without any firsthand records of the gardens' construction, archaeologists have been unable to locate any ruins in the area that prove they ever existed.

Research by scholar Stephanie Dalley suggests that efforts to find the gardens (　**28**　). Dalley translated texts written by a king named Sennacherib, who lived a century before Nebuchadnezzar. The texts describe impressive raised gardens at Sennacherib's palace. Sennacherib, however, ruled in the city of Nineveh, 300 miles from Babylon. Dalley notes that Sennacherib also constructed complex systems for transporting water into Nineveh, and she believes these could have been used to maintain the gardens there. If Dalley is correct, ancient descriptions of the Hanging Gardens of Babylon may actually refer to the gardens at Sennacherib's palace.

106

(26)
1 For example
2 Because of this
3 Nonetheless
4 In short

(27)
1 make no mention of the gardens
2 disagree about the size of the gardens
3 suggest the gardens did not last long
4 describe the gardens very differently

(28)
1 have already been successful
2 should ignore written sources
3 may be focusing on the wrong location
4 could be destroying their remains

Aquaculture and Wild Fish Stocks

For decades, the world's wild fish populations have been declining, mainly due to overfishing. As the situation has become increasingly serious, it has often been suggested that aquaculture, also known as fish farming, should be promoted as an alternative to commercial fishing. It appears, however, that the aquaculture industry has (29   ). In a recent study, researchers analyzed historical data on both aquaculture and traditional fishing over a 44-year period. In eight out of nine cases, aquaculture did nothing to relieve the pressure on wild fish populations, despite having greatly increased the production of farmed fish.

The idea that a resource can be conserved by using another, more easily replaceable one seems logical. However, cases in various industries suggest that the opposite is true. For example, it was once assumed that replacing traditional energy sources with renewable ones would lower demand for fossil fuels, but the increased supply has actually led to greater overall energy consumption. (30   ), it is now believed that the availability of farmed fish has merely encouraged people to consume fish in greater quantities.

There is also another problem related to aquaculture. For years, many aquaculture companies have focused on farming species such as salmon and tuna, which unfortunately have to be fed smaller fish that are caught in the wild. Experts say this problem (31   ), however. By focusing on farming types of fish that eat algae or other common plantlike organisms, fish farms can become more ecologically friendly instead of making the situation worse.

(29) **1** not developed as quickly as expected
  2 provided a solution to the problem
  3 not had the effect that was intended
  4 benefited from lessons learned by fishermen

(30) **1** Similarly
  2 Regardless
  3 In contrast
  4 For one thing

(31) **1** is difficult to measure
  2 has helped wild fish populations
  3 was not caused by aquaculture
  4 can easily be fixed

3 *Read each passage and choose the best answer from among the four choices for each question. Then, on your answer sheet, find the number of the question and mark your answer.*

The Rebirth of the Scottish Whiskey Industry

During the 1980s, the Scottish whiskey industry was in a slump. Falling sales led to the closure of a number of long-established whiskey makers, and many experts believed the decline to be irreversible. At that time, rival beverages, such as vodka and rum, were aggressively marketed, so they became fashionable among younger people. Prior to the 1980s, the custom of consuming whiskey had been passed down from generation to generation. This had led the whiskey industry to assume its consumer base was guaranteed, but the younger generation became less likely to follow family traditions, and the industry paid a heavy price in the form of falling sales.

A further problem was that the Scottish whiskey industry had greatly increased production in the 1970s. This was risky because whiskey requires aging, a process that can take several decades. The aging process made adjusting production to meet demand a near impossibility. By the 1980s, the falling demand for whiskey, which was made worse by an economic downturn, had created a massive surplus. Fierce competition between whiskey manufacturers led to severe price cuts and the manufacturing of new, lower-quality products that harmed the industry's overall reputation. Even famous manufacturers with long-established reputations for excellence went out of business.

Fortunately, the situation was not permanent. Scottish whiskey producers started focusing on promoting high-quality products known as single-malt whiskeys. Also important were their efforts to inform consumers about the merits of these whiskeys, why they commanded a higher price, and how they could be paired with food or cigars. This strategy was highly successful and encouraged consumers abroad to open their wallets for premium Scottish whiskeys. This, in turn, led to whiskey makers in other nations imitating the strategy and creating their own luxury brands. Today, interest in and demand for whiskey has never been stronger.

110

(32) In the years before the 1980s, the Scottish whiskey industry

1 realized it needed to focus its marketing on various age groups, rather than trying to appeal mainly to younger people.

2 mistakenly believed younger people would always consume whiskey without makers having to promote it.

3 was charging extremely high prices for its products despite the fact that many people could not afford them.

4 had cooperated with makers of other types of alcoholic beverages to prevent a decline in overall alcohol consumption and sales.

(33) What was one problem that was faced by the Scottish whiskey industry?

1 Lack of expertise made it impossible for companies to offer the level of quality that their customers expected.

2 An inability to supply the market with large quantities of whiskey caused consumers to lose interest in the product.

3 Consumers made it clear they were no longer interested in cheaper brands that were only aged for a short time.

4 Difficulties in predicting what quantity could be sold in the future caused manufacturers to produce too much.

(34) What conclusion can be made about the changes to whiskey production that have taken place since the 1980s?

1 The foreign market has shrunk because most whiskey drinkers in other countries prefer single-malt whiskeys over other types.

2 Whiskey consumers have become more aware of the value of single-malt whiskeys and are willing to pay higher prices for them.

3 Although the popularity of Scottish whiskey has been reestablished, makers in other countries have yet to experience similar growth.

4 Competition bctwccn whiskey makers has led to lower prices, which has caused overall whiskey sales to rise again.

Richard III

In 2012, the body of Richard III, king of England from 1483 to 1485, was found beneath a parking lot in the English city of Leicester. Richard was the subject of one of William Shakespeare's most well-known plays and was one of England's most infamous rulers. He is commonly remembered as a physically disabled man who was desperate to become king and murdered his brother and two nephews in order to achieve his goal. Richard's reputation does not originate in Shakespeare's play, but further back, in Thomas More's *History of King Richard III*. Modern-day experts view many of the details in More's book as highly questionable, since they were written in support of the family that won the throne from Richard, but the book's portrayal of Richard as evil became the basis for the negative reputation of him that remains to this day.

The Richard III Society, formed in 1924 with the aim of researching the king's life, strongly disputes the common image of Richard. In the hope of restoring his reputation, the society helped sponsor the research that led to the discovery of his body, and some of the findings of the society and other researchers have been particularly eye-opening. According to analysis of the skeleton, it turns out that Richard's reported physical disabilities were largely a myth. In fact, some of the injuries observed on the bones suggest that Richard likely fought in battle, which supports historical reports that suggest he was a skilled soldier.

Debate continues, however, about how Richard became king and the things he did during his two years in power. The Richard III Society points to his notable social and political reforms and claims that he is innocent of the murders that were the source of his unfortunate reputation. However, while acknowledging that some of Richard's policies were beneficial, many historians believe he was far from a generous or caring king and may very well have committed cruel acts. In the end, it is probably wisest to see Richard as a ruler who operated in a manner typical of the time in which he lived, and to realize that exactly how he came to power may not really matter that much. As Cardinal Vincent Nichols, archbishop of Westminster, explains, "In his day, political power was invariably won or maintained on the battlefield and only by ruthless determination, strong alliances and a willingness to employ the use of force."

(35) What is one thing the passage says about Thomas More's *History of King Richard III*?

1 It is not reliable because it was influenced by the play that was written about Richard III by William Shakespeare.

2 It provided many important clues that helped researchers involved in the recent discovery of the body of Richard in Leicester.

3 It strongly influenced people's image and opinion of Richard despite some of the information in it likely being inaccurate.

4 It contains evidence that proves that Richard did not actually murder his brother and other family members.

(36) As a result of analysis of Richard's body, it was learned that

1 he died in a way that was very different from that which people in the past believed to be the case.

2 not only was he mostly free from physical disabilities, but he may also have been a capable fighter.

3 the injuries he suffered in his final battle were serious, but they were probably not the cause of his death.

4 his physical appearance likely had a greater influence on people's impression of him than his ability as king.

(37) Which of the following statements would the author of the passage most likely agree with?

1 It is a mistake to judge Richard's ability based only on the losses he suffered on the battlefield and not on the reforms he introduced.

2 The historians who claim that Richard knowingly carried out terrible acts are likely to be incorrect in their assessment of him.

3 The crimes that Richard committed while he was king greatly exceed the positive things he did for the country.

4 Richard was likely no better or worse as a ruler than other kings who ruled England in the distant past.

The Temples of Jayavarman VII

At the height of King Jayavarman VII's rule, his Khmer empire covered most of Southeast Asia, with its center at Angkor, in present-day Cambodia. Prior to Jayavarman's rule, the political situation in the region had been unstable as a result of ongoing military struggles between shifting alliances of powerful local warlords, as well as battles between these alliances and the neighboring Cham people. After a Cham invasion defeated the Khmer empire's previous ruler, however, Jayavarman and his allies not only drove out the invaders but also managed to crush other warlords who hoped to rule the empire themselves. Jayavarman gained the throne in 1181.

Jayavarman's rule, which lasted for more than 30 years, brought peace and prosperity to the region, but he also seems to have been obsessed with constructing as many Buddhist temples as possible during his reign. Though promotion of religion had long been a fundamental part of Khmer culture, Jayavarman took it to a whole new level, building temples faster and in greater numbers than any previous king. Some researchers suggest he did this because he felt his time may be limited — he became king relatively late in life, at the age of 61, and he suffered from a long-term medical condition.

Jayavarman was a passionate follower of Buddhism, which was reflected in his concern for the well-being of his people. In addition to the many temples he built, he also built over a hundred hospitals, each employing doctors, pharmacists, and other healthcare professionals. The quality of care was advanced for the time: pulse readings were used to aid diagnoses, and butter and honey were prescribed as medicines. Supplies from the government arrived at these hospitals frequently, and it appears that any citizen in the empire, regardless of income or social standing, was eligible for treatment at no cost. Such a visible demonstration of generosity likely helped convert people to Buddhism as well as solidify Jayavarman's reputation as a king who had genuine compassion for his people.

While Jayavarman's time as king is considered by many to be the Khmer empire's golden age, it may also have paved the way for the empire's downfall. According to some researchers, Jayavarman's temple construction was evidence of his policy of centralizing power. As the king himself took ownership of the temples' lands, a unified, government-controlled system emerged, depriving local landowners of power. Meanwhile, construction of the temples required that tens of thousands of people relocate to cities, which meant there were far fewer people in rural areas to farm the land and produce food for the empire. Furthermore, the building projects used up a significant amount of the empire's wealth. These factors combined became a huge problem for later Khmer kings when the empire suffered because of droughts and monsoons. The highly centralized system lacked the wealth, agricultural labor force, and flexibility to overcome the effects of these natural disasters, leading to the empire's eventual collapse.

(38) What is one thing that we learn about Jayavarman VII?

1 By successfully making the Cham people allies rather than enemies, he was able to take control of the Khmer empire.

2 He was able to become the king of the Khmer empire by cooperating with other leaders in the region.

3 After tricking the previous king into attacking an enemy kingdom, he was able to take over that region as well as his own.

4 He gradually strengthened the Khmer empire in order to make it powerful enough to invade and defeat the neighboring kingdom.

(39) The passage suggests that one reason Jayavarman built so many temples was that

1 people demanded that the Khmer empire open itself up to Buddhism to stop the spread of a deadly disease.

2 he hoped to use the temples as a way to keep other Khmer rulers satisfied and prevent them from rebelling against his government.

3 he wanted to show his people that he was different from the previous ruler, who they felt had not been as religious as he should have been.

4 he likely believed that he did not have very long to live and wished to achieve as much as possible during his time as king.

(40) What is true of the hospitals built by Jayavarman?

1 They were well staffed but lacked adequate medical supplies for the large numbers of people who required treatment.

2 They provided medical treatment at the government's expense to all Khmer people who were in need of it.

3 They demonstrated that Jayavarman only had compassion for Khmer people who had accepted Buddhism.

4 They were seen by leaders in the region as an inappropriate use of funds that were supposed to be solely for the purpose of promoting Buddhism.

(41) What was one result of Jayavarman's temple building?

1 Local landowners felt betrayed by Jayavarman, causing many to refuse to support him when the Khmer empire was attacked.

2 It angered rural people who were forced to move to cities, so they attempted to remove Jayavarman from power.

3 It required the use of so many resources that it left the Khmer empire unable to deal with problems it faced in the future.

4 It proved valuable in diverting the attention of Khmer citizens away from the effects of frequent natural disasters in the region.

4
- *Write an essay on the given TOPIC.*
- *Use TWO of the POINTS below to support your answer.*
- *Structure: introduction, main body, and conclusion*
- *Suggested length: 120–150 words*
- *Write your essay in the space provided on Side B of your answer sheet.*

Any writing outside the space will not be graded.

TOPIC
Is it beneficial for workers to change jobs often?

POINTS
- Career goals
- Motivation
- The economy
- Working conditions

一次試験

──────── **Listening Test** ────────

There are three parts to this listening test.

Part 1	Dialogues: 1 question each	Multiple-choice
Part 2	Passages: 2 questions each	Multiple-choice
Part 3	Real-Life: 1 question each	Multiple-choice

※**Listen carefully to the instructions.**

Part 1 　　　▶MP3 ▶アプリ ▶CD 2 28〜41

No. 1
1　She will find it hard to get the money.
2　She barely knows the bride.
3　She can no longer attend the wedding.
4　She already bought a gift.

No. 2
1　Take the 6:30 flight.
2　Change his flight.
3　Pay extra for an upgrade.
4　Give up his window seat.

No. 3
1　She has a high fever.
2　She requested a different room.
3　The air conditioner is not working properly.
4　Room service has not arrived yet.

No. 4
1　Sharing the responsibilities.
2　Shortening Patty's visit.
3　Making the decision later.
4　Postponing the visit.

No. 5
1　The class is not challenging enough.
2　The professor is too busy to help them.
3　The study guide is not helpful.
4　The book is difficult to understand.

No. 6	1 Susan invited her coworkers to lunch.
	2 Susan's farewell party is tomorrow.
	3 The man does not know Susan's e-mail address.
	4 The man could not organize a farewell party.

No. 7	1 She is not used to being married yet.
	2 She does not like being busy at work.
	3 She needs to adjust to her new job.
	4 She is ready for another vacation.

No. 8	1 Reschedule the appointment.
	2 Come back tomorrow.
	3 Speak with his secretary.
	4 Call Mr. Phelps another time.

No. 9	1 The man should not complain about the noise.
	2 The man should not have taken the train.
	3 The other passengers should be more polite.
	4 The baby's parents should be more careful.

No. 10	1 The school he graduated from is not well known.
	2 He has never cooked French food before.
	3 He did not have a job over the summer.
	4 His résumé contained too many mistakes.

No. 11	1 The woman should prepare more for the audition.
	2 The woman's career plan is unrealistic.
	3 He chose the wrong major in college.
	4 He should have pursued a career in music.

No. 12	1 Purchase more blankets.
	2 Replace their heating unit.
	3 Call the electric company.
	4 Use the heating less at night.

Part 2 　◀» ▶MP3 ▶アプリ ▶CD 2 42~48

(A)

No. 13
1 They do not share genetic similarities.
2 They met and had children centuries ago.
3 They shared knowledge about building rafts.
4 They had little experience as sailors.

No. 14
1 A raft could be used to cross the Pacific Ocean.
2 It is unlikely Native Americans crossed the Pacific Ocean.
3 Polynesians' rafts were superior to their canoes.
4 Some Pacific islands could not be reached by boat.

(B)

No. 15
1 It has little effect on people's productivity.
2 It helps students perform better on tests.
3 It might make certain tasks more difficult to do.
4 It improves people's mental health.

No. 16
1 It can be effective during breaks.
2 It can actually make work less enjoyable.
3 It improves communication between workers.
4 It only has a small effect on concentration.

(C)

No. 17
1 They make more sounds than dolphins.
2 The sounds they make have meaning.
3 Their sounds are not very complex.
4 Their communication system has changed.

No. 18
1 They recorded the sounds that sleeping bats made.
2 They matched bat sounds to those of other animals.
3 They monitored bats in their natural environment.
4 They used a computer program to categorize bat sounds.

120

(D)

No. 19
1 The rivers and lakes there are polluted.
2 It is home to a number of rare species.
3 Important products are developed there.
4 It is no longer open to tourists.

No. 20
1 It would not affect local residents.
2 It could bring long-term benefits.
3 It would boost the tourist industry.
4 It could do more harm than good.

(E)

No. 21
1 It was discovered by chance.
2 It was smaller than archaeologists expected.
3 It is the oldest tomb in Egypt.
4 It has never been photographed.

No. 22
1 The writings in the tomb could not be translated.
2 The body of Hetepheres was not in the tomb.
3 All of the tomb's treasures had disappeared.
4 They were not allowed to study the jewelry.

(F)

No. 23
1 It causes more problems for wealthy families.
2 It has been occurring less frequently.
3 It may especially affect teenagers.
4 It has a significant impact on adults' health.

No. 24
1 Moving increases the rate of divorce.
2 Moving helps solve problems at school.
3 Moving can damage parent-child relationships.
4 Moving can lead to behavior problems.

121

||||| Part 3 |||||||||||||||||||||||||||||||||||| ◀» ▶MP3 ▶アプリ ▶CD2 49~54

(G)

No. 25

Situation: You are an international student at a US university. You want to apply for a graduate program but are worried about funding. An academic adviser tells you the following.

Question: What should you do first?

1 Apply for a scholarship.
2 Renew your visa.
3 Apply for financial aid.
4 Choose a supervisor.

(H)

No. 26

Situation: You are at an airport. Your flight to London has been canceled, but you need to get there as soon as possible. You hear the following announcement.

Question: What should you do?

1 Take the charter flight.
2 Pay for a seat upgrade.
3 Go to the airport hotel.
4 Take the flight to Amsterdam.

(I)

No. 27

Situation: You are attending an academic conference on teaching English to university students. Your main interest is student motivation. You hear the following announcement.

Question: Which room should you go to?

1 Room 210.
2 Room 212.
3 Room 214.
4 Room 216.

122

(J)

No. 28

Situation: You are a teacher. You teach classes every weekday and supervise basketball practice after school on Tuesdays. You receive the following voice mail from a colleague on Monday morning.

Question: When should you meet with your colleague?

1 During lunchtime on Tuesday.
2 On Wednesday evening.
3 On Thursday evening.
4 Next Monday.

(K)

No. 29

Situation: You want to become a volunteer language interpreter. You do not have experience volunteering. The director of a local volunteer center tells you the following.

Question: Which option should you choose?

1 Helping at hospitals.
2 The school program.
3 Helping at police stations.
4 The youth mentorship program.

面 接

問題カード（A日程）　　　▶MP3 ▶アプリ ▶CD 4 28〜32

You have **one minute** to prepare.

This is a story about a restaurant owner who wanted to make her customers happy.

You have **two minutes** to narrate the story.

Your story should begin with the following sentence:
One day, a restaurant owner was working at her restaurant.

Questions

No. 1   Please look at the fourth picture. If you were the restaurant owner, what would you be thinking?

No. 2   Do young people today tend to waste money?

No. 3   Should countries do more to lower their reliance on imported food?

No. 4   Can the development of new technology help to save the natural environment?

問題カード（C日程） ▶MP3 ▶アプリ ▶CD 4 33～36

You have **one minute** to prepare.

This is a story about a young woman who wanted to improve her career.
You have **two minutes** to narrate the story.

Your story should begin with the following sentence:
One day, a young woman was in her office.

Questions

No. 1   Please look at the fourth picture. If you were the young woman, what would you be thinking?

No. 2   Do you think more elderly people will choose to study at universities after retiring in the future?

No. 3   Do you think the media places too much emphasis on earning money?

No. 4   Are companies doing enough to reduce pollution in Japan?

2021-1

一次試験　2021.5.30実施
二次試験　A日程　2021.6.27実施
　　　　　C日程　2021.7.11実施

Grade Pre-1

試験時間

筆記：90分
リスニング：約30分

一次試験・筆記　　　　p.130～145
一次試験・リスニング　p.146～151
二次試験・面接　　　　p.152～155

＊解答・解説は別冊p.181～224にあります。
＊面接の流れは本書p.16にあります。

2021年度第1回　**Web特典「自動採点サービス」対応 オンラインマークシート**
※検定の回によって2次元コードが違います。
※筆記1～3，リスニングの採点ができます。
※PCからも利用できます（本書p.8参照）。

筆 記

1 To complete each item, choose the best word or phrase from among the four choices. Then, on your answer sheet, find the number of the question and mark your answer.

(1) *A:* Thanks for showing me the outline of your sales presentation. It's good, but it's a bit (   ) in some places.
B: I guess I do repeat some information too much. I'll try to take some of it out.
1 decisive   2 subjective   3 redundant   4 distinct

(2) Lisa went to the interview even though she thought there was a low (   ) of her getting the job. As she expected, she was not hired.
1 restoration   2 credibility   3 contention   4 probability

(3) It is sadly (   ) that, in developing countries, many of the farmers who grow nutritious crops for export do not have enough food to feed their own families.
1 indefinite   2 ironic   3 restless   4 superficial

(4) The explosion at the chemical factory (   ) great damage on the local environment. It will take years for wildlife to fully recover in the region.
1 inflicted   2 enhanced   3 vanished   4 perceived

(5) Some say the best way to overcome a (   ) is to expose oneself to what one fears. For example, people who are afraid of mice should try holding one.
1 temptation   2 barricade   3 phobia   4 famine

(6) English classes at the university were required, but students were ( ) from them if they could prove they had advanced ability in the language.

1 exempted **2** prosecuted
3 commanded **4** quantified

(7) E-mail and text messaging have ( ) the way people write. Many people shorten words and ignore traditional rules of grammar.

1 transformed **2** officiated
3 synthesized **4** disarmed

(8) Some analysts think the new treaty on CO_2 emissions is a ( ) in the fight against global warming. "This is the most important environmental treaty ever signed," said one.

1 milestone **2** vigor **3** backlog **4** confession

(9) Lying on the sunny beach with her husband on their vacation, Roberta felt ( ) happy. She had never been so content.

1 barely **2** profoundly **3** improperly **4** harshly

(10) Nadine spends an hour thoroughly cleaning her apartment every day, so the entire place is ( ).

1 spotless **2** minute **3** rugged **4** impartial

(11) After many poor performances, the rugby player was ( ) from his club's first team to its second team.

1 inclined **2** clinched **3** demoted **4** adapted

(12) With no clear winner in the election, the new government consists of a ( ) that includes socialist, liberal, and green parties.

1 gradation **2** casualty **3** coalition **4** warranty

(13) Mark spent more than a month in the hospital after becoming the victim of a (　　　) bear attack.

1 dazed　　　　**2** vicious　　　　**3** heartfelt　　　　**4** superior

(14) People have been growing a variety of plants for thousands of years, but wheat was one of the first food crops to be (　　　) by humans.

1 omitted　　　　**2** thawed　　　　**3** cultivated　　　　**4** harassed

(15) *A:* Jan, how much of a tip do you think I should leave the waiter?

B: The (　　　) has already been added to the bill, so you don't have to leave anything.

1 gratuity　　　　**2** module　　　　**3** arsenal　　　　**4** allotment

(16) Glenn had no choice but to borrow money from his father to pay his rent. He had (　　　) all his other options.

1 delighted　　　　**2** retraced　　　　**3** revolted　　　　**4** exhausted

(17) Although a smile generally (　　　) happiness, some people also smile to cover up negative emotions, such as anger.

1 monitors　　　　**2** signifies　　　　**3** vomits　　　　**4** regulates

(18) The supermarket chain's expansion plans are based on the (　　　) that consumer spending will continue to increase for the next five years at least.

1 malfunction　　　　　　　　**2** institution
3 assumption　　　　　　　　**4** transcription

(19) Some of the people living on the tropical island are the (　　　) of French sailors who arrived there 200 years ago.

1 garments　　　　　　　　**2** descendants
3 inhabitants　　　　　　　**4** compartments

(20) In the past, many people believed the sun (   ) around the earth. Advances in science and math eventually proved that, in fact, the earth moves around the sun.

    1 revolved   **2** renewed   **3** relieved   **4** restrained

(21) *A:* Why are you so (   ) to accept the job offer at DTP?

    B: Well, I'm concerned that I'd be even busier than I am now, so I'd really like something that'd give me a better work-life balance.

    1 frank   **2** reluctant   **3** spiteful   **4** righteous

(22) *A:* If you don't come to the party tomorrow night, you'll (   ) on all the fun.

    B: Sorry, I really have to finish my presentation. You can tell me about the party later.

    1 miss out   **2** add up   **3** get over   **4** join in

(23) Marty spent many hours (   ) the problem before he realized that the solution was much simpler than he thought.

    1 living down   **2** clearing out
    3 snapping off   **4** wrestling with

(24) As the suspect was being arrested by the police, he (   ) an officer's gun. Luckily, he was stopped before he could get it.

    1 went for   **2** let up
    3 picked over   **4** set off

(25) After living in a remote jungle for three months, the researcher was glad when he could finally access the Internet and (   ) the news in his home country.

    1 catch up on   **2** change out of
    3 open up to   **4** put up with

2 Read each passage and choose the best word or phrase from among the four choices for each blank. Then, on your answer sheet, find the number of the question and mark your answer.

Herbal Medicine

For thousands of years, people have taken plants and plant-based substances as medicines. Such cures are still used more commonly than modern drugs in many regions, with some 80 percent of the population in certain developing countries relying on herbal medicines. (26   ), their effectiveness is largely unsupported by science-based evidence. Many Western doctors therefore discourage their use, especially for seriously ill people. For such patients, using scientifically proven drugs can mean the difference between life and death.

Research has highlighted other problems, too. Scientists reviewed over 50 studies on herbal medicines and found that the chemicals they contain can cause organ damage, and that these medicines can be harmful when used in combination with other drugs. The scientists say such effects are generally not reported in the societies where the medicines are commonly used. This leads patients to (27   ). In fact, the majority of these people see no reason to even tell their doctors they are using the medicines, putting them at risk of dangerous side effects when the medicines interact with doctor-prescribed drugs.

Supporters of herbal medicines say the amount of data from clinical studies is increasing, and this can help people understand which medicines are safe. They also feel that herbal medicines and modern, doctor-prescribed drugs (28   ). Instead of viewing herbal medicines as an alternative to standard drugs, which are often necessary in emergencies or to fight serious infections, people should instead use them to maintain overall health and wellness. If taken properly, supporters say, both traditional and modern medicines can be safely used in combination with each other.

134

(26) 1 In exchange
2 Similarly
3 In other words
4 Nevertheless

(27) 1 do their own research
2 suddenly stop using them
3 believe the medicines are safe
4 more closely follow doctors' advice

(28) 1 are both overused
2 are essentially the same
3 should have different roles
4 both lack evidence that they work

Memory and Language

The outcomes of court cases often depend on evidence given by people who witnessed crimes or accidents. But can their memories always be trusted? In one famous psychology experiment, students were divided into groups and shown a video of a car accident. One group was asked, "About how fast were the cars going when they smashed into each other?" For another group, the words "smashed into" were replaced with "hit." The results showed that those who were asked the question with the words "smashed into" estimated an average speed of 65.2 kmh, compared with 54.7 kmh for those asked with "hit." This demonstrates that the descriptions witnesses give can depend on (**29**   ).

In a follow-up experiment, students were shown another video of an accident and asked similar questions using the words "smashed" and "hit." This time they were also asked if they had noticed any broken glass. The windows were undamaged in the video, but the students who had been asked the question using "smashed" were far more likely to report having seen broken glass. This tendency is even more disturbing because the students had (**30**   ).

Watching a video of a car crash, however, is not the same as being present at the scene of one, critics argue. They say that the students' memories were more easily influenced because they did not have the emotional experience of seeing the accident in person. (**31**   ), the students were likely less motivated to give accurate answers. Other studies have also shown that manipulative questions have less effect on people who have witnessed real crimes, suggesting that the experiments' conditions may have played a role in shaping the results.

(29) 1 who is asking the question
2 when they see an accident
3 why they are being questioned
4 how they are being asked

(30) 1 expected to be asked something different
2 been told that the accident was fake
3 remembered something that never happened
4 described the wrong part of the video

(31) 1 As a result
2 On the contrary
3 Surprisingly
4 Otherwise

3 Read each passage and choose the best answer from among the four choices for each question. Then, on your answer sheet, find the number of the question and mark your answer.

Impostor Syndrome

Many people will experience "impostor syndrome" at some point in their lives. Those who are affected by this condition have trouble accepting or believing in their own success, no matter how capable or experienced they may be. Often, they think their achievements are due to good fortune or outside circumstances rather than their actual ability. Impostor syndrome affects people of various backgrounds working in many fields, and it can have different consequences for each person. Some feel they must prove their worth by working far harder than they need to. Others fear they will lose their job when their supposed lack of skill is discovered, so they distance themselves from colleagues as much as possible.

The cause of impostor syndrome has been debated by experts. It may have something to do with people's basic personality traits, such as a tendency to worry, or it could possibly have its roots in an individual's upbringing. For instance, when children are constantly praised, even for minor achievements, it can cause them to lose faith in their real abilities. Impostor syndrome can also arise in adulthood due to factors out of a person's control. One such factor is institutional discrimination, where the atmosphere in a work or academic environment makes people who are not of a certain race, gender, or other characteristic stand out.

Several studies have shown that individuals in minority groups who report feelings of "impostorism" also experience higher levels of anxiety and depression. This may be due not only to discrimination but also to a lack of representation among professors, managers, and other authority figures. According to psychology professor Thema Bryant-Davis, when people in the working world do not see others of their gender or race in positions of power, there is no "signal of the possibility of advancement." Without this, it is often difficult to have self-confidence and maintain a positive attitude in life.

(32) What is one effect that "impostor syndrome" may have on

138

workers affected by it?

1 They feel that they have no choice but to do extra work in order to compensate for their coworkers' weaknesses.
2 They become afraid they will be fired and attempt to isolate themselves from their coworkers.
3 It becomes easier for them to dishonestly take credit for the achievements of their coworkers.
4 It can cause them to exaggerate their experience and abilities when communicating with their coworkers.

(33) One possible cause of impostor syndrome is when

1 people have difficulty finding a job, mainly due to companies discriminating against them.
2 adults tend to worry more than they should about criticism they received when they were young.
3 companies refuse to seriously consider workers' claims that they are feeling anxious or worried.
4 children are given praise too frequently, even for things that are not actually difficult to do.

(34) According to Thema Bryant-Davis, which of the following is true?

1 Individuals who avoid discrimination at school are less likely to have impostor syndrome when they start working.
2 Minorities are more likely to suffer from impostor syndrome if they are treated in the same way as those in the majority.
3 People who do not see others like themselves in higher positions are more likely to lose hope that they will be promoted.
4 Minorities are less likely to experience discrimination in schools with a greater amount of diversity.

Climate Change and the Sámi

The Sámi people, who are native to the Arctic regions of Europe, have historically made a living through fur trading and reindeer farming. However, the reindeer herds they rely on are under severe pressure due to climate change and the resulting habitat loss. Unstable temperatures in winter cause snow to melt and then freeze into ice, which prevents reindeer from accessing the plants they need for food. Though this has also occurred in the past, rapid climate change has caused it to happen more frequently. Due to this, reindeer herds are losing more animals to starvation, and lack of nutrition has reduced birthrates. Furthermore, as global warming makes northern areas more accessible, companies are moving into traditional Sámi territory to pursue mining, carry out oil and gas exploration, and promote tourism. This has further restricted the food available to the Sámi's reindeer herds, and many Sámi worry that increased activity in their traditional lands could end their way of life altogether.

The decline of reindeer herds has caused many Sámi to experience financial and emotional difficulties. Some teenagers and young adults have fled to cities for work, and these urban Sámi have found themselves alienated and the target of discrimination due to their heritage. With their lives uprooted and their cultural traditions being lost without access to vibrant Sámi social groups, many suffer from significant mental health problems. The problem extends to traditional Sámi communities, with higher-than-average suicide rates reported, especially among young males. Few seek help, though, as mental health is a taboo topic for the Sámi. Although exact numbers are unknown, surveys suggest that most Sámi have a relative or friend who has committed suicide.

Efforts are under way to tackle some of these problems, however. Social programs, for example, are being introduced to offer emotional support to young Sámi and encourage discussion about the discrimination they experience. Mental health issues in traditional Sámi communities, though, are often said to be based on economic uncertainty and worries related to the impact of climate change. To address these fears, politicians have been listening to the Sámi and taking greater care to consider the potential consequences that government decisions may have on their communities. By giving the Sámi a way to influence decisions that affect them directly, the stress and hardship associated with environmental or economic decline can be reduced. More importantly, it is hoped that the Sámi themselves can have greater control over maintaining their traditional way of life.

(35) Climate change has affected the Sámi lifestyle by

1 reducing many plant species that the Sámi rely on as a source of food when reindeer are not available.

2 impacting both the living areas and food sources of the animals that the Sámi depend on economically.

3 forcing the Sámi to adopt farming methods that are financially less rewarding than their traditional ones.

4 attracting corporations that have put pressure on the Sámi to give up their land for oil and gas exploration.

(36) According to the passage, what difficulties are the Sámi facing?

1 The organizations that provide financial support in their communities have been negatively affected by changes to their society.

2 Sámi who have been forced to move from rural regions to urban areas are choosing to reject their culture in order to be accepted.

3 The conflict between younger Sámi and the older generation regarding reindeer farming is leading many to suffer from mental health issues.

4 Younger Sámi are struggling with mental health issues caused by isolation from their families and the loss of their cultural traditions.

(37) What is being done to help the Sámi?

1 Concerns expressed by the Sámi are being used to shape government policies and actions as a way to avoid causing them further harm.

2 Volunteer groups are being established to promote wider understanding of Sámi culture throughout countries with large Sámi populations.

3 Greater efforts are being made to encourage younger Sámi to enter politics and represent their communities in local governments.

4 Financial support is being offered to Sámi suffering from mental health issues that arise due to the stress of living in urban areas.

Lemons and the Mafia

The organized-crime group known as the Mafia first appeared on the island of Sicily in the 1800s. In the years since its emergence, its illegal activities, which include bribery and fraud, have become well known, but its origins were unclear. Recent research by a group of economic historians has, however, uncovered an unexpected connection between the Mafia and a common fruit.

In the 1700s, it was discovered that lemon juice prevented a deadly disease called scurvy, leading to greatly increased demand for lemons, which caused revenues from the fruit to skyrocket. Sicily was one of the few places where lemons could grow, but lemon farming was limited to certain locations on the island due to the fruit's sensitivity to frost. In addition, the shift to large-scale lemon growing required huge financial investments to build facilities and develop irrigation systems. High walls were also constructed to protect lemon trees from thieves, as without such safeguards, an entire year's harvest could go missing overnight.

Rising demand for the fruit saw profits continue to increase in the 1800s, but the situation was complicated by the fact that Sicily was ruled by kings with ancestral ties to the Spanish royal family. The rulers were regarded as outsiders, and unpopular policies like forced military service caused dissatisfaction and unrest among the population. Local poverty and a lack of public funding, particularly in rural areas, led to an increase in crime. This forced farmers to find their own way to deal with the threat of lemon theft. They began employing local strongmen, who eventually became the Mafia, to protect their orchards, offering lemons as payment.

While the Mafia may have originally provided a legitimate service that kept lemon crops safe from thieves, that did not stay true for long. It began forcing farmers to accept its services against their will, using violence and intimidation when it encountered resistance. Mafia members then began acting as middlemen between sellers and exporters, manipulating the market to ensure substantial profits. They soon forced their way into other areas of the industry, such as transportation and wholesaling, and eventually their power grew to cover all aspects of lemon production. Some politicians attempted to address these activities, but widespread government corruption allowed the Mafia to extend its influence to many areas of politics and law enforcement.

According to researcher Arcangelo Dimico, one of the historians who researched the connection between lemons and the Mafia, the group's rise is an example of the "resource curse." He explains that the combination of a source of extreme wealth together with weak social and political systems can lead to the rise of conflicts or illegal activities, which can leave a country worse off economically than if it had not possessed the valuable resource in the first place. Examples can be seen in modern times, such as wealth from diamonds funding the growth of private armies in some African nations. Like Sicily's Mafia, these groups often employ criminal methods to gain control over resources and local populations. Using Dimico's study, economists, sociologists, and political scientists can better understand this phenomenon and help governments fight against it.

(38) What is one difficulty Sicilian farmers faced in the 1700s?

　1 While lemons had once been believed to cure a serious disease, profits from growing the fruit declined when this was discovered not to be true.

　2 Although large amounts of money could be earned from growing lemons, setting up a lemon farm could only be done at great expense.

　3 Because of Sicily's unpredictable climate, farmers new to growing lemons regularly had to throw away large amounts of bad lemon crops.

　4 Due to rules about where lemons could be grown, purchasing enough land to make the business profitable was a serious issue.

(39) Which of the following statements best describes the situation that led to the rise of the Mafia?

　1 The government was unable to provide Sicilians with suitable public services, causing some private citizens to find ways to protect their crops.

143

2 Owners of lemon farms refused to trade with those who supported Sicily's foreign rulers, causing the economy to worsen and crime to rise.

3 People were unhappy about profits from Sicilian lemons going to the Spanish royal family and did not mind when thieves stole from wealthy farmers.

4 The government's desire to profit from lemon farming caused it to accept illegal payments from farmers who were connected with criminals.

(40) The Mafia used its involvement with lemon farmers to

1 control both the people who grew lemons and those who sold them overseas as part of its way to make more money and increase its power.

2 successfully generate greater profits from the lemon industry by demanding that farmers grow larger amounts of lemons.

3 persuade a few politicians to ignore its criminal activities, despite overwhelming opposition from the government.

4 gain control over the entire lemon industry, despite being unable to obtain the cooperation of key members of the police.

(41) Arcangelo Dimico would likely say that the "resource curse"

1 is more closely related to the poor economic performance of a nation than to the level of support its government provides for social issues.

2 occurs when governments are willing to overlook criminal activities as long as they help boost the country's supply of resources.

3 is caused by a country's resources being overvalued by its leaders and then failing to generate the amount of profit that was expected.

4 can happen due to unethical groups taking advantage of a lack of governance to profit from valuable national assets.

- *Write an essay on the given TOPIC.*
- *Use TWO of the POINTS below to support your answer.*
- *Structure: introduction, main body, and conclusion*
- *Suggested length: 120–150 words*
- *Write your essay in the space provided on Side B of your answer sheet.*

Any writing outside the space will not be graded.

TOPIC
Agree or disagree: Big companies have a positive effect on society

POINTS
- Products
- The economy
- The environment
- Work-life balance

リスニング

―――― **Listening Test** ――――

There are three parts to this listening test.

Part 1	Dialogues: 1 question each	Multiple-choice
Part 2	Passages: 2 questions each	Multiple-choice
Part 3	Real-Life: 1 question each	Multiple-choice

※**Listen carefully to the instructions.**

Part 1 　🔊　▶MP3 ▶アプリ ▶CD 3 **1**～**14**

No. 1
1　The man should be more apologetic.
2　The man should have bought a present.
3　The man worries too much.
4　The man is not very reliable.

No. 2
1　She is confident.
2　She is cautious.
3　She is worried.
4　She is disappointed.

No. 3
1　She is looking for a new job.
2　She is keeping her current job.
3　She failed her job interview.
4　She started a new job.

No. 4
1　The noise is disturbing his work.
2　The air conditioner is broken.
3　The heat is making him uncomfortable.
4　The window cannot be opened.

No. 5
1　Purchase a new computer.
2　Renew their security program.
3　Help the woman with her report.
4　Take the computer in for repairs.

146

No. 6	1 Take out a loan for university expenses.
	2 Attend a community college.
	3 Work full time for two years.
	4 Go to a university out of town.

No. 7	1 Getting a new prescription from his doctor.
	2 Starting to eat more healthily.
	3 Going to see the woman's doctor.
	4 Stopping his prescription medicine.

No. 8	1 Go fishing with Ronan.
	2 Attend a teaching conference.
	3 Take his wife to a movie.
	4 Look after the children.

No. 9	1 Paying to have the driveway cleared.
	2 Looking for a new snow shovel.
	3 Starting to exercise more regularly.
	4 Having his back checked by a doctor.

No. 10	1 Increase the number of channels.
	2 Stop paying for the movie channels.
	3 Keep their current cable plan.
	4 Let their children watch only educational TV.

No. 11	1 The band did not play many hits.
	2 The band's performance lacked energy.
	3 The band's tour schedule changed.
	4 The band was rude to the audience.

No. 12	1 The woman should train her dog.
	2 The woman should buy a dog-training book.
	3 The woman's dog may have a medical problem.
	4 The woman's dog is too old to train.

|||||| Part 2 |||||||||||||||||||||||||||||||||||||||||||||||| ◀») ▶MP3 ▶アプリ ▶CD3 **15**〜**21**

(A)

No. 13
1 It gives food a bitter taste.
2 It is produced by drying plants.
3 It gives some plants their color.
4 It is found in a type of insect.

No. 14
1 It should be replaced with other options.
2 It can be harmful to plants.
3 It should be used as a medicine.
4 It is too valuable to use in cosmetics.

(B)

No. 15
1 They lasted longer than wooden houses.
2 They were easier to rebuild than stone houses.
3 They were well suited to the environment.
4 They could be constructed very quickly.

No. 16
1 They no longer exist today.
2 They were often connected to each other.
3 They could only be built on hilltops.
4 They were also popular in other countries.

(C)

No. 17
1 They combine with grease to block sewer tunnels.
2 They endanger people working in sewer tunnels.
3 They block household pipes when flushed.
4 They cannot be recycled cheaply.

No. 18
1 They were not created using laboratory tests.
2 They are not based on actual sewer-tunnel conditions.
3 The damage to sewer tunnels was not addressed.
4 The blockage issue cannot be solved with guidelines.

148

(D)

No. 19
1 Farmers are more interested in larger ones.
2 Caring for their wool requires much effort.
3 Raising them is no longer profitable.
4 The quality of their wool can vary.

No. 20
1 The rabbits often spoil it by chewing it.
2 It has to be cut at least once a month.
3 It can cause harm to the rabbits.
4 The rabbits do not like having it removed.

(E)

No. 21
1 To raise money to help hungry people.
2 To share his concerns about the government.
3 To encourage citizens to work harder.
4 To address public worries about the economy.

No. 22
1 Roosevelt used casual language.
2 Roosevelt interviewed famous people.
3 Roosevelt performed patriotic music.
4 Roosevelt visited people's homes.

(F)

No. 23
1 They no longer use traditional fishing equipment.
2 They often have their spleens removed.
3 They have a physical advantage when under the water.
4 They practice holding their breath on land.

No. 24
1 Help Bajau people adapt to new lifestyles.
2 Study Bajau people in more detail.
3 Help protect the local environment.
4 Study divers from around the world.

|||||| Part 3 |||||||||||||||||||||||||||||||||||||||||| ◀)) ▶MP3 ▶アプリ ▶CD3 **22**～**27**

(G)

No. 25

Situation: You want an apartment that is just a short walk from a train station. You need at least two bedrooms. A real estate agent tells you the following.

Question: Which apartment should you look at?

1 The one in Wilson Heights.
2 The one in Downtown Hills.
3 The one in Bronte Towers.
4 The one in Norton Villas.

(H)

No. 26

Situation: You have had stomach pain for a few days. You are busy for the next two days. You call your doctor, and he tells you the following.

Question: What should you do first?

1 Get some additional pain medication.
2 Take the medicine you received earlier.
3 Call your doctor again at a later date.
4 Book an appointment with a specialist.

(I)

No. 27

Situation: You are checking in at a resort hotel. You made a reservation online through ExTravel because they offered a 20 percent discount on a spa treatment. A receptionist tells you the following.

Question: What should you do first?

1 Make a reservation at the spa.
2 Contact ExTravel for confirmation.
3 Ask the manager for a room upgrade.
4 Print the e-mail containing the offer.

(J)

No. 28

Situation: You are enrolling your daughter in a new school. She is allergic to dairy products. The school principal tells you the following.

Question: What should you do?

1 Get a letter from a doctor.
2 List your daughter's requirements.
3 Pay for school lunch.
4 Sign up for special meals.

(K)

No. 29

Situation: It is winter, and you want to visit Alexandra Park by car this weekend. You do not own tires that can be used in the snow. You call Park Information and hear the following.

Question: What should you do?

1 Purchase snow chains for your tires.
2 Take Grand Point Road.
3 Change your tires to studded tires.
4 Rent chains in Alexandra Park.

二次試験
面 接

問題カード（A日程）　　　　◀))　▶MP3　▶アプリ　▶CD 4 37〜41

You have **one minute** to prepare.

This is a story about a man who was about to retire from his job.
You have **two minutes** to narrate the story.

Your story should begin with the following sentence:
One day, a man was arriving home after work.

Questions

No. 1　Please look at the fourth picture. If you were the man, what would you be thinking?

No. 2　Have people nowadays forgotten the importance of eating a balanced diet?

No. 3　Will more people choose to retire early in the future?

No. 4　Is cybercrime becoming a bigger problem in today's society?

問題カード（C日程） ▶MP3 ▶アプリ ▶CD 4 42〜45

You have **one minute** to prepare.

This is a story about a young woman who started working for a restaurant chain.
You have **two minutes** to narrate the story.

Your story should begin with the following sentence:
One day, a young woman was at an orientation for new employees.

Questions

No. 1   Please look at the fourth picture. If you were the young woman, what would you be thinking?

No. 2   Do you think schools are responsible for preparing students for their future career?

No. 3   Are people in modern society better at dealing with stress than people were in the past?

No. 4   Should the government do more to promote Japanese products overseas?

2020-3

一次試験　2021.1.24 実施
二次試験　A日程　2021.2.21 実施
　　　　　B日程　2021.2.28 実施

試験時間

筆記：90分
リスニング：約30分

一次試験・筆記　　　p.158〜173
一次試験・リスニングp.174〜179
二次試験・面接　　　p.180〜183

＊解答・解説は別冊p.225〜268にあります。
＊面接の流れは本書p.16にあります。

Grade Pre-1

Pre
1

2020年度第3回　Web特典「自動採点サービス」対応
オンラインマークシート

※検定の回によって2次元コードが違います。
※筆記1〜3，リスニングの採点ができます。
※PCからも利用できます（本書p.8参照）。

筆 記

---

1 *To complete each item, choose the best word or phrase from among the four choices. Then, on your answer sheet, find the number of the question and mark your answer.*

---

(1) Miriam tries to use healthy (   ) when preparing food. For example, instead of using butter to make cookies, she uses olive oil.
1 ingredients **2** attributes **3** perimeters **4** surroundings

(2) The board members failed to reach a (   ) on how much to pay the new CEO. Some felt the initial figure suggested was too high.
1 ratio **2** preview **3** consensus **4** simulation

(3) Ellen's apartment was cheap, but living there quickly became (   ). There was no air conditioning, the roof leaked, and the baby next door often cried.
1 decent **2** crucial **3** gracious **4** intolerable

(4) The deep ocean is a very (   ) environment with cold temperatures, high pressure, and no sunlight. In spite of this, many creatures manage to survive there.
1 quaint   **2** inhospitable
3 dignified **4** confidential

(5) As his grandmother's physical (   ) became more of a concern, Stuart encouraged her to move into a nursing home.
1 haze **2** canal **3** frailty **4** statistic

(6) In order to study various organisms, scientists have (   ) them according to differences and similarities. Each species is placed into a specific group.
1 saluted **2** classified **3** personified **4** extinguished

158

(7) *A:* James, our supplier said they didn't receive a payment this month.

B: Yes, I know. There was an (　　　) by the accounting department. I'll call the supplier and apologize.

1 underdog　**2** overhead　**3** upheaval　**4** oversight

(8) The man and his friend (　　　) to rob a local bank. However, someone else found out and told the police, so they were caught before they could do anything.

1 conspired　**2** inhaled　**3** diminished　**4** identified

(9) Domingo's boss told him his plan for a new factory was not (　　　). It would cost too much and take too long to finish.

1 feasible　**2** fierce　**3** inventive　**4** eventful

(10) The new mayor said he was looking forward to his first day in office, when he could begin (　　　) some of the problems that faced the city.

1 inserting　**2** tackling　**3** triggering　**4** generating

(11) When a person has major surgery, (　　　) such as infection and nerve damage are possible, so operations are usually performed only when there are no other treatment options.

1 denials　　　　　　**2** domains
3 comparisons　　　　**4** complications

(12) Henrietta is a very (　　　) reader. She loves books, and it is not unusual for her to finish several in a week.

1 passionate　**2** obscure　**3** uncomfortable　**4** feeble

(13) On the trail, hikers may occasionally (　　　) wild animals. However, it is important not to get too close to them or to offer them food.

1 scrap　**2** propel　**3** encounter　**4** seal

159

(14) Following his (   ) from the company, Todd collected unemployment insurance for a few months until he found a new job.

1 testimony   **2** tremor   **3** dismissal   **4** glossary

(15) After most of the votes were counted, it was clear the candidate could not win. He decided to (   ) the election to his opponent.

1 concede   **2** consolidate **3** foster   **4** plaster

(16) Kelly (   ) upset her host family by taking long showers. She did not realize until her host father told her they were unhappy about her using so much water.

1 sympathetically   **2** typically
3 unwittingly   **4** diagonally

(17) One side effect of the medicine is the occurrence of (   ) dreams. About 5 percent of people who take it report having intense, realistic experiences during their sleep.

1 allied   **2** vivid   **3** stout   **4** fluent

(18) Before a match, the boy always asks famous soccer players for their (   ). He waits near the locker room entrance hoping they will sign their names in his notebook.

1 telegraphs   **2** autographs   **3** editorials   **4** exhibits

(19) Many airlines require young children to have the permission of a parent or (   ) if the child is going to travel alone on an airplane.

1 guardian   **2** defendant   **3** servant   **4** commuter

(20) Many visitors to the theater complained that the stage was so low they could not see the performers. The management decided to have the stage (   ) by a meter.

1 snatched   **2** appreciated **3** elevated   **4** donated

160

(21) In ancient times, some people thought earthquakes were a ( ) warning. They believed God was telling them to change their behavior.

1 divine   **2** dutiful   **3** sparse   **4** lively

(22) The runner ( ) early from the other runners to lead the race. When she crossed the finish line to win, there was a large distance between her and the next runner.

1 broke away   **2** held down
3 bottomed out   **4** turned back

(23) The web developer hired to update the company's website did a terrible job. It took months to ( ) all the problems he had caused.

1 stumble on   **2** trade in
3 rip off   **4** straighten out

(24) Marcia went upstairs to ( ) her son, and she was very angry to find him playing video games instead of doing his homework.

1 check up on   **2** go through with
3 get away with   **4** fall back on

(25) After the two friends had a terrible argument, they did not speak to each other for a month. Eventually, though, they ( ), and now they spend even more time together.

1 kept away   **2** made up   **3** worked up   **4** played out

2

Read each passage and choose the best word or phrase from among the four choices for each blank. Then, on your answer sheet, find the number of the question and mark your answer.

The Wallet Experiment

Psychologists have developed various theories about honesty. Among the most well-known is that it (26   ). Recently, however, this idea has been questioned. While it does seem logical that people are more likely to lie, steal, or cheat if they believe they will gain something they desire by doing so, an interesting experiment has shown that this may not be true.

A team of researchers theorized that people would be more likely to keep something valuable when found rather than return it, and to test this they brought wallets to a number of public places, pretending they had found them on the street. Some contained money and some did not, but all contained a key and an e-mail address. The researchers then waited to see if they would get an e-mail informing them that the lost wallet had been found. Surprisingly, they got the most responses when there was a large amount of money in the wallet. (27   ), an even higher number of wallets were returned when the amount of money was further increased. The researchers believe this is evidence to indicate that many people value honesty over money.

Later, the researchers conducted a follow-up experiment in which the wallets all had the same amount of money. This time, though, some of the wallets contained a key — something that would only be important to the person who lost it — while others did not. Return rates for wallets containing a key were significantly higher. The researchers suggest the most likely reason for this result is that people's honesty was strongly affected by (28   ).

162

(26) **1** is related to temptation
2 relies on many connected factors
3 changes over long periods
4 depends on people's intelligence

(27) **1** Alternatively
2 In contrast
3 What is more
4 Nevertheless

(28) **1** how hard it was to return the wallet
2 whether they knew the wallet owner
3 how much they care about others
4 whether they would receive a reward

An Unusual Relationship

The black rhinoceros once roamed across much of the African continent. Today, however, it has become an endangered species due to illegal hunting. The rhinos are particularly vulnerable because, although their noses are highly sensitive, they have extremely poor vision. (**29**   ), hunters are able to approach them without being detected, as long as the wind is not blowing their scent in the animals' direction.

Behavioral science researchers investigating how rhinos avoid such situations noticed an unusual relationship with birds called red-billed oxpeckers. The birds have sharp vision and make hissing sounds if they feel threatened by approaching animals. They are drawn to rhinos due to the tiny organisms known as ticks that live on the rhinos' skin, and the oxpeckers often sit atop the animals' backs and peck at them while searching for the organisms. Rhinos with the birds perched on them were observed to be far more likely to detect the presence of approaching threats. The researchers therefore believe the (**30**   ). This may also explain why the rhinos tolerate the oxpeckers' presence.

In recent years, (**31**   ), which has been bad news for the rhinos. The ticks that oxpeckers feed on also live on cows, but farmers have been using pesticides to kill the organisms. Many oxpeckers have been killed by eating these poisoned ticks, and as a result, there are fewer and fewer of them, including in areas where the rhinos live. However, ecologists believe that reintroducing oxpeckers may be vital in helping to preserve the populations of the rhinos.

(29) **1** Otherwise
      2 Instead
      3 Consequently
      4 Similarly

(30) **1** rhinos are frightened of the birds
      2 birds provide warnings to the rhinos
      3 rhinos' survival is threatened by the birds
      4 birds are attracting ticks to the rhinos

(31) **1** animal protection laws have become weaker
      2 hunting oxpeckers has become legal
      3 the ticks have proved useful for crops
      4 oxpeckers have been disappearing

3

Read each passage and choose the best answer from among the four choices for each question. Then, on your answer sheet, find the number of the question and mark your answer.

Bike Sharing in Seattle

Seattle is an environmentally friendly city whose residents are known for their active lifestyles and love of the outdoors. It was therefore surprising to many when Pronto Cycle Share, Seattle's first bike-sharing service, ended in failure. Designed around docking stations that allowed bikes to be stored when not in use, Pronto was initially provided by a nonprofit company with help from a corporate sponsor. The public's underwhelming response, however, led to the city stepping in to purchase the service. After continued unsatisfactory results, the city announced an enlargement of the service's network to encourage usage but failed to expand it significantly. Finally, following years of criticism and financial issues, Pronto was abandoned in 2017.

The successful introduction of a new bike-sharing service called Spin some months later only raised additional questions about Pronto's demise. The proven success of bike-sharing companies in other US cities known for rainy weather and steep hills meant that Seattle's climate and terrain were not to blame; instead, Pronto's critics pointed the finger at serious issues with the locations of its docking stations. Spin's bikes could be unlocked using a smartphone and left anywhere within an authorized area, and Spin enrolled many users in areas that had lacked access to Pronto when it started operating. Furthermore, Pronto's network had failed to adequately provide service in areas ignored by Seattle's existing public transportation system.

When Spin became successful, similar services started up in Seattle, leading the city to introduce a permanent bike-sharing program in 2018. While this was a positive move for riders, it received a negative response from the companies that were forced to join the program if they wanted to continue doing business. The mandatory costs for the companies, such as permit fees and individual bike fees, proved to be too much. Two of the firms, including Spin, withdrew their services and left the city immediately following the program's introduction, putting the city's decision-making under the spotlight once again.

(32) According to the passage, what is true of Seattle's first bike-sharing service?

1 The city's continuing refusal to provide additional funding for the company made it impossible for it to survive.

2 The city finally decided to allow a nonprofit company to manage it after the service failed to gain popularity.

3 While the service was popular with the public, low profits forced the city to look for funding elsewhere.

4 When the company that operated it was unable to make it successful, the city bought and attempted to expand the service.

(33) What is one reason given for Pronto Cycle Share's failure?

1 Improvements to the city's public transportation system made it less necessary for people to use bikes to get around.

2 Gaps in its network meant that it was difficult for some residents to travel around the city easily.

3 Riders stopped using the service when many accidents were blamed on the city's hills and poor weather.

4 Problems with the smartphone software used to track the location of its bikes caused many riders to quit the service.

(34) What do we learn about the service provided by Spin?

1 The style of the service's bikes was not popular with the public, despite it being far better than that of the previous bike-sharing service.

2 The service was unable to compete with better-known companies that decided to introduce their own bike-sharing services in the city.

3 A new program introduced by the city caused the service to become too expensive to keep running for the company that was operating it.

4 While the public was positive about the service, the company that ran it was criticized by the city for the environmental damage it caused.

167

Antarctica's Wildlife

Antarctica is a vast, nearly empty continent that is mostly covered in ice. In fact, less than 1 percent of its land is permanently ice-free. This tiny area is indispensable to much of the region's wildlife, including birds such as snow petrels, because it provides the most accessible environment for species that have their young on land. Although Antarctica lacks a permanent human population, features of human presence, such as research stations, tourist camps, and waste dumps, have increasingly been threatening Antarctica's natural environment in recent years. Overall, human activity has had a negative impact on 80 percent of the ice-free area.

Among the harmful consequences of human activities are disturbances to native wildlife and pollution from waste and vehicle emissions. A major ecological concern is the unplanned introduction of foreign plant and insect species that can harm their native counterparts. Furthermore, Antarctica has relatively few species types, so local varieties are highly vulnerable to replacement by nonnative species. Another threat to the environment is oil exploration. While it is currently forbidden under the Antarctic Treaty System, the ban appears likely to be challenged in the future. Technological advances in the oil industry have made it more economical to drill in harsh environments, and oil companies are pushing to expand their operations. For example, drilling is currently under way in Alaska's North Slope, an area of sub-zero temperatures where obtaining oil was once economically impractical.

The Antarctic Treaty System has designated 55 places on the continent as protected areas, but these amount to only a tiny fraction of the ice-free land. And the designation may not mean much either: research by biologist Justine Shaw of the University of Queensland and her colleagues showed that the protections implemented in Antarctica were in the bottom 25 percent in a best-to-worst ranking of the programs designed to safeguard vulnerable areas around the world. The same study also found that all 55 protected zones are located close to areas of human activity, and 7 are considered as being at high risk for biological invasion. According to Shaw, since conserving the continent's biodiversity is essential, areas with the greatest number of species should be prioritized when establishing protected zones. It is time, Shaw warns, to realize that just because Antarctica is an isolated region, that does not mean the continent does not suffer from serious threats to its biodiversity.

(35) What is said about the significance of Antarctica's ice-free land?

    1 It has not suffered as much environmental damage as other areas of the continent that are a lot colder have.

    2 It offers more potential than other areas as a place for humans to introduce new species to the region.

    3 It is home to animals from other areas of the continent that are escaping from rising human activity.

    4 It is the easiest place to get to for certain species that need to be on land to give birth to their young.

(36) The example of the North Slope of Alaska illustrates how

    1 a protected area designation can easily be removed to allow environmentally damaging activities to occur.

    2 agreements such as the Antarctic Treaty System are necessary in resource-rich areas of the world.

    3 innovations in drilling operations have made it more cost-effective to extract oil in areas with severe climates.

    4 the introduction of outside species can fundamentally change local ecosystems over a short period of time.

(37) What does Justine Shaw recommend be done to protect nature in Antarctica?

    1 Areas with the most variety of plants and animals should be given priority when establishing protected areas.

    2 The emphasis should be changed from areas threatened by invading species to those that are lacking in diversity.

    3 The animals that live in areas near where there is human activity should be moved to areas covered in ice.

    4 A larger number of protected areas should be designated in locations that lie outside Antarctica's ice-free zone.

Darwin's Paradox

About two centuries ago, Charles Darwin sailed aboard a ship called the *Beagle* through the Indian Ocean. Although the warm, blue waters seemed like a highly suitable environment for supporting life, Darwin observed that sea creatures were scarce, seeing only the occasional fish in the clear ocean. Yet upon reaching a group of coral islands known as the Keeling Islands, he found an abundance of marine species around them. What was it, he wondered, that caused a coral island to become a fertile oasis amid the nearly lifeless desert of the ocean around it?

This mystery, which became known as "Darwin's Paradox," has long fascinated scientists. Since Darwin's time, they have determined that the very clarity of tropical seas is the reason for their lack of life, as they are not clouded by the tiny organisms known as phytoplankton, which are the main source of nutrition for marine ecosystems. In the Keelings, however, corals and other sea creatures, such as shrimp, have access to phytoplankton. Nitrogen and phosphorus — nutrients required by phytoplankton — are also present in the waters of the Keelings at levels high enough to sustain the reefs and various marine creatures. The factors supporting the growth of phytoplankton are known as the Island Mass Effect, or IME. What puzzled scientists at the time, though, was how nutrients could be maintained within the reef ecosystem rather than being washed out to the waters around them.

Researchers have finally put together all the pieces to show how the IME works. It begins with the formation of a coral reef on a high spot on the ocean floor. Corals need sunlight, so they do well in shallow water, and reef biodiversity is higher when they are located on gradual slopes rather than very steep areas. This is because gradual slopes are important for another key IME factor: upwelling, which is the movement of nutrient-rich cold water from the deep ocean to the nutrient-poor but brighter areas above. This provides food for the phytoplankton that feed corals. Sea creatures known as sponges are another key part of the process, as they suck in the waste products of both coral and phytoplankton, convert the products into substances that marine life higher up in the food chain can consume, and then expel the substances into nearby areas, where they are eaten. This keeps energy and nutrients in the closed loop of the reef

170

ecosystem. Nutrient concentrations in the reef ecosystem are further enhanced by organic matter from the creatures that live and die both onshore and on the reef.

Tropical coral reefs are an important resource for the fishing industry, but they also protect coastal areas, buffering shorelines from the effects of storms and floods. As climate change raises global temperatures and alters the movement of ocean currents around the planet, reef ecosystems will be affected significantly. It will become increasingly vital to better understand the IME and take appropriate action to preserve it so that the harmful effects of future weather patterns on coral reefs can be reduced.

(38) Which of the following statements best summarizes "Darwin's Paradox"?

1 Coral reefs that do not support much life are generally found in areas of the ocean that are home to a wide variety of marine species.

2 In spite of the lack of life in the open water around them, coral reefs are able to support large populations of sea creatures.

3 Coral reefs that form in cold water are better able to support life than those that develop where temperatures are higher.

4 Sea creatures that live alone prefer to live near coral reefs, while those found in groups prefer parts of the ocean with warmer water.

(39) Scientists were puzzled by the Island Mass Effect because

1 although sea creatures do not eat the phytoplankton found in the open ocean, they consume huge amounts of it in areas near coral islands.

2 smaller coral islands seem to be much better able to prevent the loss of phytoplankton than larger coral islands are.

3 although smaller organisms obtain enough nitrogen and phosphorus, larger organisms are unable to get sufficient quantities of them.

4 coral islands appear to be able to sustain levels of nitrogen and phosphorus that are higher than those found in the open ocean.

171

(40) What role do sponges play in the IME?

    1 They supply marine organisms with substances necessary for their survival by changing certain materials into a form that can be eaten.

    2 Because they absorb a lot of sunlight that enters the water, they are able to provide more nutrients to steep areas around the islands.

    3 The waste substances that the sponges produce are an important source of food for both corals and phytoplankton.

    4 After feeding on phytoplankton, the sponges pass the nutrients on to the larger marine animals that feed on them.

(41) How might a better understanding of the IME be useful?

    1 It could help scientists understand more clearly how global warming affects the patterns of storms and floods that form in coastal areas.

    2 It might enable scientists to lessen the harmful effects that the fishing industry has had on the ecosystems around coral reefs.

    3 It could help scientists to understand how ocean currents can be prevented from warming even though global temperatures are increasing.

    4 It might enable scientists to discover ways to protect coral reefs against shifts in ocean currents and temperatures.

- *Write an essay on the given TOPIC.*
- *Use TWO of the POINTS below to support your answer.*
- *Structure: introduction, main body, and conclusion*
- *Suggested length: 120–150 words*
- *Write your essay in the space provided on Side B of your answer sheet.*

Any writing outside the space will not be graded.

TOPIC
Agree or disagree: More people should become vegetarians in the future

POINTS
- Animal rights
- Cost
- Environment
- Health

リスニング

―――――― Listening Test ――――――

There are three parts to this listening test.

Part 1	Dialogues: 1 question each	Multiple-choice
Part 2	Passages: 2 questions each	Multiple-choice
Part 3	Real-Life: 1 question each	Multiple-choice

※**Listen carefully to the instructions.**

Part 1   ▶MP3 ▶アプリ ▶CD 3 28〜41

No. 1
1 Phone for a taxi.
2 Walk to the restaurant.
3 Wait for the rain to stop.
4 Take the subway.

No. 2
1 Cancel his meeting.
2 Take the afternoon off.
3 Wait to see if the pain decreases.
4 Go to the dentist this morning.

No. 3
1 Scientists often make wrong predictions.
2 Pollution levels do not affect the weather.
3 The high temperatures are nothing to worry about.
4 The heat wave is related to global warming.

No. 4
1 Change the dates of his business trip.
2 Arrange a picnic for the playgroup.
3 Find a park with a jungle gym.
4 Give her directions to Fairfield Park.

No. 5
1 She does not want to give their things to charity.
2 She does not want to have another yard sale.
3 She wants to change the moving date.
4 She wants to advertise in the newspaper.

No. 6

1 That she call his sister.
2 That she ask a friend for help.
3 That she start work later.
4 That she take care of Carol's kids.

No. 7

1 It will arrive no later than Friday.
2 It is being looked into.
3 It was sent back to the manufacturer.
4 It has not yet been shipped.

No. 8

1 He is now working as a teacher.
2 He quit his restaurant job.
3 He started a new career.
4 He went back to school.

No. 9

1 She will soon start work on a bigger project.
2 She prefers her new office space.
3 She wants her staff to hold fewer meetings.
4 She is looking for a new office.

No. 10

1 The class instructor is likely to fail him.
2 He is concerned he will not meet the deadline.
3 The woman refused to practice with him.
4 He is not used to making presentations.

No. 11

1 The woman should hire more staff.
2 The new file clerk might be dismissed.
3 The procedure for hiring staff is outdated.
4 The woman is too concerned about Brent.

No. 12

1 Attempt to sell the car.
2 Stay with their current insurance company.
3 Report the man's accident.
4 Cancel their insurance policy.

| Part 2 | ◀» ▶MP3 ▶アプリ ▶CD3 **42**~**48** |

(A)

No. 13
1 It causes the trees to die.
2 It is impossible in dry areas.
3 It requires considerable effort.
4 It can damage the local environment.

No. 14
1 Helped them gain business skills.
2 Found them jobs in cosmetics companies.
3 Located foreign producers for them.
4 Established schools for their children.

(B)

No. 15
1 It was the first bridge to connect two islands.
2 It was the longest bridge of its kind.
3 It was designed by a woman.
4 It was the first suspension bridge.

No. 16
1 She was familiar with bridge construction.
2 She was best qualified for the job.
3 She was appointed by her father-in-law.
4 She was representing her husband.

(C)

No. 17
1 They are less common than originally thought.
2 They are only found in cold places.
3 They can be found anywhere on Earth.
4 They can be harder than rocks from Earth.

No. 18
1 It provides useful information about our solar system.
2 It led to the discovery of a new material.
3 It shows that most micrometeorites are older than predicted.
4 It helped to prove the age of the sun.

176

(D)

No. 19
1 He was hired to steal it by an art dealer.
2 He wanted to show that the museum had poor security.
3 He thought it should be returned to Italy.
4 He believed it was a forgery.

No. 20
1 It harmed Italy's reputation.
2 It increased the *Mona Lisa*'s level of fame.
3 It lowered the value of the *Mona Lisa*.
4 It led to changes in Italian laws.

(E)

No. 21
1 It can be hard for farmers to take vacations.
2 Government funding is being reduced.
3 Crop farming is becoming less profitable.
4 Keeping animals is more difficult than growing crops.

No. 22
1 A lack of trust from farm owners.
2 Intense competition for jobs.
3 Convincing farmers to change their procedures.
4 Becoming familiar with operations on each farm.

(F)

No. 23
1 Improve air quality.
2 Reduce traffic accidents.
3 Help emergency services.
4 Increase security for pedestrians.

No. 24
1 The technology needed is not yet good enough.
2 The streetlights record people's private information.
3 The remote controls require too much electricity.
4 The streetlights are unsuitable for most cities.

|||| Part 3 ||||||||||||||||||||||||||||||||||||||||||||||| ◀» ▶MP3 ▶アプリ ▶CD3 49〜54

(G)

No. 25

Situation: You receive the following voice mail after your first interview for a university teaching position in Canada. You are a legal resident of Canada.

Question: What should you do first?

1 Send a copy of your passport.
2 Contact your previous employer.
3 Schedule your second interview.
4 Send copies of your recent publications.

(H)

No. 26

Situation: You hear the following commercial from SuperBuzz electronics store. You need a new printer for your home office and want the best deal.

Question: What should you do?

1 Make your purchase on Thursday or Friday.
2 Wait until the weekend.
3 Download the store's smartphone app.
4 Bring in a coupon from a newspaper.

(I)

No. 27

Situation: Today, you need to drive to a nearby city for a two-day conference. Your husband has left a voice mail on your cell phone. You must depart within two hours.

Question: What should you do?

1 Have the snow tires put on.
2 Borrow your husband's vehicle.
3 Purchase chains tonight.
4 Cancel your attendance.

178

(J)

No. 28

Situation: You will head your company's new branch office in Japan. The company president tells you the following.

Question: What should you do first?

1 Ask coworkers to take over your work now.
2 Begin searching for new clients in Japan.
3 Let your clients know you are leaving.
4 Identify a suitable person for your position.

(K)

No. 29

Situation: It is your first day at a new job. You have questions about the tax forms you need to complete. The office manager tells you the following.

Question: What should you do first?

1 Contact Ms. Rodriguez.
2 Ask the office manager for an ID.
3 Speak with Stephanie.
4 Meet Julia about getting an office.

面 接

問題カード（A日程）　　　　　▶MP3 ▶アプリ ▶CD 4 46〜50

You have **one minute** to prepare.

This is a story about a couple who owned a flower farm.
You have **two minutes** to narrate the story.

Your story should begin with the following sentence:
One day, a couple was working on their flower farm.

Questions

No. 1 Please look at the fourth picture. If you were the woman, what would you be thinking?

No. 2 Do you think people are too concerned about the amount of chemicals used in food?

No. 3 Is it a good idea to use agricultural land for city developments?

No. 4 Should companies be required to show how their products are made?

問題カード（B日程）   ◀)) ▶MP3 ▶アプリ ▶CD 4 51〜54

You have **one minute** to prepare.

This is a story about an elderly couple who owned a café.
You have **two minutes** to narrate the story.

Your story should begin with the following sentence:
One day, a couple was at their café.

Questions

No. 1   Please look at the fourth picture. If you were the woman, what would you be thinking?

No. 2   Do you think that people understand the responsibilities of owning a pet?

No. 3   Does society put too much pressure on people to have children?

No. 4   Is hunting animals acceptable in today's society?

旺文社の英検®書

★ **一発合格したいなら「全問＋パス単」！**
旺文社が自信を持っておすすめする王道の組み合わせです。

★ 過去問で出題傾向をしっかりつかむ！
英検®過去6回全問題集 1〜5級
[音声アプリ対応] [音声ダウンロード] [別売CDあり]

過去問を徹底分析した「でる順」！
英検®でる順パス単 1〜5級
[音声アプリ対応] [音声ダウンロード]

本番形式の予想問題で総仕上げ！
7日間完成 英検®予想問題ドリル 1〜5級
[CD付] [音声アプリ対応]

申し込みから面接まで英検のすべてがわかる！
英検®総合対策教本 1〜5級
[CD付]

大問ごとに一次試験を集中攻略！
DAILY英検®集中ゼミ 1〜5級
[CD付]

動画で面接をリアルに体験！
英検®二次試験・面接完全予想問題 1〜3級
[DVD+CD付] [音声アプリ対応]

このほかにも多数のラインナップを揃えております。

旺文社の英検®合格ナビゲーター https://eiken.obunsha.co.jp/
英検合格を目指す方のためのウェブサイト。
試験情報や級別学習法，おすすめの英検書を紹介しています。

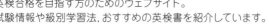

※英検®は、公益財団法人 日本英語検定協会の登録商標です。

株式会社 旺文社　〒162-8680　東京都新宿区横寺町55
https://www.obunsha.co.jp/

2023年度版

文部科学省後援

英検®準1級
過去6回全問題集

別冊解答

英検®は、公益財団法人 日本英語検定協会の登録商標です。

旺文社

2023年度版

文部科学省後援

英検®準1級
過去6回全問題集

別冊解答

英検®は、公益財団法人 日本英語検定協会の登録商標です。

旺文社

もくじ

Contents

2022年度 　第2回検定　解答・解説 …………………… 　5

　　　　　　　第1回検定　解答・解説 …………………… 　49

2021年度 　第3回検定　解答・解説 …………………… 　93

　　　　　　　第2回検定　解答・解説 …………………… 137

　　　　　　　第1回検定　解答・解説 …………………… 181

2020年度 　第3回検定　解答・解説 …………………… 225

正答率 ★75%以上 は，旺文社「英検®一次試験 解答速報サービス」において
回答者の正答率が 75%以上だった設問を示しています。

・2022 年度 第 2 回検定…全級合計約 2.4 万件の回答より
　　　　　　　　　　　　（2022 年 10 月 11 日以降の回答数）
・2022 年度 第 1 回検定…全級合計約 3.9 万件の回答より
　　　　　　　　　　　　（2022 年 6 月 6 日以降の回答数）
・2021 年度 第 3 回検定…全級合計約 4.8 万件の回答より
　　　　　　　　　　　　（2022 年 1 月 24 日以降の回答数）
・2021 年度 第 2 回検定…全級合計約 4.6 万件の回答より
　　　　　　　　　　　　（2021 年 10 月 10 日以降の回答数）
・2021 年度 第 1 回検定…全級合計約 4.0 万件の回答より
　　　　　　　　　　　　（2021 年 5 月 31 日以降の回答数）
・2020 年度 第 3 回検定…全級合計約 2.4 万件の回答より
　　　　　　　　　　　　（2021 年 1 月 22 日以降の回答数）

2022-2

一次試験
筆記解答・解説 　　　　p.6～21

一次試験
リスニング解答・解説 　p.22～44

二次試験
面接解答・解説 　　　　p.45～48

解 答 一 覧

一次試験・筆記

1
(1)	2	(10)	2	(19)	4
(2)	4	(11)	1	(20)	3
(3)	2	(12)	1	(21)	4
(4)	2	(13)	1	(22)	1
(5)	4	(14)	3	(23)	3
(6)	2	(15)	1	(24)	1
(7)	2	(16)	4	(25)	3
(8)	4	(17)	4		
(9)	3	(18)	4		

2
(26)	2	(29)	2
(27)	4	(30)	3
(28)	1	(31)	2

3
(32)	4	(35)	4	(38)	4
(33)	1	(36)	4	(39)	1
(34)	2	(37)	1	(40)	3
				(41)	3

4 　解答例は本文参照

一次試験・リスニング

Part 1
No. 1	4	No. 5	3	No. 9	3
No. 2	4	No. 6	1	No.10	2
No. 3	2	No. 7	2	No.11	2
No. 4	2	No. 8	1	No.12	4

Part 2
No.13	3	No.17	1	No.21	1
No.14	1	No.18	4	No.22	1
No.15	4	No.19	3	No.23	2
No.16	3	No.20	2	No.24	4

Part 3
No.25	3	No.28	3
No.26	4	No.29	2
No.27	2		

| 一次試験・筆記 | **1** | 問題編 p.18〜21 |

(1) ─解答 **2**

訳 A：お母さん，今夜の夕食にハンバーガーを作ってくれない？
B：いいけど，まず肉を冷凍庫から出して，それを解凍しなきゃね。

解説 〈let＋O＋動詞の原形〉「O に〜させる」の O ＝ it は肉のこと。ハンバーガーを作るのに肉を冷凍庫から出して「解凍する」必要があることから，thaw が適切。reckon「計算する」，stray「道に迷う」，shatter「粉々に壊れる」

(2) ─解答 **4**

訳 ジョセリンはいつも息子にうそをつかないよう言い聞かせた。彼女は，彼に正直であるという強い感覚を植え付けることが大切だと信じていた。

解説 it is 〜 to *do*「…することは〜だ」の構文で，目的語 sense「感覚」に合う動詞は instill「（主義・思想などを）植え付ける」。remodel「作り替える」，stumble「つまずく」，overlap「一部を覆う，部分的に重なる」

(3) ─解答 **2**

訳 ザラは彼氏にとても腹を立てていたが，彼の真剣な謝罪を聞いて彼を許した。彼女は彼が本当に申し訳ないと思っていると確信した。

解説 apology「謝罪」を修飾する形容詞はどれか。彼氏を許したことから，彼の謝罪は真剣な（earnest）ものだったと想像できる。detectable「検出できる」，cumulative「累積的な」，underlying「潜在的な」

(4) ─解答 **2**

訳 最初のうちは，スミス夫妻は裏庭のプールを楽しんでいたが，きれいに保つのが面倒になったので，たいていの場合カバーをしたままにした。

解説 〈such＋原因＋that＋結果〉の構造。2 つの it はプールのことで，カバーをしたままなのは，きれいに保つのが厄介（nuisance）になったから。bureau「（行政組織の）局」，sequel「続編」，metaphor「隠喩」

(5) ─解答 **4**

訳 歴史を通して，多くの偉大な思想家たちは，最初はその考えゆえに嘲笑されたが，最終的には真剣に受け止められた。

解説 at first と eventually の対比に着目し，嘲笑された（were ridiculed）→ 真剣に受け止められた，という流れが適切。それぞれ saturate「満たす」，flatter「お世辞を言う」，ingest「（食べ物・薬などを）摂取する」の過去分詞。なお，本文の A before B「B する前に A した」は「A し，そして B した」という意味に取るとよい。

(6) ─解答 **2**

訳 その少女は最初，スピーチコンテストで大勢の聴衆を前に恥ずかしく感

6

じていたが，1分ほどすると自信を持ち始めた。

解説 〈feel＋形容詞〉「〜に感じる」が but の前にも後ろにもあり，対照的な意味になっている。confident に対比する bashful「恥ずかしがりやの」が適切。mortal「死すべき」，pious「信心深い」，concise「簡潔な」

(7) ―解答 ② ••

訳 タイプライターは過去の遺物である。オフィスや家庭で一般的に使われていた時代からどれほどテクノロジーが進歩したかを思い知らされる。

解説 タイプライターは，テクノロジーが進歩した今となっては過去の物である。よって，relic「(過去の) 遺跡，遺物」が適切。jumble「ごちゃ混ぜ」，fraud「詐欺」，treaty「条約」

(8) ―解答 ④ ••

訳 男性がトラの檻（おり）に近づくと，その巨大な動物が低くうなった。男性はその恐ろしい声に恐れをなして後ずさりした。

解説 空所には主語 the huge animal ＝ tiger に対する自動詞が入る。第2文の the terrifying sound を手掛かりに，growl「うなる」の過去形 growled が適切。それぞれ sparkle「輝く」，leer「いやらしい目つきで見る」，disprove「反証する」の過去形。

(9) ―解答 ③ ••

訳 警察官は法律を守ることを約束しなければならない。もちろん，これには彼ら自身が法律に従うことも含まれる。

解説 目的語 the law に合う動詞は uphold「(法律などを) 支持する，守る」。第2文の themselves は警察官のことで，uphold the law と follow the law が同義になる。gravitate「引き付けられる」，detach「分離する」，eradicate「根絶する，撲滅する」

(10) ‒解答 ② ••

訳 従業員は全員，毎年義務的な健康診断を受ける。各会社は，労働者全員が確実にそれを行うようにすることを法律で義務付けられている。

解説 第2文の be required by law to do は「〜するよう法律で定められて［義務付けられて］いる」という意味で，medical checkup「健康診断」を修飾する形容詞として compulsory「義務的な」が適切。gloomy「憂鬱（うつ）にさせる」，reminiscent「連想させる」，muddled「混乱した」

(11) ‒解答 ① ••

訳 生物学の学生は，細胞分裂がどのように機能しているかを学ばなければならない。その理由は，単一の細胞が2つに分裂するこの過程が自然界で一般的に見られるためである。

解説 how ... は間接疑問で，cell (　) が S，works が V。後の a single cell splitting into two「単一の細胞が2つに分裂する」から，cell division「細胞分裂」とするのが適切。division の動詞形 divide は

7

split と同義。appliance「電化製品」，imposition「強制，（税などを）課すこと」，longitude「経度」

(12) – 解答 **1** ....

訳 2つの会社が合併した後，何人かの上級社員は不要になり，職を失った。

解説 何人かの上級社員が職を失ったのは，2つの会社が合併した（merged）からである。それぞれ pose「ポーズをとる」，conform「（習慣などに）従う」，flock「集まる」の過去形。

(13) – 解答 **1** .... 正答率 ★**75%以上**

訳 運動中に脱水症状になるのを避けるためには，常に十分な水を飲むべきである。運動時間が長ければ長いほど，より多くの水が必要である。

解説 運動中に水を飲むのは脱水症状を避けるためである。become dehydrated で「脱水症状になる」の意味。dehydrated は動詞 dehydrate「脱水症状にする」の過去分詞（形容詞用法）。eternal「永遠の」，punctuated は punctuate「句読点を付ける」の過去分詞，cautious「用心深い」

(14) – 解答 **3** .... 正答率 ★**75%以上**

訳 ケンは家ではいつも行儀が良かったので，彼の先生が彼はクラスで最も反抗的な生徒の1人だと言ったとき，彼の母親はショックを受けた。

解説 母親がショックを受けた理由は，行儀が良いはずの息子がクラスでは反抗的な（disobedient）生徒だと言われたからである。momentary「瞬間的な」，miniature「小規模の」，invincible「無敵の」

(15) – 解答 **1** .... 正答率 ★**75%以上**

訳 警察は，近くにいた誰かが何が起こったかを見ていたことを期待して，犯行現場の見物人に質問した。

解説 選択肢には人を表す語が並んでいる。犯行現場近くにいた人に質問したと考えて，bystanders「傍観者，見物人」が適切。それぞれ reformer「改革者」，mourner「追悼者」，pioneer「先駆者」の複数形。

(16) – 解答 **4** ....

訳 何人かの将軍がその国の首相を打倒しようと試みた。しかし，彼らは成功せず，彼は権力の座にとどまっている。

解説 However に着目し，首相を打倒し（overthrow）ようとしたが失敗した，という流れにするのが自然。they は Several generals，he は the country's prime minister を指す。irrigate「かんがいする」，harmonize「調和させる」，outpace「追い越す」

(17) – 解答 **4** ....

訳 カレブは，企画書の草稿を完成させたので，上司にそれを評価するよう依頼した。残念ながら，彼女はまだ多くの改善が必要だと思った。

解説 文中の he は Caleb，she は his manager を指す。2つの it は a draft

8

of his proposal のことで，上司に企画書を評価する（evaluate）よう頼んだ結果が第 2 文に書かれている。scrub「ごしごし洗う」，enchant「大いに喜ばせる」，prune「刈り込む」

(18) − 解答 ④

訳 アメリカの大統領であるトーマス・ジェファソンとジョン・アダムズは，50 年以上にわたって手紙を交換し合った。この文通は，アメリカの歴史の重要な部分である。

解説 第 1 文の exchanged letters with each other を名詞で表した correspondence「文通」が適切。matrimony「婚姻」，federation「連合」，horizon「地平線」

(19) − 解答 ④

訳 暴動の間，町は混乱状態だった。人々は通りに出てけんかをしたり窓を割ったりし，多くの店が強盗に遭った。

解説 暴動の間の町の様子が第 2 文に書かれている。その内容から，町は混乱（anarchy）していたと分かる。disclosure「暴露」，admittance「入場（許可）」，attainment「達成，獲得」

(20) − 解答 ③   正答率 ★75%以上

訳 一部の植物の花は実際に食べることができ，サラダをより美味しくするだけでなく視覚的により魅力的にするためにも使うことができる。

解説 空所後に「（一部の植物の花は）サラダをより美味しくする」とあることから，edible「食べることができる」が適切。both A and B は「A も B も」のほか，「A だけでなく B もまた」の意味にもなる。stationary「動かない」，candid「率直な」，hideous「恐ろしい」

(21) − 解答 ④

訳 その有名な科学者が講演中に多くの間違いを犯したとき，誰も驚かなかった。彼は話術が乏しいことで有名だ。

解説 第 2 文は第 1 文の理由。誰もが科学者の乏しい話術を知っているので，多くの間違いを犯しても誰も驚かなかったのである。notorious は「悪名高い」の意味で，be notorious for で「～（悪いこと）で有名だ」。treacherous「不誠実な」，momentous「重大な」，flirtatious「軽薄な，浮気な」

(22) − 解答 ①

訳 ブラッドの上司が先月彼を昇進させたとき，彼の努力や長時間労働が全て報われた。

解説 主語 ... hard work and long hours に対する動詞として，pay off「報われる」の過去形が適切。それぞれ write back「返事を書く」，chop up「～を細かく切る」，make over「～を作り直す」の過去形。

9

(23) − 解答 **3** ··

> **訳** CEO の演説があまりに漠然としていたため，ジーナは会社が深刻な財政難に陥っているという事実を理解するのにしばらく時間がかかった。

> **解説** 演説が漠然としていたという状況から，「理解」に時間がかかったと推測できる。catch on to で「～（意味など）を理解する」という意味。fill in「代理をする」，duck out「こっそり外に出る，急いで立ち去る」，give up「諦める」はいずれも〈to＋名詞〉が続かない。

(24) − 解答 **1** ··

> **訳** チームのメンバーは各自，新しいプロジェクトのためにやるべき仕事を持っているが，彼らの努力の全てをまとめ上げる責任はマネージャーにある。

> **解説** each と all に着目して，but 前後の対比をつかもう。主語 responsibility「責任」と目的語 the manager に合う動詞は，fall on「（責任などが）～に降りかかる」。それぞれ square with「～と一致する」，drop by「～に立ち寄る」，stack up「～を積み重ねる」の 3 人称単数・現在形。

(25) − 解答 **3** ··

> **訳** その従業員は，自分の罪を証明するファイルやその他の証拠を隠滅することで，会社からの窃盗を隠蔽しようとした。

> **解説** by destroying ... は，（ ）his theft from the company「会社からの窃盗を（ ）する」ための手段である。目的語の his theft に合うのは，cover up「～（罪）を隠す」である。tuck away「～をしまい込む」，latch onto「～をつかむ」，doze off「うたた寝する」

一次試験・筆記	**2**	問題編 p.22 ～ 25

全文訳 **ナブタ・プラヤのストーンサークル**

　多くの先史時代の社会がストーンサークルを建設した。これらは，太陽の動きを観測するためなど，さまざまな理由で作られた。このようなストーンサークルの中でも最古のものとして科学者たちに知られているのが，エジプトのナブタ・プラヤにある。約 7,000 年前のものであるこのストーンサークルは，おそらく世界で最も有名な先史時代のストーンサークルであるイングランドのストーンヘンジよりも 1,000 年以上前に作られた。ナブタ・プラヤの気候は現在では非常に乾燥しているが，これは常にそうだったわけではなかった。実際，ストーンサークルが建設された時期の季節的な豪雨は一時的な湖の形成につながり，これが牛を放牧する部族をこの地域に引き寄せた。

　ナブタ・プラヤの最初の入植者たちは，約 1 万年前に来た。考古学者たちは，これらの入植者たちが深い井戸のシステムを作って一年中水が得られるようにしたこと，また住居を真っすぐに並べて配置し，それらに保管スペースを備えていたことの証拠を発見

10

した。また，入植者たちは，彼らの生活に不可欠であった牛の崇拝に重きを置いた宗教を実践していた。これらの発見は，入植者たちが高度な社会を築いていた証拠である。

　研究結果は，約 7,000 年前，ストーンサークルの石の一部が 1 年で最も日が長い日に太陽に向かって一直線に並ぶようになっていたことを示している。これはストーンサークルが暦として使用されていたことを示唆している。しかし，ある宇宙物理学者は，このストーンサークルにはまた別の目的があったと信じている。彼は，ほかの石の位置が，このストーンサークルが建設された時期のオリオン座の星の位置と一致すると指摘している。このため，彼はこのストーンサークルが夜空の星の位置を示す占星術の図だったという説を提唱している。

> 語句　prehistoric「先史時代の」，predate「（時間的に）先立つ」，formation「形成」，temporary「一時的な」，cattle-grazing「牛を放牧する」，archaeologist「考古学者」，uncover「発見する，発掘する」，equip A with B「A に B を備える」，worship「崇拝」，finding「（通例複数形で）（研究や調査の）結果」，astrophysicist「宇宙物理学者」，constellation「星座」，astrological「占星術の」

(26) – 解答 ② ・・・・・・・・・・・・・・・・・・・・・・・・・・・・・・・・・・・・ 正答率 ★75%以上

解説　文頭に適切な論理マーカーを補う問題。空所前の this was not the case は「この場合はそうではなかった」という慣用句で，これに not always「常に〜とは限らない」が混じった表現。「常に乾燥していたわけではなかった」と「豪雨があった」を結ぶ表現として，In fact「実際に」が適切。ここでは前述の話題について事実を加える働きをしている。

(27) – 解答 ④ ・・・・・・・・・・・・・・・・・・・・・・・・・・・・・・・・・・・・ 正答率 ★75%以上

解説　主語の These discoveries「これらの発見」の詳細は前述にある。「深い井戸のシステムを作って一年中水が得られるようにした」や，「住居を真っすぐに並べて配置し，それらに保管スペースを備えた」などの入植者たちの行動を「高度な社会を築いていた」と表した 4 が正解。

(28) – 解答 ① ・・・・・・・・・・・・・・・・・・・・・・・・・・・・・・・・・・・・ 正答率 ★75%以上

解説　空所前の「暦として使用されていた」と空所後の「夜空の星の位置を示す占星術の図だった」は，いずれもストーンサークルの使用目的だと考えられる。よって，追加を示す another を含む 1「また別の目的があった」が適切。対照を示す however に着目して話の展開をつかもう。

全文訳　**良い道路運動**

　19 世紀後期から始まった「良い道路運動（グッドロード運動）」は，同国の道路・主要路網を生み出すことに寄与し，アメリカの風景を一変させた。この運動には意外な発端があった。今日のほとんどの人は，道路網は最初，自動車を運転する人々のニーズに応えて整備されたと思っているが，これは思い込みに過ぎない。実際には，この要求は主に自転車に乗る人の間で生まれた。近代的な自転車の発明は，1890 年代のサイクリ

ングの流行につながり，何百万人ものアメリカ人が自転車に乗るためのより良い，より安全な道路を望んだ。

　自転車に乗る人たちは，きちんと整備されず，危険なことの多かった道路の質を改善するよう自治体に圧力をかけ始めた。最初，この運動は，都市部からの自転車に乗る人たちの余暇活動を支援するために税金を使われたくなかった農家たちに抵抗された。しかし次第に農家たちは考えを改め始めた。これの理由の１つが，『良い道路の福音～アメリカ農家への手紙～』と呼ばれる影響力のあるパンフレットだった。このパンフレットは，彼らが作物を市場に輸送するのが容易になるなど，道路のメリットを強調することで多くの農家を納得させた。

　自動車が一般化するにつれて，この運動は急速に勢いを増した。特に，1900 年代初頭のフォードモデル T の発明によって多くの人が車を運転するようになり，これらの人々もより良い道路を熱望していた。これらの手ごろな車は何百万台と販売され，車を運転する人の増加は，道路を増やし，既存道路の質を改善するよう各自治体に圧力をかけた。

> [語句] transform「一変させる」，in response to「～に応えて」，myth「根拠のない話」，craze「流行」，〈pressure＋O＋to *do*〉「O に～するよう圧力をかける」，resist「抵抗する」，influential「影響力のある」，convince「納得させる」，emphasize「強調する」，momentum「勢い」，*be* eager for「～を熱望している」，existing「既存の」

(29) – 解答 **2** ....

> [解説] This movement「この運動」の内容は前述にある。空所後の While most people today assume ～, this is a myth. Actually, ... から，「～と思っているが，そうではない。実際には…」という展開をつかもう。道路ができたのは自動車ではなく自転車のためだったという趣旨で，これは意外な（surprising）事実である。よって，**2**「意外な発端があった」が適切。

(30) – 解答 **3** .... 正答率 ★75％以上

> [解説] 文中に at first が出てきたら，その後 however などが用いられて話が逆転することを予測しながら読もう。ここでは At first から Gradually, however, ... へのつながりに注目。最初，運動は農家に抵抗された→しかし次第に…→多くの農家を納得させたという趣旨から，農家の考えに変化があったことが分かる。よって，**3**「考えを改め始めた」が適切。

(31) – 解答 **2** ....

> [解説] 第 2 段落までは「自転車」のための運動の話だったが，第 3 段落では「自動車」の一般化によって運動が勢いを増したという話に発展する。空所後の Ford Model T の発明は自動車普及に寄与した具体例と考えられる。よって，具体例を示す In particular「特に」が適切。

12

一次試験・筆記 **3** 問題編 p.26 ～ 32

22年度第2回　筆記

全文訳 **顔の認識**

　人間は一般的に，顔を認識し，その表情を素早く読み取ることに非常に優れている。これは，顔の特徴を処理するのに特化した脳の特定領域があることにより実現されている。進化の観点からすると，この能力の発達は合理的である。というのも，初期の人類は，例えば周りの人間が怒っているのか，それゆえに潜在的に危険であるのかを判断する必要があったであろうからだ。しかし，意図せぬ結果の1つとして，人は，周囲の環境の中にある物体に顔が見えると思うことがよくある。人は，雲や木の幹から食べ物のかけらや電気コンセントに至るまで，さまざまな物体にこれらのいわゆる「偽顔」があるのに気付く。

　オーストラリアの研究者たちが最近，脳がどのように偽顔を処理するかについて詳しく知るための研究を実施した。先行研究では，本物の顔に関して言えば，顔がどのような感情を表しているかの判断は，その人が直前に見た顔に影響を受けるということが明らかになった。例えば，立て続けにうれしそうな顔を見ると，人は次に見る顔がうれしさを表していると評価しやすい。今回のオーストラリアの研究では，研究者たちは参加者たちに，特定の感情を表している一連の偽顔を見せた。彼らは，本物の顔と同様に，偽顔によって表された感情についての参加者たちの判断は，直前に見た偽顔に影響されることを発見した。この知見に基づき，研究者たちは，脳は本物の顔を処理するのと同様の方法で偽顔を処理していると結論付けた。

　研究者たちはさらに，人間の顔の配置 —— 目が2つあって口の上に鼻があるという配置 —— に大まかに似ているだけの特徴を持つどんな物体でも，脳が感情表現を読み取ろうとそれらの特徴を評価するきっかけとなり得ると指摘した。すなわち，脳の顔認識の基準は，特定のものというよりむしろ一般的なのである。研究者たちは，これは脳がこれほど素早く顔の表情を評価できる理由の1つだと言う。

語句 interpret「解釈する，（表情を）読み取る」，specific「特定の，具体的な」，process「処理する」，in terms of「～の観点から」，unintended「意図されたものではない」，consequence「結果」，perceive「気付く」，so-called「いわゆる」，reveal「明らかにする」，a series of「一連の～」，assess「評価する」，as with「～と同様に」，trigger「引き起こす」，criterion「（判断）基準（複数形は criteria）」

(32) – 解答 ④

問題文の訳 第1段落で，この文章の筆者はなぜ雲などの物体に言及しているのか。

選択肢の訳 **1** 人の周囲の環境が，人がどれだけよく他人の感情を判断できるかに影響を与え得るという考えを裏付けるため。

2 顔を識別できない人はほかの特定の物体を識別するのにも苦労するということを説明するため。

13

3 周囲の環境にある日常的な物体に対する私たちの反応が，脳のさまざまな領域によって制御されていることを説明するのを助けるため。

4 そこに顔が見えると人が思い込む日常的な物の例を示すため。

解説 第1段落最終文の趣旨は「人は，さまざまな物体に偽顔（false faces）が見える」ということ。そして，この a variety of objects の具体例の1つが clouds である。よって，**4** が正解。

(33) −解答 ①

問題文の訳 先行研究が示したことは

選択肢の訳 **1** 本物の顔がどんな感情を表しているかについての人の判断は，その人が直前に見たほかの本物の顔の影響を受ける。

2 人は，本物の顔よりも偽顔の方により素早く感情的な意味を結び付ける。

3 人は，本物の顔によって表された感情よりも偽顔によって表された感情の方がうれしそうで肯定的だと判断する傾向がある。

4 人は，偽顔が何も感情を表していない場合，偽顔を見分けるのにより長い時間がかかる。

解説 先行研究について書かれた第2段落第2文 Previous studies have ... から，**1** が正解。それぞれ affected を influenced に，have just seen を have seen immediately before に言い換えている。

(34) −解答 ② ･･･････････････････････ 正答率 ★75%以上

問題文の訳 オーストラリアの研究者たちは，顔によって表される感情を評価する脳の能力について何と言っているか。

選択肢の訳 **1** この能力は，生存の面では人間にもはや利点をもたらさないため，時間の経過とともに消滅する可能性が高い。

2 脳が緩い判断基準を用いて顔を識別しているという事実により，人は，顔が表す感情を素早く判断することができる。

3 脳は，顔が非常にはっきりした特徴を持っている場合にのみ，顔が表す感情を正確に識別できる。

4 過去に人間に利益だけでなく不利益ももたらしたにもかかわらず，この能力の進化は起こった。

解説 質問文の「顔によって表される感情を評価する脳の能力」は，第3段落第1文に書かれている。そして続く In other words, ... 以下では，顔を認識するための脳の判断基準は一般的（general ≒ loose）であること，またその結果として脳が素早く表情を評価できる（assess ≒ judge）ことが分かる。これらの情報を短く表した **2** が正解。〈this is one reason SV〉→〈allow＋O＋to *do*〉という因果表現の言い換えにも着目したい。

14

全文訳 **ドリアンとオオコウモリ**

　フットボール並みの大きさのドリアン果実は，その不快なにおいとクリーミーで甘い果肉でよく知られている。「果物の王様」として知られるドリアンは，ボルネオ島原産とされているが，今ではもっと広く栽培されており，世界中で消費される全てのドリアンの半分以上がタイで栽培されている。ドリアンは東南アジア全域で昔から人気があったが，その人気は今や世界各地に広がっている。ドリアンには何百もの種類があるが，ほぼマレーシアでしか栽培されていないムサンキング種は，最も価値が高い品種の１つである。ドリアンにはビタミンが豊富に含まれているため，しばしばその健康効果で宣伝されており，これが輸出の増加をもたらしている。実際，専門家たちは，次の10年間で，マレーシアから中国への出荷量だけでも50％増加すると予測している。この状況を利用するために，多くのマレーシアの農家がドリアンを生産することを選び，ヤシ油などの作物の生産をやめてしまった。

　しかし，ドリアンの木の栽培は容易ではない。ドリアンは定期的な水やりと肥料を与えることを必要とし，また温度の影響を非常に受けやすい。さらに，ドリアンは自然には群生せず，ほかの樹木や低木に混ざった方が繁茂するため，単一の作物として果樹園で栽培するのは困難をもたらす。ドリアンの木の実りを良くするために確実に花が十分授粉されるようにすることも，農家にとってはさらなる困難である。ドリアンの木の特徴の１つに，花が夜にしか花粉を放出しないという点があり，そのためミツバチなどの日中餌を求める昆虫はドリアンの受粉をしない。夜に活動する動物が受粉の役割を引き受けるが，ドリアンの木の花のうち25％ほどしか自然に受粉しない。このため，多くの農家が人の手で授粉するという多大な労働力を要する方法に頼る。

　研究によって，オオコウモリがドリアンの花の主な自然送粉者であることが分かっている。しかし，このコウモリは多くの農家に追い払われたり，駆除されたりしている。農家は，このコウモリは果実を食べることで損害を与え，利益を減らすことから，単に害獣と見なしているのだ。また，このコウモリは，食料として狩られ，売られた結果，絶滅が危惧されてもいる。というのも，東南アジアの一部の文化において，このコウモリの肉を食べることが呼吸障害を治すのに役立つと信じられているからである。オオコウモリの恩恵について人々に教えなければ，このコウモリの個数はさらに減少する可能性があり，それはドリアン栽培に深刻な結果をもたらすことになるかもしれない。

　語句 flesh「果肉」, cultivate「栽培する」, exclusively「全く，もっぱら」, take advantage of「～を利用する」, in favor of「～を選んで」, fertilizer「肥料」, *be* sensitive to「～の影響を受けやすい」, grove「小さい林」, thrive「繁茂する」, shrub「低木」, orchard「果樹園」, sufficient「十分な」, pollination「受［授］粉」, characteristic「特徴」, pollen「花粉」, pollinate「受［授］粉する」, resort to「(最終手段として) ～を用いる」, labor-intensive「多大な労動力を要する」, chase away「～を追い払う」, see A as B「A を B と見なす」, pest「害虫，害獣」, threatened「絶滅が危惧されて」, decline「減少する」

(35) －解答 ④ 正答率 ★75％以上

問題文の訳 第1段落によると，ドリアンの生産について正しいのはどれか。

選択肢の訳
1 ほかの東南アジア諸国ではもはやドリアンの栽培に利用できる十分な土地がないため，現在，ドリアンは主にマレーシアで栽培されている。
2 ドリアンは，伝統的に栽培されていた場所ではよく売れているが，ほかの国々ではまだ人気を得ていない。
3 高級品種のドリアンは，より安価な品種と同じ程度の栄養価しかないため，消費者から批判を浴びている。
4 ドリアンの需要が高まっているため，マレーシアの農家はほかの作物の栽培からドリアンの栽培に切り替えつつある。

解説 第1段落中程でドリアンの人気の高まりや出荷量の増加（＝ the increasing demand「需要の高まり」）を説明した後，最終文で「ヤシ油などの作物の生産をやめてドリアンの生産を選んだ」と続く。正解 **4** では最終文の内容を switch from A to B「A から B に切り替える」で表している。

(36) －解答 ④

問題文の訳 ドリアン農家が考慮しなければならない要因の1つは

選択肢の訳
1 ドリアンの木はほぼどんな温暖な気候でも栽培できるが，ほかの植物がほとんど生えていない場所で最もよく育つこと。
2 ドリアンの木がほかの植物を押し出す傾向があるため，先住植物の数が激減していること。
3 ドリアンの木は，ミツバチやほかの昼間の送粉者が容易に見つけられる場所で栽培するべきだということ。
4 ドリアンの木を自然に受粉させようと放っておくと，その木は大量の実をつける可能性が低いこと。

解説 ドリアンの栽培の難しさを説明した第2段落を参照。夜しか花粉を放出しないこと，また夜も25％ほどしか自然に受粉しないことから，多くの農家が人の手で授粉する。つまり，放っておいても受粉は困難→大量の実をつける可能性が低いと考えて，**4** が正解。

(37) －解答 ①

問題文の訳 この文章の筆者がオオコウモリについて言うことの1つは何か。

選択肢の訳
1 オオコウモリがドリアンの花の受粉に果たす重要な役割に関する認識が高まらなければ，ドリアンの生産が損害を被るかもしれない。
2 東南アジアでは，一部の市場で違法に販売されたコウモリの肉を食べた結果，多くの人が病気になった。
3 オオコウモリを捕獲し，その肉を販売できるように，意図的にオオコウモリを果樹園に誘引するドリアン農家もいる。
4 多くのオオコウモリが呼吸障害で死んだため，ドリアンの花の自然送

粉者が大幅に減少している。

解説 タイトルにある giant fruit bats は第３段落で初出する。オオコウモリ
はドリアンの花の主な自然送粉者である（＝重要な役割を果たす）が，
農家は害獣と見なして駆除し，また食用にも狩られるため，数が減少し
ている。オオコウモリの恩恵について人々に教えなければ（＝認識が高
まらなければ），個体数はさらに減少し，ドリアン栽培に深刻な結果を
もたらす（＝生産が損害を被る）かもしれない。よって，**1** が正解。

全文訳 **長距離砂漠挺身隊**

　第２次世界大戦中，イギリスは北アフリカの砂漠でドイツやイタリアと戦った。砂漠
での戦闘は，広範囲に展開した部隊間の小規模な戦闘が特徴で，探知されることと危険
な日中の灼熱の両方を避けるため，素早く移動したり，夜間に移動したりする必要があっ
た。この地域の広範な面積と砂の地形により，物資の輸送が難しく，水不足によって作
戦行動は深刻な制限を受けた。

　しかし，ラルフ・バグノルド少佐という１人のイギリス陸軍将校にとっては，これら
の過酷な状況は戦略的な機会を示していた。戦前，北アフリカの砂漠を何年も探検して
いたため，バグノルドはこの地形をよく知っており，敵軍を監視・追跡できる，小規模
で機動性の高い自動車化部隊が非常に有益であると確信していた。イギリスの司令官た
ちは，最初，これほどの長距離情報収集には航空機の方が適していると信じ，そのよう
な部隊を編成するという彼の提案を拒否した。しかし，バグノルドは，地上で情報収集
することは有利になると主張し，彼の粘り強さは，1940 年６月にバグノルドを司令官
とする長距離砂漠挺身隊（LRDG）の編成につながった。

　LRDG は，最初から異例の部隊だった。通例の階級による区別は存在せず，将校も一
般兵士もファーストネームで呼び合い，彼らは全員が同じ任務を遂行することを期待さ
れた。戦場で果敢に戦う兵士を求めるよりも，バグノルドは優れた体力と機転，そして
精神的な強靭さのある個人を求めた。それは例えば，飲み水の利用が限られているにも
かかわらず，長期間にわたって意欲を維持し，注意を怠らずにいられる兵士たちのこと
だった。砂漠環境に適応させた特殊トラックを有する LRDG の偵察隊は，約３週間，
1,600 キロ以上の範囲を独立して行動する態勢が整っていた。燃料，弾薬，食糧などの
必需品全てが部隊によって運ばれたため，慎重な供給計画が極めて重要であった。

　LRDG の任務は，主に敵陣深くに入り込んで敵の動きを監視することを伴った。部隊
はさまざまな兵器を利用でき，兵士たちは主に情報を収集する訓練を受けていたが，彼
らは地雷を埋めたり，敵の飛行場や燃料庫に攻撃を仕掛けたりもした。敵陣内で急襲を
行うために 1941 年に編成されたイギリス陸軍部隊である特殊空挺部隊（SAS）が，そ
の最初の任務で敵地にパラシュートで降下して多数の死傷者を出したとき，LRDG は生
存者を連れ帰る任務を負った。この救出任務は成功し，この部隊の兵士たちが持つ砂漠
に関する幅広い知識のため，LRDG はその後，SAS を陸路で目的地との間を送迎する
任務を任され，輸送と誘導の両方を行った。これはほぼ間違いなく，SAS がより大き

な成功とより少ない死傷者で急襲を達成することに寄与した。

　LRDGの最大の功績が生まれたのは1943年のことで，イギリス軍が守りの堅い敵の前線を探知されることなくうまく避けて通れるルートを同部隊が見つけ，これによってイギリス軍は敵陣の守りの弱い所を攻撃することができた。これが北アフリカにおける軍事行動で決定的な転換点となり，そこでのイギリスの勝利に大いに貢献した。LRDGは，その後も1945年までヨーロッパでの戦争遂行に多大な貢献をした。

> 語句　warfare「戦争，戦闘」，characterize「特徴付ける」，troop「（複数形で）軍隊」，detection「探知」，terrain「地形」，harsh「過酷な」，strategic「戦略的な」，convinced「確信して」，motorized unit「自動車化部隊」，invaluable「非常に有益な」，commander「司令官」，intelligence「（軍事的・政治的）機密情報」，advantageous「有利な」，persistence「粘り強さ」，unconventional「異例の」，from the outset「最初から」，distinction「区別」，resourcefulness「機転」，alert「注意を怠らない」，specialized「特殊な」，adapt A to B「AをBに適応させる」，ammunition「弾薬」，weaponry「兵器」，primarily「主に」，mine「地雷」，airfield「飛行場」，depot「貯蔵庫」，raid「急襲」，casualty「死傷者」，parachute「パラシュートで降下する」，crucial「決定的な」，turning point「転換点」，campaign「（一連の）軍事行動」

(38)－解答 ④

問題文の訳　ラルフ・バグノルド少佐がイギリス陸軍の司令官たちを説得できた内容は

選択肢の訳
1　兵士たちの砂漠での任務の成功が乏しいのは，適切な資源が供給されていないからだということ。
2　敵地上空を飛行したり砂漠で監視したりするのに使われている航空機には，大幅な改良が必要であるということ。
3　そのような環境での経験がほとんどないという事実にもかかわらず，彼は砂漠で任務を負った部隊を率いることができるということ。
4　砂漠で敵の行動に関する情報を収集するためには地上部隊を用いることが効果的な戦略だろうということ。

解説　第1段落で砂漠の過酷な環境に言及した後，Howeverで始まる第2段落で話が好転する。バグノルドは敵軍の監視・追跡に自動車化部隊（＝a ground-based unit）を用いることを提案したが，司令官たちは最初，情報収集には航空機の方が適していると信じ彼の案を拒否した。しかし，彼の粘り強さがLRDGの編成につながった（＝司令官たちを説得できた）。よって，**4**が正解。

(39)－解答

問題文の訳　長距離砂漠挺身隊（LRDG）について正しいのはどれか。

選択肢の訳　1　部隊に選ばれた兵士の特徴や作戦行動の方法が従来の部隊と違ってい

18

た。

2 予算が限られていたため，ほかの部隊よりも少ない資源と古い兵器で やりくりしなければならなかった。

3 偵察隊の兵士の数が多かったため，将校たちは管理方法の特別訓練を 受けなければならなかった。

4 その任務の成功は，敵陣の背後で定期的に LRDG へ物資が届くよう にしてくれる部隊に大きくかかっていた。

解説 LRDG の特徴を第 3 段落から読み取る。第 1 文に unconventional unit「異例の部隊」とあり，その具体的な説明が続く。「果敢に戦う兵 士より優れた体力と機転，精神的な強靭さのある個人を求めた」（＝兵士 の特徴）や，「砂漠環境に適応させた特殊トラックで約 3 週間，1,600 キ ロ以上の範囲を独立して行動」（＝作戦行動の方法）などとあり，これを 抽象的に表した **1** が正解。**4** は，物資（supplies ＝ necessary items） は LRDG の元に運ばれるのではなく，トラックに搭載して運んでいた ので不適。

(40) – 解答 ③

問題文の訳 次のうち，LRDG と特殊空挺部隊（SAS）の関係を最もよく表してい るのはどれか。

選択肢の訳 **1** 両部隊は，陸と空の急襲を同時に行えるよう，統合された。

2 作戦の性質が似ていたため，両部隊の間で競争が生まれ，助け合おう としなくなった。

3 LRDG は砂漠に関する知識を利用し，SAS が任務の有効性と安全性 の両方を向上させるのに役立った。

4 SAS が LRDG の任務に関与したことで，LRDG が敵陣に長期間と どまることがより困難になった。

解説 SAS が登場する第 4 段落を参照。LRDG ＝陸，SAS ＝空とイメージ しよう。LRDG の SAS 救出任務は成功だったことから，両部隊は良 い関係と推測できる。また，LRDG に砂漠に関する知識があることから， SAS の輸送と誘導を行い（＝ effectiveness），死傷者を減らすことに 貢献した（＝ safety）。よって，**3** が正解。陸空同時襲撃や部隊統合の 話はないので **1** は不適。また，両部隊の悪い関係を意味する **2** と **4** も不 適。

(41) – 解答 ③ 　　　　　　　　　正答率 ★75%以上

問題文の訳 この文章の筆者によると，1943 年に何が起こったか。

選択肢の訳 **1** LRDG が犯したミスにより，イギリスが獲得を望んでいた領土で敵 軍が支配力を強めることになった。

2 LRDG がヨーロッパへ移ったことで，SAS は，LRDG の支援なし に守りの堅い地域で敵軍を攻撃するしかなかった。

3 LRDGの活動により，イギリス陸軍は大きな優位性を得ることができ，その地域の敵軍を打ち負かすことにつながった。

4 イギリスの司令官たちは，LRDGは敵の行動を監視するよりも，イギリスが支配する領土を守るために使用した方がよいと判断した。

解説 1943年の出来事は第5段落参照。第1文，第2文の内容と**3**が一致。本文のthe unit, themは**3**ではそれぞれLRDG, the British armyのこと。第1文で具体的に述べられているLRDGの貢献を**3**ではmade it possible ... a significant advantageと抽象的に表し，それによってイギリスが勝利を収めたことを述べる第2文の内容をit defeating enemy forces in the areaと表している。

一次試験・筆記 **4** | 問題編 p.33

トピックの訳 人々はインターネット上の情報を信頼すべきか。

ポイントの訳 ・学習　・ニュース　・オンラインショッピング　・ソーシャルメディア

解答例 In my opinion, people should trust information on the Internet. I have two reasons to support this based on news and learning.

Firstly, Internet news sites are a fantastic source of trustworthy information. The demand for up-to-date news has led to more people submitting videos and photos of events as they happen, such as natural disasters. This information is easy to verify because it comes directly from people experiencing such events, making it easier to trust this information.

Secondly, there are many online learning courses on the Internet with content that can be trusted. To ensure their courses are reliable, educational institutions rigorously check the content of their online resources. Moreover, these courses are widely recognized, adding to their authenticity.

In conclusion, due to the increasing amount of news generated directly from the source and the high quality of learning resources online, we should trust information on the Internet.

解説 序論：第1段落では，トピックに対する自分の意見（主張）を簡潔に書く。模範解答はIn my opinion, ...「私の意見では，…」で始め，トピックの表現を利用してYesの立場を明らかにしている。その後I have two reasons to support this based on「～に基づいてこれを支持する理由

20

が2つある」という表現を使ってポイントの News と Learning を提示し，本論につなげている。

本論：本論では，序論で述べた主張を裏付ける根拠・理由を，2つの観点に沿って説明する。模範解答のように，First(ly), ..., Second(ly), ... などを使って2つの段落に分けるとよい。第2段落は News の観点でインターネットのニュースサイトの信頼性を，第3段落は Learning の観点で信頼できるオンライン学習コースについて説明している。第2段落，第3段落を見ると，因果関係を表す句動詞 lead to を用いた無生物主語構文や受動態が効果的に使われている。また，..., making it easier ... や ..., adding to ... では分詞構文が用いられている。文章にバリエーションを出したいときはぜひ分詞構文も使ってみよう。

結論：最終段落は，In conclusion「結論として」などを使って，序論で述べた主張を再確認する。模範解答では，due to「～のために」の形で2つの観点を再び取り上げて本論の内容を要約した後，we should trust ... で Yes の立場を再び明らかにして文章を締めくくっている。

そのほかの表現　「信頼する，信頼できる」を表すのにトピックの動詞 trust を繰り返し使わないように工夫したい。今回使えそうな形容詞には trustworthy, reliable, believable, authentic などがあり，反意語は false, unreliable, doubtful など，名詞には authenticity, reliability などがある。今回のトピックは No の立場でも書きやすいだろう。ポイントの News の観点では fake news「偽ニュース」について述べることができる。Social media の観点では，post [spread] false information on social media「ソーシャルメディアに偽情報を投稿［拡散］する」などの表現が使えそうだ。なお，英語では SNS ではなく social media を使うようにしよう。Online shopping の観点では，情報＝商品のレビューと捉え，Many of the buyers' product reviews are unreliable.「購入者の商品レビューの多くは信頼できない」などの視点で根拠を膨らませることが可能であろう。

一次試験・リスニング | **Part 1** | 問題編 p.34 〜 35　　▶MP3 ▶アプリ　CD 1 **1**〜**14**

No.**1** − 解答 **4**　　　　　　　　　　　　　　　　　　　正答率 ★**75%以上**

スクリプト
☆ : Leaving for lunch already, Noah?

★ : Actually, I'm on my way upstairs. We have our company medical checkups today, remember?

☆ : No, I completely forgot about them.

★ : You can still go. You don't need an appointment.

☆ : Yeah, but I had a big breakfast this morning. You're not supposed to eat before the blood test, right?

★ : Right. In fact, I'm starving. Anyway, you'll have another chance next week. They'll be back again on Wednesday.

☆ : Really? I'll make sure to remember.

Question: What will the woman probably do?

全文訳
☆ : もうランチに出るの，ノア？

★ : 実は上の階に向かっている途中だよ。今日，会社の健康診断があるの，覚えてない？

☆ : いいえ，完全に忘れていたわ。

★ : まだ行けるよ。予約は要らないから。

☆ : ええ，でも今朝いっぱい朝ごはんを食べてしまったわ。血液検査の前には食べてはいけなかったでしょ？

★ : そうだね。実際，僕は腹ぺこだよ。どっちにしても，来週も受けるチャンスがあるよ。水曜日にまた来るから。

☆ : そうなの？　絶対覚えておくわ。

質問：女性はおそらく何をするか。

選択肢の訳
1　今日，血液検査を受ける。
2　朝食を食べる量を減らす努力をする。
3　ノアとランチを食べに行く。
4　来週，健康診断を受ける。

解説
オフィス内の会話。今日の健康診断を忘れていた女性に対し，男性が来週もあると言う。女性の最後の I'll make sure ... は来週の健康診断を受けるという意図なので，**4** が正解。ノアは健康診断に行くところなので **3** は不適。本問のように，本来の予定が何らかの理由でできない→予定変更という流れでは，変更後について問われやすい。

No.**2** − 解答 **4**

スクリプト
☆ : Looks like I'll be putting in another 60-hour week. Seems like I live here at the office these days.

22

★： You do live at the office these days, and they don't pay you nearly enough. Why don't you drop a hint that you'd like to review your compensation?

☆： But I've only been working here a year.

★： In which time they've doubled your responsibilities. Come on, Laurie! You need to stand up for yourself.

☆： Well, maybe you're right.

Question: How does the man feel about the woman's situation?

全文訳 ☆： また今週も勤務時間が60時間になりそう。最近は会社に住んでいるかのようだわ。

★： 実際，君は最近会社で暮らしているし，会社は君に十分な給料を支払っているとはとても言えない。給料を見直したいとほのめかしてみたらどう？

☆： でも，まだ1年しかここで働いていないわ。

★： その1年の間に会社は君の責任を倍にしたよ。ほら，ローリー！ 自分のために立ち向かわないと。

☆： そうね，あなたの言う通りかもしれないわ。

質問：男性は女性の状況についてどう感じているか。

選択肢の訳 1 彼女はもっと休みを取る必要がある。

2 彼女はお金についてあまり心配しない方がいい。

3 彼女はそれほどの責任を負う準備ができていない。

4 彼女はもっと給料をもらうに値する。

解説 長い勤務時間に不満を述べる女性に対し，男性は Why don't you ～？ の表現で，給料を見直したい（＝増やしてほしい）と会社にほのめかすよう提案する。後ろ向きの様子の女性だが，男性は次の発言で，行動に出るようさらに後押しする。正解は **4** で，会話中の compensation「給料」を pay で表している。

No.3 – 解答 ②

スクリプト ★： Doctor, how were the test results?

☆： Not bad. It's just a sprain. Nevertheless, I still think you should avoid strenuous exercise for at least a couple of weeks after you leave the hospital today.

★： But my softball team's got a big game this Thursday.

☆： I'm afraid you're going to have to sit that one out. You should wait till you fully recover or you may make it worse.

Question: What does the doctor tell the man?

全文訳 ★： 先生，検査結果はどうでしたか？

☆： 悪くありませんよ。ただの捻挫ね。とは言っても，今日病院から出た後，やっぱり少なくとも数週間は激しい運動は避けた方がいいと思います。

★： でも，今週木曜日に所属のソフトボールチームの大きな試合があるんです。

☆： 残念だけど，その試合には参加せずにいないといけませんね。全快する
まで待たないと，悪化するかもしれませんよ。

質問：医師は男性に何と言っているか。

選択肢の訳　**1** 彼はさらなる検査を受ける必要がある。

　　2 彼は試合でプレーすることができないだろう。

　　3 彼は別の運動方法を見つける必要がある。

　　4 彼は入院しなければならない。

解説　医師と患者の会話。医師が数週間激しい運動を避けるよう助言すると，
男性は今週ソフトボールの試合があると言う。医師は I'm afraid ... で
試合には出られないと忠告しているので，**2** が正解。that one は試合の
ことで，sit ~ out は「～（活動など）に参加しない」の意味。

No.4 – 解答 ②

スクリプト　☆： Hi, Phil. I'm sorry to bother you on your day off, but I'm not
feeling well. Could you cover my shift this afternoon?

★： Unfortunately, I've already got plans.

☆： I see. Do you know who might be able to change shifts with me?

★： I'm not sure.

☆： Maybe the new guy can cover it.

★： I'd just get in touch with the manager. It's her responsibility to
deal with these issues.

☆： I know, but I hate bothering her. Maybe I should just work the shift.

★： No, don't do that. You might make everyone else sick.

Question: What does the man imply the woman should do?

全文訳　☆： こんにちは，フィル。お休みの日に邪魔して悪いのだけど，私，具合が
良くなくて。今日の午後のシフトを代わってもらえない？

★： あいにくだけど，もう予定があるんだ。

☆： そう。私とシフトを代われそうな人を知らない？

★： ちょっと分からないな。

☆： あの新人が代われるかもしれないわ。

★： 僕ならとりあえず店長に連絡を取るかな。こういう問題に対処するのは
彼女の責任だから。

☆： 分かっているけど，彼女に面倒をかけたくないの。とりあえず私がシフ
トに出るべきかも。

★： いや，それはやめて。ほかのみんなにうつしてしまうかもしれないから。

質問：男性は女性は何をすべきだとほのめかしているか。

選択肢の訳　**1** 新しい従業員に連絡を取る。

　　2 店長と話す。

24

3 彼女自身がそのシフトに出る。
  4 彼とシフトを代わる。

解説 電話での会話。具合が悪い女性が男性にシフトを代わってくれるようお願いするが，男性は代われない（→ **4** は不適）。男性の考える解決策 I'd just get in touch with the manager. から，**2** が正解。

No.5 – 解答 ③

スクリプト ☆： I'm looking forward to our business trip next week.
  ★： Me, too. I'll double-check the flight schedule tomorrow.
  ☆： Thanks.
  ★： Have you finished putting together the presentation for our meeting?
  ☆： Not yet. I was planning to get it done tomorrow.
  ★： That's a good idea. I remember trying to finish one at a hotel last year, and I couldn't connect to the Internet.
  ☆： Our hotel is supposed to have good Wi-Fi, but don't worry. It'll be done before we go.
  Question: What will the woman do before leaving for the trip?

全文訳 ☆： 私，来週の出張を楽しみにしているの。
  ★： 僕もだよ。明日，航空便のスケジュールをもう一回確認するね。
  ☆： ありがとう。
  ★： 僕たちの会議のプレゼンテーションはまとめ終わった？
  ☆： まだよ。明日終わらせようと思っていたわ。
  ★： それはいい考えだね。去年，僕はホテルで完成させようとしたことを覚えているよ。それでインターネットに接続できなかったんだ。
  ☆： 私たちが宿泊するホテルには安定した Wi-Fi があるはずだけど，心配しないで。出発する前に終わらせるから。
  質問：女性は出張に出かける前に何をするか。

選択肢の訳 1 インターネット接続についてホテルに問い合わせる。
  2 会議のスケジュールを確認する。
  3 プレゼンテーションの準備を終わらせる。
  4 航空券を買う。

解説 同僚同士の会話。来週の会議のプレゼンテーションについて聞かれた女性は，I was planning to get it done tomorrow. と答える。また，最後に It'll be done before we go. とも言っているので，正解は **3**。it と It はどちらもプレゼンテーションの準備のこと。put together は「〜（考えなど）をまとめる」という意味で，**3** では prepare で表している。

No.6 – 解答 ① 　　　　　　　　　　　　　　　正答率 ★75%以上

スクリプト ☆： Shall we order some more wine?

25

★：I'd love to, but we should probably catch the bus home soon. It's already eleven.

☆：Eleven? Oh, dear. The last one will have left by the time we get to the bus stop.

★：We can still catch the last train.

☆：That train doesn't come for another hour. I say we treat ourselves to a taxi.

★：Works for me.

☆：Great. Let's head over to the main street. We can probably catch one there.

Question: What does the couple decide to do?

全文訳 ☆：もっとワインを頼む？

★：そうしたいけど，そろそろ家に帰るバスに乗るべきかもしれない。もう11時だよ。

☆：11時？　あら，どうしよう。バス停に着くころには最終便は出発してしまっているわ。

★：まだ最終列車には乗れるよ。

☆：その列車はあと1時間は来ないでしょ。奮発してタクシーに乗りましょう。

★：僕はそれで構わないよ。

☆：よかった。大通りに向かいましょう。そこでたぶんつかまえられるわ。

質問： 夫婦は何をすることに決めたか。

選択肢の訳 1　タクシーに乗って家に帰る。
2　もっとワインを注文する。
3　最終列車に乗って家に帰る。
4　最寄りのバス停まで歩く。

解説 話題はレストランからの帰宅手段。バスには間に合わず，列車を却下した後，女性がタクシーを提案すると，男性は Works for me. と同意するので，**1**が正解。最後の We can probably catch one there. もヒントになる。one は a taxi のこと。本問のように，複数の候補を挙げて検討する会話では，最終的にどれに決めたかが問われやすい。

No.7 －解答 ② ••••••••••••••••••••••••••••••• 正答率 ★75%以上

スクリプト ★：Honey, did you see that the new restaurant down the block finally opened?

☆：I'm sorry, I can't chat right now. I need to start making dinner so it'll be ready by the time the kids get home from school.

★：Leave dinner to me.

☆：Really? But you don't cook. You aren't planning to order takeout, are you? We just bought groceries.

26

★： No. I know I'm not a good chef, but I found a cooking website for beginners. I saw a great recipe for a pasta dish I think I can make.

☆： Oh, that would be lovely!

Question: What does the man offer to do?

全文訳 ★： ねえ，1 ブロック先の新しいレストランがやっと開店したの，見た？

☆： ごめんなさい，今話せないの。子供たちが学校から帰ってくるまでにできているように，夕食を作り始めないといけないから。

★： 夕食は僕にまかせて。

☆： 本当に？　でも，あなた料理しないじゃない。テイクアウトを注文するつもりじゃないわよね？　食料品を買ってきたばかりなのよ。

★： そうじゃないよ。自分は料理がうまくないことは知っているけど，初心者向けの料理サイトを見つけたんだ。僕が作れそうなパスタ料理のすごくいいレシピを見たんだ。

☆： あら，それは助かるわ！

質問：男性は何をすると申し出ているか。

選択肢の訳 **1** 子供たちを学校に迎えに行く。

2 家族のために夕食を作る。

3 今夜の夕食のための材料を買う。

4 新しくできたレストランに料理を注文する。

解説 話題は夕食の準備。男性の申し出は，Leave dinner to me. から，夕食を作ることなので，**2** が正解。I know I'm not a good chef, but ... の発言からも，男性が料理をするつもりだと分かる。

No.**8** – 解答　①

スクリプト ☆： AFP Automotive.

★： Hi. I'm on Highway 5. My engine overheated, and it won't start. I need my car towed, and I could use a ride downtown. I have to be at a meeting in an hour.

☆： Could you tell me your policy number?

★： It's A735.

☆： I'm sorry. A car will arrive in about 10 minutes to take you downtown, but the system says you don't have towing coverage.

★： Really? I thought my plan included towing.

☆： Unfortunately, you'll have to pay out of pocket this time, but we can add it to your insurance policy in the future.

Question: What is one problem the man has?

全文訳 ☆： AFP 自動車です。

★： もしもし。今国道 5 号線にいるんですが，オーバーヒートして，エンジンがかかりません。車をレッカー移動してもらう必要があって，私はダ

ウンタウンまで送ってもらえると助かります。あと1時間で会議に出なければいけないので。
☆： 保険証書番号を教えていただけますか。
★： A735 です。
☆： 申し訳ありません。お客さまをダウンタウンに送っていく車は10分ほどで到着しますが，システムによるとお客さまはレッカー移動の補償はないようです。
★： 本当に？　私の補償プランにはレッカー移動が含まれていると思っていました。
☆： 残念ながら，今回は自己負担していただかないといけませんが，将来的に保険証書に追加していただけます。
質問：男性の抱える問題の1つは何か。

選択肢の訳
1　彼は予想外の料金を支払わなければならない。
2　彼は保険を解約した。
3　彼は会議に遅れている。
4　会社が彼の保険証書番号を見つけることができない。

解説　車が動かなくなった男性が保険会社に連絡を取っている場面。女性は，男性のプランはレッカー移動の補償がないことを伝え，you'll have to pay out of pocket this time と言う。pay out of *one's* pocket は「自腹で払う」という意味。また，I thought my plan included towing. の発言から，男性にとっては予想外の（unexpected）状況だと考えられるので，**1** が正解。

No.9 －解答

スクリプト
★： Excuse me, Professor Garcia. Could I ask you for some advice?
☆： Of course. Is it about our art classes?
★： Sort of. I'm thinking about changing my major from communications to graphic design, but I'm not sure if it's a good idea.
☆： Why are you considering the change?
★： It gives me career options. I could do advertising, marketing, or even web design.
☆： Those are good careers. What's your concern?
★： Well, I'm not confident that my artistic skills are good enough.
☆： I've seen your work. If you make the effort, I think you could be quite successful.
Question: What does the woman imply?

全文訳
★： すみません，ガルシア教授。少しアドバイスをいただけませんか。
☆： もちろんですよ。芸術の授業のことですか。

★：そんなところです。専攻をコミュニケーションからグラフィックデザインに変更しようと考えているのですが，それがいい考えか確証が持てないんです。

☆：どうして変更を考えているのですか。

★：職業の選択肢が広がります。広告もマーケティングも，それからウェブデザインさえもできます。

☆：それらはいい職業ですね。何を心配しているのですか。

★：ええと，自分の芸術スキルが通用するのか自信がありません。

☆：あなたの作品を見てきました。努力すれば大成功すると思いますよ。

質問：女性は何をほのめかしているか。

選択肢の訳　**1**　男性は専攻を変えるべきではない。

　　　　　　2　コミュニケーション分野の仕事の方が男性に向いているかもしれない。

　　　　　　3　グラフィックデザインは男性にとって良い選択である。

　　　　　　4　男性は授業の成績があまり良くない。

解説　教授と学生の会話で，質問では教授の発言意図が問われている。専攻をコミュニケーションからグラフィックデザインに変更したい学生がその理由を説明したところ，教授は Those are good careers. と言う。その後の発言からも，変更に賛成している様子なので，**3** が正解。

No.**10** 解答　**②**

スクリプト　★：Alicia, can I talk to you about that online meeting software we're using?

☆：Sure, Ben. What is it?

★：We've been using the free version, but I think we should consider paying to upgrade to the full version. The free version can be inconvenient at times.

☆：The participant limit has been a problem. Sometimes we'd like to have more than eight people in a meeting at once. Could you submit an official request with the cost?

★：Does that mean there's room in the budget for an upgrade?

☆：I'll see what I can do.

Question: What will the man do next?

全文訳　★：アリシア，僕たちが使っているあのオンライン会議のソフトウエアについて話せますか。

☆：いいわよ，ベン。どうしたの？

★：ずっと無料版を使っていますが，お金を払って完全版にアップグレードすることを検討すべきだと思うんです。無料版は不便なときがありますから。

☆：参加者数の制限が問題になっていたよね。一度に 8 人より多い人数で会議ができたらいいときもあるものね。費用を添えて正式な要望書を出し

29

てくれる？

★： つまり，アップグレードする余裕が予算にあるってことですか？

☆： 私に何ができるか検討してみるわ。

質問：男性は次に何をするか。

選択肢の訳　**1**　別のオンラインチャットツールを見つける。

2　ソフトウエアのアップグレードの要望書を準備する。

3　より多くの人にオンライン会議に参加してもらうようにする。

4　会社の予算を増やすよう依頼する。

解説　男性がオンライン会議のソフトウエアをアップグレードすることを提案すると，女性は納得した様子で，Could you submit an official request with the cost? と言って要望書を出すよう指示する。男性はこれに従うと考えて，**2**が正解。

No.11 解答 ②

スクリプト　★： Carol, I have a favor to ask you.

☆： What is it?

★： Inspectors from Mexico are coming to our plant tomorrow, and our regular interpreter is on vacation. I remember you majored in Spanish in college. Do you think you could substitute?

☆： Well, I did study Spanish, but I'm not sure I can handle all the technical terms.

★： What if we asked Barbara to do your regular work today, and you spent the rest of the afternoon brushing up on vocabulary?

☆： OK. I'll do my best.

Question: What will the woman do for the rest of the day?

全文訳　★： キャロル，お願いしたいことがあるんだけど。

☆： 何ですか？

★： 明日，メキシコから調査員がこの工場に来るんだけど，いつもの通訳が休暇を取っているんだ。君が大学でスペイン語を専攻していたことを思い出したんだ。代わりをお願いできないかい？

☆： えーと，確かにスペイン語を勉強しましたが，全ての専門用語に対応できるかは分かりません。

★： 今日の君の通常業務はバーバラにやってもらうよう頼んで，君は午後の残りの時間を語彙のおさらいに充てるというのはどう？

☆： 分かりました。最善を尽くします。

質問：女性は今日の残りの時間に何をするか。

選択肢の訳　**1**　工場に行く。

2　スペイン語を勉強する。

3　バーバラと面談する。

30

4 通訳を探す。

（解説）男性は，スペイン語の通訳が不在なので，女性にその代役を頼んでいる。女性は専門用語（technical terms）に自信がない様子だが，男性の「午後の残りの時間を語彙のおさらいに充てる」という提案（What if ...?）に同意しているので，**2** が正解。brush up on「～の能力を磨き直す」を抽象的に study と表している。

No.12 解答 ④

（スクリプト）

★： Excuse me, ma'am, this is a no-parking zone.

☆： I'm sorry, officer. I felt ill while I was driving, so I stopped my car here to take a short rest.

★： Are you OK? I can call an ambulance for you.

☆： No, thanks. I'm feeling much better now, but can I rest here for another 10 minutes or so?

★： No problem. I'll stand by in the police car until you feel well enough to leave. Honk your horn if you need help.

☆： I will. Thanks.

Question: What is the police officer going to do?

（全文訳）

★： すみません，ここは駐車禁止区域です。

☆： すみません，お巡りさん。運転している最中に具合が悪くなったので，ここに車を停めてちょっと休憩していたんです。

★： 大丈夫ですか？　救急車を呼びましょうか。

☆： いいえ，結構です。今はだいぶましになりました。でももう 10 分ほどここで休んでもいいですか。

★： いいですよ。私はあなたがここから出ていけるほど回復するまでパトカーの中で待機しています。助けが必要になったらクラクションを鳴らしてください。

☆： そうします。ありがとう。

質問：警官は何をするつもりか。

（選択肢の訳）

1 無線で救急車を呼ぶ。

2 女性の代わりに女性の車を動かす。

3 女性に駐車違反の切符を切る。

4 パトカーの中で待つ。

（解説）警官が駐車禁止区域に停車している女性に声をかけている場面。女性は具合が悪くて休んでいると知った警官は，さらに 10 分ほど休むことを許可する。警官のこの後の行動は，I'll stand by in ... から，**4** が正解。stand by は「待機する」の意味で，**4** では wait と表している。

22 年度第 2 回　リスニング

31

| 一次試験・リスニング | Part2 | 問題編 p.36〜37 | 🔊 | ▶MP3 ▶アプリ ▶CD 1 15〜21 |

A

スクリプト **The P-47 Thunderbolt**

When the P-47 Thunderbolt first appeared in World War II, American pilots worried that this extremely heavy fighter plane would be at a disadvantage against smaller, lighter German planes. The P-47 was indeed slower at low altitudes, but when it was flying high, it could outrun almost any other plane. One serious weakness early on was its limited fuel supply. Eventually, however, extra tanks were fitted onto the P-47 so that it could go on longer missions.

The P-47 had eight powerful machine guns and was able to carry an impressive selection of bombs and rockets. The real reason that pilots came to love it, though, is that it was one of the most durable planes of the war and survived many hits that would have destroyed other planes. In one extreme case, a pilot was able to land his P-47 after it was shot over 100 times.

Questions

No.13 What problem did the P-47 Thunderbolt have at first?

No.14 What did pilots like most about flying the P-47 Thunderbolt?

全文訳 **P-47 サンダーボルト**

P-47 サンダーボルトが第2次世界大戦で初めて登場したとき，アメリカのパイロットたちは，この非常に重い戦闘機がより小さく軽いドイツ機に対して不利になるのではないかと心配した。P-47 は確かに低空飛行では低速だったが，高空飛行ではほかのほとんどの戦闘機を振り切ることができた。初期の深刻な弱点の1つは，燃料の供給が限られていたことである。しかし，最終的には，より長い任務を遂行できるように，P-47 に追加のタンクが取り付けられた。

P-47 は，8基の強力な機関銃を搭載し，爆弾やロケット弾を豊富に搭載することができた。しかし，パイロットたちが P-47 を大変気に入るようになった本当の理由は，P-47 が最も耐久性のある戦闘機の1つであり，ほかの戦闘機であれば破壊されたであろう多くの攻撃に持ちこたえたからである。ある極端な例では，あるパイロットは，100回以上撃たれても P-47 を着陸させることができた。

No.13 解答 ③

質問の訳 当初，P-47 サンダーボルトが抱えた問題は何だったか。

選択肢の訳
1 十分に高く飛べなかった。
2 あまりに小さくて軽かった。
3 短い距離しか飛べなかった。
4 珍しい種類の燃料を使った。

解説 P-47 の 初 期（at first = early on） の 問 題 点 は，One serious weakness early on was ... の部分から，燃料の供給が限られていた＝短い距離しか飛べなかったと考えて，**3** が正解。続く it could go on longer missions もヒントになる。

No.14 解答 ①

質問の訳 P-47 サンダーボルトの操縦においてパイロットが最も気に入った点は何だったか。

選択肢の訳 1 ほかの戦闘機より丈夫だった。
2 新しい種類の武器を搭載していた。
3 非常に素早く着陸することができた。
4 爆弾を正確に投下することができた。

解説 パイロットが P-47 を気に入った理由は，The real reason that pilots came to love it, ... の部分にある。「ほかの戦闘機であれば破壊されたであろう多くの攻撃に持ちこたえた」とはつまり，「ほかの戦闘機より丈夫だった」と言えるので，**1** が正解。

B

スクリプト **Ascension Island**

Ascension Island lies in the middle of the Atlantic Ocean. Originally, it was nearly treeless, and fresh water was scarce, which made for tough living conditions for the first settlers. However, in the 1840s, a British scientist named Sir Joseph Hooker started a program to transform the desert island. He started importing trees and other plants that were able to survive in the island's dry environment by absorbing water from mist in the air. His program eventually resulted in an entire mountain being covered in forest. However, Hooker's plants have been so successful that several native plant species have gone extinct.

There is now a debate about the island's future. Some people say efforts must be made to preserve the plants that were originally found on the island. Others, though, want the new ecosystem to be left as is, since it has had benefits, such as increasing available water and creating the potential for agriculture.

Questions

No.15 What was one result of Sir Joseph Hooker's program for Ascension Island?

No.16 What do people disagree about regarding Ascension Island?

全文訳 **アセンション島**

アセンション島は大西洋の真ん中に位置する。もともと，そこには樹木がほとんどなく，淡水が不足していたため，最初の入植者たちにとっては厳しい生活環境をもたらした。しかし，1840 年代に，ジョセフ・フッカー卿というイギリスの科学者がこの無人

島を改造する計画を開始した。彼は，空気中の霧から水分を吸収することで島の乾燥した環境で生き抜くことができる樹木やほかの植物の移入を始めた。彼の計画は最終的に，山全体が森に覆われる結果となった。しかし，フッカーの植物があまりに成功を収めたため，幾つかの在来種の植物が絶滅してしまった。

現在，この島の将来について議論が起きている。島にもともとあった植物を保存する努力をすべきだという人もいる。しかし，新しい生態系は，利用可能な水を増やしたり農業の可能性を生み出したりするなどの利点があるため，そのままの状態にしておくことを望む人もいる。

No.15 解答 ④

質問の訳 ジョセフ・フッカー卿のアセンション島計画の成果の1つは何だったか。

選択肢の訳
1 水の供給量が減った。
2 大気の汚れが減った。
3 多くの人が島を離れなければならなくなった。
4 樹木の本数が増えた。

解説 Originally, However, eventually resulted in などの論理マーカーを手掛かりに，もともと樹木がほとんどなかった島だが，樹木や植物の移入を始め，山全体が森に覆われる結果になった，という展開をつかもう。山全体が森に覆われる→樹木が増えたと考えて，**4** が正解。

No.16 解答 ③

質問の訳 アセンション島に関して，人々は何について意見が分かれているか。

選択肢の訳
1 新しい生態系をどう分類するか。
2 水の供給を何のために使うか。
3 在来植物を保護すべきかどうか。
4 どこで農業を許可すべきか。

解説 質問の disagree about は「〜について意見が分かれる」という意味で，意見の相違は，Some people 〜. Others, ... で表されている。議論の論点は，島にもともとあった植物を保存すべきか，新しい生態系を残すべきか，であることから，**3** が適切。

スクリプト **Vivian Maier**

One of the twentieth century's greatest street photographers, Vivian Maier is known for her fascinating images of people in cities like Chicago and New York. Maier worked in childcare, but her true passion was photography. She always had her camera with her, and this habit allowed her to capture unique and unusual shots of people going about their daily lives. Her photos depict everything from strangely dressed tourists to emergency workers caring for accident victims.

Despite the incredible number of photos she took, Maier was an intensely private person. Unlike most photographers, she refused to allow others to see her work. Nevertheless, a collection of her photos was purchased at an auction in 2007, and the buyers began exhibiting her unusual work. It was not until after her death in 2009, however, that she was recognized as an artistic genius.

Questions

No.17 What is one thing we learn about Vivian Maier?

No.18 How was Maier different from other photographers?

全文訳 **ビビアン・マイヤー**

　20世紀で最も優れたストリート写真家の1人であるビビアン・マイヤーは、シカゴやニューヨークなどの都市で撮った魅力的な人物写真で知られている。マイヤーは保育分野で働いていたが、彼女が本当に情熱を注いでいたのは写真だった。彼女はいつもカメラを持ち歩き、この習慣のため、日常生活を送る人々のユニークで珍しいショットを撮影することができた。彼女の写真は、奇抜な服装をした観光客から、事故の被害者を介抱する救急隊員まで、あらゆるものを写し出している。

　膨大な数の写真を撮ったにもかかわらず、マイヤーは極めて非社交的な人物だった。多くの写真家と違って、彼女は他人が自分の作品を見ることを拒んだ。とはいえ、2007年に彼女の写真コレクションがオークションで購入され、その買い手たちは彼女の珍しい作品を展示し始めた。それでも、彼女が天才芸術家として認められるようになったのは、2009年に彼女が亡くなってからのことである。

No.17 解答 ①

質問の訳 ビビアン・マイヤーについて分かることの1つは何か。

選択肢の訳　1　彼女はどこにでもカメラを持っていった。
　　　　　　2　彼女は救急隊員と友だちになった。
　　　　　　3　彼女は世話をしている子供たちにカメラを貸した。
　　　　　　4　彼女は観光客として多くの場所に行った。

解説 ビビアン・マイヤーについての説明の She always had her camera with her の部分と **1** が一致する。文中の語句を含む選択肢 **2** と **4** や、worked in childcare から連想される **3** を選ばないように注意。

No.18 解答 ④

質問の訳 マイヤーはほかの写真家とどんな点で異なっていたか。

選択肢の訳　1　彼女はキャリアの早い段階で有名になった。
　　　　　　2　彼女は主にオークションで写真を撮った。
　　　　　　3　彼女は非常に大規模な展覧会を開いた。
　　　　　　4　彼女は自分の写真を人々に見せなかった。

解説 後半に Maier was an intensely private person とあり、この詳しい説明が Unlike most photographers, ... に続く。refused to allow others to see her work という肯定文を did not show people her photos という否定文で言い換えた **4** が正解。refuse や avoid のような否定の意味を含む語はライティングでも生かせるので確認しておこう。

D

スクリプト **The Impact of Cats**

Cats are one of the most popular pets today, but like many other pets, they affect the environment through their eating habits. As carnivores, cats primarily eat meat, the production of which releases substantial amounts of carbon dioxide gas into the atmosphere and often creates air and water pollution. According to a recent study, however, the management of cats' waste may be more harmful to the environment than their diet is.

Cat owners commonly prepare boxes for their cats that contain cat litter, a material that traps the cats' waste. However, the clay that is used in most litter is usually acquired through surface mining, a process that requires oil-powered heavy machinery and can destroy large natural areas. Recently, more manufacturers have begun producing litter made from environmentally friendly materials like wood and seeds. Nevertheless, clay-based litter is still the most used type due to its low cost and exceptional odor absorption.

Questions

No.19 What is one thing the speaker says about cat-food production?
No.20 What do we learn about the process of collecting clay?

全文訳 **猫の影響**

猫は今日最も人気のあるペットの1つだが,ほかの多くのペットと同様,その食習慣を通じて環境に影響を与えている。肉食動物であるので,猫は主に肉を食べるが,肉の生産によって大量の二酸化炭素ガスが大気中に放出され,大気汚染や水質汚染を引き起こすことがよくある。しかし,最近の研究によると,猫の食事よりも猫の排せつ物の処理の方が環境に悪い可能性がある。

猫の飼い主は,一般的に,猫の排せつ物を閉じ込める素材である猫砂を入れた箱を飼い猫のために用意する。しかし,ほとんどの猫砂に使われている粘土は,通常,露天採掘,つまり石油を動力源とする重機を必要とし,広大な自然地域を破壊し得る方法で採取される。最近では,木材や種子など,環境に優しい素材を使った猫砂を製造し始めるメーカーも増えている。とはいえ,粘土を原料とした猫砂は,その低コストと優れた臭気吸収のために,最も使用されている種類であることに変わりはない。

No.19 解答 ③ ・・・ 正答率 ★75%以上

質問の訳 キャットフードの生産について話者が言うことの1つは何か。
選択肢の訳 **1** 真水を使う必要がない。
　　　　　 2 特定の気候のもとでしかできない。

36

3 大量のガスを発生させる。

4 昔に比べて肉の使用量が少ない。

> 解説　猫の食事や排せつ物が環境に与える影響に関する文章。質問は猫の食事についてで, cats primarily eat meat, the production of which releases ... から, **3** が正解。the production of which は「肉(＝キャットフード)の生産」という意味。それぞれ本文の releases を produces に, substantial amounts of を a large amount of に言い換えている。

No.20 解答 **2**

> 質問の訳　粘土を採取する方法について何が分かるか。

> 選択肢の訳　**1** 使用する機械が非常に高価である。
> 　　　　　**2** 広大な土地に被害を与えている。
> 　　　　　**3** 近隣の農地に化学物質を放出する。
> 　　　　　**4** 作業員にとって危険な場合が多い。

> 解説　However, the clay ... natural areas. がポイント。この文を読んでいくと,「粘土」「ほとんどの猫砂に使われている」「通常 surface mining で採取される」(surface mining とは何か?)「方法」「石油を動力源とする重機を必要とする(方法)」「広大な自然地域を破壊し得る(方法)」。よって, 粘土の採取方法は **2**「広大な土地に被害を与えている」と言える。

E

（スクリプト）**Profitable Experiences**

For many young people today, experiences have become more important than material things. This has created money-making opportunities for businesses that can provide memorable and exciting experiences. One recent example is "axe-throwing bars." While axes would normally be associated with chopping wood in a forest, now people in many cities can go to special bars and throw axes like darts. Some worry about the possible dangers of this activity, but fans argue that it is a fun way to release stress.

Such businesses that sell experiences have spread across the US, but critics argue these businesses may negatively affect communities in the long run. They say the businesses are probably a short-term trend whose popularity will not last. And, when the businesses close, their employees are left without a source of income. The critics recommend that cities encourage the development of businesses that will be popular for decades, not just a few years.

Questions

No.21 What is one reason for the popularity of "axe-throwing bars"?

No.22 What is one criticism of businesses that sell experiences?

（全文訳）**有益な経験**

今日の多くの若者にとって, 形のある物よりも経験が重要になっている。そのため,

記憶に残るエキサイティングな体験を提供できる商売に金もうけの機会が生まれている。最近の例の1つに「斧投げバー」がある。斧といえば通常，森でまきを割ることが連想されるが，今では多くの都市で人々が特殊なバーに行き，斧をダーツのように投げることができるのだ。この活動の潜在的な危険性を心配する人もいるが，愛好者たちはストレスを発散する楽しい方法だと言い張る。

体験を売り物にしたこのような商売は全米に広がっているが，批評家たちは，この手の商売は長期的には地域社会に悪影響を与える可能性があると主張する。彼らは，この商売はおそらく短期的な流行で，その人気は長続きしないだろうと言う。また，商売が廃業すると，その従業員は収入源を失って残される。批評家たちは，たかが数年ではなく，何十年も人気が続くような商売の発展を各都市が奨励することを勧めている。

No.21 解答 ❶ ....

質問の訳 「斧投げバー」の人気の理由の1つは何か。

選択肢の訳 1 若者の変化する関心事。
2 若者の運動に対するニーズの高まり。
3 若者の経済状況。
4 若者の自然への情熱。

解説 今日の若者にとって「形のある物よりも経験が重要」と述べ，記憶に残るエキサイティングな体験の例として"axe-throwing bars"が挙げられる。昔の若者は「物」を重要と考えていたが，最近の若者は「体験」を重要視するように変わってきたという趣旨から，**1**が適切。理由を直接的に述べていないので判断が難しいが，消去法でも解けるだろう。

No.22 解答 ❶ ....

質問の訳 体験を売り物にする商売への批判の1つは何か。

選択肢の訳 1 長く生き残る可能性が低い。
2 都市部以外ではうまくいかない。
3 地元の人を雇用することがめったにない。
4 場所を取り過ぎる。

解説 criticism については，critics の主張を説明した部分に手掛かりがある。They say the businesses are probably a short-term trend ... から，**1**が正解。last「続く」を survive long「長く生き残る」と表している。

F

スクリプト *T. rex* **Skulls**

T. rex had two large holes at the top of its skull, which scientists used to believe held muscles that aided jaw movement. Recently, however, researchers realized that this would not have been an efficient location for jaw muscles, so they began searching for another explanation. They looked at a modern animal descended from dinosaurs: the alligator.

38

The researchers found that alligator skulls have similar holes. They are filled with blood vessels that help alligators control the amount of heat in their bodies. When alligators need to warm themselves, these areas absorb external heat, and they release heat when alligators need to cool down. Since large meat-eating dinosaurs such as *T. rex* likely tended to overheat, these holes and blood vessels could have functioned as a sort of internal air-conditioning system. Of course, we cannot observe living dinosaurs, but studies like this provide interesting clues as to what these prehistoric giants were like.

Questions

No.23 Why did the researchers decide to analyze alligators?

No.24 What do the researchers now think the holes in *T. rex* skulls were used for?

全文訳 **Ｔレックスの頭蓋骨**

　Ｔレックス（ティラノサウルス・レックス）は，頭蓋骨の上部に２つの大きな穴があり，そこには顎の動きを助ける筋肉があったと科学者たちはかつて信じていた。しかし最近，研究者たちは，これは顎の筋肉にとって効率的な場所ではなかったことに気付いたため，別の説明を探し始めた。彼らは，恐竜の子孫である現代の動物，ワニに注目した。

　研究者たちは，ワニの頭蓋骨にも同様の穴があるのを見つけた。その穴にはワニが体内の熱量を制御するのに役立つ血管が通っている。ワニが体を温める必要があるときはこの部分が外部の熱を吸収し，ワニが体を冷やす必要があるときは熱を放出する。Ｔレックスのような大型の肉食恐竜はおそらく体温が高くなり過ぎる傾向があったため，この穴と血管は体内空調システムのような役割を担っていたのかもしれない。もちろん生きている恐竜を観察することはできないが，このような研究は，これら先史時代の巨大な動物がどのようなものだったかについての興味深い手掛かりを提供してくれる。

No.23 解答 **②** ･･

質問の訳 研究者たちはなぜワニを分析することにしたのか。

選択肢の訳 **1** ワニには効率の良い顎がある。
　　　　　2 ワニは恐竜と関係がある。
　　　　　3 ワニは変わった場所に筋肉がある。
　　　　　4 ワニはＴレックスと同じ時期に進化した。

解説 used to *do* → Recently, however という対比に着目。以前はＴレックスの頭蓋骨の上部には顎の動きを助ける筋肉があったと考えていた→最近そうではないかもしれないことに気付いた→恐竜の子孫であるワニに注目した，という流れ。ワニを分析することにした理由として **2** が正解。

No.24 解答 **④** ･････････････････････････････････ 正答率 ★**75%以上**

質問の訳 研究者たちは現在，Ｔレックスの頭蓋骨の穴が何のために使われていたと考えているか。

選択肢の訳　1　食べ物の消化を助けるため。
　　　　　　2　ほかの動物の気配を察知するため。
　　　　　　3　新しい血管を作るため。
　　　　　　4　体温を調節するため。

解説　ワニの頭蓋骨にもTレックス同様の穴があり，その穴に通っている血管は，ワニが体内の熱量を制御するのに役立つと言っている。the amount of heat in their bodies を their body temperature と言い換えた **4** が正解。その後のワニが体を温める・冷やす場合の穴の働きについての説明や functioned as a sort of internal air-conditioning system の部分などもヒントになるだろう。

G

You have 10 seconds to read the situation and Question No. 25.

Welcome to Greenville. As we approach the gate, please remain in your seats with your seat belts fastened. We realize many of you have connecting flights, so we have gate agents standing by who can direct you to your connecting gates once you exit the plane. Please have your boarding passes ready to show them. If this is your final destination, you can find your luggage on the carousels in the main terminal. If you need to arrange ground transportation, look for the bus service just past the baggage claim. Customer service representatives are available throughout the airport if you need assistance.

Now mark your answer on your answer sheet.

全文訳

　グリーンビルにようこそ。ゲートに近づいていますので，シートベルトを締めてご着席のままお待ちください。乗り継ぎ便に乗られるお客さまが多いようですので，飛行機を降りましたら，乗り継ぎゲートまでご案内するゲート係員が待機しております。搭乗券をご用意のうえ，係員にご提示ください。ここが最終目的地のお客さまは，メインターミナルの回転コンベヤーで手荷物をお受け取りいただけます。地上交通機関の手配が必要なお客さまは，手荷物受け取り所を過ぎた所にあるバスサービスをお探しください。サポートが必要なお客さまは，空港内のどこでもカスタマーサービス担当者がお手伝いいたします。

No.25 解答　**3**

状況の訳　あなたは着陸したばかりの飛行機に乗っており，乗り継ぎ便に乗らなけ

ればならない。客室乗務員がアナウンスをしている。

質問の訳 あなたは飛行機を降りた後，まず何をすべきか。

選択肢の訳 1 手荷物を受け取る。

2 バスに乗って別のターミナルへ行く。

3 ゲート係員を見つける。

4 新しい搭乗券を印刷してもらう。

解説 問題用紙の「状況」から，乗り継ぎ便に関する情報を聞き取ろう。飛行機を降りたら乗り継ぎゲートまで案内してくれる係員が待機していることから，飛行機を降りて最初にすることは，**3**。放送文の exit を質問文では getting off と表している。**1** は，ここが最終目的地の場合のこと。

H

スクリプト

You have 10 seconds to read the situation and Question No. 26.

We sell four original incense brands. Bouquet Himalaya is a paper-type incense that features the scents of flowers from India. It has a deep, calming effect and helps relieve stress and anxiety. Next, Magnolia's Sanctuary is a stick-type incense that contains sweet-smelling substances. This incense will immediately lift your spirits and is perfect for creating an energizing mood. Akebono is a cone-type purifying incense made with sage, and it's popular among meditation practitioners. Finally, Shirley's Gift is a stick-type incense that was also developed specifically for releasing tension. The aroma calms the mind, creating a tranquil atmosphere.

Now mark your answer on your answer sheet.

全文訳

　当店は，オリジナルのお香ブランドを4つ販売しています。ブーケ・ヒマラヤは，インドの花の香りを特徴とする紙タイプのお香です。深い鎮静効果があり，ストレスや不安の解消に役立ちます。次に，マグノリアズ・サンクチュアリは，甘い香りの物質を含んだスティック型のお香です。このお香は，すぐに気分を高揚させ，活力を与えるムード作りに最適です。アケボノは，セージを原料とした浄化作用のある円錐型のお香で，瞑想する人たちの間で人気があります。最後に，シャーリーズ・ギフトは，こちらも特に緊張をほぐすために開発されたスティック型のお香です。香りが心を落ち着かせ，穏やかな雰囲気を作り出します。

No.26 解答 ④

状況の訳 あなたはリラックスするのに役立つスティック型のお香を買って使いたいと思っている。店員が次のように言う。

質問の訳 あなたはどのお香ブランドを買うべきか。

選択肢の訳 1 ブーケ・ヒマラヤ。

2 マグノリアズ・サンクチュアリ。
3 アケボノ。
4 シャーリーズ・ギフト。

解説 「状況」から，お香の条件として「リラックスするのに役立つ」「スティック型」の2点を押さえる。また，選択肢を見て，4つの商品が順に説明されると推測しよう。ブーケ・ヒマラヤとアケボノはスティックではないので不適。マグノリアズ・サンクチュアリは「リラックスするのに役立つ」と合わないので不適。シャーリーズ・ギフトが2つの条件に合う。

スクリプト

You have 10 seconds to read the situation and Question No. 27.

I'm calling to confirm your appointment to set up your new Internet service. It's scheduled for this Thursday. Our technician will arrive sometime between noon and 3 p.m. If this time slot is OK, no action is necessary. However, if it's not, please contact us to reschedule. Please note that we're currently experiencing high demand, so our only available appointment times would be next week. Also, our technicians are only available Monday through Friday between 9 a.m. and 6 p.m. Remember that our offices are closed on weekends. Thank you.

Now mark your answer on your answer sheet.

全文訳

お客さまの新しいインターネットサービスをセットアップする予約確認のお電話です。今週木曜日を予定しています。当社の技術者が正午から午後3時の間に伺います。この時間帯で問題ない場合は，何もする必要はありません。ですが，そうでない場合は，ご連絡いただき，予定を変更してください。現在，需要が高まっているため，予約可能な時間帯は来週になってしまうことをご承知おきください。また，技術者は，月曜日から金曜日の午前9時から午後6時の間のみ対応しています。週末は休業となっておりますのでお忘れなく。それでは。

No.27 解答 ❷

状況の訳 今日は月曜日で，あなたは新しいインタープロバイダーの担当者から音声メッセージを受け取る。あなたは今週の木曜日は正午から午後8時まで仕事をしなければならない。

質問の訳 あなたは何をすべきか。

選択肢の訳 1 今週末に予定を変更する。
2 来週の平日に予定を変更する。
3 今週木曜日の午前中に予定を変更する。
4 今週金曜日の午後6時以降に予定を変更する。

> **解説** 選択肢より，予定を変更しなければならない状況だと推測できる。our only available appointment times would be next week から，**3** と **4** は不適。週末は休みなので **1** も不適。よって，**2** が正解。**4** は，平日の午前 9 時から午後 6 時の間のみの対応という情報でも消去できる。

J

スクリプト

You have 10 seconds to read the situation and Question No. 28.

I've checked your application, and it appears that you've submitted all of the required forms that were on our website. It looks like you also paid your application fee when you submitted those documents. And we've been contacted by your high school regarding your transcripts, which should be arriving shortly. If you aren't sure what you want to major in yet, please consider attending our open-campus event next week. Otherwise, all that's left for you to do is submit a letter from a teacher or employer recommending you. Once we receive that, we can start processing your application.

Now mark your answer on your answer sheet.

全文訳

　あなたの願書を確認したところ，ウェブサイトに掲載されている必要書類は全て提出されたようですね。また，それらの書類を提出したときに，出願料も支払っているようです。あと，あなたの高校から，あなたの成績証明書について連絡がありましたので，それも間もなく届くでしょう。何を専攻したいかまだ決まっていない場合，来週のオープンキャンパスへの参加をご検討ください。そうでなければ，あとするべきことは，先生または雇用主からの推薦状を提出するだけです。私どもがそれを受け取ったら，あなたの出願手続きを開始できます。

No.28 解答 ③

状況の訳 あなたは心理学を学ぶのにある大学に出願している。入学選考事務局員があなたの願書について話している。

質問の訳 あなたは何をすべきか。

選択肢の訳 1　出願料を支払う。
2　来週の大学のイベントに行く。
3　推薦状を手に入れる。
4　高校の成績表を提出する。

> **解説** 必要書類は全て提出し，出願料も払ったので **1** は不適。高校の成績証明書は手配済みなので **4** も不適。「状況」から専攻は決まっているので，オープンキャンパスに行く必要はない→ **2** も不適。Otherwise, ...「そうでなければ（＝希望専攻が決まっていれば）」から，**3** が正解。

22年度第2回　リスニング

43

スクリプト

You have 10 seconds to read the situation and Question No. 29.

There are four local tours today. Our bus tour starting at 1 p.m. takes passengers to major sites all over the city, and it costs nothing. Next, a walking tour starts at 2:30. Local volunteer guides will escort you around the downtown area, and there's no charge. If you enjoy bike riding, join the tour starting at three. It costs $35, which includes bike rental fees and refreshments. Finally, if you take our tour starting at five, you can try various kinds of local cuisine. The participation fee is just a few dollars, but you'll have to pay for what you eat and drink at food stands or restaurants.

Now mark your answer on your answer sheet.

全文訳

本日は，現地ツアーが４つあります。午後１時発のバスツアーは，お客さまを市内各所の主要スポットに連れて行き，費用はかかりません。次に，２時30分にウォーキングツアーが出発します。地元のボランティアガイドが繁華街を案内し，無料です。自転車に乗るのがお好きなら，３時発のツアーにご参加ください。料金は35ドルで，自転車のレンタル料と軽食が含まれています。最後に，５時発のツアーに参加すると，さまざまな種類の郷土料理が試せます。参加費はわずか数ドルですが，屋台やレストランでの飲食代はご自分で払わないといけません。

No.29 解答 ②

状況の訳 あなたは海外旅行中で，無料の現地ツアーに参加したいと思っている。あなたは乗り物酔いをしやすい。ホテルのインフォメーションデスクで次のように言われる。

質問の訳 どのツアーがあなたにとって最適か。

選択肢の訳
1 午後１時からのツアー。
2 午後２時30分からのツアー。
3 午後３時からのツアー。
4 午後５時からのツアー。

解説 問題用紙の情報から，「乗り物に乗らない」「無料」ツアーは「何時」発か？がポイントだと推測しよう。１時のツアーはバスなので不適。２時30分のツアーはウォーキングで無料なので，これが適切。念のため続きを聞くと，３時と５時のツアーは無料ではないので不適。

| 二次試験・面接 | 問題カード A 日程 | 問題編 p.40〜41 | 🔊 ▶MP3 ▶アプリ ▶CD4 1〜5 |

解答例 **One day, a woman was talking with her husband.** They were sitting at the dining room table, and they both looked concerned. The woman was looking at a lot of bills they needed to pay, and she said that living in the city was very expensive. That night, her husband was using the computer. He had found a website inviting people to come to ABC Village. It said that housing was cheap there, and the couple thought it looked like a nice place to live. A few months later, the woman's family was moving into a traditional Japanese house in the countryside. It was surrounded by beautiful nature. Two old farmers were happily working in the field nearby, and they looked up to see the family. A few weeks later, however, the family members were sitting inside their house, and the children were complaining that they missed their friends in the city.

解答例の訳 ある日，女性が夫と話していました。2人はダイニングルームのテーブルに座っていて，2人とも心配そうな様子でした。女性は，支払わなければならない多くの請求書を見ていて，都会で暮らすのはとてもお金がかかると言いました。その夜，彼女の夫はコンピューターを使っていました。彼は，人々にABC村へ来るよう呼びかけるウェブサイトを見つけました。それにはそこは住宅が安いと書かれており，夫婦は住むのに良さそうな場所だと思いました。数カ月後，女性の家族は田舎の伝統的な日本家屋に引っ越していました。そこは美しい自然に囲まれていました。近くの畑では2人の年配の農家の人が楽しそうに作業をしていて，顔を上げて一家を見ました。ところが数週間後，一家は家の中で座っていて，子供たちが都会の友だちが恋しいと不平を言っていました。

解説 イラスト上部の情報から，「お金を節約したかった夫婦」の話である。各コマで押さえるべき点は，①女性が請求書（Bill）を見て，「都会で暮らすのはとてもお金がかかる」と言っている，②その夜，夫婦が「ABC村へお越しください。安価な住宅」と書かれたウェブサイトを見ている，③数カ月後，一家が田舎に引っ越している，④子供たちが「都会の友だちが恋しい」と言っている。画面や紙に書かれた文字は，It said (that) 〜 で表せる。画面のCome to ... は，解答例では〈invite＋O＋to *do*〉「O（人）に〜するよう誘う［勧める］」を使って表している。4コマ目は都会から田舎に引っ越したことで生じた問題を描写しており，howeverなどを使って話の展開を表したい。

No. 1

解答例 I'd be thinking that I should have considered my children's needs more before moving. It's natural for them to feel lonely in a village with few friends. Perhaps we can take the children to the city on the weekends.

解説 質問は「4番目の絵を見てください。もしあなたがこの女性なら，どのようなことを考えているでしょうか」。解答例は，〈I should have + 過去分詞〉を用いて「引っ越す前に子供たちの要求をもっと考えるべきだった」という後悔を表している。解決策としては，「週末に街に連れて行く」のほか，「田舎で友だちを作る手助けをする」なども考えられるだろう。

No. 2

解答例 No, renting is better. Homeowners can't easily move to a different city to change jobs, for example. This means they might miss out on some big opportunities. Also, it's a lot of work to take care of a house.

解説 質問は「住む場所を借りるより住宅を購入する方がよいと思いますか」。2択の質問の場合，「○○の方がよい」と明確にしてからそれぞれの利点［欠点］を根拠にするとよいだろう。解答例は No の立場で，「転職などで引っ越しにくい＝大きなチャンスを逃すかも」「家の手入れが大変」という購入の欠点を挙げている。

No. 3

解答例 Yes. It's clearly important to have nature in our surroundings. It gives people a place where they can relax and relieve their stress. Having large parks full of trees and other plants also helps to keep the air clean.

解説 質問は「日本は都市部に緑地を増やすべきか」。解答例は Yes の立場で，ストレスを解消する場所の提供や，木や植物は空気をきれいに保つという緑の利点を根拠にしている。It's clearly important to ... の clearly「明らかに」のような意見を強める語を用いると説得力が増す。

No. 4

解答例 Not at all. These days, workplace culture is very competitive, so most people are under huge pressure to work hard. That leaves them with very little time to spend on hobbies or with family.

解説 「最近の人々は私生活と仕事のバランスをうまく保っているか」。解答例は No の立場（全く保っていない）で，その理由として，職場での競争が激しいことや，それが原因で趣味や家族との時間がほとんどないことを挙げている。質問は特定の事象の真否を問うもので，should を含んでいないので「バランスを取るべきか」という質問ではないことに注意。

二次試験・面接 | 問題カード **C** 日程 | 問題編 p.42〜43　　▶MP3 ▶アプリ ▶CD 4 **6**〜**9**

22年度第2回　面接

解答例 **One day, a couple was taking a walk by the beach.** They passed by a fenced area, where a construction worker was putting up a sign that said a new airport was being constructed by ABC Construction. The couple was shocked to learn about the plan. A few days later, the couple joined a protest against the construction project. The husband was holding a sign that said "protect ocean life," and the wife was collecting signatures from people who opposed the construction of the airport. Six months later, the couple was at the construction site with a group of people. A sign said that the construction had been canceled, and the couple and the supporters of the protest were very pleased. A year later, the couple was looking at a newspaper at home. The wife was surprised to see an article that said ABC Construction had gone bankrupt.

解答例の訳 ある日，夫婦が海辺を散歩していました。彼らがフェンスで囲まれたエリアを通りかかると，そこでは建設作業員が ABC 建設によって新しい空港が建設中であることが書かれた看板を立てていました。夫婦はその計画を知ってショックを受けました。数日後，夫婦はその建設プロジェクトに対する抗議活動に参加しました。夫は「海の命を守ろう」と書かれた看板を手に持っており，妻は空港建設に反対する人々から署名を集めていました。6 カ月後，夫婦は集まった人々と一緒に建設現場にいました。看板には建設が中止されたと書かれており，夫婦と抗議活動の支持者たちは大喜びでした。1 年後，夫婦は自宅で新聞を見ていました。妻は，ABC 建設が倒産したという記事を見て驚きました。

解説 各コマで押さえるべき点は，①夫婦が「空港建設現場」と書かれた看板を見ている，②数日後，夫が「海の命を守ろう！」という看板を掲げ，妻が署名を集めている，③6 カ月後，人々が「建設中止」と書かれた看板を見て喜んでいる，④1 年後，夫婦が「ABC 建設倒産」と書かれた記事を見ている。2 コマ目は，飛行機に×が付いているので，建設反対運動の様子である。看板や紙に書かれた文字を適切な文で表すことがポイント。1 コマ目の Airport Construction Site は「建設中」と捉えて was being constructed，3 コマ目の Construction Canceled と 4 コマ目の ABC Construction Goes Bankrupt は解答例では had been canceled と had gone bankrupt になっている。時制の一致による動詞の形に留意したい。

47

No. 1

解答例 I'd be thinking that it was partially my fault that the company went bankrupt. However, it's extremely important to protect the ocean environment, so I still think that we did the right thing by protesting the airport's construction.

解説 質問は「4番目の絵を見てください。もしあなたがこの夫なら，どのようなことを考えているでしょうか」。解答例は，「倒産は自分のせいでもあるだろう」と責任を感じつつも，However を用いて「海の環境を守ることは大事だから正しいことをした」としている。partially や extremely などの副詞をうまく使えると表現が豊かになる。

No. 2

解答例 Yes. There are many big problems in our society, so it's essential for Japanese people to feel more comfortable discussing political issues. It's the only way for us to begin solving these problems.

解説 質問は「日本人はもっと自分の政治的意見を表明すべきだと思うか」。解答例は Yes の立場で，「社会問題の解決のためにはもっと気軽に政治問題を議論できることが不可欠だ」という意見。it's ～ for A to *do* の形で主張を述べる際は，important や necessary の代わりに essential，crucial，significant などレベルの高い多様な語を使えるようにしたい。

No. 3

解答例 No. Businesses already provide their communities with employment opportunities, and they contribute to society by developing new products. They shouldn't be expected to do more than that.

解説 質問は「企業は社会を助けるためにもっと努力すべきだと思うか」。解答例の already は，No の立場の際に，「すでにそうだ（からその必要はない）」という意見を述べるときに有効である。Yes の立場では，同様の内容で「企業は，地域社会に雇用の場を提供したり新製品を開発したりすることで，もっと社会に貢献すべきだ」と述べることが可能だろう。

No. 4

解答例 Absolutely. Reducing the amount of electricity people use at home would reduce the amount of fossil fuels burned. Things like air conditioners use a lot of energy, so limiting their use would definitely reduce global warming.

解説 質問は「個人の行動が地球温暖化の緩和に貢献することは可能か」。Yes の立場では，個人が日常生活でできることを具体的に挙げて根拠にすればよい。この解答例のように明らかに Yes（または No）の立場を示す場合は，absolutely や definitely などの強い主張を表す語が有効である。

2022-1

一次試験
筆記解答・解説　　　p.50〜65

一次試験
リスニング解答・解説　p.66〜88

二次試験
面接解答・解説　　　p.89〜92

解 答 一 覧

一次試験・筆記

1

(1)	3	(10)	3	(19)	2
(2)	1	(11)	1	(20)	3
(3)	4	(12)	1	(21)	1
(4)	4	(13)	2	(22)	2
(5)	3	(14)	4	(23)	1
(6)	3	(15)	4	(24)	1
(7)	2	(16)	1	(25)	4
(8)	4	(17)	1		
(9)	1	(18)	1		

2

(26)	4	(29)	1
(27)	1	(30)	3
(28)	2	(31)	4

3

(32)	4	(35)	3	(38)	2
(33)	2	(36)	2	(39)	1
(34)	1	(37)	4	(40)	3
				(41)	3

4　解答例は本文参照

一次試験・リスニング

Part 1

No. 1	1	No. 5	2	No. 9	2
No. 2	3	No. 6	1	No.10	4
No. 3	4	No. 7	1	No.11	3
No. 4	4	No. 8	3	No.12	2

Part 2

No.13	3	No.17	2	No.21	4
No.14	4	No.18	1	No.22	2
No.15	3	No.19	1	No.23	2
No.16	4	No.20	3	No.24	1

Part 3

No.25	3	No.28	4
No.26	1	No.29	4
No.27	1		

一次試験・筆記 **1** | 問題編 p.46〜49

(1) ― 解答 ③ ••

訳 事件を検討した後，裁判官は情けをかけることにし，その男に警告を与えただけにした。彼女は，彼が自分の犯罪に対して明らかに深く反省していると述べた。

解説 裁判官は男に何を示したか。続く「警告を与えただけ」や「すまないと思っている，反省している」から，mercy「慈悲，情け」が適切。disgrace「不名誉」，closure「閉鎖」，seclusion「隔離すること」

(2) ― 解答 ① •••••••••••••••••••••••••••••••• 正答率 ★75%以上

訳 リサは双子の姉［妹］に見た目がそっくりだが，全く違う気質がある。彼女は姉［妹］と違って，とても落ち着いていて，めったに怒らない。

解説 リサと双子の姉［妹］の比較。but があるので見た目は似ているが性格は違うという趣旨だと推測できる。temperament「気質」が適切。accumulation「蓄積」，veneer「化粧板」，glossary「用語集」

(3) ― 解答 ④ ••

訳 A：アナベル，宿題が終わったかどうか私が聞いたら肩をすくめるだけでは駄目よ。はっきりと答えなさい。
　　B：ごめんなさい，お母さん。もう少しで終わるわ。

解説 母親は don't 〜 と命令文を用い，「〜してはいけない，〜しなさい」と注意している。shrug *one's* shoulders「肩をすくめる」は欧米人の「さあね，知らない」という仕草で，「はっきりと答えなさい」につながる。echo「（音などを）反響させる」，bow「（頭を）下げる」，dump「投げ捨てる」

(4) ― 解答 ④ ••

訳 町で大規模なビジネス会議があるとき，空室のあるホテルを見つけるのはほぼ不可能だ。ほとんどのホテルはすぐに満室になる。

解説 第2文の「すぐに満室になる」から，ほぼ不可能なのは空きのあるホテルを見つけること。vacancy は可算名詞で「空室」の意味。sprain「捻挫」，segment「部分，一区切り」，transition「移行」

(5) ― 解答 ③ ••

訳 刑事は何時間もそのギャングを尋問したが，彼は誰が自分の犯罪を手助けしたか言おうとしなかった。結局，刑事は彼から情報を得ようとするのをやめた。

解説 刑事はギャングから情報を得ようとしていたことから，interrogate「尋問する」の過去形が適切。それぞれ discharge「（液体・気体などを）放出する」，convert「変換する」，affiliate「提携させる」の過去形。

50

(6) ― 解答 **3** ∙∙∙

訳 けがをした足首を治療するためには，医師は圧迫を勧める。これは，けがした部分の周りに包帯をしっかりと巻くことでできる。

解説 けがをした足首の一般的な治療法を述べた文。第 2 文にある具体的な方法から，医師が勧めたのは compression「圧縮，圧迫」。depression「憂鬱，うつ病」，progression「進行」，suspicion「疑い」

(7) ― 解答 **2** ∙∙∙

訳 A：家に帰る途中に突然雨が激しく降り始めてびしょぬれになってしまったよ。
　　B：私の忠告を聞いて傘を持って行くべきだったのに。

解説 雨にぬれて帰宅した A を，B は〈should have＋過去分詞〉「～すべきだったのに（しなかった）」を用いて非難している。heed「（助言・忠告を）聞き入れる」の過去分詞が適切。それぞれ mold「形作る」，twist「ねじる，（意味などを）ゆがめる」，yield「生み出す」の過去分詞。

(8) ― 解答 **4** ∙∙∙

訳 もっと多くの裕福な顧客を引き付ける方法として，その香水会社は主に裕福な人が読む雑誌に製品の広告を出し始めた。

解説 裕福な人が読む雑誌に製品の広告を出すことは，裕福な（affluent）顧客を引き付けるためである。文中の wealthy と同義の affluent が正解。theatrical「芝居じみた」，brutal「野蛮な」，frantic「狂乱した」

(9) ― 解答 **1** ∙∙∙

訳 先生は，幾つかのささいな間違いを除けば，その生徒のエッセーは完璧だったと言った。彼はそれに可能な限りの高い点を付けた。

解説 apart from は「～を除いて」。「エッセーは完璧だった」と続くことから，「幾つかのささいな（trivial）間違いを除けば」とする。conclusive「決定的な」，palatial「宮殿の（ような）」，offensive「不快な」

(10) ― 解答 **3** ∙∙

訳 負傷したそのサッカー選手は，自分の代わりの選手が最終戦でプレーするのをうらやましそうに見た。彼は心底プレーを続けたいと思っていた。

解説 負傷した選手が代わりの選手がプレーするのをどんな気持ちで見たか。第 2 文の内容も踏まえ，enviously「うらやましそうに」が適切。〈watch as SV〉は「S が V するのをじっと見る」の意味。substantially「実質的に」，previously「以前に」，relevantly「関連して」

(11) ― 解答 **1** ∙∙

訳 エイブラハムのアパートの前にある新しいホテルは，街の向こうの山々の眺めを遮るほど高くはない。彼はまだそれらをはっきりと見ることができる。

解説 第 2 文から，山々は実際に見えるので，ホテルは「山々の眺めを遮るほ

ど高くない」とする。not ~ enough to *do* で「…するほど~ではない」，obstruct *someone's* view で「(人) の眺め [視界] を遮る」という意味。delegate「委任する」，entangle「絡ませる」，boost「(数量などを) 増加させる」

(12) – 解答 **①** ・・・

訳 白いカーペットに赤ワインをこぼしたので，マーサはせっけんと水で染みを取り除こうとした。しかし，彼女はそれを完全には取り除くことができなかった。

解説 せっけんと水で取り除こうとしたのは，白いカーペットにこぼした赤ワインの stain「染み」。slit「切り込み」，bump「衝突 (音)，(打撲でできた) こぶ」，blaze「炎」

(13) – 解答 **②** ・・・

訳 戦争は 1 年間続いたが，どちらの側も勝利を得ることはできなかった。勝利は不可能に思えたため，両国は戦いをやめることに合意した。

解説 neither side は「戦っている 2 ヵ国のどちらも~ない」の意味。第 2 文から両国は戦いをやめることにしたので，どちらも勝つことができなかったと考える。prevail「勝つ，勝利を得る」が適切。devise「工夫する」，evolve「発展する」，reconstruct「再構築する」

(14) – 解答 **④** ・・・

訳 その指導者は，自分の支配に対するいかなる反対をも阻止することを目的とした厳格な新しい法律の導入に対する口実として，国の政情不安を利用した。

解説 国の指導者が，自分に都合の良い新法律を導入しようと，政情不安を口実 (pretext) にしたと考えられる。trance「恍惚状態」，downfall「崩壊」，rampage「大暴れ」

(15) – 解答 **④** ・・・

訳 容疑者は警察に無実を主張し続けた。彼は，犯罪が起こった場所からだいぶ離れた所にいたと繰り返し彼らに言った。

解説 第 2 文の「彼ら (＝警察) に繰り返し言った」から，無実を主張し続けたことが分かる。assert *someone's* innocence で「(人) の無実を主張する」という意味。conceal「隠す」，counter「反論する」，expire「期限が切れる」

(16) – 解答 **①** ・・・・・・・・・・・・・・・・・・・・・・・・・・・・・・・・・・・ 正答率 ★75%以上

訳 優れた作家は自分の作品から間違いをなくすために最大限の努力をするが，時には間違いを見逃し，後で修正しなければならないこともある。

解説 but があるので「作家は作品から間違いをなくす努力をするが，見逃すこともある」という趣旨だと推測できる。eliminate A from B で「B から A を取り除く」という意味。expend「費やす」，stabilize「安定さ

せる」，oppress「圧迫する」

(17) − 解答 **1** ....

訳 誘拐犯らは多額の身代金と引き換えに子供を両親に返した後，その金を持って逃げようとした。しかし，警察がすぐに彼らを捕まえ，その金を夫婦に返した。

解説 誘拐犯が子供と引き換えにするのは身代金（ransom）。空所後では the money に言い換えられている。in exchange for は「〜と引き換えに」。applause「拍手」，monopoly「独占」，prank「いたずら」

(18) − 解答 **1** ....

訳 ガスパーはある名門大学に出願した。残念ながら，成績が十分ではなかったため，あまり有名でない大学に行かざるを得なかった。

解説 対比を表す Unfortunately があるので，lesser-known「あまり有名でない」の対語となる prestigious「一流の，名門の」が適切。spontaneous「自発的な」，cordial「友好的な」，petty「わずかな，下級の」

(19) − 解答 **2** ....

訳 スパイらは気付かれずに軍事基地に入ろうと陸軍士官に変装した。

解説 in an attempt to *do*「〜しようとして」以下の内容から，disguise *oneself* as「〜に変装する」を用いる。それぞれ chronicle「年代順に記録する」，render「（人・物を）（ある状態に）する，与える」，revitalize「再活性化する」の過去形。

(20) − 解答 **3** ....

訳 ティモシーは非常に献身的な従業員だ。彼は信頼でき，手助けすることに熱心で，常に会社や同僚に忠誠心を示している。

解説 第 2 文の内容から，ティモシーは好ましい従業員だと分かる。正解は devoted「献身的な」で，後にある loyalty「忠誠心」の形容詞形 loyal と類義。grotesque「奇怪な」，defiant「反抗的な」，feeble「貧弱な」

(21) − 解答 **1** ....

訳 ポールが体重を減らすのを助けるため，医師は彼に食事を変えるよう勧めた。具体的には，彼女は，脂肪分の多い食べ物を減らし，もっと食物繊維を取るよう彼に提案した。

解説 医師の勧める減量方法は何か。具体的に述べた第 2 文の内容から，食事を変える（modify）ことである。比較級の fewer, more が変化を含意。pluck「引っ張る，（羽を）むしる」，exclaim「叫ぶ」，distill「蒸留する」

(22) − 解答 **2** ....

訳 Ａ：ずっと仕事がすごく忙しいのに，今は新入社員の教育にも対応しないといけないの。

Ｂ：それはあんまりだね。代わりに誰かほかの人がそれをできるかどう

53

か上司に聞いてみたらどうだい。

解説 A は，ずっと忙しい（現在完了）上に今は（now）新入社員の教育もしないといけないと不満を漏らしている。contend with「〜（困難）と闘う，〜（問題）に取り組む」が適切。turn over「〜をひっくり返す」，prop up「〜を下支えする」，count off「〜が全員いる［全部ある］かどうか数える」

(23) − 解答 **1**

訳 少年は割れた花瓶のことを飼い犬のせいにしようとした。しかし，彼の母親はそのうそにだまされず，彼を部屋に追いやった。

解説 However があるので，花瓶を割ったのは犬ではなく少年だと察しが付く。fall for「〜（策略など）にだまされる」が適切。hang on「〜によって決まる」，see out「〜を見届ける」，flag down「〜（車・運転手）を合図して止める」

(24) − 解答 **1**

訳 CEO（最高経営責任者）はスピーチの中で，今後5年間の会社の発展計画を打ち出した。彼は，それが会社の成長に伴い全従業員の仕事の指針となることを望んだ。

解説 map out a plan for で「〜の計画を作る［打ち出す］」という意味。第2文の this は his plan を指す。それぞれ leap in「〜に飛び込む」，rack up「〜を獲得する」，space out「〜を間隔を空けて配置する」の過去形。

(25) − 解答 **4**

訳 昨年，ハロルドは全財産を費やしてさまざまな会社の株を買った。彼は今後数年間，株価が好調に推移することに賭けていた。

解説 the stock market は動名詞 performing の意味上の主語。第1文の内容を踏まえ，bet on「〜に賭ける」の過去進行形を用いて「株価が好調に推移することに賭けていた」とする。準1級では政治・経済のテーマが扱われるので語彙力を養っておこう。それぞれ cast away「〜を投げ捨てる」，put down「〜を下に置く」，step up「〜（の量［速度など］）を増やす，上げる」の -ing 形。

一次試験・筆記 **2** | 問題編 p.50〜53

全文訳 **ピーターの法則**

　ピーターの法則として知られる理論によって，なぜ業績が悪い管理職の人が多いのかを説明できるかもしれない。この理論によると，下位職で成績の良い従業員は，自分の準備が整っていない地位にいずれ昇格する。これの理由は，従業員は通常，現職の業績に基づいて昇進するからである。この種の昇進方針は理にかなっているように見えるか

もしれないが，従業員の強みと弱みを十分に考慮することを怠ると，彼らの能力がふさわしくない地位に，彼らがゆくゆくは到達する結果になる。

　ある研究は，管理職に昇進した販売員の経歴を調べた。この研究では，予想されたように，最も優れた販売員が昇進する可能性が最も高かったことのほか，彼らが管理職では最も業績が悪かったことも判明した。この研究は，現在の業績のみに基づいて従業員を昇進させることには2つのデメリットがあることを示した。会社が最終的に無能な管理職を作り出してしまうことになるだけではなく，会社は下位職で最も優れた従業員を失うことにもなる。

　この研究を実施した研究者たちは，問題の1つは，業績の良い従業員は必然的に良い管理職になると単純に仮定してしまうという間違いを会社が犯してしまっていることだと言う。ほとんどの会社では，新入社員は仕事の仕方について専門研修を受ける。一方で，新しく管理職になった人には多くの場合において研修が全くかほとんど実施されない。これは，ピーターの法則の作用を緩和する方法の1つが新しい管理職に適切な研修を行うことであると示唆しているようである。

> 語句 principle「原理，法則」，managerial「管理者の」，result in「（結果的に）～をもたらす」，unsuited「適さない」，solely「単に，ただ」，specialized「専門化した」，lessen「減少させる」

(26) – 解答 **4**

解説 直前の who は関係代名詞で，先行詞は many people (in managerial positions)。続きを読んでいくと，下位職で成績の良い従業員が管理職（＝彼らの能力がふさわしくない地位）に昇進するという問題を論じていることが分かる。また，第2段落にも，ある研究で「管理職では最も業績が悪かったことが判明した」とあることから，**4**が適切。

(27) – 解答 **1**

解説 「この研究は，現在の業績のみに基づいて従業員を昇進させることには…ことを示した」という文意。空所後で not only A but also B「AだけでなくBも」を用いて「会社は最終的に無能な管理職を作り出してしまう」「会社は下位職で最も優れた従業員を失う」というデメリット（disadvantage）を2つ説明している。よって，**1**が適切。

(28) – 解答 **2** ・・・・・・・・・・・・ 正答率 ★75%以上

解説 文頭につなぎ言葉を入れる問題。空所前は「ほとんどの会社では，新入社員は仕事の仕方について専門研修を受ける」，空所後は「新しく管理職になった人には多くの場合において研修が全くかほとんど実施されない」という内容。most と little or no という対比に着目すると，On the other hand「一方で」が適切。

全文訳 **近視**

　近視は世界中で急速に増加している。この状態の人は，近くの物ははっきりと見るこ

とができるが，遠くの物はぼやけて見える。多くの人がこの傾向をデジタル画面の利用のせいにする。彼らは，コンピューターやスマートフォンなどのデバイスを使うことが眼精疲労につながり，また，デジタル画面が生み出すブルーライトが眼底の感光性細胞を損傷すると主張する。しかし，デジタル画面が視力に長期的影響があるとする明らかな証拠はない。

実際，近視の増加はデジタル画面が広く使われるようになる前から始まっていた。研究の中には，本当の問題は人々が屋内で過ごす時間が長過ぎることにあると示唆するものもある。これによって自然光にさらされることが少なくなる。近視は目の水晶体が伸びることにより起こり，これによって光を集める能力が低下する。しかし，脳内で産生される化学物質であるドーパミンの放出は，これが起こるのを防止することができ，自然光にさらされることはより多くのドーパミンの産生につながる。

一部の専門家たちは，1日のうち3時間ほど屋外にいることが近視の予防に役立つと言う。しかし多くの人にとって，学校や仕事のスケジュールのため，これをすることは不可能である。その代わりに，人々が家の中で使う照明の種類を変える方がより現実的かもしれない。自然光の利点をいくらか提供する照明はすでに利用可能であり，研究によって将来的により多くの選択肢が提供されることが期待される。

> 語句　nearsightedness「近視」，blurry「ぼやけた」，blame A on B「AをBのせいにする」，eyestrain「眼精疲労」，light-sensitive「感光性の」，cell「細胞」，exposure to「～にさらすこと」，lens「(眼球) 水晶体」，dopamine「ドーパミン」，practical「現実的な」，alternative「選択肢」

(29) – 解答　**1** · 正答率 ★75%以上

> 解説　第1段落第3文の Many people blame ... で，多くの人が考える近視の原因は「デジタル画面の利用」だと述べた後，However があるので，これに反する内容が続くと推測する。「デジタル画面が…とする明らかな証拠はない」という文意に合うのは **1** である。

(30) – 解答　**3** · 正答率 ★75%以上

> 解説　第2段落では，近視の原因はデジタル画面の利用以外にあると考える裏付けが書かれている。空所には「近視を増加させている本当の問題」が入る。空所後の a lack of exposure to natural light の原因として，**3** が適切。この indoors が第3段落第1文の outdoors につながる。

(31) – 解答　**4** · 正答率 ★75%以上

> 解説　第3段落は近視の予防について。空所前は，多くの人は近視の予防として1日のうち3時間ほど屋外にいることはできないという趣旨。空所後は，(屋外にいるよりも) 家の中で使う照明の種類を変える方が現実的だという内容。よって，Instead「その代わりに」が適切。

全文訳 **ナラタケ**

　地球上に現存する最も大きい生物は、クジラでもそのほかの大型動物でもない。それどころか、キノコや毒キノコを含む生物群にそれは属している。それはナラタケとして一般に知られる菌類の一種で、根のような菌糸がアメリカのオレゴン州の森の地中に広い面積にわたって広がっている。DNA検査によって、この地域のナラタケ全てが同じ生物に由来することが確認されており、その年間成長率に基づき、科学者たちはそれが8千年以上前から存在している可能性があると推定している。科学者たちはまた、仮にこれを全てひとまとめにした場合、35,000 トンほどの重さになると推定している。

　このナラタケは感銘を与えるものではあるが、森の多くの木々に問題を引き起こしている。ナラタケは木を感染させて、その根や幹から栄養を吸収し、多くの場合は最終的に枯らしてしまう。残念なことに感染した木はたいてい見つけにくく、それはナラタケが樹皮の下に隠れており、樹皮を剥がしたときに初めてその菌糸を見ることができるからである。秋の終わりごろ、ナラタケの子実体（キノコ）が木の外側に現れるが、冬の前のたった数週間だけである。木はナラタケに抵抗しようとするが、ナラタケは木の根に損傷を与えて上部に水や栄養が届かないようにするため、たいていは最終的に戦いに負ける。

　オレゴンのナラタケの完全な除去が検討されているが、費用と時間がかかり過ぎると分かるだろう。現在研究されている別の解決策は、ナラタケに対抗できる樹種を植えることである。しかし一部の専門家たちは、見方を変える必要があるかもしれないと示唆している。ナラタケの影響を否定的な観点で捉えるのではなく、むしろ人はそれを自然の成り行きの一例として考えるべきである。枯死した木々は最終的には土に返り、地域の生態系の役に立つ。

語句 fungus「菌類」, organism「有機体, 生物」, toadstool「毒キノコ」, rootlike「根のような」, filament「菌糸」, pose「(問題を)引き起こす」, infect「感染させる」, absorb「吸収する」, nutrient「栄養素」, trunk「木の幹」, spot「見つける」, bark「樹皮」, visible「目に見える」, attempt to *do*「〜しようと試みる」, resist「抵抗する」, removal「除去」, time-consuming「時間のかかる」, perspective「物事の見方」, in a negative light「否定的な観点で」, ultimately「最終的に」

(32) –解答 **4**

問題文の訳 この文章によると、オレゴン州のナラタケについて正しいことの1つは何か。

選択肢の訳 1　時間をかけて一緒に成長を始めたさまざまなキノコ種の組み合わさったものである。

2　最初はゆっくりと成長したが、過去1千年でより急速に拡大している。

3　集めた栄養を，生育している木やほかの種類の植物に分け与えている。

4　木に生育し木を常食とすることで広い範囲に広がった単一生物である。

解説　第1段落から，ナラタケは，オレゴン州の森の地中を広い面積にわたって広がっている，キノコや毒キノコを含む生物群に属する菌類の一種である。また，第2段落から，菌が木に感染し，その根や幹から栄養を吸収する（= feed on trees）ことが分かる。よって，**4**が適切。

(33) − 解答　② ⋯⋯⋯⋯⋯⋯⋯⋯⋯⋯⋯⋯⋯⋯⋯⋯ 正答率 ★75%以上

問題文の訳　ナラタケを見つけるのが困難である理由は

選択肢の訳　1　生育している木の種類によって，ナラタケが生成するキノコが色を変えるためである。

2　1年のある短期間に子実体を形成するときを除いて，ふつうは見えないためである。

3　ナラタケは地中で育つだけでなく，木の根のような見た目をしているためである。

4　ナラタケは，生育に必要な特定の気象条件のある地域でしか生存できないためである。

解説　第2段落参照。ナラタケが見つけにくいこととその理由は，Unfortunately, ... の文とその次の文 In the late fall, ... にある。「樹皮を剥がしたときだけ見える」「子実体が木の外側に現れる（=見える）のは冬の前のたった数週間だけ」という内容から，**2**が適切。**3**は，地中で育つ（ので見つけにくい）は正しいが，木の根のような見た目は見つけにくい理由ではない。

(34) − 解答　① ⋯⋯⋯⋯⋯⋯⋯⋯⋯⋯⋯⋯⋯⋯⋯⋯⋯ 正答率 ★75%以上

問題文の訳　一部の専門家たちはどう考えているか。

選択肢の訳　1　人々は，ナラタケが木に与える影響を自然で有益なプロセスと見なすべきである。

2　ナラタケに対処する唯一の現実的な方法は，除去する試みにもっと多くの時間とお金を投資することである。

3　ナラタケに感染した木は，ナラタケがそれ以上広がるのを妨げるために利用できる。

4　ナラタケは，収穫することで人々に優れた栄養源を提供できる。

解説　第3段落の Some experts have suggested, ... を参照。問題の解決策として，（ナラタケを完全除去する，ナラタケに対抗できる樹種を植えるという）見方を変える必要があると述べた後，Rather than ... people should ... で，ナラタケの影響を「自然の成り行きの一例として考えるべき」と述べている。その一例を具体的に説明した最終文の Dead trees ... ecosystem. の内容から，**1**が適切。本文の nature taking its course は「自然の成り行き」の意味。

58

全文訳 **インテンショナル・コミュニティー**

　何百年もの間，人は，しばしば「インテンショナル・コミュニティー」と呼ばれ，共通の理想，共同所有，そして資産の共同利用で特徴づけられる自立したコミュニティーを形成してきた。知られている限りの最初のインテンショナル・コミュニティーは，紀元前 6 世紀にギリシャの哲学者によって設立された。その後数世紀にわたって，社会の本流から離れて生きることを望む宗教団体によってこのようなコミュニティーが幾つも作られた。キリスト教修道院やイスラエルのキブツと呼ばれる集団農場など，これらの幾つかは何世代にもわたって成功が続いたが，他方で数年しか続かないインテンショナル・コミュニティーもあった。

　20 世紀において，1960 年代と 1970 年代の「大地へ帰れ」運動で見られたような哲学的観念論も，人々にインテンショナル・コミュニティーを形成する気にさせた。1970 年代初頭には，アメリカ合衆国だけでもそのようなコミュニティーが何千もあったと推定されているが，その多くがその後解散した。インテンショナル・コミュニティー財団には現在，アメリカにおいて 800 未満のコミュニティー，世界のその他地域において 250 弱のコミュニティーが記載されている。失敗したインテンショナル・コミュニティーは，たいてい同じような課題に直面していた。そこにとどまるために来た人の中には仕事の分担，自分たちの食料を育てること，そして集団生活の理想に傾倒している人もいたが，それほど真剣ではない人もいた。あるコミュニティーの共同創立者は「私たちは実用性はないものの高尚なビジョンを持っていたが，それは常にただ遊びに来ただけの人たちにむしばまれた」と振り返った。

　しかし，全てのインテンショナル・コミュニティーが瓦解する運命にあるわけではない。イタリアのトリノの近くにある精神的かつ芸術的な共同体であるダマヌールの現在でも続いている成功は，オープンなコミュニケーションと実際的なアプローチによるものである。ダマヌールは，その構成員を 15 〜 20 人から成る家族のようなグループに編成する。このコミュニティーでは，「家族」が 25 人より多いと親密さを生み出すのが難しくなることに気付いた。その一方で「家族」の構成員が少な過ぎると，効果的な意思決定を可能にするのに十分な集団的知性がない。ダマヌールの理想は，その憲法で述べられているが，選挙で選ばれたリーダーによって維持されている。そしてコミュニティー内の緊張は，塗料の入ったおもちゃの銃で戦う，遊び半分の模擬戦を開催することで対処される。

　うまくいっている全てのインテンショナル・コミュニティーには「常に先を考える能力」という共通する特徴があるように思われる。ダマヌールのある構成員はこう言う。「物事はうまくいかないときではなく，うまくいっているときに変えるべきである。」問題が起きる前に変化を起こすというこの戦略は，ダマヌールやその他のうまくいっているコミュニティーにとって功を奏しており，そのことはインテンショナル・コミュニティーが長期的にその構成員のニーズを満たすのにこれが効果的な方法であることを示唆している。

　語句 self-sustaining「自立した」, collective「共同の」, philosopher「哲

学者」, mainstream「主流（派）の」, monastery「（男子）修道院」, idealism「理想主義，観念論」, disband「解散する」, *be* committed to「〜に熱心である」, cofounder「共同創立者」, noble「高貴な」, undermine「むしばむ」, *be* destined to *do*「〜する運命にある」, fall apart「瓦解する」, ongoing「現在進行中の」, *be* attributed to「…の原因は〜にある」, intimacy「親密さ」, decision-making「意思決定」, outline「概要を述べる」, constitution「憲法，規約」, uphold「（慣習などを）維持する」, tension「緊張」, playful「遊び心のある」, mock「模擬の」, trait「特徴」, strategy「戦略」, fulfill「満たす」, in the long term「長期的に」

(35) – 解答 ③

問題文の訳 失敗したインテンショナル・コミュニティーが直面した共通の問題は

選択肢の訳
1 コミュニティーの大多数が誰かが参加することに賛成したが，少数の人が反対したことである。
2 人々は真の関心を持ってコミュニティーに参加したものの，効果的に貢献するためのスキルや知識が不足していたことである。
3 コミュニティーの理想に従うために一生懸命努力する構成員もいたが，共同生活に対しより軽いアプローチを取る構成員もいたことである。
4 コミュニティーは野心的なプロジェクトを完了しようと始めたが，知識と財源の不足が理由でそれを完了できなかったことである。

解説 第2段落中ほどに設問と同表現の Intentional communities that failed generally faced a similar challenge（= common issue）. がある。具体的には，続く Some people who ... but others were ... に「理想に傾倒している人もいたが，それほど真剣ではない人もいた」とあり，3が適切。2は「人は皆，真の関心を持って参加した」という意味になり，「ただ遊びに来ただけの人もいた」という本文の趣旨に合わない。

(36) – 解答 ②

問題文の訳 ダマヌールの社会構造について正しいものはどれか。

選択肢の訳
1 「家族」は自由に独自のルールを作ることができ，必ずしもコミュニティーの憲法に含まれるルールに従う必要はない。
2 グループの問題を解決し，良好な関係を維持するための最良の条件を作り出すため，「家族」の人数は制御されている。
3 意見の食い違いを解決することを目的とした模擬戦は時に深刻になり，「家族」を離れる羽目になる構成員もいる。
4 コミュニティーには，構成員が大規模グループの環境で生活するか，小規模グループの環境で生活するかを選択できるよう，さまざまな規模の「家族」がある。

解説 第3段落によると，ダマヌールの「家族」は15〜20人で，それは25人より多いと親密さを生み出すのが難しくなり，少な過ぎると効果的な意思決定をしにくいからである。これを「人数が制御されている」と表した**2**が適切。模擬戦による負の効果は述べていないので，**3**は不適。

(37) – 解答 ④

問題文の訳 この文章によると，ダマヌールはうまくいっているほかのインテンショナル・コミュニティーとどんな点で似ているか。

選択肢の訳
1 コミュニティーの構成員は，疲れ果てることがないように，ときどき責任を交換することが認められている。
2 構成員が新しいスキルを習得できるよう，収入を得るためにコミュニティーが行う仕事の種類が定期的に変更される。
3 コミュニティーの構成員は，共同所有の建物や設備の維持管理を交代で行う。
4 コミュニティーは，単に問題が発生したときに対応するのではなく，構成員のニーズを満たす方法を継続的に見つける。

解説 第4段落参照。ダマヌールやそのほかのうまくいっているコミュニティーの共通する特徴として，「物事はうまくいかないときではなく，うまくいっているときに変える」「問題が起きる前に変化を起こす」という戦略がある。続いて，この戦略について「長期的に構成員のニーズを満たすのに効果的な方法である」と述べている。本文の fulfill を正解**4**では satisfy と言い換えている。

全文訳 **インドのイギリス人**

　1600年に設立されたイギリス人所有の東インド会社は，2世紀以上の間，世界最大の会社の1つであった。インドや中国など，さまざまな国と海外貿易することによって，東インド会社はこれらの国々からぜいたく品をイギリスに輸入することができた。イギリス政府は，東インド会社の巨額の利益の一部を受け取っていたため，大いに喜んで政治的支援を与えた。何十万ものインド人の私兵集団を含む，その規模，権力，そして資金により，東インド会社はインドに圧力をかけて，だいたいにおいて同社の利益にしかならない貿易契約を受諾させた。1750年代に地元の支配者との戦いに勝利してからは，東インド会社はインドで最も裕福な州の1つを掌握した。その結果，東インド会社は企業としてのみ活動することをやめ，政治機関としても活動するようになり，インド国民に税金を同社に払うことを強制し始めた。

　東インド会社は，取引相手の国々の間で信頼できないという評判を得た。また，同社の不誠実な商習慣が中国との外交関係を悪化させたため，イギリス議会内でも人気を失いつつあった。それから，1850年代に，東インド会社の私兵集団の兵士の一部が，受けていた扱いに怒り，反乱を起こした。彼らはデリーまで行進してインド皇帝を権力の座に復帰させ，彼らの行動によってイギリス人に対する反乱はインド各地に広がった。

約２年後に反乱は結局鎮圧されたが，東インド会社の終焉（しゅうえん）の引き金となった。反乱が起こるのを許したことの責任を東インド会社に負わせたイギリス政府がインドの支配権を握り，イギリスの直接支配の時代が始まった。イギリス人は東インド会社を閉鎖し，インド皇帝を権力の座から降ろし，百年近くも続くインドの統治を始めた。

　典型的には鉄道の建設を一例として挙げて，インドはイギリス支配から恩恵を受けたと主張する人もいるが，多くの歴史家たちがインドは悪影響を受けたと主張する。イギリス文化が優れているという概念を強固なものにしようとして，インド人はイギリス人と同じ考え方や道徳，社会的選好を持つように教育された。イギリス人はまた，「分割統治」として知られる政策を実施し，これによって異なる宗教的背景を持つインド人を互いに敵対させた。イギリス政府はこの戦略を利用してインドに対する支配を維持したが，それはこれらの宗教の構成員が先の反乱時に結託したからであった。しかし，1900年代初頭からインド人の間でナショナリズムの感情が高まり，インドはついに1940年代後半に独立を獲得した。

　東インド会社が廃業したのは百年以上前のことだが，永続的な影響を及ぼしている。一部の専門家たちは，それが多国籍企業の概念の先駆けとなり，最終的には今日広まっている資本主義の経済システムにつながったと言う。さらに，イギリス政府と東インド会社の癒着は，事業目的の達成を助けるために政治的権力を利用する先例を作った。

> 〔語句〕 a portion of「〜の一部」，vast「巨大な」，be willing to do「喜んで〜する」，more than「非常に〜で」，be of benefit to「〜のためになる」，seize「奪取する」，province「州」，untrustworthy「信頼できない」，parliament「(Parliament で)(英国)議会」，rebel「反逆する」，〈restore ＋人＋to power〉「(人)を権力の座に復帰させる」，rebellion「反乱」，trigger「引き起こす」，proceed to do「〜し始める」，benefit from「〜から恩恵を受ける」，in an effort to do「〜しようとして」，reinforce「強化する」，notion「概念」，implement「実施する」，nationalist feeling「ナショナリズムの感情」，lasting「永続的な」，pioneer「先駆けとなる」，multinational「多国籍の」，capitalism「資本主義」，precedent「先例」，objective「目的」

(38) – 解答 ②

> 問題文の訳　インドが東インド会社と取引を行った結果の１つは何だったか。

> 選択肢の訳
> 1　インドは，他国と貿易取引をすることができたため，軍隊の規模を拡大する余裕があった。
> 2　インドには，自国にとって不利な商取引に合意する以外に選択肢がほとんどなかった。
> 3　インド政府は，失敗した貿易契約による損失を補うために増税しなければならなかった。
> 4　インド政府と中国との関係が悪化し，その結果，両国間の貿易が途絶えそうになった。

解説 第1段落の the company pressured India into accepting trade contracts that, in general, were only of benefit to the company 以降を参照。pressure A into -ing は「A に〜するよう圧力をかける」の意味。**2** が正解で，東インド会社がインドに圧力をかけて貿易契約を受諾させたことを，「ほぼ選択肢がない」と表し，また「東インド会社の利益にしかならない」を「インドにとって不利な」と表している。

(39) – 解答 ①

問題文の訳 イギリス政府がインドを支配することになったきっかけは何だったか。

選択肢の訳 **1** イギリス政府は，起こった反乱の責任を東インド会社に押しつけた。
2 インド国民は，国を効果的に統治するインド皇帝の能力に対する信頼を失った結果，イギリスの支配に賛成票を投じた。
3 インド国民は，インドと中国の間の戦争を防ぐために，イギリス人の協力を求めた。
4 インド皇帝は，インドの支配を維持するための政治的戦略として，イギリス人と手を組むことを決定した。

解説 第2段落後半参照。イギリスの直接支配の時代が始まった（an era of direct British rule began）きっかけは，その前の The British government, which blamed the East India Company for allowing the rebellion to happen にある。「反乱が起こるのを許したことの責任を東インド会社に負わせた」を「起こった反乱の責任を東インド会社に押しつけた」と表した **1** が適切。本文の rebellion を uprising に，happen を occur に言い換えている。

(40) – 解答 ③

問題文の訳 イギリスの支配がインドに与えた影響の1つは

選択肢の訳 **1** インド人が，自分たちの経済的・社会的ニーズを反映した政府を構築する過程に参加できたことであった。
2 学校が生徒にインドとイギリスの両文化を意識するよう教育する努力をしたことであった。
3 インド人のさまざまな集団の間に分断がもたらされ，彼らがイギリスの支配に異議を唱えるのを妨げたことであった。
4 インド政府によって建設された鉄道やそのほかの輸送システムの多くが破壊されたことであった。

解説 第3段落参照。イギリスは分割統治（統治を容易にするため被支配者の団結を妨げて分裂させること）を行い，異なる宗教的背景を持つインド人を互いに敵対させた（turned Indians from different religious backgrounds against each other）。本文 "divide and rule" の動詞 divide が正解 **3** では名詞 divisions になっている。**2** は In an effort to reinforce ... と不一致。

(41) – 解答 **3** ••••••••••••••••••••••••••••••••••••

問題文の訳 この文章の筆者は東インド会社について何と言っているか。

選択肢の訳 **1** 同社は，イギリス政府がアジアのほかの国々に支配を拡大するという目的を達成するのを妨げた。
2 同社は，その時代には成功したかもしれないが，そのビジネスモデルは今日の経済では有効ではないだろう。
3 同社は，今はもう存在しないが，現在の世界経済情勢に大きな影響を及ぼしている。
4 同社が設立されていなかったとしても，おそらく別の会社が同じような政治的・経済的影響力を持つことになっていただろう。

解説 第4段落参照。東インド会社は百年以上前に廃業した（＝ no longer exists）が，永続的な影響を及ぼしている。また，それ（東インド会社）が多国籍企業の概念の先駆けとなり，最終的には今日広まっている資本主義の経済システム（＝ the present-day global economic landscape）につながったのである。

一次試験・筆記 **4** | 問題編 p.61

トピックの訳 人の給料は仕事の成果に基づくべきか。

ポイントの訳 ・年齢　・会社の利益　・モチベーション　・スキル

解答例 In my opinion, from the perspectives of motivation and company profits, people's salaries should definitely be related to their job performance.

To begin with, while standardized salaries for workers in companies today are common, the level of motivation among employees can vary greatly. Rewarding enthusiastic employees who produce better work with higher salaries is not only fair but would also have the wider benefit of motivating other employees.

Additionally, the efforts that employees put into performing their work duties well ultimately benefit companies by increasing their profits. One of the responsibilities of a business is said to be the distribution of profits to those who contribute to its growth. Therefore, to fulfill this responsibility, companies must make sure that salaries match workers' job performance.

To conclude, when considering the importance of employee motivation and sharing company profits, I feel that people's salaries should be based on their job performance.

解説 序論：第1段落では，トピックに対する自分の意見（主張）を簡潔に書く。模範解答は In my opinion, from the perspectives of ...「私の意見では，…の観点から〜」の形でポイントの Motivation と Company profits を提示した後，「給料は仕事の成果に基づくべき」という賛成の立場を明らかにしている。definitely「間違いなく」を使うと主張が強まる。

本論：本論では，序論で述べた主張を裏付ける根拠・理由を，2つの観点に沿って説明する。模範解答の To begin with, ... / Additionally, ... のように，段落を2つに分けるとよい。第2段落は Motivation の観点で，「給料は標準化されているのが一般的だが，従業員のモチベーションは千差万別だ」と述べた後，「より良い仕事をする従業員に高い給料で報いることは，公正であるだけでなく，ほかの従業員のモチベーションを高める」と説明を続けている。while A, B と not only A but also B はいずれも B が強調されるので，主張したい内容は後ろに書くこと。第3段落は Company profits の観点で，「従業員の努力は最終的に企業に利益をもたらす」と断言した後，具体的な説明が続く。is said to be「（一般に）〜だと言われている」→ Therefore「それ故に」の展開を確認しよう。Therefore（結論）以下の companies must make sure that salaries match workers' job performance「企業は確実に給料が労働者の仕事の成果に見合うようにしなければならない」の部分は，「給料は仕事の成果に基づくべき」という主張の言い換えになっている。

結論：最終段落では序論で述べた主張を再確認する。模範解答は To conclude, で始め，when considering「〜を考慮するとき」の形で2つの観点を再び取り上げ，〈I feel that＋トピックの表現〉で締めくくっている。なお，序論と結論の「主張」でトピックの表現を用いる際，どちらかは表現を変える方がよい。模範解答では，序論で be based on を be related to に言い換えている。

そのほかの表現 ポイントの Age「年齢」を取り上げる場合，In Japan, salaries generally tend to increase with age, but ...「日本では，給料は年齢とともに上がる傾向にあるが…」のような切り口が考えられるだろう。Skills「スキル」の観点では，Many companies set salaries based on skills rather than their job performance.「仕事の成果ではなくスキルを基準として給料を設定する会社も多い」などと述べて論を展開することが考えられる。

| 一次試験・
リスニング | **Part 1** | 問題編 p.62 ～ 63 | 🔊 ▶MP3 ▶アプリ
▶CD 1 28 ～ 41 |

No.1 - 解答 ①

スクリプト
☆: Hi, Vince. Nice day for a walk, huh?

★: Yeah, it is. Actually, I'm on my way to work.

☆: I thought you drove to work. Is something wrong with your car?

★: No, I've just been putting on a bit of weight recently.

☆: I guess you have to get up pretty early now, though.

★: I don't mind that. And I feel a lot healthier.

☆: Great! And I bet walking is easier on your wallet, too.

★: Definitely! I'm planning to use the gas savings to buy a new bike.

Question: What do we learn about Vince?

全文訳
☆: こんにちは，ヴィンス。散歩日和ね。

★: そうだね。実は今仕事に向かっているんだ。

☆: 車で通勤していると思っていたわ。車に何か問題があるの？

★: いや，最近ちょっと太り気味なだけだよ。

☆: でも，今はかなり早く起きなければならないよね。

★: それは構わないんだ。それに体調がずっと良くなった気がするんだ。

☆: いいわね！　それに歩くのはきっと財布にもやさしいものね。

★: そうなんだよ！　浮いたガソリン代は新しい自転車を買うのに使うつもりだ。

質問：ヴィンスについて分かることは何か。

選択肢の訳
1 彼はもう車で通勤していない。

2 彼の車は修理中である。

3 彼はガソリンを買う余裕がない。

4 彼の新しい自転車が盗まれた。

解説
設問では，発言や話の展開を理解して，「つまりどういうことか」が問われやすい。最初の方の for a walk と I'm on my way to work から，男性は歩いて職場に向かっている。女性の「車通勤だと思っていた」や，walking is easier ... から，男性は車通勤をやめて歩くことにしたと判断して，**1** が正解。I thought ～「～だと思った」は実際［今］はそうではないことを示す表現。

No.2 - 解答 ③

スクリプト
☆: Fernando, how are you getting along with your dorm roommate?

★: Oh, he's all right, Mom, I guess. He's pretty tidy, but he's not very communicative. I never know what's on his mind.

☆: Do you ever do things together?

66

★ : Almost never. I spend more time with the other guys on my floor. They're a little crazy, but they're fun.

☆ : Well, I'm glad you're enjoying yourself, but don't forget to spend enough time on your studies.

Question: What does Fernando suggest about his roommate?

全文訳 ☆ : フェルナンド，寮のルームメートとはうまくいっているの？

★ : うん，母さん，彼は大丈夫だよ，たぶん。彼は結構きれい好きなんだけど，あまりコミュニケーションを取ってくれないんだ。何を考えているのか，さっぱり分からないんだよ。

☆ : 何か一緒にすることはないの？

★ : ほとんどない。同じ階のほかのやつらと過ごすことの方が多い。彼らはちょっとクレイジーだけど，楽しいからね。

☆ : そう，あなたが楽しんでいるのはうれしいけど，勉強に十分時間を割くことを忘れないでね。

質問：フェルナンドはルームメートについて何と言っているか。

選択肢の訳 1　彼は寮を出たいと思っている。

2　彼はパーティーを開くのが好きだ。

3　彼はあまり心を開かない。

4　彼はとても散らかす。

解説 息子と母親の会話で，話題は息子の寮（dorm）のルームメート。He's pretty tidy, but he's not very communicative. の部分を言い換えた **3** が正解。「communicative ではない」ことの説明となる I never know what's on his mind. の部分も参考になる。but 以下に話者が伝えたい内容がくることを意識して聞こう。

No.3 –解答 ④ ....

スクリプト ☆ : How are things going, Matt?

★ : Not so good. I was supposed to have a job interview yesterday, but all the trains were stopped due to an accident, so I couldn't make it.

☆ : But they'll give you another chance, won't they?

★ : No. I called the manager as soon as I got home. He said they'd already seen enough people. Looks like I'm out of luck.

☆ : That's awful.

★ : Yeah, well, I guess they have a lot of good candidates to choose from.

Question: Why did Matt not get the job?

全文訳 ☆ : 調子はどう，マット？

★ : あんまり。昨日は仕事の面接を受けるはずだったんだけど，事故で列車

が全部運休してしまって，行けなかったんだ。

☆： でも，もう一回チャンスをくれるでしょう？

★： いや。帰宅してすぐにマネージャーに電話をかけたんだ。もう十分な数の人を面接したと言っていた。僕は運がないみたいだ。

☆： それはひどいわ。

★： うん，まあ，選べるほど良い候補者がたくさんいるんだろうね。

質問：マットはなぜその仕事を得なかったのか。

選択肢の訳　**1** ほかの候補者たちの方が適任だった。

2 彼は昨日，マネージャーに電話するのを忘れた。

3 マネージャーが彼を気に入らなかった。

4 彼は面接を受け損ねた。

解説　男性は最初の発言で，昨日面接を受けられなかった理由を but 以下で説明している。can't make it は「出席［参加］できない，（約束の時間に）間に合わない」などの意味で，これを正解 **4** では miss「逃す」を使って表している。was [were] supposed to *do*「～するはずだった」は，実際はできなかったことを示す表現。マットが適任か適任でないかは話題にないので **1** は不適。

No.**4** – 解答 ④

スクリプト ☆： Professor Cranfield, can I ask you something?

★： Sure, Lucinda.

☆： It's about your intensive Spanish writing course. I feel like I'm already busy with my other classes. Doing the writing course might be too much.

★： I understand. I think you certainly have the ability, but I don't want to push you. It's not a mandatory course, but future employers would be impressed if you passed it.

☆： Thanks for your advice. I'll think it over a little more.

Question: What does the man imply about the writing course?

全文訳 ☆： クランフィールド教授，お尋ねしてもいいですか？

★： いいですよ，ルシンダ。

☆： 教授のスペイン語ライティング集中講座についてなんですが。私はほかの授業ですでに忙しいと思っていまして。ライティングの講座を受けるのは荷が重いかもしれません。

★： なるほど。私はあなたには確実にその能力があると思いますが，無理をさせたくはありません。必修の講座ではないですが，その単位を取れば，あなたの将来の雇用主も感心するでしょうね。

☆： アドバイスをありがとうございます。もう少し考えてみます。

質問：男性はライティング講座について何をほのめかしているか。

68

選択肢の訳 **1** 女性は卒業するのにその単位を取る必要がある。

2 それは女性の目標に合わない。

3 それは女性には難易度が高過ぎる。

4 その単位を取ることは女性が仕事を見つけるのに役立つかもしれない。

解説 教授と学生の会話で，話題はライティング講座。女性は I feel like ... の発言から受講に前向きではない様子。これに対する教授のアドバイスの future employers would be impressed ... から，**4** が正解。future employers は女性の将来の雇用主のことで，つまり就職に有利だという趣旨。

No.**5** – 解答 ②

スクリプト ★： Amy, I heard you're looking for a part-time job.

☆： I'm thinking about working at a restaurant as a server. I could use the money to help pay for school fees.

★： Well, I hope you like standing for long periods of time.

☆： I would get breaks, you know. I doubt it would be that bad.

★： Well, I think you should buy some comfortable shoes, just in case.

☆： I need to get the job first.

Question: What does the man imply?

全文訳 ★： エイミー，君がアルバイトを探しているって聞いたんだけど。

☆： 接客係としてレストランで働くことを考えているの。そのお金を学費の足しにできるわ。

★： そう，長時間立っているのが好きならいいけど。

☆： もちろん休憩はあるわよ。そんな悪くないと思うけど。

★： まあ，履き心地のいい靴を買っておくべきだと思うけどね，念のため。

☆： まずは仕事を得ないとね。

質問：男性は何をほのめかしているか。

選択肢の訳 **1** 女性は学校を休学すべきだ。

2 接客係として働くことは体力的にきつい。

3 飲食店の店員はあまり稼げない。

4 学生はアルバイトをするべきではない。

解説 アルバイトでレストランでの接客係をすることを検討している女性に対し，男性は，I hope you like standing for long periods of time の部分で長時間の立ち仕事を心配している。これを physically demanding と表した **2** が正解。最後の「履き心地のいい靴を買うべき」もヒントになる。男性は女性のアルバイトに賛成している様子ではないが，学生アルバイト自体を批判しているわけではないので **4** は不適。

22年度第1回 リスニング

No.6 – 解答 ①

スクリプト ☆： We still need to buy a present for Carla and Antonio's wedding. Have you checked out the gift registry yet?

★： Yes, but the only things left on the list are really expensive items, like the silver dining set.

☆： I warned you that if we didn't choose something quickly, the affordable stuff would all be gone.

★： Sorry. You were right. What should we do? Get them something cheaper that's not on the list?

☆： No. I'd rather not take any chances. We don't want to give them something they might not want.

Question: What will these people probably do?

全文訳 ☆： まだカーラとアントニオの結婚式の贈り物を買わないといけないわ。ギフト登録リストはもう確認した？

★： うん，でもリストであと残っているのはとても高価な物ばかりだよ，銀食器セットとか。

☆： 早く何かを選ばないと，手頃な物は全部なくなるってあなたに言ったわよね。

★： ごめん。君が正しかったよ。どうしたらいい？　リストにない，何か安めの物を買う？

☆： いいえ。できれば安全第一でいきたいわ。彼らが欲しくないかもしれない物をあげたくないもの。

質問：この人たちはおそらく何をするか。

選択肢の訳 **1**　リストから選んで贈り物を買う。
2　結婚式の招待を断る。
3　カーラとアントニオと話す。
4　銀食器セットを返品する。

解説 話題は友人の結婚式の贈り物。「リストに残っているのは高価な物だけ」「新郎新婦が欲しくない物をあげたくない」などの内容から，gift registry のリストには新郎新婦が欲しい物が載っていると推測できる。「リストにないものを買う？」という提案に女性は反対しているので，**1** が適切。not take any chances は「運任せにしない，安全第一でいく」の意味で，ここでは新郎新婦が欲しいもの＝リストにあるものを買うということ。

No.7 – 解答 ①

スクリプト ☆： Would you mind picking up some takeout on your way home?

★： No problem. How about burgers?

☆： Too greasy. I was thinking about that Korean restaurant we went

70

to last week.

★： That's not exactly on my way home, and it's a little pricey.

☆： I know, but the servings are huge. We'd have enough for lunch tomorrow, too. Korean food is just as good the next day.

★： All right. They're usually pretty quick with orders, so I should be home by around six.

Question: What is one reason the woman suggests the Korean restaurant?

全文訳 ☆： 帰る途中で何か持ち帰りの料理を買ってきてくれない？

★： いいよ。ハンバーガーでいい？

☆： 脂っこ過ぎるわ。先週行った韓国料理店を考えていたんだけど。

★： それは帰り道からはちょっと外れるし，少し値段も高いよ。

☆： 分かってるわ，でも量が多いでしょ。明日の昼食にも十分あるわ。韓国料理は 1 日経っても味は落ちないし。

★： 分かったよ。あの店はたいていすぐに注文を持ってきてくれるから，6時ごろには帰れると思う。

質問： 女性が韓国料理店を勧める理由の 1 つは何か。

選択肢の訳 1　量が多い。

2　自宅から車で近い。

3　ほかの飲食店よりも安い。

4　評判が良い。

解説 女性は冒頭で男性に，帰宅途中に食べ物を買ってきてくれるよう頼んでいる。burgers は Too greasy. と言って却下し，韓国料理店を提案する。その理由として the servings are huge と言っているので **1** が正解。serving と portion はいずれも「（料理の）1 人分の量」の意味。続く発言 We'd have enough for lunch tomorrow, ... もヒントになる。

No.**8** − 解答 **3**

スクリプト ☆： We should start planning our vacation for this year.

★： How about escaping the cold weather and going somewhere tropical with a nice beach?

☆： I was hoping we could go skiing.

★： Well, what did we do on our last vacation?

☆： We went camping. You caught that giant fish at the lake, remember?

★： Oh, right. And you wanted to go sightseeing in town, but the kids and I outvoted you.

☆： That's right.

★： OK. Let's do what you want this time. I'll tell the kids we're headed for the mountains.

Question: What are these people going to do for their vacation?

全文訳 ☆： 今年の休暇の予定を立て始めるべきだわ。

★： 寒い天気を逃れて，素敵なビーチのあるどこか暑い所に行くのはどう？

☆： 私はスキーに行けたらと思っていたんだけど。

★： ええと，この前の休暇は何をしたっけ？

☆： キャンプに行ったわ。あなたは湖であの巨大な魚を釣ったわ，覚えてない？

★： ああ，そうだった。それで君は町の観光をしたかったんだけど，僕と子供たちが多数決で勝ったんだ。

☆： そうよ。

★： ああ，分かった。今回は君のしたいことをしよう。子供たちには山に行くことを伝えるよ。

質問： この人たちは休暇に何をするか。

選択肢の訳 **1** ハイキングをして過ごす。

2 湖へ釣りに行く。

3 スキー旅行に行く。

4 観光に行く。

解説 男女が休暇の計画をしている。男性の希望はビーチのある南国で，女性はスキー。前回の休暇はキャンプで，女性は町の観光をしたかったが子供たちと男性の意見が通った。outvote は「（人より）多数の票を得て勝つ」の意味。男性の Let's do what you want this time. から，今回の休暇は女性の希望を通し，スキーに行くと考えられる。we're headed for the mountains は山スキーを暗示。

No.9 – 解答 ②

スクリプト ☆： Hey, Kenneth. I was looking at the latest post on our company's blog. The one about the release of our new earphones. The release date is wrong. It should be May 15th, not the 5th as stated in the post.

★： Really? That post was added by Jason last night.

☆： Well, we need to take care of it immediately so we don't mislead our customers. Ask Jason to do that right away.

★： I'm afraid he has the day off today. I'll handle it instead.

☆： Thanks.

Question: What does the woman say about the company's blog?

全文訳 ☆： ねえ，ケネス。会社のブログの最新の投稿を見ていたんだけど。あの新製品のイヤホンの発売についてのね。発売日が間違っているわ。投稿に書かれている 5 月 5 日ではなく，5 月 15 日のはずよ。

★： 本当ですか。あの記事はジェイソンが昨夜投稿しました。

72

☆： そうなの，顧客に間違った情報を与えて判断を誤らせないように，すぐに対処しないと。ジェイソンにすぐにやってもらうように頼んで。

★： あいにく彼は今日休みです。僕が代わりにやりましょう。

☆： ありがとう。

質問：女性は会社のブログについて何と言っているか。

選択肢の訳
1 一部の顧客がそれについて苦情を言った。
2 投稿の１つを修正しなければならない。
3 ケネスはその最新の投稿を編集すべきではない。
4 それはもっと頻繁に更新されるべきだ。

解説 会社員同士の会話。女性は冒頭で男性（ケネス）に，会社のブログの最新の投稿で製品の発売日が間違っていると指摘する。投稿したのはジェイソンだと分かると Ask Jason to do that right away. と指示していることから，**2** が正解。ジェイソンは不在で投稿を編集するのはケネスなので **3** は不適。選択肢の Kenneth を見て，Kenneth が話者なのか会話中に出てくる人物なのかを意識しながら聞くとよい。

No.10 解答 ④

スクリプト ☆： Excuse me, sir. Has anyone turned in a train pass today?

★： I'm afraid not. Have you lost yours?

☆： Yeah. When I used mine this morning, I was certain I put it back in my wallet, but I guess I didn't.

★： I can give you the form to purchase another one.

☆： Looks like I have no choice. It makes me so frustrated, though. I had just put $50 on it. Now, I've lost it all.

★： I'm sorry. Here's the form. It should only take a couple of minutes to fill out.

☆： Thanks. I'll do that now.

Question: Why is the woman upset?

全文訳 ☆： すみません。今日，列車の定期券を届け出た人はいませんでしたか？

★： 残念ながらいないようです。ご自分のをなくされましたか。

☆： ええ。今朝使ったときには確かに財布に戻したと思ったのだけど，そうしなかったようです。

★： 新しい定期券を購入する用紙をお渡しできますが。

☆： 選択の余地はなさそうですね。でも本当にいらいらします。50 ドルチャージしたばかりだったので。今では全部失ってしまいました。

★： お気の毒です。これが用紙です。数分で記入できると思います。

☆： ありがとう。今やります。

質問：女性はなぜいらいらしているか。

選択肢の訳
1 彼女の財布が見つからない。

73

2 彼女の列車の定期券の有効期限が切れた。

3 彼女は列車に乗り遅れた。

4 彼女はお金を無駄にした。

解説 序盤のやりとりから，女性は列車の定期券を紛失し，届けられていないか駅係員に尋ねている場面だと分かる。女性は後半で It makes me so frustrated（＝質問文の upset）と言い，その理由として「50 ドルチャージしたばかりだった」と続くので **4** が正解。

No.**11** 解答 ③ ･･････････････････････････････ 正答率 ★**75%以上**

スクリプト ★：Michelle, I'm sorry I couldn't make it to the piano concert last Sunday.

☆：No problem. I sold your ticket to Jasmine, so it wasn't wasted.

★：I'm relieved to hear that. Did you enjoy the concert?

☆：Well, the pianist was superb. Unfortunately, we were bothered by another audience member, though.

★：What happened?

☆：He was continuously whispering to the person next to him and playing with his smartphone. It was hard to concentrate.

★：Oh, that's a shame.

Question: What was the woman's problem?

全文訳 ★：ミシェル，先週の日曜日のピアノのコンサートに行けなくてごめんね。

☆：いいのよ。あなたのチケットはジャスミンに売ったから，無駄にはならなかったわ。

★：それを聞いてほっとしたよ。コンサートは楽しかった？

☆：そうね，ピアニストは素晴らしかった。でも，残念ながらほかのお客さんに悩まされたわ。

★：何があったの？

☆：彼はずっと隣の人にひそひそと話していて，スマートフォンをいじっていたの。集中しにくかったわ。

★：ああ，それは残念だね。

質問：女性の問題は何だったか。

選択肢の訳 **1** 彼女はピアニストの演奏が気に入らなかった。

2 彼女はコンサートに遅れて到着した。

3 彼女はコンサートに集中できなかった。

4 彼女はチケットを見つけることができなかった。

解説 先に選択肢を見ると，ピアノのコンサートが話題で，どれもネガティブな内容なので，何かしら問題があったことが予測できる。女性は Unfortunately, ... でほかの客に悩まされたと言い，具体的に「ひそひそと話してスマートフォンをいじっていたから（演奏を聴くのに）集中

74

しにくかった」と説明する。この concentrate を focus on と言い換えた **3** が正解。

No.12 解答 ②

(スクリプト) ☆： Hello, Jenny Williams speaking.

★： Hello. I'm calling about a package I'm supposed to deliver to your house.

☆： Oh, I see. Is there something wrong?

★： When you selected your delivery option online, you asked us to use the delivery box.

☆： Yes, I won't be home until seven tonight.

★： Unfortunately, the package won't fit in the box. Could I leave it in another location instead?

☆： Sure. If you can take it around to the side of the house, there's a bicycle shelter. You can leave it there.

Question: What does the man ask the woman to do?

(全文訳) ☆： もしもし，ジェニー・ウィリアムズです。

★： もしもし，お客さまの家にお届けすることになっている小包についてお電話しました。

☆： ああ，なるほど。何か問題が？

★： お客さまが配達方法をオンラインで選択されたとき，配達ボックスを使うことを指示されました。

☆： そうです，今夜は7時まで家に帰らないので。

★： あいにく小包がボックスに入りません。代わりに別の場所に置いておいてもいいでしょうか？

☆： いいですよ。家の横に持って回ってもらえれば，そこに自転車置き場があるわ。そこに置いてくれていいですよ。

質問：男性は女性に何をするよう頼んでいるか。

(選択肢の訳) **1** 夜に彼に折り返し電話をする。

2 彼に新しい配達指示を出す。

3 オンラインで彼女の配達方法を変更する。

4 彼女が何時に帰宅するかを彼に伝える。

(解説) Hello, 人名＋speaking. で始まる客とスタッフの電話の会話。男性配達人は女性の家に荷物を届けに来たが，女性がオンラインで指定した置き場所である delivery box に入らないと説明し，Could I leave it in another location instead? と尋ねる。別の置き場所の指示（instructions）を求めていると考えて，**2** が正解。

75

| 一次試験・
リスニング | **Part2** | 問題編 p.64 ～ 65 | 🔊 | ▶MP3 ▶アプリ
▶CD 1 42 ～ 48 |

A

スクリプト **International Rivers**

Many of the world's rivers are not contained within the borders of a single country. Because of the importance of water, international laws about how neighboring countries share these rivers are essential. Typically, all countries have equal rights to use a river that flows through their lands. Also, all countries are legally forbidden from doing anything to a river that would considerably decrease its flow of water into other countries.

However, sharing a river is not always simple. For example, the Nile River runs through a number of countries, including Ethiopia and Egypt. Ethiopia has requested international loans to build a dam on its section of the river to generate electricity. However, Egypt has used its political influence to block the loans, complaining that a dam would reduce the Nile's water flow into Egypt. At the same time, Ethiopia points out that Egypt currently uses the river for power generation, so it is unfair if Ethiopia cannot.

Questions

No.13 What is one thing the speaker says about rivers?

No.14 Why is the Nile River discussed?

全文訳 **国際河川**

　世界の河川の多くは，１つの国の境界内に収まらない。水の重要性から，近隣諸国がそういった河川をどのように共有するかについての国際法が不可欠である。通常，全ての国に自国を流れる河川を利用する平等な権利がある。また，全ての国は，他国への水の流れを大幅に減少させるようなことを河川に対して行うことを法律で禁じられている。

　しかし，１つの河川を共有することは必ずしも単純ではない。例えば，ナイル川はエチオピアとエジプトを含め，いくつかの国を流れている。エチオピアは，発電のためにナイル川の自国の部分にダムを建設するための国際融資を求めた。しかしエジプトは，ダムはエジプトに流れるナイル川の水量を減らすと訴え，その融資を阻止しようと政治的影響力を行使している。一方でエチオピアは，エジプトは現在発電のためにナイル川を利用していることから，エチオピアが利用できないのは不公平だ，と指摘している。

No.13 解答 ③

質問の訳　話者が河川について言うことの１つは何か。

選択肢の訳　**1**　多くの河川において水位が下がっている。

　　2　河川を保護するための法律を厳しくする必要がある。

　　3　河川を共有する国々は通常，同じ使用権を持っている。

76

4 河川は国境を保護するのを困難にすることが多い。

解説 Typically, all countries have equal rights to use a river ... their lands. から，**3** が正解。typically を **3** では usually に，equal rights to use を the same usage rights に言い換えている。河川や国境を保護する話はないので **2** と **4** は不適。

No.14 解答

質問の訳 ナイル川について話されているのはなぜか。
選択肢の訳
1 国境問題の解決策を提案するため。
2 貧しい国々が電力を得るために河川を必要としていることを示唆するため。
3 ダムはしばしばコストがかかり過ぎることを示すため。
4 河川の使用権がいかに複雑になり得るかを示すため。

解説 設問はパッセージの目的を問うもの。後半（However, ...）で「1つの河川を共有することは必ずしも単純ではない」と述べた後，いかに複雑かの説明が続くので，**4** が正解。not always は「必ずしも～ではない」で，**4** では simple の反意語 complicated「複雑な」を用いている。

B

スクリプト **Theriac**

For thousands of years, people believed that a substance known as theriac was a wonder drug. According to legend, it was created by an ancient king who lived in fear of being poisoned. He was said to have taken theriac daily to protect himself from all forms of poison. The use of theriac gradually spread around the ancient world, and people began to believe that it was also effective against all kinds of illnesses. Making it, however, required time and effort, as some theriac recipes contained over a hundred ingredients, some of which came from poisonous snakes.

By the fifteenth century, there were regulations in many places about how theriac could be manufactured, and in some cities, such as Venice, it had to be made in a public ceremony. Though the scientific community now believes that theriac is ineffective, the regulations on the manufacture of theriac marked an important milestone in the development of modern medicine.

Questions
No.15 What is one thing that we learn about theriac?
No.16 What is one thing the speaker says about theriac in Venice?

全文訳 **テリアック**

何千年もの間，人々はテリアックとして知られる物質を奇跡の薬だと思っていた。伝説によると，この薬は毒殺を恐れて生きていた古代の王によって作られたという。彼は，あらゆる形の毒から身を守るために毎日テリアックを飲んでいたと言われている。テリ

アックの使用は徐々に古代世界に広がり，それがあらゆる病にも効くと人々が信じ始めた。しかし，それを作るには時間と手間がかかった。というのも，テリアックのレシピには100種を超える成分を含むものもあり，その中には毒ヘビから採取したものもあったからだ。

15世紀には，各地でテリアックの製造方法に関する規制ができ，ベネチアなど一部の都市では，公の儀式で製造されなければならなかった。現在，科学界ではテリアックは効果がないと考えられているが，テリアックの製造に関する規制は，現代医学の発展における重要な節目となった。

No.15 解答

質問の訳 テリアックについて分かることの1つは何か。
選択肢の訳
1 毒として使うことができた。
2 ヘビで実験された。
3 作るのが困難だった。
4 初の医薬品だった。

解説 冒頭の a substance known as theriac was a wonder drug に続き，have taken theriac daily や effective against all kinds of illnesses などから，テリアックは「薬」だと理解しよう。Making it, however, required time and effort, ... から，作るのが難しいと分かるので，**3** が正解。パッセージ中の語 drug，poison，snakes を含む誤答に惑わされないように。

No.16 解答 4

質問の訳 話者がベネチアのテリアックについて言うことの1つは何か。
選択肢の訳
1 作るのに何日もかかった。
2 毎日少量しか作れなかった。
3 製造の規制が非常に甘かった。
4 そこの人々は，それが作られるのを見ることができた。

解説 ベネチアについて，in some cities, such as Venice, it had to be made in a public ceremony と言っている。it はテリアックのこと。public は「公の（場での）」と捉え，公の場で製造しなければならなかった＝ベネチアの人々は作られるのを見ることができたと考えて，**4** が正解。

C

  Spirit Bears

Found only in parts of Canada, spirit bears are black bears that are born with white fur due to a rare gene. Scientists estimate there may be as few as a hundred of these beautiful animals in the wild. For years, native peoples did their best to prevent the bears' existence from becoming known to the outside world. Because the bears' fur is so unusual, native peoples feared it would become a great prize for hunters and collectors.

　Spirit bears' bright fur also provides them with a unique advantage when hunting salmon. Unlike the fur of ordinary black bears, spirit bears' fur is difficult for fish to see, so the fish are less able to avoid the bears. Unfortunately, however, spirit bear numbers may decrease even further. Recent research has revealed the gene that results in spirit bears' white fur is rarer than once thought. Additionally, many spirit bears live outside the areas where they are protected.

Questions
No.17 What does the speaker say about native peoples?
No.18 What advantage do spirit bears have over ordinary black bears?

全文訳 シロアメリカグマ（精霊の熊）

　カナダの一部でしか見られないシロアメリカグマは，珍しい遺伝子のために生まれつき毛が白いクロクマである。科学者たちは，この美しい動物は野生では100頭ほどしかいないかもしれないと推定している。何年もの間，先住民たちはこのクマの存在を外部に知られないよう最善を尽くした。このクマの毛は非常に珍しいため，先住民たちは猟師や収集家の格好の獲物になることを恐れたのだ。

　シロアメリカグマの鮮やかな毛は，サケを捕る際に彼らに独自の強みも与える。通常のクロクマの毛と違い，シロアメリカグマの毛は魚には見えにくいため，魚はこのクマを避けにくいのだ。しかし残念なことに，シロアメリカグマの数はさらに減少する可能性がある。最近の研究により，シロアメリカグマの白い毛をつくる遺伝子は，かつて考えられていたよりも希少であることが明らかになったのだ。さらに，多くのシロアメリカグマは，彼らが保護されている地域の外に生息している。

No.17 解答 ②

質問の訳 話者は先住民について何と言っているか。
選択肢の訳
1　彼らは黒い毛を持つシロアメリカグマしか狩らなかった。
2　彼らはシロアメリカグマを秘密にしておこうとした。
3　彼らはシロアメリカグマを危険だと思った。
4　彼らはシロアメリカグマが自分たちを守ってくれると信じていた。

解説 For years, native peoples ... の部分から，**2**が正解。「外部に知られないようにする」を「秘密にする」と表している。先住民はシロアメリカグマを猟師から守ろうとしたので**1**は不適。spirit bear という名前からは分かりにくいが，このクマは生まれつき白い（born with white fur）ことから，spirit bears with black fur も不適。

No.18 解答

質問の訳 シロアメリカグマは通常のクロクマに比べてどんな強みがあるか。
選択肢の訳
1　シロアメリカグマの方が容易に餌を捕まえる。
2　シロアメリカグマの方が日光に強い。

3　シロアメリカグマの方が猟師に見つかりにくい。
4　シロアメリカグマの生息地は全てよく保護されている。

 シロアメリカグマの advantage「利点，強み」については Spirit bears' bright fur also provides them with a unique advantage 以降にある。通常のクロクマと比較した Unlike the fur of ordinary black bears, ... から，「魚はシロアメリカグマを避けにくい」=「シロアメリカグマは餌を捕まえやすい」と考えて，**1** が適切。対比を表す unlike「～とは違って」の使われ方を確認しよう。

D

（スクリプト） **Distributed Generation**

　In many parts of the United States, the electric power industry has been shifting away from the traditional system of centralized generation to a newer system known as distributed generation. With centralized generation, electricity is generated in one central location and then delivered to homes and businesses. Distributed generation is a network of smaller energy sources, such as solar panels or wind turbines, that produce electricity close to where it is needed. This can make the distributed-generation system more cost-effective.

　Distributed generation has some disadvantages, however. The required infrastructure takes up space in communities, and residents generally consider it unattractive. In fact, homes close to large solar-energy facilities often sell for less than homes that are farther away. In addition, some distributed-generation systems require water to run, which is a limitation in areas that experience water shortages.

Questions
No.19 What is true about distributed-generation systems?
No.20 What is one downside of distributed generation?

（全文訳）　**分散型発電**

　アメリカ合衆国の多くの地域で，電力業界は従来の集中型発電システムから分散型発電と呼ばれる新しいシステムに移行している。集中型発電では，電力は1カ所の中心的場所で生成され，家庭や企業に供給される。分散型発電は，例えばソーラーパネルや風力タービンのような，電力が必要な場所の近くで発電する，より小さなエネルギー源のネットワークである。これにより，分散型発電システムの費用対効果を高めることができる。

　しかし，分散型発電には幾つかの欠点がある。発電に必要な設備が地域社会の場所を取り，住民には概して見映えが悪いように映る。実際，大規模な太陽光発電施設付近の住宅は，遠方の住宅よりも安く売られる場合が多い。さらに，分散型発電システムの中には運用するのに水を必要とするものもあり，水不足に見舞われる地域では限界がある。

No.19 解答 1

質問の訳 分散型発電システムについて何が正しいか。
選択肢の訳
1 電力を使用する場所付近で発電する。
2 小規模事業者に好まれる。
3 太陽エネルギーを使用しない。
4 維持費が非常に高い。

解説 分散型発電に関する説明文で，前半では集中型発電と比較して概要と利点が述べられている。Distributed generation is a network of ... that produce electricity close to where it is needed. の部分から，**1**が正解。**1**の power は electricity のことで，本文の close to「～に近い」を near と表している。

No.20 解答 3

質問の訳 分散型発電の欠点の1つは何か。
選択肢の訳
1 政府はおおむねその開発に反対している。
2 エネルギー会社は通常，それから利益を得ることはない。
3 資産価値に悪影響を与える可能性がある。
4 しばしば地域の水源を汚染する。

解説 欠点（disadvantage(s) = downside）は後半の however 以下で述べられる。In fact の後には重要な内容が続くのでしっかりと聞こう。「大規模な太陽光発電施設付近の住宅は，遠方の住宅よりも安く売られる場合が多い」を「資産価値（property values）に悪影響を与え得る」と抽象的に表した**3**が正解。

スクリプト **What Zoos Can't Do**

In recent decades, zoos have been essential to efforts to save endangered animals. Several species of frogs, birds, and turtles have been saved from extinction by conservation programs that breed endangered animals in the safe environment of zoos. Unfortunately, certain species, such as tarsiers, which are animals that look like tiny monkeys, and great white sharks, cannot survive in captivity. These animals usually die quickly after being captured, making it impossible to breed them.

For this reason, the survival of tarsiers and great white sharks depends on the conservation of their natural environments. Though many of their habitats are already legally protected, the current laws are often ignored. Governments must try harder to stop the illegal destruction of the forests where tarsiers live and breed. They must also reduce illegal fishing activities that threaten great white sharks.

Questions

No.21 Why are zoos unable to breed some endangered animals?

No.22 What does the speaker say about saving tarsiers and great white sharks?

全文訳　**動物園にできないこと**

　ここ数十年，動物園は，絶滅の危機にひんした動物を救う取り組みに不可欠となっている。動物園という安全な環境で絶滅の危機にひんした動物を繁殖させる保護プログラムにより，カエル，鳥，カメなどの幾つかの種が絶滅の危機から救われた。しかし残念ながら，小猿のような見た目の動物であるメガネザルやホホジロザメなどの特定の種は，捕獲されると生き延びることができない。こういった動物は通常，捕獲直後に死んでしまうため，繁殖させることができないのだ。

　この理由から，メガネザルやホホジロザメの生存は，自然環境の保全にかかっている。すでに生息地の多くが法的に保護されているものの，現在の法律は無視されることが多い。各国政府は，メガネザルが生息・繁殖する森林の違法な破壊を阻止するためにもっと努力しなければならない。また，政府はホホジロザメを脅かす違法な漁業を減らさなければならない。

No.**21** 解答　④

質問の訳　なぜ動物園は一部の絶滅の危機にひんした動物を繁殖させることができないのか。

選択肢の訳　**1**　世話にお金がかかり過ぎる。
　　2　捕獲するのが難し過ぎる。
　　3　深刻な病気にかかる。
　　4　捕獲後長く生きることがめったにない。

解説　メガネザルやホホジロザメなどの特定の種（＝一部の絶滅の危機にひんした動物）について，These animals usually die quickly after being captured, making it impossible to breed them. と言っている。「捕獲直後に死ぬ」を「捕獲後長く生きられない」と表した **4** が適切。

No.**22** 解答　②

質問の訳　話者はメガネザルとホホジロザメを救うことについて何と言っているか。

選択肢の訳　**1**　動物園はそれらの繁殖方法を学ぶ必要がある。
　　2　政府は確実に法律が守られるようにしなければならない。
　　3　それらを新しい生息地に移動させなければならない。
　　4　それらを野生で保護することは不可能である。

解説　後半で「現在の法律は無視されることが多い」と述べた後，メガネザルとホホジロザメ保護のために政府がしなければならないこととして，森林の違法な破壊の阻止，違法な漁業を減らすことに言及している。よって，**2** が正解。**4** は「すでに生息地の多くが法的に保護されている」と合わない。

82

スクリプト **Written in Stone**

Petroglyphs are ancient drawings or carvings on rock surfaces. For researchers in the Americas, they are an important source of information about the Native Americans who lived there before the arrival of Europeans. Some of the most famous petroglyphs are those at Castle Rock Pueblo in Colorado. These images were not drawn in the style typical of the area, but in a way that was common in another settlement hundreds of kilometers away. There are also drawings of human conflict. This suggests that there may have been contact, and likely fighting, between these two communities.

Another interesting feature of the carvings is their use of light. On the longest and shortest days of the year, the carvings create specific patterns of light and shadow. This has led researchers to conclude that they were used as a type of solar calendar.

Questions

No.23 What is one thing we learn about the Castle Rock Pueblo petroglyphs?

No.24 How do researchers think the Castle Rock Pueblo petroglyphs were used?

全文訳 岩石に刻まれたもの

ペトログリフとは，岩面に刻まれた古代の線画や彫刻のことである。アメリカ大陸の研究者たちにとって，それは，ヨーロッパ人の到来以前にそこに住んでいたアメリカ先住民に関する重要な情報源である。最も有名なペトログリフとして，コロラド州のキャッスル・ロック・プエブロのものがある。その画は，その地域に典型的なスタイルではなく，何百キロも離れた別の集落でよく見られる方法で描かれた。人間同士の争いを描いた線画もある。これは，この2つのコミュニティーの間に接触，おそらく戦いがあった可能性を示唆している。

彫刻のもう1つの興味深い特徴は，太陽光の使い方である。1年で最も日が長い日と最も日が短い日に，彫刻が光と影の特定の模様を作り出す。このことから，研究者たちは，その彫刻は一種の太陽暦として使用されていたと結論付けた。

No.23 解答

質問の訳 キャッスル・ロック・プエブロのペトログリフについて分かることの1つは何か。

選択肢の訳　1　典型的なものよりも数が多い。
　　　　　　　2　遠い地域のものと似ている。
　　　　　　　3　その地域で最大である。
　　　　　　　4　ヨーロッパ人の姿が含まれている。

解説 These images were not drawn in the style typical of the area, but in a way that was common in another settlement hundreds of kilometers away. の文から，**2** が正解。those は petroglyphs のことで，「何百キロも離れた別の集落」を a distant area と表している。not A but B「A ではなく B」を含む長い 1 文だが，not の後に続けて but が聞こえたらその後をしっかりと聞くとよい。

No.24 解答

質問の訳 キャッスル・ロック・プエブロのペトログリフはどのように使用されたと研究者たちは考えているか。

選択肢の訳
1 1年の特定の時期を示すため。
2 敵に近づかないように警告するため。
3 別の集落への行き方を示すため。
4 光源を提供するため。

解説 質問は How were the Castle Rock Pueblo petroglyphs used? に do researchers think が挿入された形で，使用目的が問われている。彫刻の特徴（feature）について述べた On the longest and shortest days ... の部分から，**1** が正解。「1年で最も日が長い日と最も日が短い日」を「1年の特定の時期」と表している。

G

スクリプト

You have 10 seconds to read the situation and Question No. 25.

Hi, dear. I'm sorry, I was in a rush this morning and wasn't able to do a few things. Could you take care of them? The living room is a mess. Miranda's toys are all over the place, so could you put them away? Also, Toby's new bird food arrived this morning. I know we usually store it in that box near the kitchen shelves, but when the package was delivered, I left it at the front door. Sorry. It should still be sitting there. And can you change one of the light bulbs in the garage? When I got home last night, I saw that one was flickering.

Now mark your answer on your answer sheet.

全文訳

もしもし，あなた。ごめんなさい，今朝は急いでいてできなかったことが幾つかあるの。それらをお願いできる？　居間が散らかっているの。ミランダのおもちゃがあちこちにあるから片付けてもらえるかしら。あと，トビーの新しい鳥の餌が今朝届いたの。いつも台所の棚の近くのあの箱の中に保管しているのは知っているけど，荷物が届いたときに玄関に置きっぱなしにしちゃったの。ごめんね。まだそこにあるはずよ。それと，ガレー

ジの電球の1つを交換してくれる？　昨夜帰宅したとき，1つチカチカしていたの。

No.25 解答 ③

状況の訳　あなたはオウムのトビーに餌をやりたいと思っているが，その餌が見つからない。携帯電話を見て妻からの音声メッセージに気付く。

質問の訳　あなたはトビーの餌を見つけるのにどこへ行くべきか。

選択肢の訳　**1**　台所へ。　　　　　　　**2**　居間へ。
3　玄関へ。　　　　　　　**4**　ガレージへ。

解説　問題用紙の「状況」から，「トビー（オウム）の餌が見つからない」という状況をつかもう。妻はやり残した用事を順に説明して夫に頼んでいる。トビーの餌について「玄関に置きっぱなしにした」「まだそこにあるはず」と言っているので，**3**が正解。**1**は普段置いている場所なので不適。

H

スクリプト

You have 10 seconds to read the situation and Question No. 26.

Greta Bakken has written in various genres over her long career. I would recommend four books to a first-time reader. First, *The Moon in Budapest* is considered to be a masterpiece of romance, and it has the biggest fan base. *Along That Tree-Lined Road* is a beautifully crafted fantasy novel with a touch of mystery. If you're a travel fan, I recommend you try *Mixed Metaphors*. It's a travel journal documenting her trip to Siberia, with a number of stunning photographs she snapped along the way. Lastly, *Trishaws* is her latest book, and it has been getting great reviews from science fiction enthusiasts.

Now mark your answer on your answer sheet.

全文訳

グレタ・バッケンは長いキャリアの中でさまざまなジャンルの作品を書いてきました。初めて読まれる方にお薦めする本が4冊あります。まず，『ブダペストの月』はロマンスの傑作と考えられていて，最も多くのファン層を持つ作品です。『あの並木道に沿って』は，ちょっとミステリー風の，見事に作り上げられたファンタジー小説です。旅行好きでしたら，『混喩』を読んでみることをお勧めします。本書は彼女のシベリア旅行を記録した旅行記で，道中で彼女が撮った素晴らしい写真の数々が掲載されています。最後に，『人力三輪車』は彼女の最新作で，SFファンから素晴らしい評価を得ています。

No.26 解答 ①

状況の訳　あなたはグレタ・バッケン著の本を読みたいと思っている。彼女の最も人気のある本を読みたい。書店の店員があなたに次のように言う。

質問の訳　あなたはどの本を買うべきか。

選択肢の訳　**1**　『ブダペストの月』

2 『あの並木道に沿って』

3 『混喩』

4 『人力三輪車』

解説 「状況」から，「最も人気のある本」という条件を押さえる。店員がお薦めの本を４冊順番に説明する中で，１冊目の *The Moon in Budapest* について，it has the biggest fan base と言っている。「最も多くのファン層を持っている」＝「最も人気がある」と考えて，**1** が正解。

I

スクリプト

You have 10 seconds to read the situation and Question No. 27.

The company has decided to outsource the personnel department's services to ABC Resource Systems. There will be two main changes. First, we'll be using a new website to handle all scheduling, requests for time off, and complaints. More importantly, time-off requests will now need to be submitted two weeks in advance. These changes will apply at the end of next month, so please submit requests on the website at that time. Until then, please direct all personnel issues to the manager of your department. Thank you for your cooperation.

Now mark your answer on your answer sheet.

全文訳

　我が社は，人事部の業務を ABC リソース・システム社に外部委託することを決定しました。主な変更が２つあります。まず，全てのスケジュール管理，休暇の申請，クレームを処理するのに新しいウェブサイトを使うことになります。さらに重要なことに，休暇申請は今後，２週間前に提出する必要があります。これらの変更は来月末に適用されますので，そのときはウェブサイトで申請書を提出してください。それまでは，人事に関することは全て所属部署の部長に伝えてください。ご協力をお願いいたします。

No.27 解答 ①

状況の訳 あなたの会社の社長が事務手続きの変更について発表している。あなたは来週，休暇を取りたいと思っている。

質問の訳 あなたは何をすべきか。

選択肢の訳 **1** 部長と話す。

2 新しいウェブサイトで申請書を提出する。

3 所属部署の社員たちに E メールを送る。

4 ABC リソース・システム社に連絡する。

解説 「状況」から，「来週休暇を取りたい」ことを押さえる。「主な変更が２つある」と前置きした後，First, ..., More importantly, ... で順に説明される。まず，休暇申請は新しいウェブサイトで行うことが分かるが，

86

続く These changes will apply ... から，その変更は来月末からである。来週休暇を取りたい場合の情報を期待しながら聞き進めると，Until then に続いて「部長に伝えること」と言っている。**1** が正解で，direct「（言葉などを）向ける」を speak to と表している。

(スクリプト)

You have 10 seconds to read the situation and Question No. 28.

The course website is now accessible. On the left side, you'll see the menu. At the top of the menu, there's a news section where I'll post event reminders and assignment due dates. I've already posted a notification about a guest lecture that you can attend for additional credit. You can click on the icon to reserve a seat. Below the news section, there's a link to a page where you can check on your weekly reading assignments. Finally, in the resources section, I put some links that might help you when working on your final research project.

Now mark your answer on your answer sheet.

(全文訳)

このコースのウェブサイトにアクセスできるようになりました。左側には，メニューが表示されます。メニューの上部にはニュース欄があり，そこに私がイベントのリマインダーや課題の提出期限を掲載します。追加の単位のために出席できるゲスト講義に関するお知らせをすでに掲載しました。席を予約するにはアイコンをクリックしてください。ニュース欄の下には，毎週の読書課題を確認できるページへのリンクがあります。最後になりますが，リソース欄に，最終研究プロジェクトに取り組む際に役立ちそうなリンクを幾つか貼りました。

No.28 解答 ④

(状況の訳) あなたの教授はクラスにコースのウェブサイトを見せている。あなたは成績を上げるために追加の単位を取得したいと思っている。

(質問の訳) あなたは何をすべきか。

(選択肢の訳)
1 ウェブサイトを通して追加の研究論文を提出する。
2 追加の読書課題を完了する。
3 クラスのためにオンラインリソースを作成する。
4 ニュース欄から講義に申し込む。

(解説) 「状況」から，教授がウェブサイトの画面を見せながら説明している場面を想像しよう。「追加の単位を取得したい」という条件を押さえる。ニュース欄についての説明の中で，I've already posted a notification about a guest lecture that you can attend for additional credit. と言っており，ゲスト講義に出席すれば追加単位が取得できることが分か

る。よって，正解は **4**。

スクリプト

You have 10 seconds to read the situation and Question No. 29.

Hi, this is Bill. As you know, today's the deadline for your column. How is it coming along? If you've already finished it, please send the column directly to my office e-mail address. If you're likely to finish it by tomorrow morning, send the file to Paula. I'll be out all day tomorrow. However, if you're not likely to make it by tomorrow morning, could you call me on my office phone tonight? I'll be here until eight. Otherwise, you can reach me on my smartphone after eight. If necessary, I can give you another few days to finish it. Thanks.

Now mark your answer on your answer sheet.

全文訳

　もしもし，ビルです。知っての通り，今日はあなたのコラムの締め切り日です。どんな感じですか。すでに書き終えているなら，コラムを直接私のオフィスのEメールアドレスに送ってください。明日の朝までに書き上がりそうな場合は，ポーラにファイルを送ってください。私は明日，一日中外出しますので。でも，明日の朝までに間に合いそうにない場合は，今夜，私のオフィスの電話に連絡してもらえませんか。8時までここにいますので。そうでなければ，8時以降は私のスマートフォンで連絡が取れます。必要なら，書き終えるのにあと数日与えることもできます。では。

No.29 解答 ④

状況の訳　あなたは新聞のライターである。あなたは午後8時30分に帰宅し，編集者からの次のような音声メッセージを聞く。あなたはコラムを書き上げるのにあと2日必要である。

質問の訳　あなたは何をすべきか。

選択肢の訳
1　ファイルをビルに送る。
2　ファイルをポーラに送る。
3　ビルのオフィスの電話に電話する。
4　ビルのスマートフォンに電話する。

解説　「状況」から，「コラムを書き上げるのにあと2日必要」という条件を押さえる。メッセージは編集者＝ビルからで，執筆中のコラムについて，「〜の場合，…してください」と条件別に指示が聞こえてくる。if you're not likely to make it by tomorrow morning, ...「明日の朝までに間に合いそうにない場合…」の部分に一瞬惑わされそうだが，続く Otherwise, ... がポイント。「8時以降なのでビルのスマートフォンに連絡する」→「あと数日待ってもらえるかも」と理解して，**4** が正解。

二次試験・面接 | **問題カード A 日程** | 問題編 p.68～69 | ▶MP3 ▶アプリ ▶CD 4 **10**～**14**

解答例 **One day, a mayor was having a meeting.** The meeting was about the decreasing number of tourists. This was a problem, and the mayor asked if her staff members had any ideas. They all looked worried. That weekend, the mayor was drinking coffee and watching TV at home. The TV show was saying that camping was popular, and this gave the mayor an idea. Six months later, the mayor and one of her staff members were visiting the new ABC Town campsite. They were happy to see that there were a lot of campers using the campsite. A few months later, the mayor and the staff member were watching TV in her office. The staff member was shocked to see breaking news that a bear had entered the campsite because there was a lot of food garbage.

解答例の訳 ある日，町長が会議を開いていました。会議は観光客の減少についてのものでした。これは問題であり，町長は職員たちに何かアイデアがないか尋ねました。彼らは皆，心配そうでした。その週末，町長は自宅でコーヒーを飲みながらテレビを見ていました。テレビ番組は，キャンプが人気だと言っており，これを聞いて町長はアイデアを思い付きました。6カ月後，町長と職員の1人は，新しいABC町キャンプ場を訪問していました。彼女らはキャンプ場を利用しているキャンパーがたくさんいるのを見て満足でした。数カ月後，町長とその職員は町長のオフィスでテレビを見ていました。職員は，生ごみがたくさんあるためにクマがキャンプ場に侵入したというニュース速報を見てショックを受けました。

解説 解答に含めるべき点は以下の4つ。①町長が会議で観光客の減少を示したグラフを見せ，職員たちに Any ideas? と尋ねている，②その週末，町長は「今，キャンプが人気」と示したテレビを見てアイデアを思い付く，③6カ月後，町長と職員が ABC Town Campsite を訪問していて，満足そうな様子，④数カ月後，2人はテレビで，クマがキャンプ場に落ちているごみを食べている様子を見ている。1コマ目について描写した解答例の This was a problem, ... は，The mayor asked her staff members, "Do you have any ideas on how to solve this problem?"「町長は職員たちに『この問題の解決方法についてのアイデアはありますか』と尋ねました」のようにせりふを利用して直接話法で表してもよいだろう。

22年度第1回 面接

89

No. 1

解答例 I'd be thinking that I should've planned the campsite more carefully. It was a good way to increase the number of tourists who come to our town, but I should've asked experts for advice about how to avoid problems with wildlife.

解説 質問は「4番目の絵を見てください。もしあなたが町長なら，どのようなことを考えているでしょうか」。解答例は，〈I should've + 過去分詞〉を用いて「もっと慎重に計画すべきだった」「専門家にアドバイスを求めるべきだった」という後悔を表している。should've は should have の短縮形。ごみを出さないなどの具体的な対策を話すこともできるだろう。

No. 2

解答例 Yes. These days, people spend a lot of time inside using computers and tablets. People should learn about the natural world, and personal experiences can be more effective for learning than the Internet or books.

解説 質問は「人々は自然について学ぶためにもっと屋外で過ごすべきだと思いますか」。解答例は Yes の立場で，最近は屋内で過ごす時間が多いという理由を述べた後，「学ぶにはインターネットや本よりも個人的な体験の方が効果的」という意見を述べている。No の立場の理由では，周りに自然がないことや屋外で過ごす時間がないなどの内容が考えられる。

No. 3

解答例 Yes, I think so. These days, many people damage their health by working too hard, so it's important for people to relax and take care of themselves. By doing so, their performance at work will naturally improve, too.

解説 質問は「企業は労働者にもっと休暇を与えるべきですか」。解答例は Yes の立場で，過労による健康被害に言及し，リラックスして自分をケアすることで仕事のパフォーマンスも上がると述べている。It's important for A to *do*「A にとって～することは重要だ」は万能に使える表現。

No. 4

解答例 I don't think so. Unfortunately, the government has more important responsibilities. Taking care of people's problems should be the priority. Besides, the government already spends a lot of money protecting endangered animals.

解説 「政府は絶滅の危機にひんした動物を保護するためにもっと努力すべきですか」という質問。Yes / No ではなく解答例のように I (don't) think so. と始めてもよい。解答例は No の立場で，「政府には（動物の保護）より重要な責務がある」「すでに多くのお金を使っている」という2つの理由を述べている。

| 二次試験・面接 | 問題カード **C** 日程 | 問題編 p.70〜71 | 🔊 ▶MP3 ▶アプリ ▶CD 4 **15**〜**18** |

解答例 **One day, a woman was talking with her company's CEO in the office.** He was telling her that she was promoted to manager, and she looked happy to hear that. That evening, she was at home with her husband and baby. She showed her husband that she had gotten a promotion. He said that he could pick up their baby from the day care center instead. A month later, the woman was working in her new position as manager. She got a message from her husband at 7 p.m. saying that he had picked up their baby from day care, and she was glad that she could continue working. A few days later, she was working on a project, and her husband called her at seven. He seemed very busy, and he told her that he could not pick up the baby that day.

解答例の訳 ある日，女性がオフィスで会社の CEO と話していました。彼は，彼女がマネージャーに昇進したことを伝えており，彼女はそれを聞いてうれしそうでした。その日の晩，彼女は夫と赤ん坊と一緒に自宅にいました。彼女は自分が昇進したことを夫に伝えました。彼は，代わりに託児所に赤ん坊を迎えに行けると言いました。1 カ月後，女性はマネージャーとして新しい役職で働いていました。彼女は，午後 7 時に夫から，託児所に赤ん坊を迎えに行ったと伝えるメッセージを受け取り，引き続き仕事ができることを喜びました。数日後，彼女はあるプロジェクトに取り組んでいたところ，7 時に夫から電話がありました。彼はとても忙しそうで，その日は赤ん坊を迎えに行けないと彼女に言いました。

解説 解答に含めるべき点は以下の 4 つ。① CEO が女性にマネージャーへの昇進を伝えている，②その日の晩，女性が夫に昇進を伝え，夫は「僕が（君の）代わりに赤ん坊を迎えに行けるよ」と言っている，③ 1 カ月後，女性は仕事中に携帯電話を見て，夫が託児所で赤ん坊を引き取ったことを知る，④数日後，夫は仕事が忙しそうで，電話で「今日は迎えに行けない」と女性に話している。2 コマ目の instead から，昇進前に女性が赤ん坊を迎えに行っていたことを推測しよう。3 コマ目と 4 コマ目は同じ午後 7 時の出来事であること，また，3 コマ目は携帯電話のメッセージで，4 コマ目は電話で直接話しているという違いも押さえよう。

22年度第1回　面接

No. 1

解答例 I'd be thinking, "Neither of us can go to pick up our baby from the day care center. The same problem is probably going to happen again. Maybe I shouldn't have accepted the promotion to manager."

解説 質問は「4番目の絵を見てください。もしあなたがこの女性なら，どのようなことを考えているでしょうか」。解答例は，〈I shouldn't have＋過去分詞〉を用いて「昇進を受け入れるべきではなかった」という後悔を表している。2人とも迎えに行けない問題に対し，「定時以降は自宅で働いてよいか交渉しよう」など具体的な解決法を話すこともできるだろう。

No. 2

解答例 I think so. Parents these days try to control every part of their children's lives, so children never get a chance to make their own decisions. As a result, the younger generation is becoming less independent.

解説 質問は「近ごろ，親は子供に対して過保護ですか」。解答例はI think so. で始まるYesの立場で，「親は子供の生活のあらゆる面をコントロールしようとしているため，子供は自分で決定を下す機会が全くない」という意見。A, so B.「Aなので，B」やAs a result「その結果」などの因果関係を表す表現の使い方を確認しよう。

No. 3

解答例 Yes. Especially in big cities, it seems like people never have time to relax. I think that the biggest reason is the work culture. This definitely has a negative effect on people's mental and physical health.

解説 「現代の速いペースの生活は人々に悪影響を及ぼしていますか」という質問。解答例はYesの立場。大都市に焦点を絞り，具体的な悪影響として「リラックスする時間がない」と述べた後，I think that the biggest reason is ... の形でその理由を説明している。速いペースの生活＝多忙と考えて，睡眠や食事への悪影響も根拠にできるだろう。

No. 4

解答例 I think so. The government realizes the decreasing birth rate is a problem, and it's spending money to encourage people to have more children. Also, companies provide more childcare leave these days.

解説 質問は「今後，日本の出生率は減少が止まると思いますか」。解答例はYesの立場で，政府の対策や企業の育児休暇制度を根拠にしている。「減少し続けると思う」というNoの立場では，未婚化・晩婚化や子育ての負担など，少子化の原因を取り上げて説明できるだろう。

2021-3

一次試験
筆記解答・解説　　　p.94〜109

一次試験
リスニング解答・解説　p.110〜132

二次試験
面接解答・解説　　　p.133〜136

解 答 一 覧

一次試験・筆記

1

(1)	2	(10)	4	(19)	1
(2)	2	(11)	1	(20)	4
(3)	3	(12)	1	(21)	1
(4)	2	(13)	3	(22)	1
(5)	2	(14)	3	(23)	2
(6)	2	(15)	4	(24)	1
(7)	3	(16)	4	(25)	2
(8)	1	(17)	3		
(9)	2	(18)	2		

2

(26)	2	(29)	3
(27)	4	(30)	1
(28)	1	(31)	3

3

(32)	1	(35)	4	(38)	3
(33)	2	(36)	2	(39)	4
(34)	2	(37)	1	(40)	1
				(41)	2

4　解答例は本文参照

一次試験・リスニング

Part 1	No. 1	4	No. 5	3	No. 9	1
	No. 2	1	No. 6	1	No.10	2
	No. 3	1	No. 7	3	No.11	1
	No. 4	1	No. 8	4	No.12	4

Part 2	No.13	3	No.17	1	No.21	3
	No.14	1	No.18	2	No.22	3
	No.15	1	No.19	2	No.23	2
	No.16	4	No.20	1	No.24	1

Part 3	No.25	3	No.28	4
	No.26	4	No.29	2
	No.27	1		

一次試験・筆記 **1** 問題編 p.74 〜 77

(1) ― **解答** **2**

訳 ロベルトは真の愛国者だったので，自国が隣国に攻撃されると直ちに陸軍への入隊を志願した。

解説 隣国に攻撃されるという非常事態に自ら入隊して戦おうとする人はどんな人かと考えると，patriot「愛国者」が正解。villain「悪人」，spectator「観客」，beggar「物乞いする人」

(2) ― **解答** **2**

訳 「今から休憩を取りましょう」と議長は言った。「次の議題について話し合うため，約15分後に会議を再開します」

解説 休憩を取った後で次の議題について話し合うということは，約15分の中断後に会議を再開する（resume）ことになる。parody「パロディーを作る，面白おかしく真似る」，impede「妨げる」，erect「建てる」

(3) ― **解答** **3**

訳 ダンは，初めてスキーに挑戦したときは難しいと思ったが，その後スキーに出かけるたびに上達した。今では彼はスキーの達人だ。

解説 最初は難しかったが次第に上達して今では達人だという流れから，「それに続く，その後の」（subsequent）スキー旅行のたびにと考えるのが自然。sufficient「十分な」，arrogant「尊大な」，prominent「卓越した」

(4) ― **解答** **2**

訳 その教授は自分の分野では専門家だが，常軌を逸した振る舞いがもとで同僚たちを（同僚として）恥ずかしい気持ちにさせている。「彼はいつも妙なことをしたり言ったりしている」と1人の同僚は述べた。

解説 第2文の always doing or saying strange things に相当する形容詞を考えると，eccentric「常軌を逸した」が適切。secular「世俗の」，vigilant「用心深い」，apparent「明白な」

(5) ― **解答** **2**

訳 その野菜の売店は販売している野菜がオーガニックだと証明することができなかったので，エディはそこの野菜を買うのを拒んだ。オーガニック食品だけを食べるのが彼の厳格なポリシーだった。

解説 オーガニック食品しか食べないエディが野菜を買わなかったのは，野菜の売店が野菜はオーガニックだと証明する（certify）ことができなかったから。diverge「分岐する」，evade「回避する」，glorify「美化する」

(6) ― **解答** **2**

訳 学校の進路相談員として，ペレイラさんは生徒たちが天職を見つける支援をすることを専門にしている。人は自分の個性とスキルに合ったキャ

94

リアを持つべきだと彼女は考えている。

解説 第 2 文の careers that fit their personality and skills がヒント。自分にぴったり合った職業を vocation「天職」と言う。boredom「退屈」，insult「侮辱」，publicity「一般に知れ渡ること」

(7) ―解答 ③

訳 そのマラソンランナーはレース後とても喉が渇いていたので，大容量のスポーツドリンクをわずか数口でがぶ飲みしてから，すぐにもう 1 本欲しいと言った。

解説 喉が渇いて 1 本では足りなかったのだから，ランナーは最初のスポーツドリンクを数口のがぶ飲み（gulps）で飲み干したと考えられる。それぞれ herd「群れ」，lump「塊」，sack「袋」の複数形。

(8) ―解答 ①

訳 眠っていた赤ん坊は，兄の部屋から聞こえる大音量の音楽にびっくりした。彼女は泣きながら目を覚まし，再び寝入るまでに長いことかかった。

解説 赤ん坊が目を覚ましたのは，大きな音に驚いたからだと考えられる。startle「びっくりさせる」の過去分詞 startled が正解。それぞれ improvise「即興的に作る」，prolong「長引かせる」，tolerate「許容する」の過去分詞。

(9) ―解答 ②

訳 A：もうこのアパートには 1 年住んでいて，賃貸契約がそろそろ切れるんだ。住み続けるべきか引っ越すべきか，決めなくちゃならない。
B：家賃が変わらないなら，契約を更新して住み続けることを勧めるよ。

解説 1 年住んだアパートに住み続けるか引っ越すかという会話なので，間もなく切れるのは lease「賃貸契約」。B の言う contract「契約」は lease のこと。token「代用貨幣」，vicinity「近隣」，dialect「方言」

(10) ―解答 ④

訳 その大統領候補は，停滞した景気は現大統領の責任だとした。当選したら景気を改善すると彼は約束した。

解説 第 2 文の it は the (　) economy を指す。それを改善する（improve）と言っていることから，景気は停滞した（sluggish）状態だと考えられる。bulky「かさばった」，functional「機能の」，ethnic「民族の」

(11) ―解答 ①

訳 A：アニー，元気だった？　去年のイタリア旅行は楽しかったかい？
B：楽しかったわよ，パブロ。実はね，すごく気に入ったので，あちらに移り住もうと考えているの。息子が高校を卒業するまで待たなければならないだろうけど。

解説 contemplate -ing で「〜しようと考える」という意味。イタリアを気に入った B は移住を検討していることになる。それぞれ emphasize「強

調する」, vandalize「故意に破壊する」, illustrate「説明する」の -ing 形。

(12) – 解答 **1**

訳 全上院議員がその新法を支持すると述べたので，彼らが満場一致で賛成票を投じたのは全く意外ではなかった。

解説 senator は「上院議員」。その全員が新法支持を表明したのだから，投票の際は満場［全員］一致で（unanimously）賛成したはず。abnormally「異常に」，mockingly「あざけって」，savagely「残酷に」

(13) – 解答 **3**

訳 A：マーカム教授の講義に行った？
B：行ったけど，あまりに退屈で 15 分しか耐えられなかった。その後は退出してカフェに行ったよ。

解説 講義が退屈で 15 分しか「耐える，我慢する」（endure）ことができず，途中で教室を出てカフェに行ったという流れ。execute「実行する，（通例受動態で）処刑する」，discern「見分ける」，relay「伝達する」

(14) – 解答 **3**

訳 寒冷地に建てられた家は，冬の間驚くほど暖かく居心地がいいことがある。暖炉と木の家具と立派なじゅうたんが，暖かくて快適な感じを家々に与えている。

解説 第 2 文の warm, comfortable に相当する cozy「暖かく居心地のいい」が適切。rigid「厳格な」，rash「向こう見ずな」，clumsy「不器用な」

(15) – 解答 **4**

訳 ウィルソンさんは息子が窓を割ったとき怒ったが，やったのは別の人だと言って息子が彼女をだまそうとしたことにむしろがっかりした。

解説 息子は窓を割ったのに自分はやっていないとうそをついたわけだが，その目的は人をだます（deceive）こと。pinpoint「正確に示す」，suppress「抑圧する」，reroute「別のルートで輸送する」

(16) – 解答 **4**

訳 ワンダが 1 カ月で 3 度目の遅刻をした後，上司は時間厳守の大切さについて彼女と長時間話した。

解説 遅刻が多いワンダが上司と話して理解すべきことは，「時間厳守，時間を守ること」（punctuality）の重要性である。congestion「密集」，drainage「排水」，optimism「楽観主義」

(17) – 解答 **3**

訳 その若い作家は慣習的な物語の書き方のルールには従わないと決め，自分の小説を唯一無二のスタイルで書いた。

解説 唯一無二の（unique）スタイルで書いたのだから，従わないと決めたのは慣習的な（conventional）ルールと考えられる。vulnerable「傷つきやすい」，clueless「何も知らない」，phonetic「音声の」

96

(18) – 解答 **2** ･･･････････････････････････････････ 正答率 ★75%以上

訳 箱の中の品物は壊れやすいのでていねいに梱包されていたが，それでもそのうち幾つかは配達中に破損した。

解説 ていねいに梱包したのに破損したということは，それらの品物は壊れやすい（fragile）物だったと考えられる。coarse「（粒などが）粗い，（肌などが）きめの粗い」，immovable「動かせない」，glossy「つやのある」

(19) – 解答 **1** ･･･

訳 女王は顧問を宮殿に呼び出したが，到着まで長時間かかると激怒した。

解説 〈summon＋人＋to〉で「（人）を～に呼び出す」という意味。問題文のqueen のように，主語は権威を持つ人が普通である。それぞれ hammer「ハンマーで打つ」，mingle「混ざる」，tremble「震える」の過去形。

(20) – 解答 **4** ･･･

訳 自軍が戦闘に負けそうだと将軍には分かっていたので，退却するよう自軍に命じた。ひとたび軍が戦場から無事に離れると，彼は敵を破るための新しい計画を練った。

解説 将軍は劣勢の軍に何を命じたか。第 2 文の「戦場から無事に離れると」から，命令が退却する（retreat）ことだったと分かる。entrust「任せる」，discard「捨てる」，strangle「絞め殺す」

(21) – 解答 **1** ･･･････････････････････････ 正答率 ★75%以上

訳 大学に入学してから，ビルは高等数学を学ぶ能力が自分にはないとすぐに気付いたので，専攻を地理学に変更した。

解説 ビルが専攻を変えた理由を考えると，高等数学を学ぶ能力（capacity）がないと気付いたからだと思われる。capacity to *do* で「～する能力」という意味。novelty「目新しさ」，bait「餌」，chunk「塊」

(22) – 解答 **1** ･･･

訳 お金を盗んだと強引に認めさせるため，容疑者に暴力を振るってはどうかと相棒が言ったとき，その警官はショックを受けた。そのように暴力を用いることは許されなかった。

解説 第 2 文の Using violence から，相棒の提案は容疑者に暴力を振るう（rough up）ことで罪を認めさせることだと分かる。give out「～を配る」，break up「～をばらばらにする，～を解散させる」，take over「～を引き継ぐ，～を支配する」

(23) – 解答 **2** ･･･

訳 バードウオッチングの初日に珍しいワシを見ることができてジュリアスは幸運だった。しかし，彼が同じ種類のワシをもう 1 羽目にするまで20 年が過ぎた。

解説 ～ go by before ... は「…まで～（の時間）が過ぎる」という意味。goを過去形にした went by が正解。それぞれ hold out「持ちこたえる」，

97

lay off「～を解雇する」，cut off「～を切り取る」の過去形。

(24) —解答 **1**

訳　A：週末にビーチへ出かけるのは中止するの？　台風が来ているよ。
　　B：まだ行く可能性を排除したわけじゃない。台風がどの方向に向かうか次第だね。

解説　B は台風の方向次第と言っているので，まだ諦めていない。つまり，ビーチに行く可能性を排除した（ruled out）わけではないことになる。それぞれ stand down「証言台を降りる」，drag into「(drag ～ into で) ～を…に引きずり入れる」，scoop up「～をすくい上げる」の過去分詞。

(25) —解答 **2**

訳　失業したら頼りにするものがあるよう，ジュンはいつもできる限り多くのお金を貯めた。

解説　fall back on は「（最後の手段として）～に頼る」という意味。失業して収入を絶たれた場合に備えて貯金したということ。look up to「～を尊敬する」，come down with「～（軽い病気）にかかる」，do away with「～を取り除く」

一次試験・筆記 **2** ｜ 問題編 p.78 ～ 81

全文訳　寄付者返礼品

　近年，慈善団体が，お金を寄付してくれた人たちに寄付者返礼品 —— コーヒーマグのようなちょっとしたプレゼント —— を渡すのが一般的になっている。多くの慈善団体が返礼品を出しており，寄付者返礼品をもらう場合に人はより多くを寄付すると広く考えられている。しかし，寄付者返礼品には寄付者たちの態度を変える傾向があると研究者たちは言う。ほとんどの人が最初にお金を寄付するのは，世界をより良い場所にしたり，自分より恵まれない人たちを助けたりしたいからである。だがプレゼントをもらうと，人は利己心と欲求に動機付けられるようになり始めることがある。実際，将来的に寄付する可能性が低くなるかもしれないのである。

　しかし，この問題を避ける方法があるかもしれない。寄付した後にプレゼントをもらえると教えることは，人が将来確実に寄付するようにする最善の方法ではないことが，研究で証明されている。ある研究では，プレゼントを予想していなかったときに，寄付者たちはプレゼントをもらうことにより良い反応を示した。さらに，そうした人たちからの将来的寄付は最大 75% 増えた。一方，寄付の後にプレゼントをもらえると知っていた寄付者たちは，そのプレゼントが何であるかにかかわらず，プレゼントを高く評価しなかった。

　寄付者返礼品には間接的なメリットもあるかもしれない。プレゼントは慈善団体の宣伝に役立つことがあると専門家たちは言う。例えば，慈善団体のロゴが入った凝ったデ

ザインの買い物袋といった品物は，寄付者が特別な人たちだけのグループの一員だと示す。そうしたプレゼントは寄付者たちを満足させておくだけでなく，慈善団体に対する一般大衆の認識も向上させる。

(語句) donor「寄付者」，premium「景品，返礼品」，initially「初めは」，motivate「動機を与える」，regardless of「～にかかわらず」，fancy「（デザインなどが）凝った」，signal「示す」，exclusive「特定の人に限られた」，awareness「認識，意識」

(26) – 解答 **2** ･･････････････････････････ 正答率 ★75%以上

解説　第1段落前半では，返礼品は寄付を増やすという想定が述べられている。空所文は However で始まるので，空所後はその想定とは異なる内容のはず。無私の気持ちで寄付を始めた人が，返礼品をもらうと「利己心と欲求」が動機となり，寄付しなくなる可能性もあるのだから，返礼品には「寄付者たちの態度を変える」傾向があることになる。

(27) – 解答 **4** ････････････････････････････････････

解説　第2段落では，返礼品があると知っていた場合と知らなかった場合を比較した研究が紹介されている。空所の前は，寄付者たちが返礼品を予想していなかった場合に反応が良かったという内容で，空所の後は，そうした人たちからの寄付は以後増えたという内容。前述の内容を補強する副詞 Furthermore「さらに」が適切である。

(28) – 解答 **1** ･･････････････････････････ 正答率 ★75%以上

解説　第3段落第1文の indirect benefits「間接的なメリット」は，返礼品が寄付を増やすという直接的なメリットと対比したもの。空所後では，慈善団体のロゴ入り買い物袋の例を挙げ，寄付者の満足感を保ち，人々の慈善団体への認識を高めるという2つの効果があるとしている。これらは，「慈善団体の宣伝に役立つ」間接的なメリットだと考えられる。

(全文訳) **政府の政策と交通安全**

　シートベルトなどの安全対策の導入により，アメリカでは交通関連死が減少した。しかし，政府の政策に批判的な多くの人は，政府による規制をより厳しくすれば不慮の死者をさらに減らせるであろうと主張する。実際，制限速度に関する現在の政府の政策は危険な運転を助長するかもしれないと言う人たちもいる。これは，制限速度がしばしば「運行速度方式」を用いて設定されているからである。この方式では，制限速度はその道路を利用する車両が実際に移動する速度に基づいて決定され，危険を増大させるかもしれない道路の特徴にはほとんど注意が払われない。残念なことだが，つまり，制限は時に安全でないレベルで設定されていることになる。

　車両の安全規定に関してはアメリカは他国より遅れている，とも批判的な人たちは指摘する。アメリカでは，安全規定は車両の中にいる人を守る目的で作られている。一部の車両は大型化し形状が変化したというのに，そうした車両が歩行者にもたらす危険が

増大したことを反映するように法律が変わっていない。批判的な人たちは，車両の乗員の安全だけを規定するのは無責任だし，歩行者の死亡防止に役立てるために取り得る簡単な対策があるのに，歩行者の死亡は増えたと言う。

　交通安全を向上させる1つの対策は，赤信号で停止しないドライバーを見つけるため，信号機でカメラを用いることである。1990年代に多くのそうしたカメラが設置され，命を救うことが証明されている。それにもかかわらず，そうしたカメラの数は近年減少している。その1つの理由は，プライバシーへの懸念から，カメラに反対する声がしばしば人々から上がることである。

> 語句　fatality「不慮の死（者）」, pose「（問題などを）投げかける」, pedestrian「歩行者」, regulate「規制する」, occupant「（乗り物などに）乗っている人」, irresponsible「無責任な」, detect「見つける，検出する」

(29) – 解答 ③ ・・・・・・・・・・・・・・・・・・・・・・ 正答率 ★75%以上

> 解説　政府の政策に批判的な人たちの主張について述べた前の文を In fact と受けていることから，空所には「制限速度に関する現在の政府の政策」を批判する内容が入ると分かる。道路の危険要因を考慮せずに設定されている制限速度は安全なレベルではないこともある，という記述から，現在の政策は「危険な運転を助長する」可能性があると考えられる。

(30) – 解答 ①

> 解説　第2段落では別の批判が述べられている。空所後によると，法律は車両の変化による歩行者への危険の増大に対応しておらず，歩行者の死亡は増えている。つまり，vehicle-safety regulations（第1文）は vehicle occupants（第4文）を守るための規定である。**1** の those inside vehicles は vehicle occupants の言い換え。

(31) – 解答 ③ ・・・・・・・・・・・・・・・・・・・・・・ 正答率 ★75%以上

> 解説　空所の前は，1990年代に多くのカメラが信号機に設置され，交通安全に役立っているという内容で，空所の後は，最近はカメラの数が減っているという内容。カメラが有用であれば増えてもよさそうであるがその想像に反する内容なので，**3**「それにもかかわらず」が適切。

一次試験・筆記 **3** | 問題編 p.82～88

全文訳　カリグラ

　「狂気の皇帝」としても知られるローマ皇帝カリグラはあまりに悪名高くなったので，その人生に関する事実と伝説とを区別するのは難しい。カリグラは在位中に，「脳炎」と言われているものを患った。この病気が原因で彼は正気を失ったとしばしば言われてきたが，この主張は，病後の一見不合理な彼の振る舞いに裏付けられている。しかし今日では，彼の行動はよく練られた，巧妙で恐ろしいほど暴力的な政治戦略の一部だった

のかもしれない，と主張する歴史家たちもいる。

　カリグラは病気の後，膨大な数の市民を，軽い犯罪であっても拷問にかけ処刑するようになった。また彼は，自分は生ける神だと主張した。これらの行動は精神的不安定を示唆するのかもしれないが，別の解釈としては，自らの地位を守ることを意図したものであったとも考えられる。カリグラが病気の間，生き延びることはないであろうと思われていたので，彼を（別の人を皇帝にして）交代させる計画が立てられ，その結果おそらく彼は裏切られ脅かされていると感じたのだろう。同様に，自分は神であると主張することは確かに狂気の兆候のように思われるが，多くのローマ皇帝は死ぬと神になると考えられていたのであり，カリグラは敵に暗殺を思いとどまらせるためにその主張をしたのかもしれない。

　一般的に信じられているように，カリグラが愛馬インキタトゥスを政府の有力な地位に任命しようとしたさまの話も，彼に精神疾患があった証拠として挙げられることがある。しかしカリグラは，動きにくい服を着て彼の戦車の前を走るといったことをさせて，ローマ元老院の議員たちにしばしば屈辱を与えたと言われている。愛馬を彼らよりも高位に昇進させることは，自分が無価値だと元老院議員たちに感じさせる別の方法だったのだろう。しかし最終的に，カリグラの振る舞いは度を越し，彼は殺害された。彼を歴史から消し去るために精力が注がれ，現代の歴史家たちが研究するための信頼できる資料はほとんど残っていない。その結果，彼が本当に狂気の皇帝だったのかどうかは決して分からないかもしれない。

> 語句 infamous「悪名の高い」，reign「在位期間，治世」，insane「正気でない，狂気の」，irrational「不合理な」，deliberate「計画的な，故意の」，horribly「恐ろしく，ひどく」，torture「拷問にかける」，offense「（軽微な）犯罪」，instability「不安定」，betray「裏切る」，insanity「狂気」，assassinate「暗殺する」，supposedly「おそらく，推定では」，humiliate「恥をかかせる」，senate「(the Senate で) 元老院」，chariot「（馬が引く2輪の）戦車」，elevate「昇進させる」，go too far「度が過ぎる」，erase「（記憶などから）拭い去る」

(32) – 解答 ①

問題文の訳 一部の現代の歴史家たちは次のように主張する。

選択肢の訳
1　カリグラの一見正気でない行動は，実際は入念に考え抜かれた計画の一部だったのかもしれない。
2　カリグラが患った「脳炎」は，当初考えられていたより重かった。
3　カリグラは精神疾患があった期間に基づいて判断されるべきでない。
4　カリグラが実行したと伝えられる暴力行為の多くは，ほかのローマ皇帝たちが行ったものだった。

解説 第1段落最終文に，問題文とほぼ同じ some historians argue という表現がある。この文の his actions は前文の his seemingly irrational behavior を指す。つまり，カリグラの狂気は，実際はよく練られた戦

略の一部だったというのが一部の歴史家たちの主張である。**1**では本文の irrational を crazy と，deliberate を carefully thought-out と言い換えている。

(33) −解答 ②

問題文の訳　何がカリグラの病気の1つの結果だったかもしれないか。

選択肢の訳
1　死にかけたことが原因で，彼は神々と宗教以外は何にも関心を持たなくなった。
2　彼はもう誰も信頼できないと感じ，その結果統治するやり方を変えることになった。
3　やはり彼は死ぬだろうとローマ市民は思っていたので，彼は神々が自分を守ってくれると彼らに示そうと試みた。
4　彼はローマ皇帝に関する古い考えに疑問を抱き始め，それが政府のほかのメンバーたちとの深刻な対立につながった。

解説　第2段落の「裏切られ脅かされていると感じた」を「もう誰も信頼できないと感じ」と言い換え，多くの市民を拷問・処刑し自分は神だと主張したことを「統治するやり方を変えた」とまとめた**2**が正解。

(34) −解答 ②

問題文の訳　この文章によると，カリグラはローマ元老院の議員たちのことをどう感じていたか。

選択肢の訳
1　彼を敵から守るためなら彼らは何でもするのだから，民衆は彼らをもっと尊敬すべきだと彼は感じていた。
2　彼は彼らに対する支配力を見せつけたかったので，自分には価値がないと彼らに感じさせる方法をしばしば見つけた。
3　彼らは身体的に弱くファッションセンスに乏しいと彼は感じていたので，彼は彼らが嫌いだった。
4　彼は彼らの支援に感謝していたので，彼らをたたえるために戦車競走などのイベントを催した。

解説　第3段落第2文の humiliated「屈辱を与えた」が，元老院議員たちへのカリグラの考え方を端的に示している。馬を高位に就けようとする，議員たちに戦車の前を走らせるといった行為は，「支配力を見せつけ」る方法だったと考えられる。**2**の no value は本文の worthless に相当。

全文訳　**エディ・コイルの友人たち**

1970年にアメリカの作家ジョージ・V・ヒギンズは，小説第1作『エディ・コイルの友人たち』を発表した。この犯罪小説はヒギンズが弁護士として働いて過ごした年月に着想を得たもので，彼はその期間，自身がかかわった事件に関連する何時間もの警察の監視カメラのテープと口述の書き起こしを精査した。彼が聞きそして読んだのは普通の犯罪者たちの日常の話し言葉で，当時テレビの犯罪ドラマの台本に書かれたせりふと

102

は全くの別物に聞こえた。ヒギンズは本物の犯罪者たちの話し方を覚え，彼らの独特でしばしば乱雑な言葉遣いのパターンは『エディ・コイルの友人たち』の基礎となった。この小説の生々しいリアリズムは，当時ベストセラーリストの上位を占めていた洗練された犯罪小説から大きくかけ離れていた。ヒギンズは罪を犯す登場人物の人生を美化したり，警察や連邦捜査官たちをことさら英雄的に描いたりはしなかった。

　『エディ・コイルの友人たち』をほかの犯罪小説から際立たせる１つの側面は，ほぼ全編が会話で書かれていることである。犯罪ものというジャンルがサスペンスを作り上げる綿密に組み立てられた物語に依拠することを考えれば，これは非常に独創的な手法だった。重要な出来事は直接述べられず，その代わり，小説の登場人物たちの会話を通して紹介される。従って読者は，エディ・コイルとその犯罪仲間たちの話をこっそり盗み聞きしているという感覚になる。アクションシーンすら会話で描かれ，地の文が必要なところでは，ヒギンズは言葉をわずかしか用いず，読者が筋を追うのに必要なだけの情報しか与えない。焦点は主に登場人物たち，彼らが住む世界，そして彼らが従う行動規範に当てられる。

　ヒギンズの最初の小説はたちまちヒットしたものの，全ての読者が著者の文体 —— 彼が続く著作でも用いた文体 —— を好んだわけではなかった。多くの人は，彼のその後の小説には分かりやすい筋がなく，アクションが少な過ぎると不平を述べた。だがヒギンズは，物語を語る上で最も人を引き付ける方法は登場人物たちの会話を通してで，そうすれば読者は話されていることに細心の注意を払わざるを得ないからだ，という信念に忠実であり続けた。ヒギンズは多くの小説を書いたが，デビュー作の成功を再現することはかなわなかった。晩年に近づくと，彼は自分の著作が注目と評価を受けないことに落胆しいら立った。それにもかかわらず，『エディ・コイルの友人たち』は，これまでに書かれた犯罪小説の大傑作の１つだと今では多くの人に見なされている。

> 語句　surveillance「監視」，transcript「（口述などの）書写」，scripted「台本のある」，messy「汚い，雑な」，gritty「生々しい，どぎつい」，removed「かけ離れた」，polished「洗練された」，dominate「支配する」，glamorize「美化する」，portray「描写する」，heroic「英雄的な」，dialogue「対話，会話」，given「〜を考慮すれば」，reliance「依存」，plot「（小説などの）筋を組み立てる；筋」，listen in on「〜を盗み聞きする」，depict「描く」，narration「語り」，sparingly「控えめに」，inhabit「住んでいる」，code of conduct「行動規範」，(be) committed to「〜に献身する，〜に忠誠を誓う」，engaging「人を引き付ける」，replicate「繰り返す」，appreciation「評価」

(35) – 解答 ④ 　　　　　　　　　　　　　　　　　　　　正答率 ★75%以上

問題文の訳　この文章によると，ジョージ・V・ヒギンズが『エディ・コイルの友人たち』を書いたのは，

選択肢の訳　**1**　この小説がベストセラーになり，弁護士業を辞めて作家活動に専念できると考えたからである。

103

2 アメリカの犯罪活動の規模に関する意識が普通のアメリカ人に欠けていることにいら立った後のことである。

3 犯罪の被害者たちを守るために弁護士たちがどれだけ熱心に働いているかを読者に教えたかったからである。

4 彼が弁護士だったころに行った調査中に見つけたことに着想を得た後のことである。

解説 第1段落によると，ヒギンズは弁護士時代に犯罪者が実際に使う言葉を知り，それを基にして小説を書いた。事件に関連する警察の監視カメラのテープと口述の書き起こしから犯罪者の言葉遣いを知ったという本文の内容を，選択肢**4**では「調査中に見つけたこと」と漠然と言い換えている。

(36) – 解答 ② ······································ 正答率 ★75%以上

問題文の訳 第2段落から『エディ・コイルの友人たち』について何が分かるか。

選択肢の訳 **1** ヒギンズは，犯罪小説に関する伝統的ルールが現代でもなお有効だと証明する小説を生み出したかった。

2 この小説が普通と違うのは，特定の出来事を詳細に描写するのではなく，登場人物たちの言葉のやりとりを通してヒギンズが物語を語っているからである。

3 ヒギンズが小説全編を通して会話に大きく依拠したのは，長い地の文を書く自信がなかったからである。

4 この小説は犯罪世界を忠実に描写しているが，ヒギンズは真の犯罪小説とは見なしていなかった。

解説 第2段落冒頭に書かれているように，この小説の特徴はほとんどが登場人物の会話で成り立っていること。**2**ではそれを interactions「言葉のやりとり」と表している。**2**の「特定の出来事を詳細に描写するのではなく」は本文の「重要な出来事は直接述べられず」に対応している。narration が少ないのは，第3段落で述べられている通りヒギンズが会話を重視していたからで，**3**のように自信がなかったからではない。

(37) – 解答 ①······································

問題文の訳 この文章の筆者は以下の記述のどれに同意する可能性が最も高いか。

選択肢の訳 **1** 文体を変えればヒギンズはより広い読者層を引き付けることができたかもしれない可能性があったにもかかわらず，彼は自分の創造的ビジョンに忠実であり続けた。

2 ヒギンズが生み出した最初の著作は出来が悪かったが，彼の作品の質はそれに続く年月で着実に向上した。

3 犯罪小説作家たちがほかのジャンルの作家たちと同レベルの名声と称賛を得ることが決してないのは必然である。

4 最初に出版された数十年後になっても自分の作品が読者に受けるであ

ろうと犯罪小説作家たちが考えるのは非現実的である。

解説 第3段落では，ヒギンズのその後が書かれている。独特の文体が多くの読者に不評だったのに，彼はそれを変えようとしなかった。つまり，文体を変えれば読者が増えたかもしれないのに，会話を通して物語を語ることにこだわる「創造的ビジョン」を守り抜いた，というのがこの文章の筆者のヒギンズ評と考えられる。**1**の true は本文の committed の言い換え。

全文訳 **マミーブラウン**

　数千年もの昔，古代エジプト人は mummification（ミイラ製作）── 死者の体を完全に乾燥させ，さまざまな物質で処理し，保存するためにくるむ手順 ── を行い始めた。これは死者の魂が来世に入るのを助けると考えられていた。しかし，12世紀から，ミイラの部位を用いて作った薬の需要がヨーロッパで生じると，多くの古代のミイラが奇妙な目に遭った。人々は，ミイラの色が黒なのは瀝青（れきせい）── 中東で天然に産出し，古代社会が病気の治療に用いた黒い石油由来の物質 ── で処理されていたからだと思い込んでいた。しかし，確かに古代エジプト人はミイラを瀝青でコーティングして保存したこともあったが，この手法はヨーロッパに運ばれたミイラの多くには使われていなかった。さらに，アラビア語の原典が不正確に翻訳された結果，ミイラの処理に使われた瀝青は実際にミイラの体内に入ると誤って信じられた。

　18世紀になるころには，医学的知識が進歩したことで，ヨーロッパ人はミイラ由来の薬の使用をやめていた。それにもかかわらず，フランスの指導者ナポレオン・ボナパルトがエジプトで軍事作戦を率いると，ヨーロッパ大衆のミイラへの関心は新たな高みに達した。軍事作戦には大規模な科学調査遠征も含まれており，重要な考古学的発見と古代の人工遺物の記録をもたらした。裕福な観光客たちは，私的コレクション用に古代人工遺物を入手しようと，エジプトを訪れさえした。実際，私的なパーティーでミイラを包んだ布を解きミイラを見せることが，人気の催しになった。ミイラは，作物の肥料や鉄道機関車の燃料に変えるといった，さまざまなほかの方法でも用いられた。

　ミイラの特に珍しい1つの利用法は，茶色の絵の具を作るための顔料としてであった。すりつぶしたミイラを用いて作られたこの顔料はマミーブラウンとして知られるようになり，その需要が伸びたのはナポレオンのエジプト戦役の時代前後だが，早くも16世紀には使われていた。その色は一部のヨーロッパの芸術家たちに称賛され，彼らは今日美術館で見ることのできる芸術作品にこの顔料を使った。それでも，この顔料を批判する人たちの方が熱狂的な支持者たちよりも多かった。多くの芸術家たちは，この顔料の乾く力が弱いことやほかの好ましくない特性について不平を述べた。さらに，亡くなった人で作った顔料で絵を描くことは非礼だと次第に考えられるようになった ── マミーブラウンを使ったある有名な英国人画家は，その製造に本物のミイラが用いられていたと知ると，持っていた絵の具のチューブを直ちに地面に埋めた。

　死んだ動物の体の部位がミイラの部位として売られることもあったので，マミーブラ

ウンに異論のない芸術家たちですら，それが本物のミイラから作られたものだと常に確信できたわけではなかった。また，いろいろな製造業者がミイラのいろいろな部位を使って顔料を製造していたことは，販売されているさまざまなバージョンの間にほとんど一貫性がないことを意味した。加えて，死体を保存するために使われる物質を含めてミイラ製作の手順それ自体が，時とともに変化を経た。まさにこれらの要因が，特定の絵画におけるマミーブラウンの存在を今日の研究者たちが検出することをほぼ不可能にしている。しかし，顔料の物議を醸す出所を考えると，自分たちが称賛する絵画のどれかにこの顔料が使われたと知ったなら，もしかすると芸術愛好家たちはショックを受けるかもしれない。

語句　mummy「ミイラ」，dry out「〜をすっかり乾かす」，afterlife「来世」，bitumen「瀝青」，fascination with「〜に魅了されること」，military campaign「軍事作戦」，expedition「遠征（隊）」，archaeological「考古学的な」，documentation「文書［資料］による裏付け，（収集した）参考資料，証拠書類提出」，artifact「人工遺物」，unwrapping「包装を解くこと」，fertilizer「肥料」，pigment「顔料」，ground-up「すりつぶした」，artwork「芸術作品」，deceased「死去した」，disrespectful「礼節を欠く，失礼な」，genuine「本物の」，consistency「首尾一貫性」，undergo「（変化などを）経る」，controversial「物議を醸す」

(38) – 解答 3

問題文の訳　この文章の筆者によると，なぜ古代エジプトのミイラはヨーロッパで薬を作るために使われたのか。

選択肢の訳　**1** 当時ヨーロッパでは病気がまん延していたので，ヨーロッパ人はよく効く薬を作るためなら何でも試すことをいとわなかった。
2 ミイラは大昔のものであるにもかかわらず黒く変色していなかったので，健康にメリットがあるかもしれないとヨーロッパ人は思い込んだ。
3 ヨーロッパ人は，医学的メリットがあると考えられる物質が全てのミイラに存在すると誤って信じた。
4 ミイラが古代エジプト人にとって宗教的意義を持っていたことが原因で，ヨーロッパ人はミイラに特別な力があると信じた。

解説　第1段落後半に，ヨーロッパ人がミイラで薬を作るようになった経緯が書かれている。瀝青は，古代社会で病気の治療に用いられ，ミイラの処理に使われることもあった。しかし，「ヨーロッパに運ばれたミイラの多くには使われていなかった」。この事情に合う説明は**3**で，瀝青を「医学的メリットがあると考えられる物質」と言い換えている。**2**は「黒く変色していなかった」が本文の記述と食い違う。

(39) – 解答 4

問題文の訳　ナポレオン・ボナパルトのエジプトでの軍事作戦について分かることの1つは何か。

106

選択肢の訳 1 数人の指導者たちが，これは自分たちもエジプトを侵略する理由になると考え，そのため多くの古代人工遺物が破壊されることになった。

2 ミイラから作った薬についてのヨーロッパ人の見解を変えさせることとなった，古代エジプト文化に関する情報を明らかにした。

3 自分たちの古代人工遺物コレクションが破壊される結果を招くと思った裕福なヨーロッパ人に反対された。

4 ミイラへの関心を高まらせるとともに，幾つかの目的にミイラを利用するようヨーロッパ人を触発した。

解説 第2段落によると，ナポレオンのエジプトでの軍事作戦はヨーロッパ人のミイラ熱を再燃させた。ミイラは，富裕層の私的展示物にされたり，肥料や燃料といった「さまざまなほかの方法」で利用されたりした。これを「幾つかの目的」と表した**4**が正解。**2**の「古代エジプト文化に関する情報を明らかにした」は正しいが，第1文に書かれているようにヨーロッパ人はすでにミイラから作った薬を使わなくなっていたのだから，見解が変わったのはナポレオン以前のことである。

(40) – 解答 ①

問題文の訳 この文章の筆者が英国人画家に言及しているのは，

選択肢の訳 1 マミーブラウンの使用が死者に対する敬意の欠如を示すということで，一部の人たちから反対されたさまを例示するためである。

2 技術的性能が良くないにもかかわらず，マミーブラウンが有名な芸術家たちの間で人気があり続けた理由を説明するためである。

3 マミーブラウンは独特な成分のためほかの絵の具顔料より優れていたという説に裏付けを与えるためである。

4 一部の芸術家たちが，当初は使うのを拒んだが後にマミーブラウンについて肯定的な見解を持つようになった1つの理由を説明するためである。

解説 第3段落後半はマミーブラウンを批判する人たち（= critics）に関する記述で，英国人画家はその流れの中で登場する。彼がミイラを使った絵の具を地面に埋めた理由は，「亡くなった人で作った顔料で絵を描くことは非礼だ」と考えたからである。従って**1**が正解。選択肢では本文のdeceased peopleをthe deadと，disrespectfulをa lack of respectと言い換えている。

(41) – 解答 ②

問題文の訳 絵画がマミーブラウンを含むかどうかを確定するのを難しくしていることの1つは何か。

選択肢の訳 1 色を良くするため顔料に加えられた物質が，検証すれば検知できた可能性のあった一切の生物学的証拠を破壊した。

2 古代エジプト人がミイラをつくる方法が変化したので，顔料の内容物

107

が一貫していなかった。

3 芸術家たちはその顔料を絵に塗る前にほかの種類の絵の具と混ぜたので，顔料はごくわずかな量しか存在しないだろう。

4 その結果が絵画の価値に影響するかもしれないという懸念から，芸術業界は研究者たちに絵画の検証を行わせないようにしてきた。

解説 第4段落では，マミーブラウンの検出をほぼ不可能にしている These same factors「まさにこれらの要因」として次の3つが挙げられている。①ミイラではなく死んだ動物が用いられた顔料もあった，②顔料は製造業者によってばらつきがあった，③保存用の物質を含めてミイラ製作の手順は変化を繰り返していた。**2**の内容が③と一致する。「顔料の内容物が一貫していなかった」の部分は，保存用の物質も含めて変化したという記述に相当する。

一次試験・筆記 **4** 問題編 p.89

トピックの訳 **人々は動物から作られた商品の使用をやめるべきか。**

ポイントの訳 ・**動物の権利** ・**絶滅危惧種** ・**製品の質** ・**伝統**

解答例 　I believe that the quality of alternative products and respecting animal rights are reasons why people should not use goods made from animals.

　Many products made from animals are being replaced by artificial goods, and technological advancements have greatly improved the quality of these man-made goods. For example, the quality of fake fur is almost the same as that of real fur. Such high-quality alternative goods mean that using animal products is unnecessary.

　Furthermore, some animal products come from animals living in conditions that restrict their freedom. However, animals deserve the right to live freely, and this right should not be ignored for the sake of commercial gain. Therefore, stopping the use of animal-based goods is an effective way to protect animal rights.

　In conclusion, the high quality of other types of products and the importance of protecting animal rights mean that people should stop using goods made from animals.

解説 序論：第1段落では，トピックに対する自分の意見を簡潔に書く。模範解答は，ポイントの Product quality と Animal rights を用いている。

108

これらに alternative「代替の」や respecting「尊重すること」という語を加えて本論での記述を先取りし，トピックに賛成だと表明している。I believe that ～ are reasons why ...「私は～が…である理由だと考える」は序論で最も使いやすい表現の1つで，～に2つのポイントを，...に自分の意見を表す文を入れる。模範解答のように，トピックの stop using「使用をやめる」を not use「使わない」に言い換えたり，that are を省略したりといった工夫ができるとよい。

本論：本論では，序論で述べた主張の理由・根拠を説明する。Product quality を取り上げた第2段落では，序論で alternative という語を用いているように，動物を使わない代替製品について述べている。科学技術の進歩によって artificial「人工の」あるいは man-made「人造の」商品の品質が大幅に向上しているので，動物から作る商品は不要だという意見である。フェイクファーの品質は本物の毛皮の品質とほぼ同じだ，と具体例を示していることで説得力が増している。Animal rights を扱う第3段落は Furthermore で始め，自由を制限された状況で生きている動物から作られた製品もあるという問題を指摘している。そこから，動物には自由に生きる権利がある，動物由来の商品の使用をやめることは動物の権利を守るのに有効だ，という展開となっていて分かりやすい。第2文の冒頭に However，第3文の冒頭に Therefore という副詞を置いていることも，論理の流れを明快にしている。

結論：最終段落では，トピックに対する自分の意見を再び主張する。模範解答は In conclusion「結論として」で始めて，序論・本論で使った alternative を other types of「ほかの種類の～」と言い換えた上で2つのポイントに改めて言及し，トピックの表現を繰り返してまとめている。第2段落でも用いられている A mean(s) that B「A は B ということを意味する，A ということはつまり B ということである」は，理由（A）と結果・結論（B）をシンプルに結ぶ表現として使えるようにしておきたい。

(そのほかの表現) 模範解答では，動名詞を用いた主部が，respecting animal rights，using animal products，stopping the use of animal-based goods と3つ登場する。第3段落の stopping the use of ... は，it を使って it is an effective way to protect animal rights to stop the use of animal-based goods とすると，to 不定詞が2つあってやや分かりにくい文になる。

| 一次試験・リスニング | **Part 1** | 問題編 p.90～91 | 🔊 ▶MP3 ▶アプリ ▶CD 2 **1**～**14** |

No.**1** – 解答 ④

スクリプト ★: Dr. Jenkins, could I speak with you for a moment?

☆: Sure, Eric. What's on your mind?

★: I'm embarrassed to say this, but I'm having a hard time keeping my eyes open in class. I have to work two part-time jobs to make ends meet, and your class is so early in the morning.

☆: So are you thinking about dropping the class? That would be a shame, considering that your test scores have been pretty good.

★: No, not that. I need this class in order to graduate next year. Actually, I was wondering if you could arrange your seating chart so I'm sitting right up in front. That should help me pay better attention in class.

☆: I think I can probably do that.

Question: What is the student concerned about?

全文訳 ★: ジェンキンズ先生，ちょっとお話しできますか？

☆: いいわよ，エリック。気になることでもあるの？

★: こんなことを言うのは恥ずかしいんですが，授業中目を開けているのがつらいんです。お金のやりくりをするのにアルバイトを2つしなければならなくて，先生の授業は午前中のすごく早い時間なんです。

☆: じゃあ，授業に出るのをやめようと考えているの？ ずっとテストでかなりいい点を取っていることを考えると残念だわ。

★: いいえ，そうじゃないんです。来年卒業するためにはこの授業が必要です。実は，僕が最前列に座れるよう，座席表を調整していただけないかと思いまして。それならきっと授業中注意力が上がると思うんです。

☆: それならたぶんできると思う。

質問：この学生は何を心配しているか。

選択肢の訳 1 最近のテストの点数。

2 その授業に出るのをやめなければならないこと。

3 仕事を見つけること。

4 授業中目を覚ましていること。

解説 男子学生が相談に来たのは，アルバイトで忙しいのに教師の授業が「午前中のすごく早い時間」なので，「授業中目を開けているのがつらい」から。そのため，注意力が上がるよう最前列に座らせてもらえないかと依頼している。keeping my eyes open を Staying awake と言い換えた **4** が正解。seating chart は「座席表」。

110

No.2 — 解答 ①

スクリプト ☆： You're not sending a personal e-mail from your office computer, are you, Allen?

★： It's just a quick note to my mom — it's her birthday tomorrow.

☆： Didn't you read the memo from the CEO? Using office computers for private communications could get you fired. I heard they're looking for excuses to cut staff.

★： I doubt if they'd take a birthday message that seriously, but thanks for the warning.

☆： Better safe than sorry.

Question: Why is the woman concerned?

全文訳 ☆： 会社のパソコンから私用Eメールを送っているんじゃないよね，アレン？

★： 母にさっと短信を書いただけだよ ― 明日は母の誕生日なんだ。

☆： CEOからの回覧を読まなかった？　会社のパソコンを個人的通信に使うと首になるかもしれない。人員削減する口実を探しているらしいよ。

★： 誕生日のメッセージをそんなに深刻には考えないだろうと思うけど，ご忠告には感謝するよ。

☆： 用心するに越したことはないわよ。

質問：女性はなぜ心配しているのか。

選択肢の訳
1　男性は失業するかもしれない。
2　男性は母親の誕生日を忘れた。
3　男性は彼女のEメールに返信しなかった。
4　男性はCEOに好かれていない。

解説　会社のパソコンで母親にEメールを送ることについて，男性本人は大したことだとは思っていないが，女性は could get you fired「首になるかもしれない」と心配している。これを could lose his job と表した **1** が正解。Better safe than sorry. は「後で悔やむより今安全策を取った方がいい」という意味のことわざ。

No.3 — 解答 ①

スクリプト ☆： Sam, next week, it's my turn to drive us to work, but my car's in the shop.

★： What's wrong with it?

☆： Oh, I had an accident over the weekend.

★： Nothing too serious, I hope.

☆： No. Just a fender bender.

★： OK. Well, why don't I do the driving next week, and you can take your turn once your car's fixed?

☆： That would be great. Thanks a lot.

Question: What do we learn about these people?

全文訳 ☆: サム，来週は私があなたを乗せて車で出勤する番なんだけど，車が修理中なのよ。

★: 車がどうかしたの？

☆: うん，週末の間に事故を起こしちゃって。

★: それほどひどい事故じゃなかったのならいいけど。

☆: うん，大丈夫よ。ほんのちょっとした事故なの。

★: 分かった。そうだね，来週は僕が運転を担当するのはどうだろう，そして，車の修理が済み次第君の番にすればいい。

☆: そうしてもらえると助かるわ。どうもありがとう。

質問：この人たちについて何が分かるか。

選択肢の訳 1 交替で車を運転する。

2 大きな事故を起こした。

3 自動車修理工場で働いている。

4 2人とも来週は運転できない。

解説 女性の「来週は私があなたを乗せて車で出勤する番」や男性の「来週は僕が運転を担当する」などから，2人は毎週交替でそれぞれの車に相手を乗せて通勤していると分かる。従って 1 が正解。fender bender は「（フェンダーが曲がる程度の）ちょっとした事故」なので 2 は誤り。

No.4 －解答 ① ·········· 正答率 ★75%以上

スクリプト ☆: I'm sorry, sir, but your credit card was declined.

★: I don't understand why. It was fine yesterday.

☆: Perhaps you've reached your limit. It happens quite often.

★: I don't know. That's certainly possible, I suppose.

☆: Anyway, I suggest you call your card issuer. Do you have a debit card or a personal check you'd like to use for today's purchases?

★: No, I'll just pay with cash.

Question: What's the man's problem?

全文訳 ☆: 申し訳ございませんが，お客さまのクレジットカードは通りませんでした。

★: 理由が分かりません。昨日は大丈夫だったんですよ。

☆: もしかすると限度額に達したのかもしれません。ありがちなことです。

★: どうでしょう。確かにそれはあり得るとは思いますが。

☆: ともかく，カードの発行会社に電話することをお勧めします。本日のご購入分にお使いになりたいデビットカードか個人小切手はお持ちですか？

★: いいえ，現金で払います。

質問：男性の問題は何か。

選択肢の訳 1 クレジットカードを使えない。

112

2 カードの発行会社に連絡するのを忘れた。

3 今日は現金が足りない。

4 デビットカードを紛失した。

解説 女性の your credit card was declined がポイント。be declined「断られる」はクレジットカードについて用いると，カードを読み取り機に通しても利用が承認されないという意味になる。つまり，男性はクレジットカードが使えなかったと分かる。

No.**5**-解答 ③ ・・

スクリプト ☆： How's the job-hunting going, Tyler? You know your dad and I can't support you forever.

★： Actually, I've been offered a second interview for a call-center job. I'm not sure it's my thing, though.

☆： It doesn't have to be. The more jobs you try your hand at, the more you'll learn about the working world.

★： But what if I take it and end up missing out on my dream job?

☆： You can keep applying to other places while you work.

★： Fair enough. I'll call them back and schedule the second interview.
   Question: What is the woman's opinion about her son?

全文訳 ☆： 職探しの調子はどう，タイラー？　お父さんも私も，いつまでもあなたを養うわけにはいかないんだからね。

★： 実は，コールセンターの仕事で二次面接に呼ばれているんだ。それが自分向きかは分からないけど。

☆： そうである必要はないわ。チャレンジする仕事が多ければ多いほど，それだけ仕事の世界のことをたくさん学べるもの。

★： だけど，その仕事に就いたあげくに夢の仕事を逃すことになったら？

☆： 働きながら別のところに応募し続ければいいじゃない。

★： もっともだ。こちらから電話して二次面接の予定を決めるよ。
   質問：息子に関する女性の意見は何か。

選択肢の訳 **1** コールセンターの仕事に向いていない。

2 間違った面接のテクニックを学んでいる。

3 呼ばれている面接に行くべきだ。

4 夢の仕事を見つけることを優先すべきだ。

解説 求職中の息子はコールセンターの仕事が自分に向いているか分からないと言っているが，母親は，とにかくいろんな仕事をやってみることを勧めている。最後に息子も二次面接を受けることに決めているので，**3** が正解。one's thing「一番好きな［合っている］こと」，try one's hand at「～を初めてやってみる」といった表現を理解できるかどうかがポイントになる。

113

No.6 – 解答 ① .... 正答率 ★75%以上

[スクリプト]
☆ : Hello, Sergio. What brings you to the clinic today?

★ : My energy's been really low recently, so I thought I should have a checkup.

☆ : Any major changes since your last appointment?

★ : I got promoted to a new position that's pretty stressful and requires a lot of business trips. I've been eating unhealthy food, too.

☆ : I see. Getting adequate nutrition can be a challenge when you're traveling.

★ : What should I do?

☆ : Let's get a few tests done, and then we'll look at your options once the results come in.

Question: What is the doctor going to do next?

[全文訳]
☆ : こんにちは，セルジオ。今日はどういったことで来院されたんですか？

★ : 最近全然元気が出ないので，健康診断を受けた方がいいと思いまして。

☆ : 前回の予約から何か大きな変化は？

★ : 結構ストレスがたまって多くの出張が必要な新しいポストに昇進しました。ずっと不健康な食事もしています。

☆ : なるほど。出張のときは，十分な栄養を取るのが難しいこともありますね。

★ : どうすればいいでしょう？

☆ : 幾つか検査を終わらせて，それから結果が出次第，選択肢について検討しましょう。

質問：医師は次に何をするか。

[選択肢の訳]
1 男性に幾つか検査を受けさせる。
2 もっと運動するよう男性に促す。
3 仕事に関連するストレスについて男性にアドバイスする。
4 専門医に行くよう男性に勧める。

[解説] 元気が出ないという男性の話を聞いた医師は，最後に Let's get a few tests done と言っている。これを言い換えた **1** が正解。検査結果が出たら options「選択肢」を検討すると言っているが，次にするのは検査である。

No.7 – 解答 ③ ....

[スクリプト]
☆ : Jasper? I thought you were on vacation this week.

★ : Officially, I am. My manager was planning to take some time off, so I thought I'd do the same. Unfortunately, she's still working, which means she's asking me to do stuff.

☆ : She's making you work during your vacation? You should complain to the personnel department.

114

★：But I've only been here a year. I want to prove I'm committed to the company.

☆：Well, be sure to set aside a little time for yourself this week. You are technically on vacation.

★：I will. Thanks.

Question: What is one thing we learn about the man?

全文訳 ☆：ジャスパー？ 今週は休暇を取っていると思っていたけど。

★：表向きにはそうなんだ。上司が少し休みを取る予定だったので，僕も同じようにしようと思ったんだ。あいにく彼女はまだ仕事をしていて，ということは，あれこれするよう僕に頼んでいるというわけ。

☆：休暇中にあなたを働かせているの？ 人事部に苦情を言った方がいいよ。

★：だけど僕はここに来てまだ1年だし。会社に忠誠心があると証明したいんだよ。

☆：うーん，今週は必ず自分のために少し時間を取りなさいよ。厳密に言うとあなたは休暇を取っているんだから。

★：そうするよ。ありがとう。

質問：男性について分かることの1つは何か。

選択肢の訳 1 今年もっと後になってから休暇を取る。
2 人事部長と面談する。
3 上司からするように頼まれたことをする。
4 女性に助けてくれるよう頼む。

解説 休暇中なのに会社にいる男性を見て女性は驚いている。男性は，休暇を取りやめて働いている上司に仕事を頼まれていると言い，まだ入社1年なので I'm committed to the company「会社に忠誠心がある」と証明したいと説明している。つまり，**3** のように，男性は上司に頼まれたことをやろうと思っていることになる。technically は「規則を厳密に適用すると」という意味。

No.8 – 解答 ④

スクリプト ★：What do you think of the proposed design for our new company logo?

☆：I quite like the style of the lettering, but the logo doesn't have enough impact. How about you?

★：The colors are appealing, but I think the shape of our current logo represents our company better.

☆：I heard there's a trend toward simplicity these days, but the designers have gone too far in that direction.

★：Agreed. We should talk to them again.

Question: What do these people think about the proposed logo?

21年度第3回 リスニング

115

全文訳 ★： うちの会社の新しいロゴだけど，提案されたデザインについてどう思う？

☆： 文字のスタイルはとても好きだけど，ロゴ（マーク）に十分なインパクトがないわ。あなたはどう？

★： 色使いは引き付けるものがあるけど，今のロゴの形の方がうちの会社をよく表していると思う。

☆： 近ごろはシンプルさを求めるのがトレンドらしいけど，デザイナーたちはそっち方面に行き過ぎたわね。

★： 同感だ。デザイナーたちともう一度話した方がいいな。

質問： この人たちは提案されたロゴについてどう思っているか。

選択肢の訳 **1** もっと明るい色が必要だ。

2 会社のイメージに合っている。

3 現在のロゴに似過ぎている。

4 デザインのやり直しが必要だ。

解説 提案された新しいロゴのデザインについて，女性は文字のスタイルは好きだがロゴにインパクトが足りないと言い，男性は色はいいがロゴの形は今の方がいいと言っている。これらから，最後に男性が言っている We should talk to them again. は，デザインを再考するようデザイナーたちに話すという意味だと考えられる。それを redesign という動詞で表した **4** が正解。

No.9 – 解答 ①

スクリプト ★： Sheena, are you going to Alice's book-launch party on Wednesday?

☆： Of course. It's taken her a decade to write, but the book turned out great!

★： You've already read it? That's not fair! But I suppose you two have been friends since kindergarten.

☆： And I helped with research for one of the chapters.

★： I guess I'll just have to read it when it's available to the general public.

☆： You only have to wait a few days.

Question: What is one thing we learn about the man?

全文訳 ★： シーナ，水曜日のアリスの出版記念パーティーには行くの？

☆： もちろん。彼女は執筆に 10 年かかったけど，本は素晴らしい出来なのよ！

★： もう読んだの？ 不公平だよ！ だけど君たち 2 人は幼稚園からの友だちなんだよね。

☆： それに私は章の 1 つの調査を手伝ったの。

★： 一般の人たちが読めるようになったら，僕も読まなきゃなあ。

☆： 2，3 日待つだけでいいわよ。

質問： 男性について分かることの 1 つは何か。

116

選択肢の訳　**1**　まだアリスの本を読んでいない。
　　　　　2　アリスのパーティーに出席できない。
　　　　　3　アリスとはもう友だちではない。
　　　　　4　アリスの本にがっかりした。

解説　book-launch party は launch a book「本を刊行する」から来た表現で，「出版記念パーティー」のこと。アリスの本について，男性は You've already read it? That's not fair! と言っているので，まだ読んでいないことが分かる。手に入るようになったら読むと言っていることからも裏付けられる。従って **1** が正解。

No.**10** 解答 ②

スクリプト　☆：Morning. Sorry to be late.

★：No problem. Was your train delayed again?

☆：Yes, for the third time this month. I take an early train, but there are always big delays on weekdays during rush hour.

★：Isn't there another train line in your area?

☆：Yes, but the station on that line is a 45-minute walk from my house.

★：Perhaps you could ride your bicycle there.

☆：That's an idea. If I did that, I could catch a later train than I do now.

★：Cycling would be good exercise, too.

☆：Good point. I think I'll give it a try.

Question: What will the woman probably do in the future?

全文訳　☆：おはよう。遅れてごめん。

★：構わないよ。また電車が遅れたの？

☆：うん，今月3度目。早い電車に乗るんだけど，平日のラッシュアワーはいつもすごく遅れるのよね。

★：君の住んでいる地域に別の路線はないの？

☆：あるけど，その線の駅はうちから45分歩くの。

★：そこまで自転車で行くのもありかもしれない。

☆：いい考えね。そうすれば，今より遅い電車に乗れる。

★：サイクリングはいい運動にもなるだろうし。

☆：確かに。やってみようかな。

質問：女性は今後おそらく何をするか。

選択肢の訳　**1**　確実にもっと早い電車に乗るようにする。
　　　　　2　違う路線を使う。
　　　　　3　自転車で会社に行く。
　　　　　4　週末に会社に入る。

117

解説 電車がよく遅れるので遅刻が多い女性に，男性は別の路線の駅まで自転車で行くことを提案している。女性は男性の提案に乗り気である。選択肢の中でこの内容に合致するのは**2**。男性は自転車で会社まで行くのがいいとは言っていないので，**3**は誤り。

No.11 解答 ①

スクリプト ☆ : What're you doing with those garbage bags, Ronan?

★ : I was just about to put them outside. Wednesday is collection day, right?

☆ : Actually, they've switched over to a 14-day schedule. There was an announcement in the local paper last month.

★ : They're only collecting every two weeks now? I sometimes wonder what we pay our taxes for.

☆ : I know what you mean, but I guess the city needs to reduce spending. They're also talking about lowering the number of bags you can put out.

Question: What is one thing we learn from the conversation?

全文訳 ☆ : そのごみ袋，どうするの，ローナン？

★ : 外に出そうとしていたんだ。水曜日は収集日だよね？

☆ : 実はね，14日間のスケジュールに切り替わったの。先月地元紙に告知があったよ。

★ : 今じゃ隔週にしか収集してないってこと？　何のために税金を払っているんだろうとときどき思うよ。

☆ : 言いたいことは分かるけど，市は支出を減らす必要があるんだと思う。外に出せる袋の数を減らそうという話もしているよ。

質問：この会話から分かることの1つは何か。

選択肢の訳 1　ごみ収集の頻度が減った。

2　ごみ袋の価格が高くなる。

3　地方税が間もなく上がりそうだ。

4　新聞の配達スケジュールが変わった。

解説 Wednesday is collection day だと思ってごみ袋を外に出そうとしている男性に，女性は they've switched over to a 14-day schedule と言っている。その後で男性が every two weeks と言い換えているように，毎週水曜日だったごみの収集日が，2週間に1回に減ったことが分かる。それを less frequent と表した **1** が正解。

No.12 解答 ④

スクリプト ★ : Hey, Sharon. Are you OK? You look exhausted.

☆ : Hi, Ranjit. Yeah, I can't sleep because of my upstairs neighbors. They're awake at all hours of the night. Even earplugs haven't

118

worked, so I'm going to complain to the landlord.
★: Have you thought about writing a polite note to them first? They might get upset if you go directly to the landlord.
☆: I hadn't thought about that. Have you ever tried something like that?
★: No, but I've read online that it can be quite effective.
☆: Thanks. I think I'll do that.

Question: What will the woman most likely do?

全文訳 ★：やあ，シャロン。大丈夫？　疲れ果てた顔だよ。
☆：こんにちは，ランジット。うん，上の階の住人のせいで眠れないの。夜の間ずっと起きているんだもの。耳栓をしても効き目がなかったから，大家に苦情を言うつもり。
★：まずその住人にていねいな手紙を書くことは考えた？　大家のところに直行すると，住人は腹を立てるかもしれないよ。
☆：それは考えなかった。そういったことをしてみた経験があるの？
★：ないけど，かなり効果的なこともあるってネットで読んだんだ。
☆：ありがとう。やってみようと思う。
質問：女性は何をする可能性が最も高いか。

選択肢の訳　1　耳栓を使ってみる。
　　　　　　2　ランジットに彼女の上の階の住人と話してもらう。
　　　　　　3　大家について苦情を言う。
　　　　　　4　上の階の住人にメッセージを書く。

解説　上の階の住人が夜の間ずっと起きていて眠れないので大家に苦情を言うつもりだ，と話す女性に対し，男性は Have you thought about writing a polite note to them first? と別の方法を提案している。その後はこの提案に関するやりとりが続くので，女性が最後に言っている I think I'll do that. の that は男性の提案ということになる。note を message と言い換えた **4** が正解。

A

 Picky Eaters

Some children are picky eaters. They will only eat a few foods and refuse to eat anything else, and this is generally considered unhealthy. Researchers have found that genetics may be one cause of this behavior, but the environment in which children are raised may also be important. Parents, for example, serve as role models for their children, so it can be damaging if their children see them following limited, unhealthy diets.

Once children form such eating habits, how can they be changed? Parents often use rewards. For example, they will tell their children they can have ice cream if they eat their vegetables. However, some experts warn against doing this. They say it does little to change children's negative attitudes toward foods they dislike. Instead, these experts recommend involving children in the growing, purchasing, and preparation of these foods. This may help children develop a positive relationship with healthy meals.

Questions

No.13 What may be one reason children become picky eaters?

No.14 What is one thing that some experts recommend?

全文訳 **偏食家**

偏食家の子供がいる。食べるのは数種類の食べ物だけで，ほかのものは一切食べようとせず，これは健康に悪いと一般に考えられている。遺伝的体質がこの行動の1つの理由かもしれないと研究者たちが発見したが，子供が育つ環境も重要かもしれない。例えば，親は子供のロールモデルとなるので，親が限られたものしか食べない不健康な食生活を送るのを子供が見れば有害なことがある。

子供がそうした食習慣を身に付けてしまったら，どうしたら変えられるのだろう。親はしばしば褒美を用いる。例えば，出された野菜を食べたらアイスクリームを食べてもいいと親は子供に言ったりする。しかし，そういうことはしないように警告する専門家たちもいる。嫌いな食べ物に対する子供の否定的態度を変えるのに，これはほとんど役に立たないと彼らは言う。代わりにこれらの専門家たちはこうした食べ物の栽培と購入，そして調理に子供を関与させることを勧める。これは，子供が健康的な食事と前向きな関係を築くのに役立つかもしれない。

No.**13** 解答 ③

質問の訳 子供が偏食家になる理由の1つかもしれないのは何か。

選択肢の訳 **1** 手に入る食べ物の選択肢が多過ぎる。
2 学校がしばしば面白味のない食べ物を用意する。
3 子供は親の食習慣を真似る。
4 子供には減量したいという願望がある。

解説 picky eaters の意味が分からなくても，They will only eat a few foods ... と説明されているので慌てないこと。子供が偏食家になる理由として，2つの可能性が挙げられている。1つは genetics「遺伝的体質」。もう1つは the environment in which children are raised で，続けて具体例が紹介されている。親は子供のロールモデルなので，親の偏食を見ることは子供に有害な影響を与え得る。それを copy「真似る」と

120

No.14 解答 ①

いう動詞を使って表した **3** が正解。

質問の訳 一部の専門家たちが勧めることの1つは何か。
選択肢の訳
1 子供に自分の食事を作る手伝いをさせること。
2 もっと多くのスポーツをするよう子供に促すこと。
3 ときどき子供に不健康な食べ物を食べさせてやること。
4 野菜を食べたことで子供に褒美を与えること。

解説 these experts recommend 以下が専門家たちが勧めることの内容。嫌いな食べ物の the growing, purchasing, and preparation に子供をかかわらせることを勧めている。このうち preparation「食事の準備」，つまり「調理」にかかわらせることに相当する **1** が正解。

B

スクリプト **Ching Shih the Pirate**

It is sometimes said that a Chinese woman named Ching Shih was one of history's most successful pirates. Her husband was also a pirate. Following his death in 1807, Ching Shih took control of their pirate operations, which grew rapidly. The Chinese government then ordered its navy to capture her. The sea battle that followed, however, went badly for the government. Ching Shih's pirates captured several naval vessels, which increased Ching Shih's power.

However, it is thought that Ching Shih began having difficulty controlling her huge forces. In 1810, therefore, she came to an agreement with government officials in which she promised to end her operations. In exchange, she was allowed to keep her wealth, and she and most of her followers were given their freedom. While many pirates throughout history died violently, Ching Shih avoided that fate.

Questions
No.15 What was one result of the sea battle?
No.16 What did Ching Shih do in 1810?

全文訳 海賊・鄭氏

　鄭氏という名の中国人女性が歴史上最も成功した海賊の1人だったと時に言われる。彼女の夫も海賊だった。1807年に夫が死んだ後，鄭氏が彼らの海賊業の支配権を握り，海賊業は急速に成長した。すると中国政府は，彼女を捕らえるよう海軍に命じた。しかし，それに続く海戦は政府に不利に運んだ。鄭氏の海賊たちは軍艦数隻を捕獲し，それが鄭氏の力を増大させた。

　しかし，鄭氏は自身の巨大な軍勢の制御に苦労するようになったと考えられている。そのため，彼女は1810年に，海賊業を終わりにすると約束する協定を政府の役人たちと結んだ。引き換えに，彼女は財産の保持を許され，彼女と手下のほとんどは自由を与えられた。歴史を通して多くの海賊が惨死した一方で，鄭氏はその運命を免れたのだ。

No.15 解答 ①

質問の訳 海戦の結果の1つは何だったか。

選択肢の訳
1 鄭氏の海賊たちが船を何隻か手に入れた。
2 多くの海賊の指揮官たちが捕らえられた。
3 海賊たちのほとんどが死んだ。
4 鄭氏が中国海軍を助けることに同意した。

解説 海賊と中国海軍の間の海戦は went badly for the government なので，海賊側が優勢だったことが分かる。captured several naval vessels を gained a number of ships と言い換えた **1** が正解。

No.16 解答 ④

質問の訳 鄭氏は1810年に何をしたか。

選択肢の訳
1 処罰を逃れるため中国を去った。
2 財産を差し出した。
3 新たな海賊組織を作った。
4 海賊業をやめることに同意した。

解説 1810年に鄭氏は政府の役人たちと協定を結んだが，その内容は she promised to end her operations というものだった。operations は前半に出てくる pirate operations のことなので，**4** が正解。

C

スクリプト **The Canada Lynx**

The Canada lynx is a type of wildcat found mainly in Canada and the northern United States. The animals are skilled at avoiding humans, so they are rarely seen in the wild. However, lynx sightings increase roughly every 10 years. This is because the population of animals called snowshoe hares rises and falls in a roughly 10-year cycle. Lynx hunt snowshoe hares, and when there are more hares to hunt, the lynx population tends to grow.

It was long believed that Canada lynx live their whole lives in one particular area. However, scientists have discovered that lynx can journey thousands of kilometers to establish new territories. Some scientists think it is likely that these animals are following hares. However, lynx have also been observed making long journeys at other times, so there may be another reason why they travel.

Questions

No.17 What does the speaker say about Canada lynx?

No.18 What did scientists discover about Canada lynx?

全文訳 **カナダオオヤマネコ**

カナダオオヤマネコは，主にカナダとアメリカ北部に生息するヤマネコの一種である。この動物は人間を避けるすべにたけているので，野生ではめったに見られない。しかし，

122

オオヤマネコの目撃例はおよそ 10 年ごとに増加する。これは，カンジキウサギという動物の個体数が，およそ 10 年周期で増減するためである。オオヤマネコはカンジキウサギを狩り，狩るウサギが多いほどオオヤマネコの個体数は増える傾向がある。

　カナダオオヤマネコは生涯ある特定の地域に生息すると長い間考えられていた。しかし，オオヤマネコは新たなテリトリーを築くために数千キロの旅をすることができると科学者たちが発見した。一部の科学者たちは，おそらくこの動物はウサギを追っているのだろうと考えている。しかし，オオヤマネコはほかのときにも長旅をしているのが観察されているので，彼らが移動する別の理由があるのかもしれない。

No.17 解答 ①

質問の訳 話者はカナダオオヤマネコについて何と言っているか。

選択肢の訳 1 ある特定の時期に数が増える。
2 人間に狩られている。
3 生息地が最近狭くなった。
4 食べるカンジキウサギの数が減ってきている。

解説 話者がカナダオオヤマネコについて話している情報は，主にカナダとアメリカ北部に住んでいること，ほとんどない目撃例が約 10 年ごとに増えること，それは餌となるウサギの数が増えるのでカナダオオヤマネコも増えるからだということ。個体数が約 10 年ごとに増えることについて，**1** が population を numbers と言い換え，「約 10 年ごとに」を at certain times と抽象的に表している。

No.18 解答 ②

質問の訳 科学者たちはカナダオオヤマネコについて何を発見したか。

選択肢の訳 1 食べ物を探すときだけ移動する。
2 時に長距離を移動する。
3 ほかのヤマネコよりずっと長生きする。
4 常に最初のテリトリーに戻る。

解説 scientists have discovered that 以下が科学者たちが発見した内容。「新たなテリトリーを築くために数千キロも旅をすることができる」と述べられている。この内容を journey → travel, thousands of kilometers → long distances と言い換えた **2** が正解。**1** は，ほかのとき（＝食べ物を探す以外のとき）にも長旅をするのが観察されているので誤り。

D

スクリプト **The Catacombs of Priscilla**

In Rome, there are networks of tunnels that were built around the beginning of the second century AD. These tunnels were used as burial places for people of many religions. However, the tunnels became especially important for

Christians. Their religion was not officially recognized at the time, so Christians used the tunnels to hold religious ceremonies.

One famous section of tunnels is called the Catacombs of Priscilla. In this section, there are some early Christian paintings. One of the paintings seems to show a woman dressed in a priest's robe, and others show women performing religious ceremonies. Some people believe the paintings are proof of female priests in the church in ancient times. This is significant because some Christian churches today do not allow women to become priests. Other observers, however, say that we cannot be sure exactly what the paintings show.

Questions

No.19 What is one thing we learn about the tunnels?

No.20 What do some people believe the paintings show?

全文訳 **プリシッラのカタコンベ**

ローマには，紀元2世紀初頭前後に造られた地下トンネル網がある。これらのトンネルは，多くの宗教の人々の埋葬所として用いられた。しかし，トンネルはキリスト教徒にとって特に重要になった。彼らの宗教は当時公式には認められていなかったので，キリスト教徒は宗教儀式を行うためにトンネルを用いた。

トンネルのある有名な区画は，プリシッラのカタコンベと呼ばれる。この区画には，幾つかの初期キリスト教絵画がある。絵の1つは，祭服に身を包んだ女性を描いているように思われ，ほかの絵は宗教儀式を執り行う女性たちを描いている。これらの絵は古代の教会に女性聖職者がいた証拠だと考える人もいる。今日のキリスト教の教派には女性が聖職者になることを許さないところもあるのだから，これは重要なことである。しかし，ほかの評者たちは，これらの絵が何を描いているのか，はっきりとは分からないと言う。

No.**19** 解答 ② ⸺⸺⸺⸺⸺⸺⸺⸺⸺⸺⸺⸺⸺ 正答率 ★75％以上

質問の訳 トンネルについて分かることの1つは何か。

選択肢の訳　**1**　現代の埋葬所はそのトンネルの設計に基づいている。
　　　　　　2　宗教的目的で用いられた。
　　　　　　3　非キリスト教徒によってのみ用いられた。
　　　　　　4　入り口はつい最近見つかったばかりだ。

解説　catacomb は「地下墓所」の意味で，特に初期キリスト教のものは「カタコンベ」と呼ばれる。ただし，この語の意味が分からなくても問題はなく，トンネルの話だと理解できれば十分である。そのトンネルは多くの宗教の burial places「埋葬所」で，またキリスト教徒は religious ceremonies「宗教儀式」に用いたと言っていることから，**2** が正解となる。

124

No.20 解答 ①

質問の訳 絵が何を描いていると一部の人は考えているか。

選択肢の訳 1 昔は女性が聖職者だった。
2 トンネルは教会として用いられなかった。
3 初期キリスト教徒に女性はほとんどいなかった。
4 かつては聖職者たちが絵を制作していた。

解説 トンネルにある絵には祭服を着た女性や宗教儀式を行う女性が描かれているように見える，という話に続いて，絵が proof of female priests in the church in ancient times だと一部の人は考えている，と言っている。この内容から **1** が正解。

E

スクリプト **Happiness and Success**

Many people believe that only by working hard and having a successful career can they find happiness. However, trying to make a lot of money or get promoted at work may not make people truly happy. People who focus on such success often prioritize work over other activities. Consequently, they may lose opportunities to enjoy the things that make life truly enjoyable, such as simple, relaxing times with their families.

After reviewing many studies, researchers recently concluded that success may actually follow happiness. They believe that happy people are more energetic and confident because they experience frequent positive moods, and that this leads to success. Of course, success also depends on factors such as intelligence and social support. More research is needed, but it may be that those whose happiness leads them to success are more likely to stay happy.

Questions

No.21 What does the speaker say about people who focus on success?

No.22 What did researchers recently conclude about happy people?

全文訳 **幸福と成功**

多くの人は，一生懸命働いてキャリアで成功を収めることによってのみ幸福を見いだすことができると考えている。しかし，大金を稼ごうとしたり仕事で昇進しようとしたりすることは，人を真に幸福にはしないかもしれない。そうした成功に注力する人は，ほかの活動より仕事を優先することが多い。それゆえ，家族と過ごす飾らないほっとする時間といった，人生を真に楽しいものにする物事を楽しむ機会を失ってしまうかもしれない。

多くの研究を精査した後，最近研究者たちは，成功は実際には幸福の後に来るのかもしれないという結論を出した。幸福な人は前向きな気分をしばしば経験するので，より活力と自信があり，これが成功につながると研究者たちは考えている。もちろん，成功は知能やソーシャルサポートといった要因にも依拠している。さらなる研究が必要だが，

幸福によって成功に導かれる人たちの方が幸福でい続ける可能性が高いのかもしれない。

No.21 解答 3

質問の訳 話者は成功に注力する人について何と言っているか。

選択肢の訳 1 しばしば成功した家族がいる。
2 しばしばストレスレベルが低い。
3 飾らない喜びを楽しむチャンスを逃しているかもしれない。
4 周囲の人を幸福にするかもしれない。

解説 People who focus on such success 以下で，そういう人は仕事を優先することが多く，家族と過ごすといった人生の楽しみを味わう機会を失ってしまうかもしれないと言っている。**3**がそれと一致する。放送文の lose opportunities を miss chances と言い換え，the things that make life truly enjoyable を pleasures の1語でまとめている。

No.22 解答 3

質問の訳 最近研究者たちは幸福な人についてどんな結論を出したか。

選択肢の訳 1 幸福でい続けるために家族の支援を必要としない。
2 収入はおそらく多くない。
3 前向きな気分が彼らをより活動的にする。
4 不幸な人より知能が高い。

解説 研究者たちの結論は success may actually follow happiness で，続けて詳しく説明されている。すなわち，幸福な人の前向きな気分が活力と自信を生み，それが成功につながる，と述べている。energetic を active と言い換えた**3**が正解である。なお，social support は行政による金銭的・制度的支援というより，家族や友人など社会的なつながりがある人たちからの精神的支援という意味合いが強い。

F

スクリプト **Ancient Oysters**

For thousands of years, Native Americans along what is now called the US East Coast used oysters as a food source. Today, however, oyster stocks have been greatly reduced. Overharvesting, pollution, and disease have caused oyster populations to fall, especially since the late 1800s, when European settlers introduced new harvesting methods. These methods included dredging, which involves removing huge numbers of oysters from the seabed. This process also damages the ecosystem in which the oysters live.

In recent years, archaeologists have studied Native American harvesting practices. The archaeologists found that Native Americans did not harvest young oysters. Instead, Native Americans waited for oysters to grow and reproduce before they harvested them. The archaeologists also discovered that

126

average shell size increased until the 1800s, which indicates that Native American practices helped ancient oysters to become larger. This finding surprised the archaeologists, who expected oyster shells to gradually get smaller in response to being harvested.

Questions

No.23 What do we learn about oysters along the US East Coast today?

No.24 What is one thing the archaeologists discovered?

全文訳 **古代のカキ**

　数千年の間，今ではアメリカ東海岸と呼ばれる所に沿って住んでいたネイティブアメリカンは，カキを食料源として利用していた。しかし今日では，カキ資源は大きく減少している。乱獲と汚染，そして病気が原因で，特にヨーロッパからの入植者が新しい収穫方法を持ち込んだ 1800 年代後期以降，カキの個体数が落ち込んだ。これらの方法には桁網漁業（漁具で海底を引っかいて漁獲する漁法）も含まれていたのだが，桁網漁業は海底から膨大な数のカキを取り去ることを伴う。このプロセスは，カキがすむ生態系にもダメージを与える。

　近年，考古学者たちがネイティブアメリカンの収穫のやり方を研究している。ネイティブアメリカンは若いカキを収穫しなかったことを考古学者たちは突き止めた。その代わり，ネイティブアメリカンはカキを収穫する前に，カキが成長して繁殖するのを待った。考古学者たちは平均的な殻のサイズが 1800 年代までは大きくなっていたことも発見したが，これは，ネイティブアメリカンのやり方が古代のカキの大型化を助けたことを示している。カキの殻は収穫されるのに対応して次第に小型化するはずだと考古学者は思っていたので，この発見は彼らを驚かせた。

No.23 解答 **2** ....

質問の訳　今日のアメリカ東海岸沿いのカキについて何が分かるか。

選択肢の訳　**1**　病気と闘うのがよりうまくなってきている。

　　　　　　2　数が以前より少ない。

　　　　　　3　カキの多くは食用に収穫されない。

　　　　　　4　カキがすむ水域がきれいになってきている。

解説　東海岸のカキの現在の状況については，oyster stocks have been greatly reduced や have caused oyster populations to fall と言っていることから，数が減っていると分かる。それを「以前より少ない」と表した **2** が正解。減った理由として disease を挙げているので **1** は不適。pollution や生態系へのダメージを挙げているので **4** も不適である。

No.24 解答 **1** ....

質問の訳　考古学者たちが発見したことの 1 つは何か。

選択肢の訳　**1**　ネイティブアメリカンの収穫のやり方はカキが大きくなるのを助けた。

　　　　　　2　ネイティブアメリカンの収穫方法は桁網漁業を含んでいた。

127

3 ネイティブアメリカンは今でもカキを収穫する。
4 ネイティブアメリカンは若いカキしか収穫しなかった。

解説 考古学者たちの発見は2つ。1つは、ネイティブアメリカンは若いカキを収穫せずカキが成長するのを待ったこと。もう1つは、そうしたやり方がカキの大型化を助けたことである。2つ目の発見の大型化(become larger) を 1 が grow と言い換えている。

一次試験・リスニング Part 3　問題編 p.94～95　

###

スクリプト

You have 10 seconds to read the situation and Question No. 25.

This bus goes around town all day, so you can just hop on and off anytime. The castle can be accessed from stop 4, and the medieval library is also just a five-minute walk away from that stop. If you're interested in the San Giovanni church, stop 7 is the nearest. It's also normally the meeting place for our 30-minute guided walking tour, but please note that due to an ongoing construction project, that tour will begin from stop 9, just in front of Montalto Gardens. Stop 13 offers access to famous sights like the Gravina Bridge and the town fountain.

Now mark your answer on your answer sheet.

全文訳

このバスは終日町を巡りますので、いつでも乗り降りしていただけます。お城は4番バス停からアクセスでき、中世の図書館もそのバス停からわずか徒歩5分の距離です。サン・ジョバンニ教会に興味がおありなら、7番バス停が最寄りです。そこは通常は当社のガイド付き30分徒歩ツアーの集合場所でもありますが、進行中の建築事業のため、そのツアーはモンタルト庭園の正面、9番バス停から始まります。13番バス停からは、グラビーナ橋や町の泉などの名所にアクセスできます。

No.25 解答 ③

状況の訳 あなたはイタリアで町を巡るツアーバスに乗るところである。ガイド付きの徒歩ツアーに参加したい。次のようなアナウンスが聞こえる。

質問の訳 あなたはどのバス停で降りればよいか。

選択肢の訳
1 4番バス停。
2 7番バス停。
3 9番バス停。
4 13番バス停。

128

解説 状況から,「ガイド付きの徒歩ツアー」がポイントになる。stop 7 が教会の最寄りのバス停であるという説明に続いて It's also normally the meeting place for our 30-minute guided walking tour と言っているが, normally「通常は」から, 今は違う事情があるのだと予想できる。すると続けて, 建築事業のためツアーは 9 番バス停から始まるとアナウンスしているので, **3** が正解となる。なお, hop on は「飛び乗る」, hop off は「飛び降りる」だが, 途中で乗降可能なツアーバスについて「乗る」「降りる」の意味でも用いられる。

H

スクリプト

You have 10 seconds to read the situation and Question No. 26.

You can apply online to renew your working-holiday visa. However, there are some things you should prepare before you apply. You'll need to provide proof that you've had a medical examination by a qualified doctor and have no serious health issues. Once you've done that, you'll also have to present evidence of your employment until now. You mentioned you had all of your salary statements, so those should be sufficient. Since you're applying from within the country, proof that you've saved enough to cover your living costs will not be required this time around.

Now mark your answer on your answer sheet.

全文訳

ワーキングホリデービザの更新はオンラインで申請できます。ですが, 申請する前に用意しておいた方がいいものが幾つかあります。有資格医師から健康診断を受け, 健康に重大な問題がないことの証明を提出する必要があります。それが済んだら, 現在までの雇用の証拠も提示しなければなりません。給与明細は全てお持ちだというお話でしたから, それで十分でしょう。国内から申請することになるので, 生活費を賄うのに足りるだけのお金を貯めたという証明は, 今回は必要とされません。

No.26 解答 ④

状況の訳 あなたはワーキングホリデープログラムで外国にいる。ビザの更新について入国管理事務所に電話し, 次のような話をされる。

質問の訳 あなたはまず何をすべきか。

選択肢の訳 1 オンラインで申請書に記入する。
2 雇用主に給与明細を要請する。
3 貯蓄の証明を見せる。
4 健康診断証明書を取得する。

解説 「まず」何をすればいいかに集中して聞く。話者は before you apply「申請する前に」用意するものを幾つか挙げ, まず medical

129

examination の証明が必要だと言っている。Once you've done that「それが済んだら」雇用の証拠の提示だが，すでに持っている salary statements で足りる。貯蓄の証明は不要だと最後に言っている。従って，まず **4** をしてから申請に移ることになる。

スクリプト

You have 10 seconds to read the situation and Question No. 27.

The new security cameras, warning signs, and staff training have all worked. Shoplifting of most products is much lower than in the last quarter. However, stock records for low-cost fruit items like bananas and oranges and expensive things like avocados and mangoes don't match the sales records. This usually means some customers at the self-checkout registers are entering false information to get costly items at a cheaper price. I recommend extra guidance for staff observing the self-checkout stations. If this doesn't work, you may have to think about checking customers' receipts at the exit.

Now mark your answer on your answer sheet.

全文訳

新しい監視カメラと警告の掲示，そしてスタッフの訓練は全て効果が出ています。ほとんどの商品の万引きは，前の四半期よりかなり減っています。ですが，バナナやオレンジなど低価格の果物の品目と，アボカドやマンゴーなど値の張るものの在庫記録が，販売記録と合いません。これは普通，セルフレジの一部の客が，高価な商品をより安い価格で手に入れるため，偽りの情報を登録していることを意味します。セルフレジコーナーを見張るスタッフに追加の指導をすることをお勧めします。それでも効果がなければ，出口で客のレシートを調べることを検討しなければならないかもしれません。

No.27 解答 ①

状況の訳　あなたはスーパーマーケットの店長である。窃盗が原因の損失を減らしたいと思っている。警備アナリストが次のように言う。

質問の訳　あなたはまず何をすべきか。

選択肢の訳
1　スタッフの一部にもっと訓練を受けさせる。
2　もっと多くの監視カメラを設置する。
3　出口で客のレシートをよく調べる。
4　果物の価格をはっきりと表示する。

解説　アナリストは，セルフレジで高い果物を安い果物だと偽って登録する客がいるため損失が起きている可能性があると指摘している。それに対する提案は extra guidance for staff observing the self-checkout stations なので，extra guidance を more training と言い換えた **1** が正解。staff training はすでに効果が出ていると最初に言っているが，

それでは足りないということになる。**3**は**1**でも効果がない場合の対策。

(スクリプト)

You have 10 seconds to read the situation and Question No. 28.

Welcome to our summer sale. We're offering great discounts on all brands, including Rannexe and Duplanne. Interested in a new vacuum cleaner? Use the coupon available on our smartphone app to get $50 off any brand. How about a new washing machine? This month, exchange your used Rannexe washing machine for a $100 credit toward any new Rannexe product. During the month of August, exchange any old Duplanne appliance and get $150 off a new one. Finally, we are offering $75 cash back on any new dishwasher until the end of August.

Now mark your answer on your answer sheet.

(全文訳)

当店の夏のセールにようこそ。ラネックスとデュプランを含め，全ブランドを大幅値引き中です。新しい掃除機に関心がおありですか。当店のスマートフォンアプリで手に入るクーポンをご利用いただくと，どんなブランドも50ドル引きになります。新しい洗濯機はいかがですか。今月は，お使いのラネックスの洗濯機を，ラネックスのどんな新しい製品にも使える100ドル分のクレジットと交換してください。8月の間は，古いデュプランの家電製品をどれでも交換していただくと，新しいものが150ドル引きになります。最後に，8月末まで，新しい食器洗い機にはどれも75ドルのキャッシュバックをご提供中です。

No.28 解答 ④

(状況の訳) あなたは新しい洗濯機が欲しい。現在はデュプランの洗濯機を所有している。7月に電器店を訪れ，次のようなアナウンスを聞く。

(質問の訳) お金を最も節約するには，あなたは何をすべきか。

(選択肢の訳)
1 店のスマートフォンアプリをダウンロードする。
2 キャッシュバックがある得な買い物を申し込む。
3 今月洗濯機を交換する。
4 8月に新しいデュプランの洗濯機を買う。

(解説) Duplanneの洗濯機を所有していることだけでなく，今はJulyだということもポイントになると予測して聞く。スマホアプリのクーポンが使えるのは掃除機だけ。100ドル分のクレジットは，Rannexeの洗濯機と交換と言っているので該当しない。続いて，8月中にDuplanneの製品を買い替えると150ドル引きになると言っている。最後のキャッシュバックは食器洗い機のみ。以上から，最も節約になるのは8月にDuplanneの洗濯機に買い替えることである。**3**のthis monthは7月

なので不適。creditは，その店で使える金券やポイントなどのこと。

スクリプト

You have 10 seconds to read the situation and Question No. 29.

This suit is a clearance item, so we only have what's here on the shelves. Our other location may still have one in your size, though. If you'd like, I can check online for you. If our other store has one, you could go there, if you don't mind driving out of town. The other option would be to reserve one for you and have it sent over to this store at no extra cost. That might take a few days, but if you give me your number, I can call you when it arrives.

Now mark your answer on your answer sheet.

全文訳

このスーツは売り尽くしの商品なので，ここの棚のものしかありません。ですが，ほかの店舗ならお客さまのサイズがまだあるかもしれません。よろしければ，オンラインでお調べできます。ほかの店にあれば，車で町の外まで行っていただいても差し支えなければ，そちらに行かれるのがいいでしょう。もう1つの選択肢は，スーツを取り置きして，追加料金なしで当店に送ってもらうことになります。2, 3日かかるかもしれませんが，お電話番号を教えていただければ，届いたら電話でお知らせできます。

No.29 解答 ②

状況の訳 あなたは近所の店で欲しいスーツを目にするが，あなたのサイズのスーツがない。町の外には出かけたくない。店員が次のように言う。

質問の訳 あなたは何をすべきか。

選択肢の訳
1 店が新しい在庫を入れるまで待つ。
2 店員にほかの店を調べてもらう。
3 オンラインストアにスーツを注文する。
4 スーツを自宅に配達してもらう。

解説 スーツはclearance itemだと店員は言っており，**1**の可能性はない。他店舗ならあるかもしれず，オンラインで調べられると言っていることから**2**が正解。If our other store has one以下では他店舗にあった場合のことが詳しく述べられているが，それに該当する選択肢はない。**3**は放送文のonlineを使った引っかけ。スーツがあったらthis storeに送ってもらうと言っているので，**4**も不適。

132

二次試験・面接　問題カード **A** 日程　問題編 p.96〜97

解答例　**One day, a husband and wife were going on a walk together.** They saw a group of volunteers picking up garbage in the park. The husband and wife looked pleased to see them cleaning up the area. The next day, the couple was walking around their neighborhood again, and they saw a poster. It said that volunteers were wanted to help at the city marathon. The couple thought it was a good opportunity for them, so they decided to volunteer. At a volunteer staff meeting, the couple was listening to an explanation about their duties at the marathon. A man was explaining that volunteers would help with tasks like working at water stations and at the information booth. The couple seemed to be looking forward to volunteering at the marathon. The day before the marathon, however, the wife was speaking with her manager at work. He told her that she needed to meet a client the next day.

解答例の訳　ある日，夫婦が一緒に散歩に出かけていました。彼らはボランティアたちが公園でごみ拾いをしているのを見かけました。彼らが地域をすっかりきれいにしているのを見て，夫婦はうれしそうでした。翌日，夫婦はまた近所を散歩していて，ポスターを見かけました。市のマラソン大会を手伝うボランティアを募集していると書かれていました。自分たちにとっていい機会だと夫婦は思ったので，ボランティアをすることにしました。ボランティアスタッフの打ち合わせで，夫婦はマラソン大会での自分たちの任務に関する説明を聞いていました。ボランティアは給水所や案内所で働くといった作業の手伝いをする，と男性が説明していました。夫婦はマラソン大会でボランティアをするのを楽しみにしているようでした。しかしマラソン大会の前日，妻は職場で上司と話していました。翌日彼女は顧客と会う必要がある，と彼は彼女に告げました。

解説　解答に含めるべき点は以下の4つ。①散歩中の夫婦がボランティアの清掃活動を見かける，②翌日，夫婦はマラソン大会のボランティア募集のポスターを見かける，③ボランティアスタッフの打ち合わせで，マラソン大会での任務の説明を夫婦が聞いている，④マラソン大会の前日，妻は，翌日は顧客に会う必要があると上司に言われる。人物の表情や発言，掲示物の内容などを基に，夫婦の気持ちを想像しよう。解答例は，1コマ目について pleased，3コマ目について looking forward to と，前向きな気持ちを示す表現を用いている。

No. 1

解答例 I'd be thinking that I should have talked about becoming a volunteer with my boss first. Now I can't fulfill my responsibilities to both my work and the marathon. I should be more careful about my schedule in the future.

解説 質問は「4番目の絵を見てください。もしあなたがこの妻なら，どのようなことを考えているでしょうか」。解答例は〈I should have ＋ 過去分詞〉を使って上司にあらかじめ話しておかなかった後悔を表している。

No. 2

解答例 Yes. It's a chance for parents to better understand their children's relationships with their classmates. This is good for building strong family relationships. It also gives parents and teachers an opportunity to communicate.

解説 質問は「親は運動会などの学校行事に参加すべきだと思いますか」。解答例は Yes の立場で，自分の子供とクラスメートの関係をより良く理解できる，家族の関係が強まる，親と教師の意思疎通の機会になる，と3つの利点を挙げている。No の立場では，親は仕事を優先しなければならないこともある，行事の数が多過ぎる，といった理由が考えられる。

No. 3

解答例 No. The purpose of public libraries is to give people access to information, but I think we can achieve the same goal using digital libraries online. That way, we don't need to spend a lot of money maintaining library buildings.

解説 質問は「公共図書館は今でも地域社会で重要な役割を果たしていますか」。解答例は No の立場で，デジタル図書館で情報を提供することができるのだから，図書館の維持に大金を費やす必要はないとしている。That way「そうすれば」というつなぎ言葉を効果的に使っている。Yes の立場では，誰もが気軽に情報を得たり，子供に読書習慣をつけたりなどの機能は今でも有効だ，などと述べることができる。

No. 4

解答例 Definitely. It might not be realistic for some companies, but I think in many cases having a more flexible schedule is an easy way to increase employee satisfaction. This will especially help employees who have young children.

解説 質問は「より多くの企業が従業員に柔軟な仕事のスケジュールを提供すべきですか」。Definitely.「絶対にそうです」は Yes. より強い肯定表現。従業員の満足感を高め，特に小さい子供のいる従業員は助かるとしている。ほかに，仕事の効率が上がる，在宅勤務はコスト削減につながる，などの理由も考えられる。

二次試験・面接　問題カード **C** 日程　問題編 p.98～99　▶MP3 ▶アプリ ▶CD 4 24～27

21年度第3回　面接

解答例 **One day, a woman was talking with her friend.** They were sitting at a table, and her friend was holding a brochure for a beach resort. The woman's friend suggested they go together, but the woman looked worried about the price. Later that evening, the woman was looking at her computer, and she saw that she could earn money by doing some part-time work before the trip. According to the calendar, the woman's trip was just a few weeks away. Two weeks later, the woman was working at a restaurant. She was taking an order while her manager looked on. A few days later, the woman's suitcase was almost packed, and she was nearly ready for her trip. She was talking on the phone with her manager. The manager had an injured leg and was telling her that the restaurant would need her help the next day.

解答例の訳 ある日，女性が友人と話していました。彼女らはテーブルに座り，友人はビーチリゾートのパンフレットを持っていました。女性の友人は一緒に行くことを提案しましたが，女性は料金が心配そうな表情でした。その後その日の晩，女性はパソコンを見ていて，旅行の前にパートタイムの仕事をしてお金を稼ぐことができると知りました。カレンダーによると，女性の旅行はわずか数週間先でした。2週間後，女性はレストランで働いていました。店長がそばで見ている中，彼女は注文を取っていました。数日後，女性のスーツケースはほぼ荷造りが終わっていて，彼女は旅行の準備がほとんどできていました。彼女は店長と電話で話していました。店長は脚をけがしていて，レストランは翌日彼女の手伝いが必要になると彼女に話していました。

解説 解答に含めるべき点は以下の4つ。①女性の友人がビーチリゾートに一緒に行こうと誘うが，女性はお金の心配をしている，②その日の晩，女性はパソコンを見ていて，パートタイムの仕事でお金を稼げばいいと思い付く，また，カレンダーによると旅行まで半月ほどある，③2週間後，女性はレストランで働いている，④数日後，旅行の前日になって，荷造り中の女性に店長から電話があり，脚をけがしたので翌日手伝ってほしいと言われる。1コマ目の友人のLet's go together! を suggest を使って言い換えているが，その後の動詞が they go と仮定法現在になることに注意。3コマ目の描写のように接続詞 while を用いると，同時に起きている2つのことを1つの文ですっきりと表現できる。

135

No. 1

解答例 I'd be thinking, "I'm sorry to hear that my manager hurt his leg, but it's impossible for me to work tomorrow. I've already booked everything for the trip, including the plane ticket and hotel reservation."

解説 質問は「4番目の絵を見てください。もしあなたがこの女性なら，どのようなことを考えているでしょうか」。解答例は，店長のけがは気の毒だが，航空券やホテルなどをすでに予約してあるのだから，明日仕事をするのは無理だ，という内容。ほかには，旅行のことを店長に伝えていなかったので話しておくべきだった，などの考えがあり得るだろう。

No. 2

解答例 It depends. Classwork should always come first. However, some university students have a lot of free time. In such cases, getting a part-time job is a good way to earn extra money and learn responsibility.

解説 質問は「大学生がアルバイトをするのはいいことだと思いますか」。解答例は It depends.「状況次第だ」という立場。学業第一であるべきだとした上で，自由な時間があるのならアルバイトをするのもよい，と述べている。ほかにも，社会経験は将来役に立つ，親の経済的負担を減らせる，といった Yes の立場などが考えられる。

No. 3

解答例 No. These days, there are many different types of theft on the Internet. Even large online businesses have had their information stolen by hackers. Traditional, face-to-face businesses are safer.

解説 質問は「オンライン企業に個人情報を渡すことは安全だと思いますか」。解答例は No の立場で，インターネット上では情報が盗まれるので従来の対面式が安全だという意見。Yes の立場では，企業のコンプライアンスは向上した，ネットの安全対策は強化された，などの理由が考えられる。

No. 4

解答例 I don't think so. Companies should only hire as many employees as they need. Hiring too many workers would mean the companies become less efficient. In addition, the unemployment rate in Japan is not so bad.

解説 質問は「日本の雇用率を上げるために政府はより多くのことをすべきですか」。解答例は，過剰に従業員を雇用するとその会社の効率が下がることになるという考えと，日本の雇用率は悪くないという現状認識から，政府の積極的介入に反対する立場である。

136

2021-2

一次試験
筆記解答・解説　　　p.138〜153

一次試験
リスニング解答・解説　p.154〜176

二次試験
面接解答・解説　　　p.177〜180

解 答 一 覧

一次試験・筆記

1

(1)	2	(10)	1	(19)	1
(2)	4	(11)	3	(20)	1
(3)	2	(12)	3	(21)	3
(4)	2	(13)	4	(22)	3
(5)	3	(14)	3	(23)	1
(6)	4	(15)	2	(24)	3
(7)	4	(16)	4	(25)	4
(8)	1	(17)	1		
(9)	2	(18)	3		

2

(26)	3	(29)	3
(27)	1	(30)	1
(28)	3	(31)	4

3

(32)	2	(35)	3	(38)	2
(33)	4	(36)	2	(39)	4
(34)	2	(37)	4	(40)	2
				(41)	3

4 解答例は本文参照

一次試験・リスニング

Part 1					
No. 1	1	No. 5	4	No. 9	1
No. 2	2	No. 6	4	No.10	3
No. 3	3	No. 7	1	No.11	2
No. 4	2	No. 8	4	No.12	4

Part 2					
No.13	2	No.17	2	No.21	1
No.14	1	No.18	4	No.22	2
No.15	3	No.19	2	No.23	3
No.16	1	No.20	4	No.24	4

Part 3			
No.25	3	No.28	3
No.26	1	No.29	2
No.27	3		

一次試験・筆記 **1** 問題編 p.102〜105

(1) ―解答 ②

訳 ケビンの上司は，安全の必要性は，危険を冒すことを伴う時間の節約**よりも重要である**と考えている。彼は不注意による事故よりも建設事業の遅延に対処したいと思うだろう。

解説 それぞれ第 2 文の careless accidents が第 1 文の safety に，delays が the time savings に対応している。空所に outweighs「（重要性が）勝る」を入れて，「安全の必要性が時間の節約よりも重要」とする。それぞれ grasp「把握する」，declare「宣言する」，captivate「魅了する」の 3 人称単数・現在形。

(2) ―解答 ④ ･･････････････ 正答率 ★**75%以上**

訳 A：なぜ引っ越したいの？　君のアパートはすごくいいのに。
B：もっと**広々とした**所がいいの。この場所は私の持ち物全部を入れるには狭過ぎるわ。

解説 B はアパートを引っ越したい理由を話している。第 2 文の too small から，もっと「広々とした」場所を必要としているのである。spacious = space（空間）＋-ous（〜の多い）。tragic「悲劇的な」，legible「判読可能な」，tentative「暫定的な」

(3) ―解答 ②

訳 『自然愛好家』誌の出版元は，その**発行部数**を心配している。読者数は 5 年前には 40,000 人を超えていたのが現在では 15,000 人にまで減少している。

解説 第 2 文で読者数の減少を述べていることから，出版元の心配の種は circulation「発行部数」である。aviation「航空学」，commencement「開始」，imprisonment「投獄」

(4) ―解答 ②

訳 その若い政治家には少ないながらも**熱狂的な**支持者がいる。彼の支持者たちは彼の選挙イベントで非常に熱心で，彼が話すのを聞くためだけに長距離を移動する。

解説 第 1 文の following と第 2 文の supporters はいずれも「支持者」の意味。支持者の特徴として，第 2 文の enthusiastic に近い意味の fanatical「熱狂的な」が適切。holistic「全体論の」，mellow「（音・色などが）豊潤な」，illogical「非論理的な」

(5) ―解答 ③

訳 **頑丈**に作られた棚ならサルマの重い本を支えられたであろうが，彼女が使うことにした安物の棚は，その重さで壊れてしまった。

138

解説 would have supported は仮定法過去完了で，過去の事実と反する内容を表す。つまり，A (　) built shelf は使わなかった＝代わりに安物の棚を使った，という文意。重い本を支えられる棚は，頑丈に（sturdily）作られていると考えられる。built は過去分詞で shelf を前置修飾している。loyally「忠実に」，fondly「愛情を込めて」，vastly「非常に」

(6) ― 解答 **4**

訳 大使は，二度と戦争をしないように，両国の緊密な関係を育むために一生懸命努力した。

解説 so that 以下の「二度と戦争をしないように」という内容から，大使は両国の緊密な関係を育む（nurture）努力をしたのである。tickle「くすぐる」，swallow「飲み込む」，litter「散らかす」

(7) ― 解答 **4** ・・・・・・・・・・・・・・・・・・・・・・・・ 正答率 ★**75%以上**

訳 その気候の専門家は，自動車排ガスが地球温暖化の主な原因であると述べた。彼は，自動車が毎年どれだけの二酸化炭素を環境に放出しているかを示すデータを提示した。

解説 地球温暖化の原因を考えると，vehicle emissions「自動車排ガス」が適切。第2文の how much CO_2 cars released の release「放出する」もヒントになる。それぞれ withdrawal「撤退，（預金の）引き出し」，collision「衝突」，settlement「解決，入植地」の複数形。

(8) ― 解答 **1** ・・・・・・・・・・・・・・・・・・・・・・・・ 正答率 ★**75%以上**

訳 ロバートは非常に人里離れた地域にある丸太小屋に住んでいる。一番近い村まで車で90分以上かかる。

解説 第2文の内容から，村から非常に遠い所に住んでいることが想像できる。remote「人里離れた，辺ぴな」が正解。virtual「実質上の，仮想の」，blunt「切れ味の悪い，ぶっきらぼうな」，swift「敏速な」

(9) ― 解答 **2** ・・

訳 昨日，レットは庭仕事をしている間に気を失った。彼が目を覚ますと，妻と子供たちが心配そうな顔つきで彼の周りに立っていた。

解説 家族が心配する状況であることと，「目を覚ますと」とあることから，fainted「気を失った」が適切。それぞれ dilute「薄める」，persist「言い張る，持続する」，correct「訂正する」の過去形。

(10) ― 解答 **1** ・・

訳 筆者は，明確にするために自分のエッセーに手を加え，特に努力して文章の理解しにくい部分を改善した。

解説 自分の書いた文章について，理解しにくい部分を分かりやすくした＝明確にしたのである。clarity「明確さ」は clear「明確な」の名詞形。appetite「食欲」，shelter「避難所」，preference「好み」

21年度第2回　筆記

139

(11) – 解答 **3**

訳 その会社は昨年，売り上げの低下があったため，顧客を取り戻すべく，より積極的な広告キャンペーンを始めた。

解説 積極的な広告キャンペーンを始めたのは，売り上げの「低下」が原因である。名詞 dip は価格などの一時的な「下落，低下」の意味。suite「一組，一続きの部屋」，coma「昏睡（状態）」，ramp「傾斜路」

(12) – 解答 **3**

訳 ランディーは常習的に嘘をつくことで有名だったため，彼の信じられないような旅行の話は，本当だったのにもかかわらず，誰も信じなかった。

解説 本当の話を信じてもらえなかったのは，普段よく嘘をつくからで，habitual「習慣的な，常習的な」が適切。miserly「けちな」，sacred「神聖な」，stale「（飲食物が）新鮮でない」

(13) – 解答 **4**

訳 若いころ，ステファノは非常に虚栄心が強かった。彼は自分の外見を気にするあまり，給料のほとんど全てを服や靴，スキンケア製品に費やした。

解説 第2文に書かれているような行動から，ステファノがどんな性格だったのかを考える。vain は「無駄な」のほか，人について用いて「虚栄心の強い，（容姿・能力を）自慢する」の意味がある。crafty「ずる賢い」，inopportune「（時機が）不適当な」，unsound「不健全な」

(14) – 解答 **3**

訳 スザンヌは夜空の明るく青い光に戸惑ったが，科学者として，その光には合理的な説明があるはずだということは分かっていた。

解説 選択肢の中で explanation「説明」と意味的に合うのは rational「合理的な」のみである。steep「急勾配の」，lawless「無法の，違法な」，downcast「落胆した，うつむいた」

(15) – 解答 **2**

訳 その大学の教職員たちは評判が高く，彼らに教わろうと全国各地から若者が集まってくる。

解説 文の最後の them は The (　) members at the college を指す。faculty (members) で「（大学の）教員陣」という意味。custody「親権」，retainer「（弁護士などの）依頼料」，seizure「つかむこと，発作」

(16) – 解答 **4** ・・・・・・・・・・・・・・・・・・・・・・・・・・・・・ 正答率 ★75%以上

訳 バートとエヴァは，40年の関係を維持してこられた方法を尋ねられたとき，大事なことはいつも誠実にコミュニケーションを取ることだと言った。

解説 they said ... の部分で夫婦は，40年間の良好な関係の秘訣^{ひけつ}を話していることから，sustain「維持する」が適切。dispatch「派遣する」，mistrust「信頼しない，疑う」，impair「（力や質・量を）減じる，損なう」

140

(17) – 解答 **1** ・・・・・・・・・・・・・・・・・・・・・・・・・・・ 正答率 ★**75%以上**

訳　その新聞社では，編集者たちは交代制で働いている。1カ月間，何人かは早番で働き，何人かは遅番で働く。そして翌月，彼らは交代する。

解説　第2～3文は rotating shifts「交代制（勤務）」の説明である。rotating は動詞 rotate「（仕事で人が）持ち回る，交代する」の -ing 形で，ここでは形容詞的に用いられている。それぞれ dissolve「溶ける」，devote「（努力・時間などを）ささげる」，exert「発揮する」の -ing 形。

(18) – 解答 **3** ・・・

訳　ノラはそのホラー映画を見るのを楽しまなかった。恐ろしいことが起こるたびに，彼女は叫びたい衝動を抑えなければならなかった。

解説　第2文はホラー映画を楽しまなかった理由。resist the impulse to *do* で「～したい衝動を抑える」という意味。pessimism「悲観（主義）」，pitch「投げること，音程」，vacuum「真空（状態）」

(19) – 解答 **1** ・・・

訳　その男は森の中を歩いているのを止められ，不法侵入で逮捕された。彼は誤って政府の所有する土地に入ってしまっていたとは知らなかった。

解説　「誤って政府の所有地に入って逮捕された」という文意から，trespassing「不法侵入」が適切。trespassing は trespass「不法侵入する」の -ing 形で，名詞的にも使われる。それぞれ endorse「是認する，支援する」，sway「揺れる」，convene「招集する」の -ing 形。

(20) – 解答 **1** ・・・

訳　リオはチェス大会の最終戦でいいプレーをしたが，相手を出し抜くことができなかった。彼女はあまりに優秀だった。

解説　but があるので「いいプレーをしたが勝てなかった」という文意だと推測できる。outsmart は「出し抜く，（知恵を使って）勝つ」という意味。inflame「（感情などを）かき立てる」，update「最新にする」，shepherd「（羊の）番をする」

(21) – 解答 **3** ・・・

訳　マーティンは4時間かけて庭を掃除していた。半分しか終わっていないことに気付いたとき，急にとても疲れたように感じた。

解説　庭掃除に4時間もかけたこと，また「半分しか終わっていないと気付いた」という文脈から考える。weary は重労働などで肉体的に「疲れた」の意味。steady「安定した」，hasty「急ぎの」，sly「ずる賢い」

(22) – 解答 **3** ・・・

訳　男性は，若い女の子がボートから落ちるのを見たとき，すぐに海に飛び込み，彼女を救出しようと泳いだ。

解説　ボートから落ちた女の子をどうやって救出しようとしたかを想像すると，the sea が続くので，plunged into「～に飛び込んだ」が適切である。

21年度第2回　筆記

141

それぞれ wheel out「～（使い古した説など）を持ち出す，（台車などに載せて）～を運び出す」，whip up「～（感情など）を刺激する」，tuck in「～（衣服など）の端を押し込む」の過去形。

(23) − 解答 ①

訳 Ａ：この風はたこを揚げるのに最適だね。
Ｂ：うん，そうだね。風が弱まる前に公園に行こう。

解説 空所前の it はたこ揚げに最適な「風」のことで，「風が弱まる前に…」という文意が適切。die down は「（風や音・騒ぎが）徐々にやむ，弱まる」の意味だが，down のイメージから選べるだろう。それぞれ act up「正常に動作しない」，fall apart「ばらばらになる」，peel away「剥がれる」の３人称単数・現在形。

(24) − 解答 ③　　正答率 ★75%以上

訳 Ａ：ねえ，今週の家族でのピクニックを中止しなければならないかもしれない。天気予報では雨になるそうよ。
Ｂ：それなら，代わりに自宅でピザパーティーをしたらいいよ。

解説 予報では雨なので，今週のピクニックを中止する（call off）ことを話している。これに対しＢは，中止した場合の代案を答えている。get by「通り抜ける，～に容認される」，opt for「～の方を選ぶ」，play up「～を重視する」

(25) − 解答 ④　　正答率 ★75%以上

訳 グレッグはカフェでのパートタイムの仕事を楽しんでいたが，もらっている給料で生活することができないことに気付き，フルタイムの仕事を探し始めた。

解説 フルタイムの仕事を探し始めたのは，パートタイムの仕事の給料ではやっていけないからである。live on「～（金額など）で生活する」が適切。roll around「転げ回る」，rip up「～を引き剥がす」，wash down「～を洗い流す」

一次試験・筆記 ２ 問題編 p.106 ～ 109

全文訳　バビロンの空中庭園

　紀元前５世紀に，世界で最も見事な美術品や建築物の一覧がギリシャの文献に現れ始めた。最も有名なそのような一覧は，７つの特に素晴らしい遺跡について記述している。これらの「古代世界の七不思議」のうち，エジプトのギザのピラミッド群ただ１つだけが現存している。とはいえ，歴史家たちや考古学者たちは，あと５つが実際に存在していたことを裏付ける十分な証拠を発見している。しかし，７番目のバビロンの空中庭園はいまだ謎のままである。

この庭園は，現在のイラクにあった都市バビロンに，ネブカドネザル2世によって建造されたと長らく考えられていた。しかし，ネブカドネザルの治世の時代の文書の記録には，この庭園についての言及が全くない。この庭園はさまざまな古文書で言及されており，複数の層から成る高い構造物で植物が並んでいると記述されているが，これらは全て庭園が建造されたとされる時期より何世紀も後に作成されたものである。庭園の建造に関する直接の記録がないため，考古学者たちはその場所で空中庭園が存在したことを証明する遺跡を何も見つけることができないでいた。

学者であるステファニー・ダリーの研究は，この庭園を見つける努力が間違った場所に焦点を当てている可能性があることを示唆する。ダリーは，ネブカドネザルより1世紀前に生きたセンナケリブという王によって書かれた文献を翻訳した。これらの文献は，センナケリブの宮殿にある見事な高台の庭園について記述している。しかし，センナケリブはバビロンから300マイル離れた都市ニネヴェを治めていた。センナケリブはニネヴェに水を輸送するための複雑な仕組みも建造したとダリーは指摘し，これらがそこの庭園を維持するために使用されていた可能性があると考えている。ダリーが正しければ，バビロンの空中庭園に関する古代の記述は実際はセンナケリブの宮殿にあった庭園を指しているかもしれない。

語句 architecture「建築」，archaeologist「考古学者」，sufficient「十分な」，present-day「今日の」，rule「治世；統治する」，multileveled「複数の層から成る」，vegetation「植物，草木」，firsthand「（情報などが）直接に得られた」，ruins「遺跡」，refer to「～のことを指して言う」

(26) – 解答 ③ •

解説 文頭につなぎ言葉を入れる問題では空所前後の論理展開がポイント。「古代世界の七不思議」のうち1つだけ現存→（空所）→残りのうちの5つは実際に存在した→7番目は謎のまま，という流れから，nonetheless「とはいえ，もっとも」が適切。**1**「例えば」，**2**「このため」，**4**「要するに」はどれも文脈に合わないので，消去法で解いてもよいだろう。

(27) – 解答 ① •

解説 however があるので，空所を含む文は前文と対立する内容になる。空中庭園はネブカドネザル2世によって建造されたと考えられていた→しかし→ネブカドネザル王の時代の文書の記録には「庭園についての言及がない」という流れが適切。空所後の Without any firsthand records of the gardens' construction も手掛かりになる。**3** の「庭園は長く持たなかった」は庭園の存在は謎だという本文の主旨に合わない。

(28) – 解答 ③ •

解説 第3段落の空所後は，バビロンの空中庭園は実際はニネヴェにあった庭園を指している可能性があるという研究について述べている。これを，庭園を見つける努力が「間違った場所に焦点を当てている可能性がある」と表した**3**が適切。

全文訳 **水産養殖と天然の魚資源**

　何十年もの間，主に乱獲により，世界の天然魚の個体数が減少してきている。状況がますます深刻になってきたため，養魚としても知られる水産養殖が商業漁業に代わるものとして推進されるべきであるとしばしば提案されている。しかし，水産養殖業は意図された効果がないようである。最近の研究で，研究者たちは44年間にわたる水産養殖と従来の漁業の両方に関する史料を分析した。9件のうち8件で，水産養殖は養殖魚の生産を大幅に増加させたにもかかわらず，天然魚個体群への圧迫を緩和するのに何の役にも立っていなかった。

　もっと容易に置き換え可能な別の資源を利用することで，ある資源が保全できるという考えは，論理的に思える。しかし，さまざまな産業の事例は，その逆が真実であることを示唆している。例えば，従来のエネルギー源を再生可能なエネルギー源に置き換えることが化石燃料の需要を減少させると考えられていたことがあったが，増加した供給によって実際にはさらに全体のエネルギー消費が増えることにつながった。同様に，今では養殖魚の普及は人々により多くの魚を消費させるようにしたに過ぎないと信じられている。

　水産養殖に関連した問題がもう1つある。何年も，多くの水産養殖会社がサケやマグロなどの品種の養殖に重点を置いてきたが，これらには残念ながら天然ものの小魚を餌として与える必要がある。しかし専門家たちは，この問題は容易に解決できると言う。藻類やその他よくある植物性の生物を食べる魚の品種の養殖に重点を置くことで，養魚場は状況を悪化させるのではなく，より環境に配慮したものになることができる。

語句 aquaculture「水産養殖」，overfishing「乱獲」，alternative「代わるもの，代替手段」，out of「〜（ある数）の中から」，despite「〜にもかかわらず」，conserve「保存［保護］する」，replaceable「取り換え可能な」，logical「論理的な」，renewable「再生可能な」，fossil fuel「化石燃料」，overall「全体の」，consumption「消費」，merely「単に〜に過ぎない」，alga「藻（複数形はalgae）」，organism「生物」，ecologically friendly「環境に配慮した」

(29) – 解答 **3** ●●●●●●●●●●●●●●●●●●●●●●●●●●●●●●●●●●●●●●

解説 however の前後は相反する内容になることから，商業漁業を水産養殖に置き換え→しかし→水産養殖業は「意図された効果がない」という流れにするのが適切。またこの後，水産養殖の効果がない具体的な説明が述べられていることからも，**3** が正解。

(30) – 解答 **1** ●●●●●●●●●●●●●●●●●●●●●●●●●●●●●●●●●●●●●●

解説 第2段落第2文の the opposite is true は，その前の内容から，「資源は別の資源に置き換えても保全できない」という意味。そして，For example の後に，資源（従来のエネルギー源）を別の資源（再生可能なエネルギー源）に置き換えても効果がない具体例が続く。さらに，空所後の「養殖魚の普及は人々により多くの魚を消費させるようにしたに

144

過ぎない」も，資源（天然ものの魚）を別の資源（養殖魚）に置き換え
ても効果がない例なので，空所には Similarly「同様に」が適切。

(31) – **解答** ④ ••

解説 ここも however が示す論理展開に着目。第3段落冒頭では水産養殖の
別の問題に言及しているが，空所後ではそれを解決する具体的な方法が
述べられている。よって，**4**「（この問題は）容易に解決できる」が適切。

一次試験・筆記 **3** | 問題編 p.110 ～ 116

全文訳 **スコッチウイスキー業界の復活**

1980年代，スコッチウイスキー業界は低迷していた。売り上げの落ち込みは，あま
たの老舗ウイスキー製造所の閉鎖につながり，多くの専門家たちがこの低落からは回復
できないと考えていた。そのころ，ウォッカやラムなどの競合飲料が積極的に販売され
たため，それらが若い人たちの間で流行した。1980年代より前は，ウイスキーを飲む
習慣は世代から世代へと受け継がれてきた。これはウイスキー業界に，消費者基盤が保
証されていると思わせていたが，若い世代は一家のしきたりに従わないことが多くなり，
ウイスキー業界は売り上げ減少という形で大きな代償を払うことになった。

さらなる問題は，スコッチウイスキー業界が1970年代に大幅に増産していたことで
ある。ウイスキーには何十年もかかることがある熟成という工程が必要なため，これは
リスクを伴うものであった。この熟成の工程により，需要に見合うように生産を調整す
ることがほとんど不可能だった。1980年代になるころには，景気の低迷によってさら
に悪化したウイスキーの需要の落ち込みにより，多大な余剰が生まれた。ウイスキーメー
カー同士の激しい競争が熾烈な値下げや，業界全体の評判を害する低品質の新製品の製
造につながった。優良の評判を長く確立してきた有名メーカーでさえも廃業した。

幸いにも，この状況は永続的なものではなかった。スコッチウイスキー生産者たちは，
シングルモルトウイスキーとして知られる高品質な製品の販促に注力し始めた。もう1
つ重要だったのは，これらのウイスキーの長所，なぜこれらのウイスキーが高価格なの
か，またどのように食べ物や葉巻と組み合わせられるかについて消費者に伝えるための
生産者たちの取り組みである。この戦略は非常に成功し，高級スコッチウイスキーに海
外の消費者の財布を開かせる一助となった。その結果，これはほかの国のウイスキー生
産者たちがこの戦略に倣い，独自の高級ブランドを生み出すことにつながった。今日で
は，ウイスキーに対する関心と需要がかつてないほど高まっている。

語句 rebirth「復活」，slump「下落，落ち込み」，closure「（商売などの）閉
鎖」，long-established「長い歴史を持つ」，irreversible「元に戻せな
い」，beverage「飲料」，aggressively「積極的に」，fashionable「流行
している」，aging「熟成」，downturn「（景気の）低迷」，massive「極
めて多い」，surplus「余剰」，fierce「激しい」，go out of business「廃

業する」，permanent「永続的な」，strategy「戦略」，premium「上等な」，
in turn「その結果」，imitate「模倣する」

(32) – 解答 ②

問題文の訳 1980年代以前，スコッチウイスキー業界は

選択肢の訳
1 主に若い人々にアピールしようとするのではなく，さまざまな年齢層への売り込みに注力する必要があることに気付いた。
2 生産者たちが宣伝しなくても，若い人々はいつまでもウイスキーを消費すると誤って信じていた。
3 多くの人々に買う余裕がなかったという事実にもかかわらず，製品を非常に高い価格にしていた。
4 アルコールの消費と販売全般における落ち込みを防ぐため，ほかの種類のアルコール飲料の生産者たちと協力し合っていた。

解説 第1段落のPrior to the 1980s以下を参照。ウイスキーを飲む習慣は世代から世代へと受け継がれてきた→ウイスキー業界は消費者基盤が保証されていると（誤って）信じていた→しかし（but），若い世代は飲まなくなった，という流れである。よって，**2**が正解。

(33) – 解答 ④

問題文の訳 スコッチウイスキー業界が直面した問題の1つは何だったか。

選択肢の訳
1 専門知識不足のため，企業は顧客が期待するレベルの品質を提供できなかった。
2 市場に大量のウイスキーを供給できなかったため，消費者が製品への興味を失った。
3 消費者が短期間しか熟成されていない安いブランドにはもはや興味がないことを明確に示した。
4 将来的に売れる量を予測することが困難だったため，メーカーが生産し過ぎた。

解説 第2段落第1文から，スコッチウイスキー業界が1970年代に大幅に増産していたことが分かる。読み進めると，熟成には何十年もかかり，将来的な需要に見合うように生産を調整するのはほぼ不可能であると分かる。問題は，1970年代に大量に仕込んだウイスキーが，消費されるころには需要の落ち込みで大量に余ったこと。よって，**4**が正解。

(34) – 解答 ②

正答率 ★75%以上

問題文の訳 1980年代以降に起こったウイスキー生産の変化についてどのような結論が得られるか。

選択肢の訳
1 他国のウイスキー愛飲家の大半がほかの種類よりもシングルモルトウイスキーを好むため，海外市場が縮小した。
2 ウイスキーの消費者は，シングルモルトウイスキーの価値をいっそう認識するようになり，喜んでより高い価格で購入している。

3 スコッチウイスキーの人気は回復したが，他国の生産者たちはまだ同様の成長を遂げていない。

4 ウイスキー生産者間の競争によって価格が下がり，その結果ウイスキー全体の売り上げが再び上昇した。

解説 第3段落は Fortunately で始まり，第2段落のネガティブな問題から話が好転する。生産者たちが始めたシングルモルトウイスキーの販促が成功し，ウイスキーに対する関心と需要が高まっているという話なので，**2** が正解。シングルモルトウイスキーについては high-quality products, a higher price, luxury brands などの語句から高価格だと分かる。また，シングルモルトウイスキーの販促戦略が成功したと述べられており，「消費者が価値をいっそう認識するようになった」と言える。

全文訳 **リチャード3世**

1483年から1485年までイングランド王であったリチャード3世の遺体が2012年にイングランドの都市レスターにある駐車場の下で発見された。リチャードは，ウィリアム・シェークスピアの最もよく知られた劇の題材の1つで，イングランドで最も悪名高い支配者の1人でもあった。彼は，王になることに必死になり，自らの目的を達成するために自分の兄や2人の甥を殺害した，身体的な障害のある男性として一般的に記憶されている。リチャードの評判はシェークスピアの劇に端を発するものではなく，もっと前の，トマス・モアの『リチャード三世伝』に由来する。現代の専門家たちは，モアの本の内容がリチャードから王座を勝ち取った一家を支持して書かれたものであったため，その詳細の多くを非常に疑問視しているが，この本におけるリチャードを悪とする描写が今日まで残る彼の悪評の基礎となった。

リチャード王の人生を研究することを目的として1924年に発足したリチャード3世協会は，リチャードの一般的なイメージに強く異議を唱えている。王の名誉を回復することを願って，同協会は王の遺体の発見につながった調査の支援に協力し，同協会やそのほかの研究者たちの調査結果の中には特に目を見張るようなものがあった。骨格の分析によると，報告されているリチャードの身体障害がほとんど作り話であったことが判明している。実のところ，骨に見られた損傷の幾つかは，リチャードがおそらく参戦したことを示唆しており，これは彼が腕の立つ軍人であったと示唆する歴史報告を裏付けている。

しかし，リチャードがどのようにして王になったのか，そして権力の座にあった2年間で彼が行ったことについては議論が続いている。リチャード3世協会は，彼の注目に値する社会的・政治的改革を指摘して，彼の残念な評判の源である殺人について彼が無実であると主張する。しかし，リチャードの政策の一部が有益であったことを認める一方で，多くの歴史家が，リチャードは，決して寛大な王または思いやりのある王ではなく，残酷な行為を行ったと十分に考えられると信じている。結局のところ，リチャードを彼が生きた時代の典型的なやり方で動いた支配者と見なし，彼が具体的にどのようにして

21年度第2回 筆記

147

権力の座に就いたのかはさほど重要な問題ではないと気付くことがおそらく最も賢明である。ウェストミンスター大司教であるヴィンセント・ニコルズ枢機卿が説明するように、「彼の時代において、政権とは、常に戦場で、それも無慈悲な決断、強力な同盟、および武力を行使する心意気によってのみ、勝ち取られたり維持されたりするものであった」。

語句 ruler「支配者」, disabled「(身体) 障害のある」, *be* desperate to *do*「~しようと必死である」, murder「殺害する」, view A as B「A を B と見なす」(= see A as B), in support of「~を支持して」, throne「王座」, portrayal「描写」, dispute「異議を唱える」, in the hope of「~を願って」, restore「回復する」, sponsor「後援する」, eye-opening「目を見張るような」, skeleton「骨格」, myth「作り話」, skilled「腕の良い」, in power「政権の座にある」, notable「注目に値する」, reform「改革」, acknowledge「認める」, beneficial「有益な」, far from「決して~ではない」, may very well *do*「~することは十分に考えられる」, commit「(悪事を) 行う」, cruel「残酷な」, invariably「常に」, ruthless「無慈悲な」, alliance「同盟」, willingness「意欲, 進んで~する気持ち」, employ「(手段を) 用いる」, use of force「武力行使」

(35) – 解答 ③

問題文の訳 この文章がトマス・モアの『リチャード三世伝』について述べていることの 1 つは何か。

選択肢の訳
1 ウィリアム・シェークスピアがリチャード 3 世について書いた劇の影響を受けているため、信頼できない。
2 レスターでの最近のリチャードの遺体発見にかかわった研究者たちの助けとなる重要な手掛かりを多く提供した。
3 それに含まれる一部の情報はおそらく不正確であるにもかかわらず、人々のリチャードに対するイメージや意見に強い影響を与えた。
4 リチャードが実際には自分の兄やほかの家族を殺害しなかったことを証明する証拠が含まれている。

解説 *History of King Richard III* という本の特徴を読み取る。第 1 段落最終文の Modern-day ... はかなり長いが、A but B の構造を意識して読むと、専門家たちが本の内容の多くを疑問視→しかし→その本のリチャードを悪とする描写が彼の悪評の基礎になっている、という主旨。正解は **3** で、but の代わりに despite を用いて表している。

(36) – 解答 ② ★正答率 75%以上

問題文の訳 リチャードの遺体を分析した結果分かったことは、

選択肢の訳
1 彼は過去の人々がそうであったと信じていたのとは非常に異なる死に方をした。
2 彼は身体的な障害がほとんどなかっただけでなく、有能な戦士だった

可能性もある。

3 彼が最後の戦いで負った大けがは深刻だったが，おそらくそれは死因で
はなかった。

4 彼の外見は，王としての能力よりも，人々の彼に対する印象におそら
く大きな影響を与えた。

解説 第2段落の According to ... を参照。〈it turns out that SV〉「～と判
明する」と設問の〈it was learned that SV〉が同様の意味。分析の結
果リチャードの身体障害がほとんど作り話だったこと，また In fact, ...
から，リチャードが腕の立つ軍人だった可能性があると分かる。**2** が正
解で，skilled soldier を capable fighter に言い換えている。

(37) – 解答 **4** ••

問題文の訳 次の文のうち，この文章の筆者が最も同意しそうなのはどれか。

選択肢の訳 **1** リチャードの能力を，戦場で被った損失だけに基づいて判断し，彼が
導入した改革に基づいて判断しないのは間違いである。

2 リチャードが意図的にひどい行為をしたと主張する歴史家たちは，彼
に対する評価が間違っているように思われる。

3 リチャードが王だった間に犯した罪は，彼が国のために行った有益な
ことをはるかに超えている。

4 リチャードは，遠い昔にイングランドを統治したほかの王たちに比べ，
おそらく支配者として良くも悪くもなかった。

解説 リチャードがどうやって王になったかや，残酷な行為を行ったことにつ
いて，筆者は，第3段落の In the end, it is ..., and to realize that ...
で持論を述べている。「リチャードを彼が生きた時代（＝遠い昔）の典
型的なやり方で動いた支配者と見なす」「どうやって王になったかは重
要ではない」とあり，つまり，ほかの王たちと比べて際立って良い面や
悪い面があったわけではないと考えていると判断できるので，**4** が正解。

全文訳 **ジャヤヴァルマン7世の寺院**

　ジャヤヴァルマン7世の治世の最盛期には，彼のクメール帝国は，現在のカンボジア
のアンコールを中心に，東南アジアの大半を占めていた。ジャヤヴァルマンの統治前は，
強力な地方武将の変わり続ける同盟間の継続的な軍事闘争と，これらの同盟と隣のチャ
ム族との戦闘により，この地域の政情は不安定だった。しかし，チャム族の侵攻により
クメール帝国の前支配者が倒された後，ジャヤヴァルマンと彼の盟友たちは，侵略者た
ちを追い出しただけではなく，帝国の覇権を狙うそのほかの武将たちも何とか鎮圧した。
ジャヤヴァルマンは1181年に王座に就いた。

　30年以上続いたジャヤヴァルマンの治世は，この地域に平和と繁栄をもたらしたが，
彼は治世中はできるだけ多くの仏教寺院を建設することに取りつかれていたようでもあ
る。宗教の推進は長らくクメール文化の根幹を成すものではあったが，ジャヤヴァルマ

ンはそれまでのどの王よりも速いスピードでより多くの寺院を建設し，それを全く新し
いレベルに導いた。彼がこれを行ったのは，自分の時間が限られているかもしれないと
感じていたからとする研究者たちもいる。というのも，彼は比較的晩年の61歳のとき
に王になり，また，長期にわたる疾患を患っていたからである。

　ジャヤヴァルマンは熱心な仏教徒であり，これは彼の国民の健康に対する気遣いにも
表れていた。彼が建設した多くの寺院に加え，彼は百を超える病院も建て，各病院には
医者，薬剤師，その他医療の専門家を雇用した。当時にしては，医療ケアの質は進んで
いた。脈を測って診断に役立てたり，薬としてバターとはちみつが処方されたりした。
政府からの物資が頻繁にこれらの病院に届き，収入や社会的地位にかかわらず帝国民は
誰でも無料で治療を受けられたようである。このような目に見える形で気前の良さを示
すことは，人々を仏教に改宗させるだけでなく，国民に対して偽りのない思いやりを持
つ王としてのジャヤヴァルマンの評判を確固たるものにするのにも役立ったと思われる。

　ジャヤヴァルマンの王としての時代は，多くの人からクメール帝国の黄金時代と見な
されている一方で，帝国の崩壊へ道を開いた可能性もある。一部の研究者たちによると，
ジャヤヴァルマンの寺院建設は，彼の権力集中化政策の証拠であった。王自身が寺院の
土地の所有権を持つことにより，統一された政府管理体制が生まれ，地元の地主たちか
ら権力を取り上げた。その一方で，寺院の建設は何万人もの人々を都市部に移住させる
必要があり，これは農村部で農業をして帝国のために食料を生産する人がはるかに少な
くなったことを意味した。さらに，建設事業は帝国の富の相当量を使い果たした。これ
らの組み合わさった要因が，干ばつやモンスーンで帝国が苦しんだときに後続のクメー
ル帝国の王たちにとって大きな問題になった。この高度に集中化された体制は，財力も，
農業の労働力も，これらの自然災害の影響を乗り越えるための柔軟性もなく，帝国の最
終的な崩壊につながった。

(語句) ongoing「継続的な」, warlord「武将」, invasion「侵略」, defeat「打
　　　ち負かす」, ally「盟友，同調者（複数形は allies）」, drive out「～を
　　　追い出す」, invader「侵略者」, crush「鎮圧する」, prosperity「繁栄」,
　　　be obsessed with「～で頭がいっぱいである」, reign「治世」,
　　　fundamental「基本的な」, passionate「熱心な」, follower「信奉者」,
　　　reflect「反映する」, pharmacist「薬剤師」, pulse「脈」, diagnosis「診
　　　断（複数形は diagnoses）」, prescribe「処方する」, regardless of「～
　　　にもかかわらず」, be eligible for「～に対して資格がある」,
　　　demonstration「証明，示すこと」, generosity「寛大さ」, convert A
　　　to B「A（人）を B に改宗させる」, solidify「固める」, genuine「偽り
　　　のない」, compassion「思いやり」, downfall「破滅」, centralizing
　　　power「権力集中化」, unified「統一された」, emerge「現れる」,
　　　deprive A of B「A から B を奪う」, relocate to「～に移住する」,
　　　drought「干ばつ」, flexibility「柔軟性」, collapse「崩壊」

(38) – 解答 **2**

問題文の訳 ジャヤヴァルマン7世について分かることの1つは何か。

選択肢の訳 **1** チャム族をうまく敵ではなく盟友にすることで，彼はクメール帝国の支配権を握ることができた。

2 彼はその地域のほかの指導者たちと協力することで，クメール帝国の王になることができた。

3 前任の王をだまして敵対する王国を攻撃させた後，彼は自分の国だけでなくその地域も支配することができた。

4 彼は，隣の王国を侵略して打ち負かすのに十分な力が持てるよう，クメール帝国を徐々に強化した。

解説 ジャヤヴァルマンが王になった経緯が書かれた第1段落の第3〜4文の内容と**2**が一致する。**2**の other leaders in the region は本文の his allies（ジャヤヴァルマンの盟友たち）に当たる。「チャム族を盟友にした」や「前任の王をだました」という記述はないので**1**と**3**は不適。また隣のチャム族が侵略してきたり，その侵略者を追い出したとは書かれているが，隣の王国を侵略する話や国を徐々に強化したという記述はないので**4**も不適。

(39) – 解答 **4** ··· 正答率 ★75%以上

問題文の訳 この文章が示唆するところによると，ジャヤヴァルマンがこれほど多くの寺院を建てた理由の1つは，

選択肢の訳 **1** 致命的な病気の蔓延を食い止めるために，クメール帝国が仏教に門戸を開くことを国民が要求したからである。

2 彼は，クメールのほかの支配者たちを満足させておき，彼らの政府に対する反乱を防ぐ方法として寺院を使用したいと思ったからである。

3 彼は，国民が信心深さに欠けると感じていた前支配者と自分は違うことを国民に示したかったからである。

4 彼は，自分の命はあまり長くないと思っており，王としての時代の間にできるだけ多くのことを成し遂げたいと願ったからであろう。

解説 寺院の建設について，第2段落第1文に constructing as many Buddhist temples as possible「できるだけ多くの仏教寺院を建設する」とあり，その理由として研究者たちは，「自分の時間が限られているかもしれないと感じていたから」と述べている。

(40) – 解答 **2**

問題文の訳 ジャヤヴァルマンによって建てられた病院について正しいのはどれか。

選択肢の訳 **1** 十分な人員が配置されていたが，治療を必要とする多数の人々のための十分な医療品がなかった。

2 政府の費用で医療を必要とする全てのクメール国民に医療を提供した。

3 ジャヤヴァルマンは仏教を受け入れたクメール国民にのみ思いやりが

21年度第2回 筆記

151

あることを示した。
  4 仏教の普及のためだけに使われるはずの資金を不適切に使用していると地域の指導者たちに見なされた。

解説 第3段落には，ジャヤヴァルマンが国民のために多くの病院を建てた話が書かれている。第4文の it appears that any citizen ...「帝国民は誰でも無料で治療を受けられたようである」から，**2** が正解。at no cost「無料で」を at the government's expense「政府の費用で」と表している。

(41) – 解答

問題文の訳 ジャヤヴァルマンの寺院建設の結果の1つは何だったか。
選択肢の訳
  1 地元の地主たちはジャヤヴァルマンに裏切られたと感じ，クメール帝国が攻撃されたときに多くの人が彼を支援することを拒否した。
  2 都市部への移住を余儀なくされた農村部の人々を怒らせ，彼らはジャヤヴァルマンを権力の座から降ろそうとした。
  3 多くの資源の使用を必要としたため，クメール帝国がこの先直面する問題に対処できなくなった。
  4 その地域で頻繁に発生する自然災害の影響からクメール国民の目をそらすのに役に立つと判明した。

解説 第4段落は While A, B. で始まり，ジャヤヴァルマンの負の側面に話が展開される。寺院建設のため多くの人を都市部に移住させたことで食料生産不足になり，また帝国の富の相当量を使い果たした（＝多くの資源の使用を必要とした）。そして最終的に，自然災害など（＝この先直面する問題）に対処できず，帝国の崩壊につながった。よって，**3** が正解。

一次試験・筆記 4 問題編 p.117

トピックの訳 頻繁に転職するのは労働者にとって有益か。
ポイントの訳 ・キャリア目標　・モチベーション　・経済　・労働条件

解答例
　　Changing jobs regularly is an overall benefit for workers because there are clear advantages in terms of career goals and working conditions.

　　Firstly, changing jobs is one of the best ways for workers to achieve their career goals. A worker's chances of promotion or broadening their work duties depend heavily on the company, so staying in one job can limit their career progression. Switching jobs allows people to explore different employment opportunities, which can positively impact their career development.

　　Secondly, moving to a new company exposes workers to a

variety of working conditions. Some companies may expect their employees to follow strict rules, which can cause workers to feel stressed. Changing jobs, however, allows workers to experience better working conditions and improve their well-being.

Therefore, considering career goals and positive experiences gained through various working conditions, changing jobs is beneficial for workers.

解説 序論：第1段落では，トピックに対する自分の意見を簡潔に書く。模範解答は，〈主張（Yes または No）＋because＋理由〉の構造で，まず「定期的に転職することは労働者にとって全体的なメリットがある」と述べることで Yes の立場を明らかにした上で，理由の部分では in terms of 「～の点で」を用いてポイントの Career goals と Working conditions の観点を取り上げている。トピックの意味を勝手に変えるとマイナス評価につながるが，often「頻繁に」→ regularly「定期的に」程度なら良い。本論：本論では，序論で述べた主張の理由を2つの観点に沿って説明する。模範解答では Firstly / Secondly を用いている。第2段落は Career goals の観点で，「転職は労働者がキャリア目標を達成するのに最良の方法の1つだ」と述べた後，1つの仕事にとどまることのデメリットに続けて，「さまざまな雇用機会を模索できることがキャリア形成にプラスの影響を与える」という，転職のメリットを述べている。第3段落は Working conditions の観点で，厳格な規則による労働者のストレスという労働環境の悪例を挙げた後，however を用いて「転職によってより良い労働条件を経験し，幸福感（well-being）を高めることができる」と転職のメリットを説明している。また，～, which can cause A to *do*「～が原因で A が…し得る」はぜひこのまま覚えておきたい。結論：最終段落では，トピックに対する意見を再び主張する。模範解答は Therefore, ... で始めて，considering「～を考慮すると」を用いて2つの観点を再び取り上げた後，「転職は労働者にとって有益だ」と締めくくっている。

そのほかの表現 主張を述べる部分では，there are advantages「利点がある」よりも there are clear advantages「明らかな利点がある」のような表現の方が強い主張が伝わる。主張を強める表現はほかに，It is clear [obvious] that ～「～は明らかだ」などがある。また，トピックの beneficial を模範解答では名詞の benefit や advantage（反意語は disadvantage）に言い換えている。理由・根拠を述べる部分では「利点・欠点」を説明することはよくあるので，これらの語は使えるようにしておこう。関連語：good point「良い点」，good effect「良い効果」，good influence [impact]「良い影響」 ※ good（⇔ bad）は positive（⇔ negative）にも置き換えられる。

153

| 一次試験・
リスニング | **Part 1** | 問題編 p.118～119 | ▶MP3 ▶アプリ
▶CD 2 **28**～**41** |

No.**1** – 解答 ① ···

スクリプト ☆： Yusuke, I'm going to a Japanese-style wedding next month. What kind of present should I buy?

★： It's pretty easy here in Japan. We just give cash wrapped in a special envelope.

☆： Really? Is that all?

★： Yeah, it's the custom here. How close are you to the couple?

☆： The bride is my best friend in Japan.

★： Ah. In that case, you're looking at around 30,000 yen.

☆： That much!? I'll have to cut way back on expenses this month so I can cover that.

★： Well, good luck.

Question: What does the woman tell Yusuke?

全文訳 ☆： ユウスケ，来月日本式の結婚式に行くんだけど，どんなプレゼントを買えばいいかな。

★： ここ日本では結構簡単だよ。特別な封筒に現金を包んで渡すだけなんだ。

☆： 本当に？　それだけ？

★： そう，それがここの慣習だよ。ご夫婦とはどれぐらい親しいの？

☆： 新婦は日本での親友よ。

★： そう。その場合，だいたい３万円ぐらいだね。

☆： そんなに!?　それを賄えるように今月は支出をずっと抑えないといけないわ。

★： そう，がんばって。

質問： 女性はユウスケに何と言っているか。

選択肢の訳 **1** 彼女はお金を得るのに苦労するだろう。

2 彼女は新婦のことをほとんど知らない。

3 彼女はもはや結婚式に出席できない。

4 彼女はすでに贈り物を買った。

解説 女性は結婚祝いに３万円も必要だと知って驚く。最後に「支出を抑えないと」と言っていることからも，お金を用意するのは簡単ではないことが分かるので，**1** が正解。新婦は親友なので **2** は不適。この barely は「ほとんど〜ない」の意味で hardly と同意。

No.**2** – 解答 ② ·· 正答率 ★**75%以上**

スクリプト ☆： Good evening, sir. May I see your ticket, please?

★： Here you are. I'm taking the 6:30 flight to Boston. I'd like an aisle

154

seat, if possible.

☆： Ah, that flight is overbooked.

★： Do you mean I can't get a seat?

☆： No, your seat is confirmed. But we are asking all passengers whether they can help us out this evening. If you agree to take the 9:30 flight, we will give you a complimentary $100 travel voucher.

★： That would be fine.

☆： Thank you very much, sir.

Question: What does the man agree to do?

全文訳 ☆： こんばんは。チケットを拝見します。

★： はい，どうぞ。6 時 30 分のボストン行きの便に乗ります。できれば通路側の席をお願いしたいのですが。

☆： ああ，その便はオーバーブッキングされています。

★： 席が取れないってことですか。

☆： いえ，お客さまの座席は取れています。ですが，全ての乗客の皆さまに今晩ご協力願えないかお尋ねしています。9 時 30 分の便に乗ることに同意していただけたら，100 ドルの無料旅行券を提供いたします。

★： それで結構です。

☆： ありがとうございます，お客さま。

質問：男性は何をすることに同意しているか。

選択肢の訳 1　6 時 30 分の便に乗る。

2　便を変更する。

3　アップグレードのために余分に払う。

4　窓側の席を諦める。

解説 空港での航空会社の女性スタッフと男性客の会話。女性は男性が乗る予定の 6 時 30 分の便はオーバーブッキングのため，条件付きで 9 時 30 分の便に変更できるか尋ねている。これに対し男性は That would be fine. と受け入れている。つまり，6 時 30 分から 9 時 30 分に「便を変更する」ことに同意しているので，**2** が正解。

No.3 – 解答 ③ ･･････････････････････････ 正答率 ★75%以上

スクリプト ★： Hello, front desk. Can I help you?

☆： Yes, I'm in room 302. It's so hot in here I can hardly breathe.

★： I assume you've tried adjusting the temperature already.

☆： Several times. It's at the lowest possible setting, but it doesn't seem to be having any effect. I'm boiling up here.

★： That's very strange. I sincerely apologize. I'll have someone from our maintenance staff go up and look at it right away.

21 年度第 2 回　リスニング

155

☆： Thanks. I'd appreciate that.

Question: What is the woman's problem?

全文訳 ★： もしもし，フロントです。ご用件を伺います。

☆： はい，302号室の者ですが，室内がすごく暑くてとても息苦しいです。

★： もうすでに温度を調節しようとしてみたのですね。

☆： 何度も。一番低い設定になっていますが，何の変わりもないみたいです。ここはうだるように暑いですよ。

★： それはとても妙ですね。心からお詫びいたします。当ホテルのメンテナンススタッフから誰かを向かわせて，すぐに調べさせます。

☆： ありがとう。助かります。

質問： 女性の問題は何か。

選択肢の訳 **1** 彼女は高熱がある。

2 彼女は違う部屋を頼んだ。

3 エアコンが正常に動いていない。

4 ルームサービスがまだ来ない。

解説 女性がホテルの客室からフロントに電話をかけている場面。女性の最初の発言から，室内が暑いことが分かる。air conditioner という語句は出てこないが，男性の I assume you've tried adjusting the temperature already. や女性の It's at the lowest possible setting はエアコンの温度調整のことと考えられる。よって，**3** が正解。

No.4 - 解答 ②

スクリプト ★： Honey, I'm going to invite my sister to stay with us this summer.

☆： Don't I have a say in this matter?

★： Uh, sure you do, but I thought you liked Patty.

☆： Of course, but a whole summer? I'm the one who has to cook for an extra person.

★： I get the point. How about a couple of weeks in July, then?

☆： Well, that might be better.

Question: What does the woman suggest to the man?

全文訳 ★： ねえ，妹［姉］を今年の夏一緒に過ごさないか誘おうと思っているんだ。

☆： この件について私に口出しする権利はないの？

★： ああ，もちろんあるよ。でも君はパティーを気に入っていると思ってたけど。

☆： もちろんよ，でも夏の間ずっと？　もう1人分の料理を作らなければならないのは私なのよ。

★： 言いたいことは分かった。そしたら7月に数週間はどう？

☆： そうね，その方がいいかな。

質問： 女性は男性に何を示唆しているか。

156

選択肢の訳　**1**　責任を分担すること。

2　パティーの訪問期間を短くすること。

3　後で決めること。

4　訪問を延期すること。

解説　男性が夏に妹［姉］を呼ぶ話をすると，女性は少々不満げな受け答えをし，a whole summer? と言っていることから，期間が長いことに不満がある様子である。これに対し男性は，（夏の間ずっとではなく）7月の数週間ならどうか（＝期間を短くする）と提案しており，女性は「その方がいい」と言っている。よって，**2** が正解。

No.5 -解答 ④

スクリプト　★：Hey, Abigail. Are you having as much trouble as I am with our sociology class?

☆：Big trouble! What's with the book the professor assigned?

★：I spent ages just trying to understand the introduction. It's all I can do to get through a single chapter!

☆：Yeah, the author just seems to go around in circles.

★：I agree. He never seems to make a point.

☆：Hey, maybe there's a study guide on the Internet . . .

★：That's an idea.

　　Question: Why are these students complaining?

全文訳　★：ねえ，アビゲイル。社会学の授業，僕と同じぐらい苦労してる？

☆：すごく大変！　教授が指定したあの本，一体どうなってるの？

★：導入部を理解しようとするのだけでもすごく時間がかかったよ。たった1章を読み終えるのがやっとだ。

☆：そうなの，著者はただ堂々巡りしているみたい。

★：そうそう。何を言いたいのかはっきりしないんだ。

☆：ねえ，ネット上に学習の手引があるかもしれない…

★：それも1つの手だね。

　　質問：これらの学生はなぜ文句を言っているか。

選択肢の訳　**1**　授業があまりやりがいのあるものではない。

2　教授が忙し過ぎて彼らを助けられない。

3　学習の手引が役に立たない。

4　本を理解するのが難しい。

解説　最初のやりとりから，2人は社会学の授業に苦労していることが分かる。女性が教授指定の本のことを言うと，男性も導入部の理解が難しいことや読むのに時間がかかると答えている。よって，**4** が正解。What's with ...?，I spent ages，It's all I can do to ...，go around in circles などの話し言葉特有の表現の理解がポイント。

21年度第2回　リスニング

157

No.6 - 解答 ④

スクリプト

★： I get the feeling Susan's upset with me.

☆： What happened?

★： I was trying to organize a farewell party for her, but I had to give up. We just couldn't find a date or time that everyone could agree to.

☆： She doesn't blame you for that, does she? I mean, with how busy she is, her schedule is probably the hardest to work around.

★： Exactly, but when I suggested calling it off, she seemed hurt. I e-mailed her a couple of days ago and said maybe we could all have lunch instead, but I haven't heard from her since.

☆： Well, she's very busy, so maybe she just hasn't gotten around to answering you yet.

★： Maybe, but her last day is tomorrow!

Question: What do we learn from the conversation?

全文訳

★： スーザンが僕に腹を立てている気がする。

☆： 何があったの。

★： 彼女のために送別会を手配しようとしていたんだけど，諦めなければならなくなってね。どうしても全員が同意できる日時がなかったんだよ。

☆： 彼女は，それがあなたのせいだって思ってないわよね？ というか，彼女の忙しさからして，彼女のスケジュールが一番合わせるのが難しいと思うんだけど。

★： その通りなんだけど，取りやめることを提案したら傷ついたみたいだった。何日か前に彼女にEメールを送って代わりに皆でランチでも行こうって言ったんだけど，それ以来彼女から何の連絡もない。

☆： まあ，彼女はとても忙しいから，まだ返事できる時間がないだけかも。

★： そうかもしれないけど，彼女の最後の日は明日なんだよ！

質問：この会話から何が分かるか。

選択肢の訳
1　スーザンは同僚たちをランチに誘った。
2　スーザンの送別会は明日である。
3　男性はスーザンのEメールアドレスを知らない。
4　男性は送別会を手配できなかった。

解説　男性の発言の I was trying to organize a farewell party for her, but I had to give up. から，彼がスーザンの送別会を諦めた（＝手配できなかった）ことが分かる。その後，理由を話す中で I suggested calling it off と言っていることからも，**4** が正解。call off は「〜を取りやめる，中止する」。

158

No.7 – 解答 ①

スクリプト ★： Hi, Samantha, welcome back.

☆： Hi, Jack. Thanks. How's work been?

★： Pretty busy, as always. So tell me, how's married life?

☆： Well, the honeymoon was great. But now I'm adjusting to living with another person. Plus, we moved into a new house. The whole situation is quite a change.

★： I remember going through a similar thing. It takes a while to get used to it.

☆： Well, I hope things settle down soon.

Question: What do we learn about the woman?

全文訳 ★： やあ，サマンサ。おかえり。

☆： こんにちは，ジャック。ありがとう。仕事はどうだった？

★： いつも通り，結構忙しいよ。で，教えてよ。結婚生活はどう？

☆： そうね，新婚旅行は素晴らしかったわ。でも今は他人と暮らすことに順応しているところ。それに，新しい家に越したの。この状況全部が大きな変化よ。

★： 僕も似たようなことを経験したことを思い出すよ。慣れるのにしばらくかかる。

☆： そうね，そのうち落ち着くといいのだけど。

質問：女性について何が分かるか。

選択肢の訳 1 彼女はまだ結婚していることに慣れていない。

2 彼女は仕事で忙しいのは好きではない。

3 彼女は新しい仕事に順応する必要がある。

4 彼女は別の休暇の準備ができている。

解説 男性の welcome back，how's married life?，女性の How's work been?，the honeymoon was great などから，女性は結婚したばかりで新婚旅行から戻って職場に復帰した場面だと想像できる。女性の「他人（＝夫）と暮らすことに順応しているところ」「新しい家に越した」や，男性の「慣れるのにしばらくかかる」という発言から，**1** が正解。get used to は「～に慣れる」。

No.8 – 解答 ④

スクリプト ★： Good morning. My name is Tom Hendricks. I'm here to see Mr. Phelps.

☆： I'm sorry, Mr. Hendricks. Mr. Phelps is out of town today. Did you have an appointment to see him?

★： Well, I thought so. I had my secretary schedule it last week.

☆： Let me check. . . . Oh, it seems he's scheduled to meet you tomorrow at this time.

★ : Really? I guess I must have written it down wrong. Well, could you please see that he gets these brochures? I'll call him later in the week to discuss them.

☆ : I'll see that he gets them.

Question: What does Mr. Hendricks say he will do?

全文訳 ★ : おはようございます。私はトム・ヘンドリクスと申します。フェルプスさんに会いに来ました。

☆ : 申し訳ございません，ヘンドリクスさん。フェルプスさんは本日不在です。彼と会うお約束がございましたか。

★ : はい，そう思っていたのですが。先週，私の秘書に予定を入れさせました。

☆ : 確認しますね…。あら，彼は明日のこの時間にあなたと会う予定のようです。

★ : 本当に？　私が間違って書き留めてしまったようですね。では，彼がこれらのパンフレットを受け取るようにしていただけますか。今週後ほど彼に電話をしてこれらについて話し合います。

☆ : 彼がこれらを受け取るようにします。

質問：ヘンドリクスさんは何をすると言っているか。

選択肢の訳 1　約束の予定を変更する。

2　明日戻ってくる。

3　彼の秘書と話す。

4　別の機会にフェルプスさんに電話をする。

解説 男性が会う約束をしたはずのフェルプスさんが不在で，日時を確認すると，約束は明日だと分かった。男性はパンフレットを残し，「今週後ほど彼（＝フェルプスさん）に電話をします」と言っていることから，**4** が正解。会話中の later in the week を another time と言い換えている。電話で話し合うと言っており，約束を変更するとは言っていないので **1** は不適。

No.**9** ‒解答　**1** •••••••••••••••••••••• 正答率 ★**75％以上**

スクリプト ★ : That baby behind us has been crying the whole trip. The noise is driving me crazy!

☆ : Don't you remember what our kids were like when we traveled on trains with them?

★ : I thought they were fairly quiet and well behaved, weren't they?

☆ : You're kidding, right? They used to start up as soon as we sat down.

★ : Really? I don't remember that at all. Did other passengers complain?

☆： No. They were more polite than that.

★： OK. I get your point.

Question: What does the woman imply?

全文訳 ★： 僕たちの後ろのあの赤ちゃん，この旅の間ずっと泣いているよ。やかましくて気が変になりそうだよ！

☆： 子供たちと電車で旅をしたときにあの子たちがどうだったか覚えてない？

★： あの子たちはわりと静かで行儀善くなかった？

☆： 冗談でしょ？　座ったらすぐに泣き始めたものだわ。

★： 本当に？　それは全く覚えていないよ。ほかの乗客たちは文句を言った？

☆： いいえ，彼らは礼儀正しかったからそんなことはしなかったわ。

★： うん，言いたいことは分かったよ。

質問：女性は何をほのめかしているか。

選択肢の訳 **1** 男性はやかましいことに文句を言うべきではない。

2 男性は電車に乗るべきではなかった。

3 ほかの乗客たちはもっと礼儀正しくするべきだ。

4 赤ちゃんの両親はもっと気を付けるべきだ。

解説 電車内の赤ちゃんがずっと泣いていることに対して夫が文句を言うと，妻は自分たちの子供も同じだった（から文句を言うべきではない）と夫を諭す。正解 **1** の the noise は赤ちゃんの泣き声のこと。They were more polite than that. は，文句を言う夫は礼儀正しくないという意図が含まれている。

No.**10** 解答 **3**

スクリプト ☆： How was your job interview at the restaurant?

★： Pretty good, I think. But they have a lot of other chefs to interview.

☆： Well, you graduated from a famous school, and you trained at that French restaurant while you were studying.

★： But I made a mistake by not working over the summer. The interviewers asked me what I did. I wish I'd gotten a part-time job instead of spending my time on the beach.

☆： Yeah, it would've made your résumé look better.

Question: What is the man's concern?

全文訳 ☆： レストランの仕事の面接はどうだった？

★： 結構うまくいったと思う。でも，ほかにも面接するシェフがたくさんいるからなあ。

☆： でも，あなたは有名な学校を卒業しているし，学生の間はあのフランス料理店で研修を受けたでしょう。

★： でも夏の間働かなかったという間違いをしてしまったんだよ。面接官た

21年度第2回 リスニング

161

ちは，僕が何をしていたかを尋ねたんだ。ビーチで過ごすんじゃなくてアルバイトをしていればよかった。

☆： そうね，そうすれば履歴書の見栄えが良くなっていたわね。

質問：男性の心配事は何か。

選択肢の訳　**1** 彼が卒業した学校は有名ではない。
2 彼は以前にフランス料理を作ったことがない。
3 彼は夏の間仕事をしなかった。
4 彼の履歴書はあまりにも間違いが多かった。

解説　最初のやりとりから，男性はシェフとしてレストランの面接を受けたことが分かる。男性の心配事は2番目の発言の I made a mistake by not working over the summer から，**3** が正解。最後の方の I wish I'd gotten ... や it would've made your résumé ... では仮定法過去完了が使われており，実際には夏の間仕事をしなかったことを表す。

No.11 解答 ②

スクリプト　★： How are things, Felicity?

☆： Great! I just got invited to audition for another movie.

★： That's exciting. But what about college?

☆： I'm thinking about dropping out. These days, I have so many auditions that I'm sure to get a part soon.

★： I don't think that's a good idea.

☆： You should understand. You lived for playing music when you were in high school.

★： Yeah, but I eventually realized a college degree would give me a better chance to make a steady living.

☆： That's true enough. But I just don't want to have regrets later.

Question: What does the man imply?

全文訳　★： 調子はどう，フェリシティ？

☆： すごくいいわ！　また別の映画のオーディションに招待されたばかりなの。

★： それはわくわくするね。でも大学はどうなの？

☆： 退学することを考えているわ。最近，本当にたくさんのオーディションがあるから，すぐに役をもらえると思うの。

★： それはいい考えとは思わないな。

☆： あなたなら分かるでしょ。高校のとき音楽の演奏に生きていたじゃない。

★： そうだけど，結局のところ大学の学位の方が安定した生計を立てやすいってことに気付いたよ。

☆： 確かにその通りね。でも私はただ後で後悔したくないの。

質問：男性は何をほのめかしてるか。

162

選択肢の訳　**1**　女性はもっとオーディションの準備をするべきだ。

2　女性のキャリアプランは現実的でない。

3　彼は大学で間違った専攻を選んだ。

4　彼は音楽の道を追い求めるべきだった。

解説　女性が映画出演のために大学を退学するつもりだと言うと，男性は I don't think that's a good idea. と言って，大学の学位の方が大事だ（から退学すべきでない）と助言する。**2** が正解で，女性の「退学して俳優の道を進みたい」という career plan を unrealistic と表している。

No.**12** 解答 ④

スクリプト　★：You're looking very serious. What's the matter?

☆：It's our electric bill. It was over $250 last month.

★：Well, it was the coldest month this winter.

☆：Yes, but that still seems high. Maybe I'll call the electric company.

★：I'm sure the bill's correct. I think we should start turning down the temperature at night. We have extra blankets we can use to keep warm.

☆：I guess we can start with that and see if it helps.

Question: What does the couple decide to do first?

全文訳　★：すごく深刻そうな顔をしているね。どうしたの？

☆：電気代よ。先月は 250 ドルを超えていた。

★：まあ，この冬で一番寒い月だったから。

☆：そうだけど，それでも高いと思う。電気会社に電話してみようかしら。

★：請求書は合っていると思うよ。これからは，夜は温度を下げるべきだと思う。余分にある毛布を使って暖かくしよう。

☆：とりあえずそれをやってみて，効果があるか見ましょう。

質問：夫婦はまず何をすることにしたか。

選択肢の訳　**1**　もっと多くの毛布を買う。

2　暖房機器を取り換える。

3　電気会社に電話する。

4　夜の暖房の使用を減らす。

解説　話題は先月の高い電気代。夫の「夜は（暖房の）温度を下げよう」という提案に妻は同意しているので，**4** が正解。**1** は毛布で暖かくするのは正しいが，すでにあるので Purchase という動作が不適。**3** の「電気会社に電話する」は妻の発言にあるが，夫は「請求書は合っていると思う（から電話しなくていい）」と受け答えているので不適。

21年度第2回　リスニング

163

| 一次試験・リスニング | **Part2** | 問題編 p.120～121 | ▶MP3 ▶アプリ ▶CD 2 42 ～ 48 |

A

スクリプト **Pacific Links**

Researchers have long considered the possibility of ancient contact between Polynesian people of the South Pacific and Native Americans of South America. A recent study strongly supports such a theory. The study's researchers analyzed DNA samples from hundreds of Polynesians and Native Americans. They found genetic evidence that these peoples met and produced children together around 800 years ago.

What remains unclear is which group crossed the thousands of kilometers of ocean to make such contact possible. Polynesians were known for their canoes. They made long sea voyages and settled on many islands in the Pacific Ocean. However, in 1947, an explorer showed it was possible to cross the Pacific Ocean from South America on a raft. Native Americans, who used rafts, may therefore also have made great voyages.

Questions

No.13 What did the researchers confirm about Polynesians and Native Americans?

No.14 What did an explorer demonstrate in 1947?

全文訳 **パシフィックリンク**

研究者たちは長い間，南太平洋のポリネシア人と南米のアメリカ先住民が古代に接触した可能性について考えてきた。最近の研究によって，その説に強い裏付けが示されている。この研究の研究者たちは，何百人ものポリネシア人とアメリカ先住民の DNA サンプルを分析した。彼らは，800 年ほど前に両民族が出会い子孫を残したという遺伝的証拠を発見した。

依然として不明な点は，そのような接触を可能にするのに，どちらの民族が何千キロもの海を渡ったかということである。ポリネシア人はカヌーで有名である。彼らは長い航海をし，太平洋の多くの島々に定住した。しかし 1947 年に，ある探検家が筏で南米から太平洋を横断することができることを証明した。つまり，筏を使用していたアメリカ先住民も大航海をした可能性がある。

No.**13** 解答 ②

質問の訳 研究者たちは，ポリネシア人とアメリカ先住民について何を確認したか。

選択肢の訳 1 遺伝的な類似点がない。

2 何世紀も前に出会い子孫を残した。

3 筏作りの知識を共有した。

4 船乗りとしての経験がほとんどなかった。

解説 選択肢の主語 They は質問文の Polynesians and Native Americans を指す。放送文の these peoples met and produced children together around 800 years ago の these peoples も Polynesians and Native Americans のことで，**2** が正解。around 800 years ago を centuries ago と言い換えている。

No.14 解答

質問の訳 1947年，探検家は何を実証したか。
選択肢の訳
1 太平洋を横断するのに筏を使うことができた。
2 アメリカ先住民が太平洋を横断した可能性は低い。
3 ポリネシア人の筏は彼らのカヌーより優れていた。
4 一部の太平洋の島々はボートでたどり着けなかった。

解説 探検家について述べた an explorer showed it was possible to cross ...「ある探検家が筏で南米から太平洋を横断することができることを証明した」から，**1** が正解。it was possible to *do* を **1** では could で表している。この後「筏を使用していたアメリカ先住民も大航海をした（＝太平洋を横断した）可能性がある」とあるので，**2** は不適。

B

スクリプト **Music and Work**

It has often been claimed that listening to music during work can improve focus and productivity. Recent research, however, suggests this may only be true of people performing highly repetitive tasks. For more-creative jobs, or those requiring intense concentration, listening to music might be harmful. In addition, other studies have found that the test scores of students who listen to music while completing reading tasks are lower than the test scores of students who read without music.

According to neuroscientist Daniel Levitin, many people are unaware that music might be causing them to get less done. Although listening to music while working may be enjoyable, Levitin says popular music with lyrics is especially bad for concentration. However, he believes that listening to music helps workers relax during rest periods between tasks, so it can improve their overall ability to concentrate.

Questions
No.15 What is one thing recent research has revealed about listening to music?
No.16 What does Daniel Levitin believe about listening to music?

全文訳 **音楽と仕事**

仕事中に音楽を聴くことで，集中力や生産性が向上するとよく言われてきた。しかし，最近の研究では，これは反復性の高い作業をしている人にしか当てはまらない可能性が

あることを示唆している。より創造性の高い仕事，あるいは高い集中力を要する仕事の場合，音楽を聴くことは有害かもしれない。また，ほかの研究では，読解の課題をしながら音楽を聴く学生たちのテストの点数は，音楽なしで読む学生たちのテストの点数よりも低いことが分かった。

　神経科学者のダニエル・レヴィティンによると，多くの人は，音楽が成し遂げられる仕事の量を減らす原因になっている可能性に気付いていない。仕事中に音楽を聴くのは楽しいかもしれないが，レヴィティンは，歌詞の付いたポピュラー音楽は特に集中するのに良くないと言う。しかし彼は，音楽を聴くと労働者たちは作業の合間の休憩時間にリラックスできるため，全体的な集中力を高めることができると考えている。

No.15 解答 ③

質問の訳　音楽を聴くことについて最近の研究が明らかにしたことの1つは何か。
選択肢の訳
1　人々の生産性にほとんど効果がない。
2　学生たちがテストでより良い点数を取るのに役立つ。
3　特定の作業をよりやりにくくする可能性がある。
4　人々のメンタルヘルスを改善する。
解説　仕事中に音楽を聴くことについて，「（有益な効果は）反復性の高い作業にしか当てはまらない」，「創造性の高い仕事や高い集中力を要する仕事には有害」と述べている。この後者の内容を表した **3** が正解。「創造性の高い仕事や高い集中力を要する仕事」を certain tasks と抽象化している。前者の内容から，反復性の高い作業では生産性に効果があるので，**1** は不適。

No.16 解答 ①

質問の訳　ダニエル・レヴィティンは音楽を聴くことについてどう考えているか。
選択肢の訳
1　休憩時間に効果的になり得る。
2　実際に作業を楽しくないものにし得る。
3　労働者間のコミュニケーションを向上させる。
4　集中力にわずかな効果しかない。
解説　質問文と同じ believe を含む最後の部分（However, he believes that …）に手掛かりがある。「音楽を聴くことで，労働者は作業の合間の休憩時間にリラックスできる」＝効果があり得る，と考えて，**1** が正解。

スクリプト **The Language of Bats**

　Some animals, such as dolphins, are thought to communicate using sounds that can express specific meanings. However, it was long believed that the sounds made by some other animals, such as bats, were random. A study of Egyptian fruit bats suggests that their communication system is actually quite complex.

The bats were kept in captivity, and the scientists conducting the study used a computer program to analyze the sounds that the bats made. The sounds were grouped into categories based on context. For example, certain sounds tended to be produced in the presence of food. Other sounds occurred during what appeared to be arguments between bats over where the bats would sleep. In the future, the scientists hope to monitor bats in their natural habitat to see whether the sounds they make change.

Questions

No.17 What did the study of Egyptian fruit bats suggest?

No.18 How did the scientists conduct their analysis?

全文訳 **コウモリの言語**

　イルカなど一部の動物は，特定の意味を表し得る鳴き声を使ってコミュニケーションを取ると考えられている。一方で，コウモリなどのほかの動物が発する鳴き声は無原則だと長く考えられてきた。エジプトルーセットオオコウモリの研究は，このコウモリのコミュニケーションシステムは実際には非常に複雑であることを示している。

　このコウモリは飼育され，研究を行う科学者たちは，コンピュータープログラムを使ってコウモリの発する鳴き声を分析した。その鳴き声は，状況に応じてカテゴリーに分類された。例えば，特定の鳴き声は，食べ物があるときに発せられる傾向があった。寝る場所を巡ってコウモリ同士がけんかしているような感じのときには別の鳴き声が発せられた。将来的に科学者たちは，生息環境にいるコウモリを観察し，コウモリの発する鳴き声が変わるかどうかを調べたいと思っている。

No.17 解答 ②

質問の訳　エジプトルーセットオオコウモリの研究は何を示したか。

選択肢の訳　**1**　コウモリはイルカよりも多くの鳴き声を発する。

　　2　コウモリが発する鳴き声には意味がある。

　　3　コウモリの鳴き声はあまり複雑ではない。

　　4　コウモリのコミュニケーションシステムが変化した。

解説　冒頭では，特定の意味を表し得る鳴き声を使ってコミュニケーションを取る動物に言及し，エジプトルーセットオオコウモリの研究についての説明が続く。「コウモリの発声を状況に応じてカテゴリーに分類した」と述べ，2つの異なる場面での鳴き声が説明されていることから，**2**が正解。

No.18 解答 ④

質問の訳　科学者たちはどのようにして分析を行ったか。

選択肢の訳　**1**　眠っているコウモリが発する鳴き声を録音した。

　　2　コウモリの鳴き声をほかの動物の鳴き声と一致させた。

　　3　自然環境にいるコウモリを観察した。

167

4 コンピュータープログラムを使ってコウモリの鳴き声を分類した。

解説 分析方法については，後半の the scientists conducting the study used a computer program to analyze the sounds that the bats made と，続く The sounds were grouped into categories based on context. の部分を簡潔に表した **4** が正解。選択肢では category （categories はその複数形）の動詞形 categorize が使われている。

D

スクリプト **Wilderness Protection**

The Boundary Waters Canoe Area Wilderness, located in a US national forest, contains over a thousand lakes and rivers. It offers visitors the chance to experience nature in an undisturbed state and provides an important habitat for endangered plants and animals. The area also contains large amounts of valuable metals underground. Such metals could be mined and used to make products ranging from electronics to aircraft engines. However, conservationists worry that mining would release harmful substances into nearby waterways.

Local residents are split over whether to allow mining in the area. Some say it could improve the economy by creating jobs, while others believe protecting nature should be the priority. According to a study by an economist, mining may indeed bring short-term economic benefits. However, the study found that such benefits would be smaller than the long-term negative impact mining would have on the tourist industry.

Questions

No.19 What is true about the area described by the speaker?

No.20 What did the study suggest about allowing mining in the area?

全文訳 **自然区域の保護**

アメリカの国有林内にあるバウンダリー・ウォーターズ・カヌー・エリア・ウィルダネスには，1,000 を超える湖や川がある。ここは，訪れる人々に手付かずの自然を体験する機会を提供し，また絶滅危惧種の動植物にとって重要な生息地にもなっている。またこの地域は，地下に大量の貴重な金属が眠っている。これらの金属は，採掘され，電子機器から航空機エンジンに及ぶ製品を作るのに使うことができる。しかし，自然保護団体らは，採掘によって有害物質が周辺の水路に流れ込むことを懸念している。

地域住民の間では，この地域での採掘を許可するかどうかを巡って意見が分かれている。採掘によって雇用が創出され，経済が改善し得ると言う人たちがいる一方で，自然保護を優先すべきだと考える人たちもいる。ある経済学者の調査によると，採掘は確かに短期的な経済的利益をもたらし得る。しかし，その調査によると，そのような利益は，採掘が観光産業に与える長期的な悪影響より小さいであろうことが分かった。

168

No.19 解答 ②

質問の訳 話者が説明する地域について何が正しいか。

選択肢の訳
1 そこの川や湖は汚染されている。
2 そこには多くの希少種が生息している。
3 そこでは重要な製品が開発されている。
4 もはや観光客には開放されていない。

解説 冒頭で長い固有名詞（The Boundary Waters Canoe Area Wilderness）が出てくるが，located in a US national forest と続くことから，国有林の一部の地域だとイメージして聞き進めよう。この地域の説明の中の It ... provides an important habitat for endangered plants and animals. から，**2** が正解。habitat を be home to を使って，endangered plants and animals「絶滅危惧種の動植物」を rare species「希少種」に言い換えている。

No.20 解答 ④

質問の訳 調査はこの地域での採掘を許可することについて何を示したか。

選択肢の訳
1 地域住民には影響を与えないだろう。
2 長期的な利益をもたらすかもしれない。
3 観光産業を後押しするだろう。
4 益となるよりも害となるかもしれない。

解説 調査について述べた According to a study by an economist, ... がポイント。採掘について，「短期的な経済的利益をもたらし得る」（益）→ However（対比）→「利益は観光産業に与える長期的な悪影響より小さいだろう」（害）という流れから，**4** が正解。

E

スクリプト A Discovery in Egypt

Hetepheres was an important Egyptian queen who lived more than 4,000 years ago. However, the location of her burial place was long a mystery. It was finally discovered in the 1920s by a photographer who, when setting up his camera, noticed something unusual under his camera stand. Upon investigation, he discovered it was a covering over some steps that led down to the tomb of Hetepheres.

Thanks to the photographer's unexpected discovery, archaeologists found items of ancient furniture and jewelry, some of which had writings on them. The archaeologists also found evidence that the tomb had been broken into after Hetepheres was buried there. Many items appeared to have been stolen. In fact, even the body of Hetepheres was missing. Although the archaeologists were disappointed by this, the writings and remaining objects in the tomb have helped to expand our knowledge of ancient Egypt.

Questions

No.21 What is one thing the speaker says about the tomb of Hetepheres?

No.22 What is one reason the archaeologists were disappointed?

全文訳 **エジプトでの発見**

　ヘテプヘレスは，4,000 年以上も前に存命していたエジプトの重要な女王であった。しかし，彼女の埋葬場所は長らく謎であった。ついに発見されたのは 1920 年代のことで，ある写真家が，カメラを設置していたときにカメラスタンドの下にある妙なものに気付いた。調べると，彼は，それがヘテプヘレスの墓に続く幾つかの段を覆っているものだと分かった。

　その写真家の予期せぬ発見のおかげで，考古学者たちは古代の家具や宝石類を発見し，中には文字が書かれているものもあった。また，考古学者たちは，ヘテプヘレスがそこに埋葬された後に墓が侵入された形跡も発見した。盗まれた品も多いようだった。それどころか，ヘテプヘレスの遺体さえも消えていた。これには考古学者たちもがっかりしたが，墓の文字や残された品々は，私たちの古代エジプトの知識を広げるのに役立った。

No.21 解答 ①

質問の訳 ヘテプヘレスの墓について話者が言うことの 1 つは何か。

選択肢の訳
1 偶然発見された。
2 考古学者たちが予想したよりも小さかった。
3 エジプトで最も古い墓である。
4 一度も写真撮影されたことがない。

解説 ヘテプヘレスの埋葬地が発見された経緯は，It was finally discovered in the 1920s by a photographer who, ... の部分にある。写真家がカメラを設置しているときに偶然発見したことから，**1** が正解。

No.22 解答 ②

質問の訳 考古学者たちががっかりした理由の 1 つは何か。

選択肢の訳
1 墓に書かれた文字が解読できなかった。
2 ヘテプヘレスの遺体が墓になかった。
3 墓の宝物が全て消えていた。
4 宝石類を調べることが許されなかった。

解説 考古学者たちががっかりした話は Although the archaeologists were disappointed by this の部分にある。この this は前の the body of Hetepheres was missing を受けているので，**2** が正解。

F

スクリプト **Moving during Childhood**

Moving to a new home can be difficult for children. Researchers are learning more about the problems it causes and which children are most at risk. Studies in the UK have shown that children forced to move more than once in a single

170

year are especially affected. The impact of moving is the same whether children come from wealthy or poor backgrounds. However, some of the studies have also shown that teenagers may experience the most serious negative effects of moving.

The findings of a study using data from Denmark showed that moving more than once can increase a child's risk of criminal activity later in life. Moving to a new area and having to form social relationships at a new school can be difficult and stressful for children. More research is needed to determine how to prevent these negative effects.

Questions
No.23 What have some studies in the UK shown about moving?
No.24 What was learned from the data from Denmark?

全文訳 **子供時代の引っ越し**

新しい家に引っ越すのは子供にとって困難な場合がある。研究者たちは，引っ越しが引き起こす問題や，どんな子供が最もリスクにさらされているのかについて，さらに詳しく調べている。イギリスの研究によると，1年に2回以上の引っ越しを余儀なくされた子供が特に影響を受けることが分かった。引っ越しの影響は，裕福な家庭の子供でも貧しい家庭の子供でも同じである。しかし，中には，ティーンエイジャーが最も深刻な引っ越しの悪影響を受けている可能性を示す研究もある。

デンマークのデータを用いた調査の結果，2回以上引っ越しをすると，のちに子供が犯罪を引き起こすリスクが高まる可能性があることが分かった。新しい地域に引っ越し，新しい学校で社会的関係を築かなければならないことは，子供にとって困難でストレスとなり得る。このような悪影響を防ぐ方法を突き止めるにはさらなる研究が必要である。

No.23 解答 　　　　　　　　　　　　　　　　　　　正答率 ★75%以上

質問の訳　イギリスの研究は引っ越しに関して何を示したか。
選択肢の訳　1　裕福な家庭により多くの問題を引き起こす。
　　　　　　2　行われる頻度が減ってきている。
　　　　　　3　特にティーンエイジャーに影響を与える可能性がある。
　　　　　　4　大人の健康に重大な影響を及ぼす。

解説　イギリスの研究の説明の中で，However, some of the studies have also shown that teenagers may experience the most serious negative effects of moving. とあり，**3**が正解。名詞 effects が **3** では動詞の affect を使って表されている。

No.24 解答 **4**　　　　　　　　　　　　　　　　　　　

質問の訳　デンマークのデータから何が分かったか。
選択肢の訳　1　引っ越しは離婚率を上げる。
　　　　　　2　引っ越しは学校での問題の解決に役立つ。

3 引っ越しは親子関係を損なう可能性がある。
4 引っ越しは行動の問題を引き起こす可能性がある。

解説 調査の結果（findings），引っ越しが及ぼす影響について ... can increase a child's risk of criminal activity later in life「のちに子供が犯罪を引き起こすリスクが高まる」と言っている。これを「行動の問題を引き起こす」と抽象化した **4** が正解。

一次試験・リスニング　Part**3**　問題編 p.122 ～ 123　

G

You have 10 seconds to read the situation and Question No. 25.

　Well, your grades are good enough to qualify, and you might even be entitled to a scholarship based on your academic record so far. You can apply for one, but you'll need to be accepted into the program first. In the meantime, if you're concerned about the cost of the program, you can apply for other forms of financial aid, like a student loan. That can be done right away, and the approval process is quick. Your visa shouldn't be an issue, and as for your supervisor, one will be appointed for you depending on your course of study.

　Now mark your answer on your answer sheet.

全文訳
　ええと，あなたの成績は基準を満たすのに十分ですし，これまでの学業成績に基づいて奨学金を受ける資格も得られるかもしれません。奨学金を申請することはできますが，まずは課程に合格する必要があります。それまでの間，もし学費が心配なら，学生ローンのようなほかの形の学資援助を申請することができます。それはすぐに行うことができますし，審査も迅速です。ビザは問題にならないでしょう。また指導教官については，あなたの研究コースに応じて選任されます。

No.**25** 解答　**3**

状況の訳 あなたはアメリカの大学の留学生である。大学院課程に出願したいと思っているが，学費を心配している。履修指導員が次のように言う。

質問の訳 あなたはまず何をすべきか。

選択肢の訳
1　奨学金を申し込む。
2　ビザを更新する。
3　学資援助を申請する。
4　指導教官を選ぶ。

解説 状況から，大学院課程に出願したいと思っており，「学費を心配している」

という状況を押さえる。質問文に do first とあるので，最初にすべきことを聞き取るようにする。「奨学金を申請できるが，まず課程に合格する必要がある」と言っているので，**1** は不適。放送文の中ほどで In the meantime, ... you can apply for other forms of financial aid, like a student loan. That can be done right away, ... と言っていることから，**3** が正解。

スクリプト

You have 10 seconds to read the situation and Question No. 26.

We apologize for the cancellation of the flight to London. All passengers can take the same flight tomorrow, and free accommodation will be provided at an airport hotel for tonight. Passengers wishing to leave today have two options. First, a charter flight will leave in one hour and arrive in London this evening. This flight has economy-class seats only. Second, there are first-class and business-class seats available on a flight to Amsterdam. A connecting flight to London will arrive in the early hours of tomorrow morning. You can use your existing ticket for both of these options.

Now mark your answer on your answer sheet.

全文訳

ロンドン行きの便が欠航になったことをお詫び申し上げます。全ての乗客の皆さまは明日の同じ便にご搭乗いただけます。また今夜は空港ホテルに無料でご宿泊いただけます。本日出発を希望される乗客の皆さまには，2つの選択肢があります。1つ目は，チャーター便が1時間後に出発し，今夜ロンドンに到着します。この便の座席はエコノミークラスのみです。2つ目は，アムステルダム行きの便で，ファーストクラスおよびビジネスクラスの座席があります。ロンドン行きの乗り継ぎ便は明日の早朝に到着します。どちらの選択肢もお手持ちの航空券をご利用いただけます。

No.26 解答 ①

状況の訳 あなたは空港にいる。あなたが乗るロンドン行きの便は欠航になったが，できるだけ早くそこに行かなければならない。次のようなアナウンスが聞こえる。

質問の訳 あなたは何をすべきか。

選択肢の訳
1 チャーター便に乗る。
2 座席アップグレードの代金を支払う。
3 空港ホテルに行く。
4 アムステルダム行きの便に乗る。

解説 航空便が欠航になった場面。代替案が順に説明されるので，「できるだけ早く行きたい」という条件に合うものを判断する。空港ホテルに泊まっ

て明日の便に乗るのでは遅いので，**3** は不適。Passengers wishing to leave today ...「本日出発を希望される乗客の皆さまには…」の後がポイント。今夜ロンドンに着くチャーター便に乗るという選択肢が最適なので，**1** が正解。アムステルダム行きの便に乗るという選択肢は，到着が明日になるので不適。

I

スクリプト

You have 10 seconds to read the situation and Question No. 27.

That concludes this morning's opening session. The next session will begin at 1 p.m., following the lunch break. There are four excellent options to choose from, each focusing on a different theme. The first seminar will focus on factors that affect English pronunciation and will be held in room 210. The second will focus on teaching grammar to beginners and will be held in room 212. In room 214, participants will learn how to create motivating lessons using realistic situations that inspire students to use English. Finally, in room 216, there'll be a discussion on testing in relation to class placement.

Now mark your answer on your answer sheet.

全文訳

以上で，午前中のオープニングセッションは終了です。次のセッションは，昼休みの後，午後1時に始まります。セッションには4つの素晴らしい選択肢があり，それぞれ異なるテーマに焦点を当てます。1つ目のセミナーは，英語の発音に影響を与える要因に焦点を当てるもので，210号室で行われます。2つ目のセミナーは，初学者に文法を教えることに焦点を当てるもので，212号室で行われます。214号室では，参加者たちは，学生たちが英語を使う気になるような現実的な状況を用い，やる気を起こさせる授業の作り方を学びます。最後に216号室では，クラス分けに関連したテストについてのディスカッションを行います。

No.27 解答 ③ ••••••••••••••••••••••••••••••••••• **正答率 ★75%以上**

状況の訳 あなたは大学生への英語指導に関する学会に出席している。あなたの主な関心は学生のモチベーションである。次のようなアナウンスが聞こえる。

質問の訳 あなたはどの部屋に行くべきか。

選択肢の訳 1　210号室。
2　212号室。
3　214号室。
4　216号室。

解説 状況から，「学生のモチベーション」に関心があることを押さえ，選択肢からは部屋番号（数字）の聞き取りが重要になることを理解しよう。

174

午後のセッションはテーマが4つあり，The first seminar ... The second ... と説明が続く。そして3つ目の In room 214, ... に create motivating lessons や inspire students to use English とあり，これが関心のある内容だと判断できる。

(スクリプト)

You have 10 seconds to read the situation and Question No. 28.

Hi, Lance here. I know we'd planned our meeting about the new curriculum for this evening, but something's come up. I've had to book an after-school meeting with a parent, so I need to reschedule. Unfortunately, I have lunchroom duty every day this week, so that time slot is out. I know you're really busy, but could we meet tomorrow after school? I have another evening meeting on Wednesday, but Thursday evening would also work. We can't leave it until next week because I need to confirm the curriculum with the principal by next Monday.

Now mark your answer on your answer sheet.

(全文訳)

もしもし，ランスです。新しいカリキュラムに関する打ち合わせを今日の夕方に予定していたことは知っているのですが，急用ができてしまいました。保護者との放課後の面談を予約しなければならなくなったので，予定を変更しなければなりません。あいにく，今週は毎日食堂の当番があるので，その時間帯は無理です。すごくお忙しいのは分かっているのですが，明日の放課後に会えますか。水曜日の夕方は別の打ち合わせが入っていますが，木曜日の夕方でもいいです。来週の月曜日までに校長先生とカリキュラムを確認しなければならないから，来週までは延ばせませんね。

No.28 解答 ③

(状況の訳) あなたは教師である。平日は毎日授業があり，火曜日の放課後はバスケットボール部の顧問をしている。月曜日の朝に同僚から次のような音声メッセージを受け取る。

(質問の訳) あなたはいつ同僚に会うべきか。

(選択肢の訳)
1 火曜日の昼休み中。
2 水曜日の夕方。
3 木曜日の夕方。
4 来週の月曜日。

(解説) 状況から，「平日は毎日授業」，「火曜日の放課後は部活」を押さえよう。同僚が提案する日時の中で条件に合うのは，木曜日の夕方（Thursday evening would also work）である。1と2は話者（同僚）の都合が悪い日時として説明しているので不適。

175

K

スクリプト

You have 10 seconds to read the situation and Question No. 29.

Thank you for applying to be a volunteer. There are a number of options that might interest you. Mainly, we need people who can work at hospitals to assist new immigrants with paperwork, which requires at least a year of experience. For people new to volunteer work, there's a program in schools to help children with different language backgrounds. We also need people to help out at police stations, which requires at least two years of experience. There's also the youth mentorship program, which is open to people with experience participating in similar programs.

Now mark your answer on your answer sheet.

全文訳

ボランティアにご応募いただきありがとうございます。興味を持っていただけそうな選択肢が幾つかあります。主に，新しく移民として来た人たちの事務処理を手伝うのに病院で働ける人を必要としていまして，これには最低でも1年の経験が必要です。ボランティア活動が初めての人には，さまざまな言語背景を持つ子供たちを支援するプログラムが学校にあります。あと，警察署で手伝ってくれる人も必要ですが，これには最低2年の経験が必要です。同様のプログラムに参加した経験のある人を対象とした，若者向け指導プログラムもあります。

No.29 解答 ②

状況の訳 あなたはボランティアの言語通訳者になりたいと思っている。ボランティアの経験はない。地元のボランティアセンターの所長が次のように言う。

質問の訳 あなたはどの選択肢を選ぶべきか。

選択肢の訳
1 病院での手伝い。
2 学校のプログラム。
3 警察署での手伝い。
4 若者向け指導プログラム。

解説 やりたいのは通訳者のボランティア。「経験がない」という条件から，最低1年の経験が必要な **1**，最低2年の経験が必要な **3** は不適。For people new to volunteer work, there's a program in schools ... が経験がなくてもできる活動で，**2** が正解。最後の open to people with experience participating in similar programs はボランティアの経験がないとできないことを意味するので，**4** も不適。

176

二次試験・面接　問題カード **A** 日程　問題編 p.124 〜 125　　▶ MP3 ▶ アプリ　▶ CD 4 28 〜 32

解答例 **One day, a restaurant owner was working at her restaurant.** The customers were enjoying the restaurant's hamburgers. However, she overheard an old couple walking past the restaurant. The old woman said to the man that the restaurant's food was unhealthy, and she didn't seem interested in eating there. That weekend, the owner was shopping at a supermarket. She saw a display of organic vegetables, and it gave her an idea. A few weeks later, the owner and an employee were putting a sign outside the restaurant. The sign announced the restaurant's new organic vegetable hamburger set. The next week, the owner and the employee were in the restaurant after it closed for the night. They were looking at a list of the restaurant's top sets for that week. The organic vegetable hamburger set was not as popular as they had expected. The employee told the owner that the new set was too expensive.

解答例の訳 ある日，レストランの店主がレストランで働いていました。客たちはレストランのハンバーガーを楽しんでいました。しかし，彼女はレストランを通りかかった老夫婦の話を小耳に挟みました。高齢の女性は男性に，ここのレストランの食事は不健康だと言い，そこで食事をすることに興味がない様子でした。その週末，店主はスーパーで買い物をしていました。彼女は，有機野菜の陳列棚を見て，あるアイデアを思い付きました。数週間後，店主と従業員はレストランの外に看板を出していました。看板は，レストランの新しい有機野菜ハンバーガーセットを知らせていました。翌週，店主と従業員は夜間のため閉店した後，レストランにいました。彼らはその週のレストランの人気セットのリストを見ていました。有機野菜ハンバーガーセットは，彼らが期待したほど人気がありませんでした。従業員は店主に，新セットは高過ぎると言いました。

解説 解答に含めるべき点は以下の4つ。①高齢の男女がレストランを通りかかり，女性が「ここの食事はどれも不健康だ」と言っている，②その週末，店主の女性はスーパーの有機野菜を見てアイデアを思い付く，③数週間後，店主と従業員が，新メニューの有機野菜ハンバーガーセットの看板を出している，④翌週，今週の人気セットのリストを見て，従業員が「新しいセットは高過ぎる」と言っている。4コマ目のリストは販売ランキングを表しており，新メニューのセットが低い順位であること，その原因が高価格にあると言っていることを理解しよう。

21年度第2回　面接

177

No. 1

解答例 I'd be thinking, "Many people don't know about our new organic vegetable hamburger set yet, so we should keep promoting it. It'll probably become more popular once health-conscious people learn about it."

解説 質問は「4番目の絵を見てください。もしあなたがこのレストランの店主なら，どのようなことを考えているでしょうか」。解答例は，新メニューの不人気の理由を「多くの人がまだ知らないから」とし，「宣伝を続けるべき」という考え。ほかには，「価格を抑える工夫をすべき」や，「別の健康に良い商品を検討しよう」などの考えもあり得る。

No. 2

解答例 Yes. Young people these days want to buy popular products they see on social media, but social-media trends are changing all the time. This means young people often buy clothes and only wear them once or twice.

解説 質問は「今日の若者はお金を無駄にする傾向にありますか」。解答例はYesの立場で，ソーシャルメディアで見た人気商品を買う傾向を根拠にした後，「1，2回しか着ない服を買う」という具体例が続く。Noの立場では，「高品質の物を買って大事にする人もいる」など，お金は使うが浪費している（waste）訳ではない点を説明してもよいだろう。

No. 3

解答例 No, I don't think so. Some countries don't have good climates for growing food, so there might not be enough food for everyone without imports. Importing food from other countries is a good way to maintain the food supply.

解説 質問は「各国は，輸入食品への依存を減らすのにもっと努力すべきですか」。解答例はNoの立場で，気候の面で輸入食品を必要とする国に言及し，「食品輸入は食料供給を維持するための良い方法だ」という意見。質問文のreliance「依存」は動詞relyの名詞形で，「輸入食品に依存している」はbe dependent on imported foodという表現も可能。

No. 4

解答例 I think so. Scientists could develop environmentally friendly technologies to replace harmful ones. For example, new manufacturing technology could reduce air pollution. Better electric cars will also help the environment.

解説 「新しい技術の開発は自然環境を救うのに役立つことができますか」という質問。解答例はYesの立場で，「有害な技術に取って代わる環境に優しい技術の開発ができる」と述べた後，For exampleを使って，大気汚染を減らす製造技術と，より優れた電気自動車を挙げている。

二次試験・面接 | 問題カード **C** 日程 | 問題編 p.126〜127 | ▶MP3 ▶アプリ ▶CD 4 33〜36

解答例 **One day, a young woman was in her office.** She and some of her coworkers were reading a poster on the wall that was about a self-development program. It said that workers could get a qualification through the program. The young woman was determined to do this so she could advance her career. A few days later, the young woman was in her room. It was past midnight, but she was studying hard for the qualification test. The next day, the young woman was getting ready to leave work at six o'clock because she wanted to go home and study more. One of her coworkers was surprised that she was leaving work so early. At the monthly sales meeting, the sales manager presented the young woman and her team with a chart with their sales data, which showed that the team's sales had dropped. She said the team needed to do better.

解答例の訳 ある日，若い女性がオフィスにいました。彼女と同僚の何人かが壁に張られた自己啓発プログラムに関するポスターを読んでいました。従業員たちはそのプログラムを通じて資格を得ることができると書いてありました。若い女性はキャリアアップのためにこれをしようと決意しました。数日後，若い女性は自分の部屋にいました。夜中の12時を過ぎていましたが，彼女は資格試験に向けて猛勉強していました。翌日，若い女性は家に帰ってもっと勉強したかったので，6時に職場を出る支度をしていました。同僚の1人が，彼女がそんなに早く退社することに驚いていました。月次営業会議で，営業部長は，若い女性と彼女のチームに，チームの売り上げが減少したことを示す売り上げデータのグラフを提示しました。彼女は，チームはもっと成績を上げる必要があると言いました。

解説 解答に含めるべき点は以下の4つ。①女性が社内で「自己啓発プログラム・資格を得よう」と書かれたポスターを見ている，②数日後，自宅で夜中の12時過ぎに試験勉強をしている，③翌日，6時に退社しようとする女性に同僚［上司］が「帰るの？」と言っている，④月次営業会議で，営業部長が売り上げ減少を示すグラフを見せて「あなたのチームはもっと成績を上げる必要がある」と言っている。カード上部の This is a story ... から，女性はキャリアアップを望んでいることを押さえよう。4コマ目は，「売り上げの低下を示すグラフ」を表す a graph that showed the drop in sales や a graph showing sales had fallen などの表現も使える。

21年度第2回　面接

179

No. 1

解答例 I'd be thinking, "I need to focus more on doing my work well. Otherwise, the sales manager is going to have a bad opinion of me. Just getting a qualification won't lead to a promotion."

解説 質問は「4番目の絵を見てください。もしあなたがこの若い女性なら，どのようなことを考えているでしょうか」。解答例は，「もっと仕事をがんばらないといけない」「資格を取っただけでは昇進できない」という反省の気持ちを表している。そのほか，「残業したら勉強時間が確保できるだろうか」などの不安な気持ちを表すこともできるだろう。

No. 2

解答例 I don't think so. Many retired people are interested in learning new things, but it's easier for them to learn on their own through the Internet. Studying at a university may also be too expensive.

解説 質問は「今後，定年退職後に大学で学ぶことを選択する高齢者が増えると思いますか」。解答例は No の立場で，「（大学よりも）ネットを使って独学する方が楽だ」「大学で勉強するのは費用がかかり過ぎる」という2つの理由を述べている。Yes の立場では，高齢化社会（aging society）によって高齢者向けの大学や講座が増えていることなどを根拠にできるだろう。

No. 3

解答例 Yes. Many news programs and articles promote expensive products. This makes people feel they need to earn a lot of money to be happy. Publishing companies also release many books on how to become rich.

解説 質問は「メディアはお金を稼ぐことに重点を置き過ぎていると思いますか」。解答例は Yes の立場で，media について具体的に「ニュース番組や記事」と「本」の観点で意見を述べている。No の立場では，「メディアはお金以外の大事な事柄も大いに扱っている」などの意見があり得る。

No. 4

解答例 No. Air pollution in Japan sometimes makes people sick. Also, the water in areas such as Tokyo Bay has a lot of pollution in it. Most of this pollution is caused by companies, not by individual people.

解説 「日本において企業は汚染を減らすために十分な努力をしていますか」という質問。汚染の種類には大気汚染，海洋汚染，土壌汚染などがある。解答例は No の立場で，大気汚染に苦しむ人々がいるという事例を挙げた後，「東京湾」という具体的な地域を取り上げて水質汚染について述べている。「汚染の大半は個人ではなく企業によって引き起こされている→だから企業は十分な努力をしていない」という論理展開である。

2021-1

一次試験
筆記解答・解説　　　p.182〜197

一次試験
リスニング解答・解説　p.198〜220

二次試験
面接解答・解説　　　p.221〜224

解 答 一 覧

一次試験・筆記

1

(1)	3	(10)	1	(19)	2
(2)	4	(11)	3	(20)	1
(3)	2	(12)	3	(21)	2
(4)	1	(13)	2	(22)	1
(5)	3	(14)	3	(23)	4
(6)	1	(15)	1	(24)	1
(7)	1	(16)	4	(25)	1
(8)	1	(17)	2		
(9)	2	(18)	3		

2

(26)	4	(29)	4
(27)	3	(30)	3
(28)	3	(31)	1

3

(32)	2	(35)	2	(38)	2
(33)	4	(36)	4	(39)	1
(34)	3	(37)	1	(40)	1
				(41)	4

4　解答例は本文参照

一次試験・リスニング

Part 1

No. 1	4	No. 5	2	No. 9	1
No. 2	1	No. 6	2	No.10	1
No. 3	2	No. 7	3	No.11	2
No. 4	3	No. 8	4	No.12	1

Part 2

No.13	4	No.17	1	No.21	4
No.14	1	No.18	2	No.22	1
No.15	3	No.19	2	No.23	3
No.16	2	No.20	3	No.24	2

Part 3

No.25	2	No.28	1
No.26	2	No.29	1
No.27	4		

| 一次試験・筆記 | **1** | 問題編 p.130～133 |

(1) ─ 解答 ③

訳 Ａ：販売プレゼンテーションの概要を見せていただきありがとうございます。よくできているのですが，一部の箇所が少し冗長です。

Ｂ：確かに幾つかの情報を繰り返し過ぎていると思います。いくらか取り除こうと思います。

解説 Ａ は Ｂ のプレゼンテーションの概要を見て感想を述べている。Ｂ の応答の「繰り返し過ぎ」に相当する redundant「冗長な」が適切。decisive「決定的な」，subjective「主観的な」，distinct「目立つ」

(2) ─ 解答 ④

訳 リサはその職を得る可能性が低いと思ったが，面接に行った。予想した通り，彼女は雇われなかった。

解説 第 2 文の「予想した通り雇われなかった」という文脈から，彼女の予想は「職を得る可能性（probability）が低い」だったと判断できる。restoration「修復」，credibility「信頼性」，contention「争い」

(3) ─ 解答 ②

訳 発展途上国において，輸出用に栄養価の高い作物を栽培している農家の多くが自分の家族を養うのに十分な食料がないことは，悲しいことに皮肉である。

解説 It is ～ that ...「…なのは～だ」の構文。作物を栽培している農家に十分な食料がないのは，皮肉な（ironic）状況だと言える。indefinite「不定の」，restless「落ち着きのない」，superficial「表面的な」

(4) ─ 解答 ①

訳 化学工場での爆発は，地域の環境に甚大な被害を与えた。その地域で野生生物が完全に回復するには何年もかかるだろう。

解説 第 2 文の「回復に何年もかかる」にうまくつなげるには，環境に被害を「与えた」という文意にするのが自然。inflict「（苦痛・打撃などを）与える」の過去形が適切。それぞれ enhance「強化する」，vanish「消える」，perceive「気付く」の過去形。

(5) ─ 解答 ③

訳 恐怖症を克服する最善の方法は，恐れているものに身をさらすことだと言う人たちもいる。例えば，ネズミが怖い人はネズミを手に持ってみるべきだ。

解説 空所には克服する（overcome）べきものが入る。fears や afraid などの語句，また For example, ... で示された具体例から，克服すべきは恐怖症（phobia）である。temptation「誘惑」，barricade「障害物」，

182

famine「飢饉」

(6) ― 解答 **1**

訳 大学の英語の授業は必須だったが，その言語の高い能力を証明できれば，学生はその授業を免除された。

解説 空所後の them は English classes を指す。高い英語力を証明できたら英語の授業を「受けなくてよい」という文意がふさわしい。*be* exempted from「～を免除される」が適切。それぞれ prosecute「起訴する」，command「命令する」，quantify「量を計る」の過去分詞。

(7) ― 解答 **1**　　　　　　　　　　　　　　正答率 ★75%以上

訳 Eメールや携帯メッセージは，人々の文章の書き方を変えた。多くの人々は，言葉を短くし，伝統的な文法の規則を無視している。

解説 第2文は，Eメールや携帯メッセージがもたらした書き方の「変化」を表している。transform「変える，転換する」の過去分詞が正解。それぞれ officiate「職務を果たす」，synthesize「総合する」，disarm「（人の）武器を取り上げる」の過去分詞。

(8) ― 解答 **1**

訳 アナリストの中には，二酸化炭素排出に関するその新条約は，地球温暖化との闘いにおける画期的な出来事だと考える人たちもいる。そのうちの1人は，「これは，これまでに調印された中で最も重要な環境条約だ」と述べた。

解説 第2文の「これまでに調印された中で最も重要な環境条約」から，新条約の説明として milestone「画期的な出来事，節目」が適切。vigor「活力」，backlog「未処理の仕事」，confession「告白」

(9) ― 解答 **2**

訳 休暇中，夫と一緒に太陽が降り注ぐビーチに横たわり，ロベルタは心から幸せに感じた。彼女はこれほど満足したことはなかった。

解説 空所には happy を修飾する副詞が入る。第2文の内容からポジティブな感情だと判断し，profoundly「心から，深く」が適切。barely「かろうじて」，improperly「不適切に」，harshly「厳しく」

(10) ― 解答 **1**

訳 ナディーンは毎日，1時間かけてアパートを徹底的に掃除するので，部屋中がピカピカである。

解説 徹底的に掃除された部屋はどんな状態かを想像すると，spotless が適切。spot（染み，汚れ）＋ less（～のない）。minute「取るに足らない」，rugged「ごつごつした，頑丈な」，impartial「公平な」

(11) ― 解答 **3**

訳 度重なる振るわないパフォーマンスの末，そのラグビー選手は所属クラブのトップチームから2番目のチームに降格させられた。

183

解説 demote は「降格させる」という意味で，ここではスポーツの文脈で「下部リーグに下げる」という意味となる。これを受動態で表すと空所後の「トップチームから2番目のチームに」という文意に合う。それぞれ incline「傾ける」，clinch「（くぎを）打ち曲げる」，adapt「適応させる」の過去分詞。

(12) − 解答 ③

訳 選挙で明確な勝者がいなかったため，新政権は社会党，自由党，緑の党を含む連立で成り立っている。

解説 「新政権は〜で構成されている」という文意と，空所後の「社会党，自由党，緑の党を含む」という説明を考慮すると，coalition「（2つ以上の政党の）連立，連合」がふさわしい。gradation「段階，グラデーション」，casualty「死傷者，犠牲者」，warranty「保証」

(13) − 解答 ②

訳 マークは容赦ないクマの攻撃の被害者となり，1カ月以上も入院した。

解説 1カ月以上の入院の原因は，「ひどい，残酷な」（vicious）クマの攻撃の被害者になったためである。dazed「ぼんやりした」，heartfelt「心のこもった」，superior「優れた」

(14) − 解答 ③　　　　　　　　　　　　　正答率 ★75%以上

訳 人間は何千年もの間，さまざまな植物を育ててきたが，小麦は人類によって最初に栽培された食用作物の1つだった。

解説 〈the first＋名詞＋to *do*〉「〜する最初の（名詞）」では名詞と *do* が主語と動詞の関係になる。またここでは to 不定詞が受動態になっている。crop（作物）は栽培されるものなので，cultivated が適切。それぞれ omit「省略する」，thaw「解凍する」，harass「困らせる」の過去分詞。

(15) − 解答 ①

訳 A：ジャン，ウエーターにチップをいくら置いていくべきだと思う？
B：チップはすでに勘定書に加えられているから，何も置いていく必要はないよ。

解説 ウエーターにチップをいくら払うかについて，B は「すでに勘定書に加えられている」と言う。よって空所には「チップ」と同意になる語がふさわしい。正解の gratuity「心付け，チップ」は tip の改まった表現。module「モジュール」，arsenal「兵器」，allotment「割り当て」

(16) − 解答 ④

訳 グレンは，家賃を払うのに父親からお金を借りるしかなかった。彼はほかの選択肢を全て使い果たしてしまったのだ。

解説 第1文（結果）＋第2文（理由）の関係。父親からお金を借りるしかなかったのは，ほかの選択肢を使い果たした（exhausted）からである。それぞれ delight「喜ばす」，retrace「引き返す」，revolt「（人に）反感を

184

抱かせる」の過去分詞。

(17) – 解答 **2**

訳 笑顔は一般的に幸福の表れであるが，怒りなどの否定的な感情を隠すためにほほ笑む人もいる。

解説 smile と happiness の関係から，signify「表れである，意味する」の3人称単数・現在形である signifies が適切。それぞれ monitor「監視する」，vomit「吐く」，regulate「規制する」の3人称単数・現在形。

(18) – 解答 **3**

訳 そのスーパーマーケットチェーンの拡大計画は，消費者支出が少なくとも向こう5年間は増加し続けるという仮定に基づいている。

解説 空所直後の that は同格を表す。未来を表す will に着目し，「消費者支出が増加し続けるという仮定（assumption）」とするのが適切。malfunction「誤動作」，institution「機関」，transcription「転記」

(19) – 解答 **2**

訳 その熱帯の島に住む人々の中には，200年前にそこに到着したフランス人船員の子孫もいる。

解説 Some of the people living on the tropical island は今住んでいる人々のことだが，French sailors who arrived there 200 years ago は過去の人々のことなので，descendants「子孫」が適切。それぞれ garment「衣服」，inhabitant「住民」，compartment「区画」の複数形。

(20) – 解答 **1**

訳 昔，多くの人々は，太陽が地球の周りを回っていると信じていた。科学や数学の進歩により，実際には地球が太陽の周りを回っていることがようやく証明された。

解説 第2文の moves に相当する revolve「周回する」の過去形が適切。対比を表す eventually と in fact を意識して読もう。それぞれ renew「更新する」，relieve「緩和する」，restrain「抑える」の過去形。

(21) – 解答 **2**

訳 A：どうして DTP の仕事のオファーを受け入れるのをそんなに渋っているの？

　　B：まあ，今よりさらに忙しくなるんじゃないかという不安があってね，どうしても仕事と生活のバランスがより良く取れる仕事がしたいんだ。

解説 B は発言内容から，仕事のオファーに消極的な様子である。*be reluctant to do*「～するのに気が進まない」が文意に合う。frank「率直な」，spiteful「意地悪な」，righteous「正義の」

(22) – 解答 **1** 　正答率 ★75%以上

訳 A：明日の夜のパーティーに来ないと，せっかくの楽しみを逃してしまうよ。

185

B：ごめん，どうしてもプレゼンテーションを終わらせないといけないんだ。パーティーのことは後で教えて。

解説 パーティーに行かないということは，楽しみを逃す（miss out）ことを意味する。add up「～を合計する」，get over「～を乗り越える」，join in「～に参加する」

(23) − 解答 **4**

訳 マーティーは，何時間も費やしてその問題**に取り組ん**だ末，解き方が思ったよりはるかに単純であることに気付いた。

解説 問題の解き方が分かる前にすることは，問題を「解こうとする」ことである。wrestle with「～（困難・問題など）と格闘する，～に取り組む」の -ing 形が適切。それぞれ live down「～（失敗・恥など）を克服する」，clear out「～の中を掃除する，～（人など）を追い出す」，snap off「～をポキリと折る」の -ing 形。

(24) − 解答 **1**

訳 容疑者は，警察に逮捕されそうになっていたとき，警官の銃**を取ろうとした**。幸い，彼はそれを手にできる前に止められた。

解説 第2文の get it の it は an officer's gun を指し，空所には get につながる go for の過去形が入る。「～を求めて（for）行く（go）」のイメージから，「～を取りに行く，～を得ようとする」などの意味になる。それぞれ let up「和らぐ，弱まる」，pick over「～を細かく調べる」，set off「～（出来事など）を引き起こす，出発する」の過去形。

(25) − 解答 **1** ・・・・・・・・・・・・・・・・・・・・・・・ 正答率 ★**75%以上**

訳 その研究者は，人里離れたジャングルで3カ月生活した後，ようやくインターネットにアクセスして母国のニュース**を知る**ことができて喜んだ。

解説 空所に入る語句は access と並列。インターネットがつながってできることを想像すると，ニュースを「手に入れる」といった意味がふさわしい。catch up on「～（近況など）を知る，～（遅れ・不足）を取り戻す」が適切。change out of「～から着替える」，open up to「～（人）に打ち明ける」，put up with「～を我慢する」

一次試験・筆記 **2** 問題編 p.134 ～ 137

全文訳 **植物薬**

　何千年もの間，人は植物や植物由来の物質を薬として服用してきた。そのような治療剤は今でも多くの地域で近代薬剤より一般的に使用されており，特定の発展途上国各国の人口の80％ほどが植物薬に頼っている。**それにもかかわらず**，植物薬の有効性は科学に基づく証拠による裏付けがほとんどない。そのため多くの西洋の医者が，重篤な人

186

に対して特に，その使用に反対している。そのような患者たちにとって，科学的に証明された薬剤を使うことは生と死の分かれ目になり得る。

　また，研究によってほかの問題も浮き彫りになった。科学者たちは植物薬に関する50以上の研究を調べ，植物薬に含まれる化学物質が臓器障害を引き起こすことがあること，さらにこれらの植物薬がほかの薬剤と併用されると有害になり得ることを突き止めた。科学者たちはこれらの薬が一般的に使用されている社会ではそのような作用はほとんどの場合報告されていないと言う。これによって，患者たちはこれらの薬が安全だと信じてしまうのである。実際，これらの人々の大多数は植物薬を使っていることを医者に言うことすらする理由は何もないと考えており，植物薬が医者によって処方された薬と相互作用した場合の危険な副作用のリスクにさらされている。

　植物薬の支持者たちは，臨床試験からのデータの量が増えてきており，これはどの薬が安全かを人々が把握する助けになり得ると言っている。彼らは植物薬と近代的で医者に処方される薬は，異なる役割があるはずだとも感じている。緊急時や重篤な感染症と闘うためにしばしば必要な標準薬の代わりとして植物薬を捉えるのではなく，人々は全体的な健康や健康状態を維持するためにそれらを代わりに用いるべきである。支持者たちは，適切に服用されれば，伝統薬と近代薬の両方ともが互いに安全に併用できると言う。

（語句）substance「物質」，cure「治療（法［薬］）」，effectiveness「有効性」，unsupported「裏付けのない」，highlight「強調する」，side effect「副作用」，supporter「支持者」，wellness「健康であること」

(26) – 解答 **4** ・・・・・・・・・・・・・・・・・・・・・・・・・・・・・・・・・　正答率 ★75%以上

（解説）第1段落：植物薬の概要・事実 → 第2段落：植物薬のマイナス面→第3段落：支持者たちの見解，という段落構成。空所はコンマで区切られており，文頭に適切なつなぎ表現を入れるパターン。空所前の「多くの人が植物薬に頼っている」と，空所後の「有効性は科学に基づく証拠による裏付けがほとんどない」は対照的な内容なので，Nevertheless「それにもかかわらず」が適切。

(27) – 解答 **3** ・・

（解説）〈lead＋O＋to *do*〉「Oに～させる，（主語が原因で）Oが～する」は因果関係を表し，to不定詞部分が空所になっている。主語のThisは前述の内容を受けており，植物薬が引き起こす負の作用が報告されていない結果，患者たちがどうするかと考えると，**3**「これらの薬が安全だと信じてしまう」が適切。

(28) – 解答 **3** ・・

（解説）空所はthat節の主語の「植物薬と近代的で医者に処方される薬は」に対する述部の部分。この後，「近代的で医者に処方される薬」は緊急時や重篤な感染症と闘うため，「植物薬」は全体的な健康や健康状態を維持するために用いるべき，とそれぞれの用途が対比的に述べられている。これを「異なる役割」と表した**3**が適切。

全文訳 **記憶と言語**

　訴訟の結果はしばしば犯罪や事故を目撃した人による証言に左右される。しかし彼らの記憶は常に信頼の置けるものなのだろうか。ある有名な心理学の実験で，学生たちはグループに分けられ，自動車事故の動画を見せられた。グループの１つは「互いに衝突したとき，車はどれぐらい速度を出していましたか」と尋ねられた。別のグループは「衝突した」という言葉を「ぶつかった」に代えられて質問された。その結果，「ぶつかった」で質問された学生たちは平均して時速54.7キロメートルと推測したのに対して，「衝突した」という言葉で質問された学生たちは平均して時速65.2キロメートルと推測した。これは，目撃者たちの描写が**どのように質問されるか**に左右される可能性があることを示している。

　追跡実験では，学生たちは別の事故の動画を見せられ，「衝突した」と「ぶつかった」という言葉を使った同様の質問をされた。このときはさらに，彼らは割れたガラスに気付いたかも尋ねられた。動画では窓は損傷を受けていなかったが，「衝突した」を使った質問をされた学生たちの方が割れたガラスを見たと報告することがはるかに多かった。学生たちが**全く起きていないことを覚えていた**ということなので，この傾向は（ただ正確に覚えていないということよりも）さらに悩ましい。

　しかし，自動車の衝突事故の動画を見ることと，事故現場にいることは同じではない，と批判する人々は主張する。彼らは学生たちの記憶は，直接事故を目撃するという感情的な体験がなかったために影響を受けやすかったと言う。**その結果**，学生たちは正確な答えを出すことに対する動機付けがおそらく薄かったとみられた。そのほかの研究でも，実際の犯罪を目撃した人に対して誘導的な質問は効果が低いことが示されており，これは実験の条件が結果を形成するのに一役買ったかもしれないことを示唆している。

> **語句** outcome「結果」，witness「目撃する」，smash into「～に衝突する」，compared with「～に対して，～と比較して」，demonstrate「証明する」，follow-up experiment「追跡実験」，tendency「傾向」，disturbing「心を悩ませる，迷惑な，心配な」，critic「批判する人」，argue「主張する，異論を唱える」，〈motivate＋O＋to *do*〉「Oが～する動機付けとなる，Oを～する気にさせる」，manipulative「巧みに扱う，操作的な」

(29) – 解答 **4** ・・・・・・・・・・・・・・・・・・・・・・・・・・ 正答率 ★75%以上

> **解説** 主語のThisは前述の内容を指す。実験において，自動車事故の動画を見た学生たち（＝目撃者）がsmashed intoとhitという言葉を使って尋ねられたときの違いについて説明されている。つまり，目撃者の描写が**4**「どのように質問されるか」によって異なることを示している。

(30) – 解答 **3** ・・・

> **解説** 主語のThis tendency「この傾向」は，動画では実際には窓は割れていなかったのにsmashedを使って尋ねられると割れたガラス（＝全く起きていないこと）を見たと報告することがはるかに多かったことを指している。よって，正解は**3**。

188

(31) – 解答 ① ･･････････････････････････････ 正答率 ★75%以上

解説 第3段落は動画と実際の事故現場を対比的に論じている。事故現場での感情的な体験がなかった（原因）→ 影響を受けやすかった（結果）= 正確な答えを出さなかった（= 全く起きていないことを報告した），という意味関係から，空所には As a result「その結果」が適切。

一次試験・筆記 **3** 問題編 p.138 ～ 144

全文訳 インポスター症候群

　多くの人が人生のある時点で「インポスター症候群」を経験する。この状態に陥った人は，自分がどれほど有能であったり，または経験豊富であっても自分の成功を受け入れたり，信じたりすることが難しい。多くの場合，彼らは自分の成果が自分の実際の能力ではなく，幸運や外的状況によるものだと信じる。インポスター症候群は，多くの分野で働くさまざまな背景を持つ人たちに起こり，それぞれに異なる結果をもたらし得る。ある人たちは，必要以上に極度にがんばって自分の価値を証明しなければならないと感じる。またある人たちは，自分の能力がないこと —— それは自分が思い込んでいることなのだが —— が判明すると仕事を失くすのではないかと心配し，なるべく同僚たちと距離を置く。

　インポスター症候群の原因は，専門家たちに議論されてきた。それは，心配性であるとか，人の基本的な性格特性に関係があるのかもしれないし，個人の育ちに根本的な原因があるのかもしれない。例えば，子供が常にちょっとした成果でさえ褒められていると，自分の本当の能力に対する信頼を失うことがある。インポスター症候群は，人の力の及ばない要因により，成人してからも起こることがある。そのような要因の1つが制度化した差別であり，職場または学術の環境の雰囲気が，特定の人種，性別，またはそのほかの特性であってもとにかくそうではない人たちを目立たせるということだ。

　幾つかの研究が，「インポスターイズム」の気持ちを訴える少数派集団の個々人は，程度の高い不安とうつも経験していることを示している。これは差別のみではなく，教授や管理職，その他権威のある人物たちの中に（自分たちの人種や性別を）代表する人がいないことにも原因がある可能性がある。心理学教授テイマ・ブライアント=デイヴィスによると，社会人は自分の性別または人種の人物が権力を持つ立場にいないと，「出世の可能性の表れ」がない。これなしでは，自信を持って人生に前向きな姿勢を維持することはしばしば困難である。

　語句 imposter「（他人の名や身分をかたる）詐欺師，詐称者」, syndrome「症候群」, capable「有能な」, experienced「経験豊富な」, background「背景」, consequence「結果」, colleague「同僚」, trait「特性」, upbringing「養育，育ち」, faith「信頼」, institutional「制度化された，慣習化された」, discrimination「差別」, stand out「目立つ」,

minority「少数（派）の」，representation「代表（者）」，authority figure「権威のある人」

(32) – 解答 ②

問題文の訳 「インポスター症候群」に陥った労働者たちにそれが与え得る影響の1つは何か。

選択肢の訳
1 彼らは同僚の弱点を補うために余分に働かざるを得ない気分になる。
2 彼らは首になるのではないかと心配になり，同僚から距離を置こうとする。
3 彼らは同僚の成果を不正に自分の手柄にすることが容易になる。
4 同僚と意思疎通を図る際に自分の経験や能力を誇張する原因となり得る。

解説 第1段落のインポスター症候群の具体的な説明の中で，最終文 Others fear ... の内容と **2** が一致する。それぞれ本文の fear が become afraid に，lose their job が be fired に，distance（動詞）が isolate に言い換えられている。supposed lack of skill の supposed は「（事実と）思われている」という意味で，自分に能力がないことを同僚に知られたくないのだが，それは実は自分の思い込みなのである。

(33) – 解答 ④

問題文の訳 インポスター症候群の原因の1つとして考えられるのは，

選択肢の訳
1 主に会社が彼らを差別しているために，人々が就職するのが困難な場合である。
2 大人が若いときに受けた批判について必要以上に心配する傾向がある場合である。
3 不安や心配を感じるという従業員たちの主張を会社が真剣に検討することを拒む場合である。
4 実際にはするのが難しくないことでさえも，あまりにも頻繁に子供が褒められる場合である。

解説 インポスター症候群の原因を述べた第2段落を参照。具体例を示した For instance, ... 「子供が常にちょっとした成果でさえ褒められていると，自分の本当の能力に対する信頼を失うことがある」の部分から，**4** が正解。things that ... は本文の minor achievements の言い換えである。

(34) – 解答 ③

問題文の訳 テイマ・ブライアント＝デイヴィスによると，次のうちどれが正しいか。

選択肢の訳
1 学校で差別を避けている人たちは，社会人になってからインポスター症候群になる可能性が低い。
2 少数派の人たちは，多数派の人たちと同様に扱われるとインポスター症候群になる可能性が高い。
3 自分と同じような人が上の立場にいない人たちは，出世するという希

190

望を失う可能性が高い。

4 少数派の人たちは，多様性の高い学校では差別を受ける可能性が低い。

解説 第3段落の According to psychology ...「社会人は自分の性別または人種の人物が権力を持つ立場にいないと，『出世の可能性の表れ』がない」の部分から，**3** が正解。それぞれ others of their gender or race と others like themselves, in positions of power と in higher positions, advancement と be promoted が対応している。

全文訳 **気候変動とサーミ族**

　ヨーロッパの北極地方に先住するサーミ族は，歴史的に毛皮の売買とトナカイの牧畜で生計を立ててきた。しかし，彼らが頼るトナカイの群れは，気候変動とその結果起きている生息地の消失により非常に追い詰められている。冬季の不安定な気温は雪を溶かして凍らせ，これによりトナカイは食料として必要な植物が得られなくなる。これは以前にも起こったことがあるが，急速な気候変動によってより頻繁に起こるようになった。これにより，トナカイの群れは飢餓によって個体数を減らし，栄養不足により出生率が減少している。さらに，地球温暖化により北方地域へ行き来しやすくなるにつれ，企業が採鉱を推進し石油とガスの探査を行い，また観光事業の促進のために，昔からサーミ族の土地だったところに進出しつつある。これにより，サーミ族のトナカイの群れが得られる食料はますます制限され，多くのサーミ人は，彼らの昔からある土地での企業活動が増えたことが彼らの生活様式を完全に終わらせるかもしれないことを心配している。

　トナカイの群れが減少したことにより，多くのサーミ人が経済的，精神的困難を経験している。10代の若者や若年層の大人たちの中には仕事を求めて都市に逃れたサーミ人もいるが，これらの都会のサーミ人たちは彼らの生来の立場によって疎外されたり差別の対象になったりしている。今までの生活から追いやられ，活気のあるサーミ族の社会集団へのアクセスがなくなって文化的伝統が失われ，多くが深刻なメンタルヘルスの問題を抱えている。この問題は伝統的なサーミ族のコミュニティーにも広がっており，平均より高い自殺率が報告されており，特に若い男性の間で顕著である。それでも，サーミ族にとってメンタルヘルスはタブーの話題であるため，ほとんどの人は助けを求めない。正確な人数は不明だが，調査によると，ほとんどのサーミ人には自殺した親戚または友人がいることが分かっている。

　しかし，これらの問題の一部に対処するための取り組みが進行している。例えば，若いサーミ人に心の支えを提供し，彼らが経験している差別について話し合うことを促すために社会プログラムが導入されている。そうは言うものの，伝統的なサーミ族のコミュニティーにおけるメンタルヘルスの問題は，気候変動の影響に関係する経済的な不透明感と不安に基づいているとしばしば言われている。これらの不安に対処するため，政治家たちはサーミ族に耳を傾け，政府の決定が彼らのコミュニティーにもたらし得る潜在的な結果を考慮するよう，よりきめ細かく注意を払っている。サーミ族に直接影響がある決定にサーミ族が関与できる方法を提供することで，環境上または経済的な衰退に関

21年度第1回　筆記

連するストレスや困難を減らすことができる。さらに重要なのは，サーミ族自身が彼らの伝統的な生活様式を維持することに，よりしっかりと手綱を握れるようになることが望まれている。

語句 reindeer「トナカイ」，herd「（動物の）群れ」，starvation「飢餓」，birthrate「出生率」，territory「土地，領地」，pursue「追求する」，alienate「仲間外れにする」，heritage「（人が生まれながらにして持つ）地位，立場」，uproot「追い出す」，vibrant「活気のある」，tackle「（問題に）取り組む」，uncertainty「不確かさ，不透明感」，(be) related to「～に関係する」，(be) associated with「～と関連している」

(35) – 解答 **2**

問題文の訳 気候変動がサーミ族の生活様式に影響を与えたのは，

選択肢の訳
1 トナカイが手に入らないときの食料源としてサーミ族が依存している多くの植物種を減らしたことによる。
2 サーミ族が経済的に依存している動物の生活圏と食料源の両方に影響を与えたことによる。
3 サーミ族に彼らの伝統的な農法よりも経済的に見返りの少ない農法の採用を余儀なくさせたことによる。
4 石油とガスの探査のために土地を手放すようサーミ族に圧力をかける企業を引き寄せたことによる。

解説 冒頭から，サーミ族はトナカイの牧畜で生計を立ててきたことが分かる。そして続く内容から，気候変動によりトナカイの生息地が消失し，食料が得られず個体数が減っていることが分かる。これらの状況がサーミ族の生活様式に悪影響を及ぼしていることから，**2**が正解。

(36) – 解答 **4**

問題文の訳 この文章によると，サーミ族はどのような困難に直面しているか。

選択肢の訳
1 彼らのコミュニティーで経済的支援を提供している組織が，彼らの社会の変化によって悪影響を受けている。
2 農村部から都市部への移動を余儀なくされたサーミ人が，受け入れてもらうために自分たちの文化を拒否することを選んでいる。
3 トナカイの牧畜に関する若いサーミ人と上の世代のサーミ人との対立により，多くの人がメンタルヘルスの問題を抱えている。
4 若いサーミ人が，家族からの孤立や文化的伝統の喪失によって引き起こされるメンタルヘルスの問題にもがき苦しんでいる。

解説 メンタルヘルスの問題を抱えている若者について説明した第2段落の第2～3文を参照。「生来の立場によって疎外されたり差別の対象になったりしている」や「サーミ族の社会集団へのアクセスがなくなって文化的伝統が失われている」という内容を，正解の**4**では「家族からの孤立や文化的伝統の喪失」と表している。**2**は，文化的伝統が失われているの

192

はサーミ族の社会集団へのアクセスがなくなったことが原因であって，受け入れてもらうために自ら文化を拒否することを選んでいるわけではないので不正解。

(37) – 解答 ①

問題文の訳 サーミ族を支援するために何が行われているか。

選択肢の訳
1 サーミ族にさらなる危害を与えないようにする方法として，政府の政策や行動を形成するために，サーミ族が表明した懸念が利用されている。
2 サーミ族の人口が多い国々で，サーミ族の文化へのより幅広い理解を促すために，ボランティア団体が設立されている。
3 若いサーミ人が政界に入り，地方自治体で彼らのコミュニティーを代表することを奨励する取り組みがますます行われている。
4 都市部での生活のストレスからくるメンタルヘルスの問題に苦しむサーミ人に経済的支援が提供されている。

解説 サーミ族への支援について述べられている第3段落を参照。サーミ族が抱える問題に対処するため，社会プログラムが導入されたり，政治家たちがサーミ族に耳を傾け（＝サーミ族が表明した懸念を利用し），サーミ族に直接影響がある政府の決定にサーミ族が関与できる方法を提供したりする取り組みを行っている。これらの内容から，**1**が正解。

全文訳 **レモンとマフィア**

　マフィアとして知られる組織的犯罪集団は，1800年代に初めてシチリア島に現れた。その登場以来，贈賄と詐欺を含め，その違法な活動がよく知られるようになったが，その発祥ははっきりとしなかった。しかし，ある経済歴史学者のグループによる最近の研究が，マフィアとある一般的な果物との間の意外なつながりを明らかにした。

　1700年代に，レモンの果汁が壊血病という死に至る病を予防することが発見され，これがレモンの需要の大幅な増加につながり，この果物による収益が飛躍的に増大した。シチリア島はレモンが育つことのできる数少ない場所の1つであったが，レモンが霜に弱いことからレモン栽培は島の特定の場所でしかできなかった。さらに，大規模なレモン栽培への転換には施設を建設したり，かんがいシステムを開発したりするのに莫大な財政投資が必要であった。レモンの木を泥棒から守るために高い壁も建築された。というのも，そのような保護対策がないと，丸1年分の収穫が一晩で消える可能性もあったからだ。

　レモンの需要増大によって1800年代には利益は増加し続けたが，シチリアがスペイン王室を祖先とする王たちによって支配されていたという現実のために状況は複雑だった。これらの支配者たちはよそ者と見なされており，強制兵役などの不人気な政策は島民の間で不満と騒乱を引き起こした。現地の貧困と公的資金の欠如は，特に農村部では，犯罪の増加につながった。これによって農家は自らレモンの盗難の脅威に対処する方法

21年度第1回　筆記

193

を見つけざるを得なかった。彼らは果樹園を守るためにレモンを対価に地元の強い男たちを雇い始め，これがのちにマフィアになった。

マフィアももともとはレモンを泥棒から守るまっとうなサービスを提供していたかもしれないが，それは長くは続かなかった。マフィアは農家の意に反してサービスを受け入れることを農家に強要し始め，抵抗に遭うと暴力と脅しを使った。それからマフィアの構成員たちは販売者と輸出者との間の仲介者として振る舞うようになり，相当な利益を確実に得るために市場を操作した。間もなく彼らは，輸送や卸売など産業の別の領域にも無理やり入り込み，最終的に彼らの力はレモン生産のあらゆる側面を網羅するほど大きくなった。政治家たちの中にはこれらの活動に対処しようとした者もいたが，蔓延していた政府の汚職はマフィアが政治や警察のさまざまな面に影響力を伸ばすことを許した。

レモンとマフィアとの間のつながりを調査した歴史学者たちの１人である研究者アルカンジェロ・ディミコによると，この集団の台頭は「資源の呪い」の一例である。彼は，非常に大きな富の源と弱い社会・政治体制との組み合わせは紛争や非合法活動の発生につながることがあり，そもそもその貴重な資源を保有していなかった場合よりも国を経済的に厳しい状況にすることがあると説明する。現代でもこのような例は見られ，例えば一部のアフリカの国々で民間武装組織の成長の資金を供給するダイヤモンドから得られる富がそうである。シチリアのマフィアのように，これらの集団はしばしば犯罪的な手段を使って資源や地域住民を支配する。ディミコの研究を利用することで，経済学者や社会学者，政治学者たちはこの現象をより良く理解し，政府がそれに立ち向かう手助けができる。

語句 bribery「賄賂の授受行為」，fraud「詐欺」，uncover「明らかにする」，revenue「収益」，skyrocket「飛躍的に増加する」，sensitivity「感度」，frost「霜」，irrigation「かんがい」，safeguard「安全措置」，ancestral「先祖の」，tie「つながり，関係」，dissatisfaction「不満」，unrest「混乱」，strongman「強い男，（独裁的）実力者」，orchard「果樹園」，legitimate「合法の，合理的な」，will「意思」，intimidation「脅迫」，encounter「遭遇する」，resistance「抵抗」，middleman「仲介者」，manipulate「操作する」，substantial「（数量や程度が）かなりの」，wholesaling「卸売」，widespread「広がった」，corruption「汚職」，law enforcement「法執行機関，警察」，curse「呪い」，conflict「紛争」，in the first place「まず第１に，そもそも」，employ「（手段を）用いる」

(38) – 解答 ②

問題文の訳 1700年代にシチリアの農家が直面した困難の１つは何か。

選択肢の訳
1 レモンはかつて深刻な病気を治すと信じられていたが，これが真実ではないことが判明したとき，レモン栽培の利益は減少した。
2 レモンを栽培することで多額のお金を稼ぐことができたが，レモン農場の設立は多大な費用をかけないとできなかった。

3 シチリア島の予測不可能な気候のため，レモンの栽培を始めたばかりの農家は，しばしば大量の質の悪いレモンを捨てなければならなかった。

4 レモンを栽培できる場所に関する規則により，事業を収益化するのに十分な土地を購入することは深刻な問題だった。

解説 第1段落でマフィアについて導入した後，第2段落でレモンの話に展開される。1700年代の様子について，第1文の「レモンによる収益が飛躍的に増大した」，第3文の「施設を建設したりするのに莫大な財政投資が必要だった」という内容から，**2**が正解。

(39) − 解答 ①

問題文の訳 マフィアの台頭につながった状況を最もよく表しているのは次の文のうちどれか。

選択肢の訳
1 政府はシチリア島民に適切な公共サービスを提供することができなかったため，一部の民間人は自分たちの作物を守る方法を見つけた。
2 レモン農場の所有者たちは，シチリアの外国人支配者たちを支持する人々との取引を拒否したため，経済が悪化し，犯罪が増加した。
3 人々は，シチリアのレモンから得た利益がスペイン王室に渡ることに不満を抱き，泥棒が裕福な農家から盗んでも気にしなかった。
4 レモン栽培で利益を得たいという願望から，政府は犯罪者と関係のある農家から違法な支払いを受け入れた。

解説 第3段落ではレモンとマフィアの関係に発展する。シチリア島民は政府の政策に不満を抱き，貧困と公的資金の欠如が犯罪の増加をもたらし，その結果「農家は自らレモンの盗難の脅威に対処する方法を見つけざるを得なかった」とある。また果樹園を守るのに雇い始めた強い男たちがマフィアの前身である。よって，**1**が正解。

(40) − 解答 ①

問題文の訳 マフィアは，レモン農家とのかかわりを利用して，

選択肢の訳
1 より多くのお金を手に入れ，権力を増大させる手段の一環として，レモンを栽培する人々と海外に販売する人々の両方を支配した。
2 農家により多くのレモンを栽培するよう要求することで，レモン産業からより大きな利益を生み出すことに成功した。
3 政府からの圧倒的な反対にもかかわらず，一部の政治家を説得して犯罪行為を無視させた。
4 警察の主要メンバーの協力を得ることができなかったにもかかわらず，レモン産業全体を支配した。

解説 第4段落からの出題。第3文の「マフィアの構成員たちは販売者と輸出者との間の仲介者として振る舞うようになり，相当な利益を確実に得るために市場を操作した」という内容から，**1**が正解。sellers and exporters を the people who grew lemons and those who sold them overseas と表している。

(41) – 解答 ④

問題文の訳 アルカンジェロ・ディミコがおそらく言うことは，「資源の呪い」は，

選択肢の訳
1 社会問題に対して政府が提供する支援のレベルというより，国の低調な経済活動に密接に関連している。

2 犯罪活動が国の資源供給量を増やすのに役立つ限りにおいて，政府がその犯罪活動を見逃すことをいとわない場合に起こる。

3 国の指導者たちによってその国の資源が過大評価され，期待された額の利益を生み出せない場合に起こる。

4 貴重な国の資産から利益を得るために統治・管理体制の欠如を利用する非倫理的な集団が原因で起こり得る。

解説 第5段落第1文によると，マフィアの台頭は "resource curse" の一例である（マフィアの例では「資源」＝レモン）。第2文に「非常に大きな富の源と弱い社会・政治体制（＝統治・管理体制の欠如）との組み合わせは紛争や非合法活動の発生につながる」とあり，またこの状況を利用して，マフィアのような非倫理的な集団が犯罪的手段を使って貴重な国の資産から利益を得ようとすると言える。よって，**4** が正解。

一次試験・筆記 **4** | 問題編 p.145

トピックの訳 賛成か反対か：大企業は社会に良い影響を与える

ポイントの訳 ・製品　・経済　・環境　・仕事と生活のバランス

解答例 I agree that big companies have a positive effect on society. There are two major areas where this effect can be seen: the economy and work-life balance.

Large companies generate huge amounts of money, both for national economies and for the global economy as a whole. Developing countries, in particular, benefit from the extra commerce created by such corporations. Furthermore, governments receive considerable tax sums from these corporations, which can be used to fund public projects.

The existence of big companies also leads to better conditions for workers. Large corporations employ thousands of people and are more likely to have the resources to keep their employees satisfied. Offering access to on-site gyms or implementing policies that limit overtime work, for example, significantly improves employees' work-life balance.

Therefore, from the broader economic advantages to the individual benefits for workers, the effect that big companies have on society is most certainly positive.

解説 序論：第1段落では，トピックに対する自分の意見を簡潔に書く。模範解答では，〈I agree that＋トピックの表現〉の構造で賛成の立場を明らかにした後，There are two ... の形でポイントの The economy と Work-life balance の2つの観点を取り上げている。

本論：本論では，序論で述べた主張の理由・根拠を，2つの観点を使って説明する。模範解答の第2段落は The economy の観点で，「大企業は国内外の経済に莫大な金額を生み出している」と説明している。in particular「特に」で焦点を絞ったり，Furthermore, ... で情報を追加したりしていく方法を確認しよう。第3段落は also を用いて Work-life balance の観点を説明している。「大企業には従業員を満足させ続けるためのリソースがある」と抽象的に述べた後，for example を用いて社内のスポーツジムや残業の制限などの具体例を挙げている。トピックの companies は corporations に言い換えるなど，同じ表現は繰り返さないように工夫しよう。

結論：最終段落では，トピックに対する意見を再び主張する。模範解答は Therefore, ...「従って」で始め，from the broader economic ... for workers「広い意味での経済的メリットから労働者の個人的メリットまで」の部分で2つの観点を盛り込みつつ，the effect that big companies ...「大企業が社会に与える影響は間違いなく有益なものだ」と主張している。意見を強調したいときは most certainly のような強意的な表現を使うとよい。序論でトピックの表現をそのまま使った場合，結論では別の表現を使うようにしよう。結論の書き出しはほかに In conclusion「結論として」，For these reasons「これらの理由で」などがある。

そのほかの表現 模範解答の in particular や for example，however などの接続副詞は文頭・文中・文末で用いることができる。解答例では Furthermore, ... や Therefore, ... があり，in particular や for example を文中で用いることでバリエーション豊かな文章になっている。また，lead to，cause，result in などの因果関係を示す（句）動詞は無生物主語の文で使われやすいため，積極的に使う練習をしておこう。反対の立場では，大企業が社会に悪い影響を与える例や，中小企業でも社会に良い影響を与え得ることなどを根拠にできるだろう。

197

一次試験・リスニング Part 1　問題編 p.146〜147

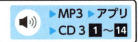

No.1 — 解答 ④

スクリプト
☆ : Hey, honey, did you mail my mom's present like I asked you to?
★ : Uh, I'll do it tomorrow on my way to work.
☆ : I can't believe it. This is the third time I've reminded you.
★ : I know. I know. I just got busy and it slipped my mind. Sorry. It won't happen again.
☆ : It happens almost every time I ask you to do something.
Question: What does the woman imply?

全文訳
☆ : ねえ，あなた。頼んでおいたように私のお母さんへのプレゼントを送ってくれた？
★ : ああ，明日仕事に向かう途中でしておくよ。
☆ : 信じられない。あなたに言うのはこれで3度目よ。
★ : 分かってる，分かってるよ。忙しくて忘れてしまっただけだ。ごめんね。二度と忘れないから。
☆ : 私が何かしてって頼むたびにたいてい忘れてるんだけど。
質問： 女性は何をほのめかしているか。

選択肢の訳
1　男性はもっと申し訳なさそうにするべきだ。
2　男性はプレゼントを買うべきだった。
3　男性は心配し過ぎである。
4　男性はあまり信頼が置けない。

解説　男性に頼んだことをまだしていないことを知って，女性は怒っている様子である。また，最後の It happens ... から，男性は普段から頼まれたことを忘れることが多いと分かる。これを not very reliable「あまり信頼が置けない」と表した 4 が正解。

No.2 — 解答 ① 正答率 ★75%以上

スクリプト
☆ : I finally found the ideal spot for my new hair salon. I just signed the lease today.
★ : You're opening another shop? The first one must be doing quite well.
☆ : Business is great. My new salon will have a special focus, though. We'll offer haircuts exclusively for children.
★ : I didn't know there was a demand for that.
☆ : The children's beauty market is so hot now. I just figure I can't lose.
★ : I'd be wary of trends. They often don't last long. Anyway, how

198

does one make the haircutting experience different for children?

☆ : We make the environment fun. The salon chairs will be in the shape of animals, and kids can choose from various scented shampoos.

★ : Well, I wish you luck!

Question: How does the woman feel about her new business project?

全文訳 ☆ : とうとう私の新しい美容室にぴったりの場所を見つけたわ。今日リース契約をしてきたばかりよ。

★ : また店舗をオープンするのかい？　１号店がかなりうまくいっているんだね。

☆ : ビジネスは成功しているわ。でも新店舗は特殊化しようと思っているの。子供専門のヘアカットを提供するの。

★ : それに需要があるとは知らなかったよ。

☆ : 今，子供の美容市場はとても熱いわ。負けられないと思っただけよ。

★ : 僕なら流行には慎重になるな。多くの場合，長続きしないからね。とにかく，どうやって散髪体験を子供向けに差別化するの？

☆ : 環境を楽しい感じにするのよ。サロンの椅子は動物の形にして，子供はいろんな香りのするシャンプーから選べるの。

★ : まあ，がんばってね！

質問：女性は自分の新しい事業計画についてどう感じているか。

選択肢の訳 1 自信満々である。

2 慎重である。

3 不安である。

4 落胆している。

解説 話題は女性が新しい美容室の店舗をオープンさせること。男性は「自分なら流行に慎重になる」と後ろ向きだが，女性は「ビジネスは成功している」「熱い子供の美容市場で負けられない」と言って張り切っている様子なので，**1** が正解。

No.3 −解答 ②

スクリプト ☆ : Hey, John. Did you hear whether Stacey got the job or not? I haven't seen her for a while.

★ : I had lunch with her yesterday. Apparently, the company offered her the job, but she turned them down.

☆ : You're kidding! She seemed really interested when I last spoke to her.

★ : I know, but after the interview, she reconsidered and decided she's better off where she is now.

21年度第1回　リスニング

199

☆： Well, I did wonder why she wanted to change jobs in the first place.

Question: What do we learn about Stacey?

〈全文訳〉
☆： ねえ，ジョン。ステーシーがあの職に受かったかどうか聞いた？ しばらく彼女に会ってないの。

★： 昨日彼女と一緒に昼食を取ったよ。どうも会社は彼女に内定を出したけど，彼女は断ったみたいだよ。

☆： うそでしょ！ 最後に彼女と話したときはすごく興味があるみたいだったのに。

★： 知ってる，でも面接の後に考え直して，今の仕事の方がいいって思ったんだ。

☆： そう，そもそも何で転職したいと思ったのかも疑問だったのよね。

質問：ステーシーについて何が分かるか。

〈選択肢の訳〉
1 新しい職を探している。
2 今の仕事を続けている。
3 仕事の面接に落ちた。
4 新しい仕事を始めた。

〈解説〉放送を聞く前に選択肢を見て，女性の就職に関する話だと予測できれば効率よく聞けるだろう。2 人はステーシーという共通の知人について話しており，ステーシーが新しい職の面接に受かって内定をもらったが断った（turned them down）という流れ。男性の she reconsidered and decided she's better off where she is now の部分が決め手で，**2** が正解。

No.**4** −解答 ③

〈スクリプト〉
★： Is it boiling in here or is it just me?

☆： I'm all right, but we can open a window if you want.

★： No, it'll be too noisy. Why don't we just turn on the air conditioner?

☆： Company policy. The air conditioner is set to come on automatically at 28 degrees.

★： Really? It feels like an oven in here. I can't concentrate.

☆： Tell you what. I'll turn on the fan.

★： OK. At least it'll move the air around.

Question: What is the man's complaint?

〈全文訳〉
★： ここってすごく暑い？ それとも僕だけ？

☆： 私は大丈夫だけど，よかったら窓を開けてもいいわよ。

★： やめておくよ，うるさいだろうから。ちょっとエアコンつけてみない？

☆： 会社の規則よ。エアコンは 28 度で自動的につくように設定されているの。

★： そうなの？　ここはオーブンの中にいるみたいだよ。集中できない。

☆： こうしましょう。扇風機をつけるわ。

★： 分かった。少なくとも空気が循環するね。

質問：男性の不満は何か。

選択肢の訳　**1**　騒音が仕事の邪魔になっている。

2　エアコンが故障している。

3　暑さが彼を不快にさせている。

4　窓を開けることができない。

解説　男性の Is it boiling in here ...? や It feels like an oven in here. という発言がポイント。hot という語は出てこないが，これらの表現や，エアコンや扇風機をつけるという話の流れから，男性は部屋の中がすごく暑いと思っていることが分かる。これを uncomfortable「不快な」と表した **3** が正解。

No.**5** – 解答 ②

スクリプト ☆： Hi, Frank. I'm sorry to bother you at work. Did you do something to our home computer? I'm trying to get a report done, and the whole system is really slow.

★： The security software expired a few days ago, and I haven't had a chance to renew it yet. We may have picked up a virus or something.

☆： We'd better renew it right away. I'd do it, but I don't really know how.

★： I'll do it when I get home this evening.

Question: What will Frank do tonight?

全文訳 ☆： こんにちは，フランク。仕事中に邪魔してごめんなさい。あなた，家のコンピューターに何かした？　レポートを終わらせようとしてるんだけど，システム全体がすごく遅いの。

★： セキュリティー・ソフトウエアの期限が数日前に切れて，まだ更新できていないんだ。ウイルスか何かに感染したかもしれない。

☆： すぐに更新しないとね。私がやってもいいけど，やり方がよく分からないわ。

★： 夕方に帰宅したら僕がやるよ。

質問：フランクは今夜，何をするか。

選択肢の訳　**1**　新しいコンピューターを買う。

2　セキュリティー・プログラムを更新する。

3　女性のレポートを手伝う。

4　コンピューターを修理に出す。

解説　話題は男女の自宅のコンピューター。女性は仕事中の男性に電話をかけ

21年度第1回　リスニング

201

て，システム全体が遅いと伝える。女性の発言の We'd better renew it right away. の it はセキュリティー・ソフトウエアのことで，これを受けて男性は，「帰宅したらやる（＝更新する）」と答えている。よって，男性が今夜することとして，**2** が正解。

No.6 – 解答 ②

スクリプト ☆： Hi, Vince. Come in and have a seat. I heard you're concerned about your future university expenses.

★： That's right, Ms. Merkley. My parents can't really afford to help me much.

☆： I see. Instead of taking out a big loan, you might want to consider a community college for your first two years. The tuition is very reasonable, and you could continue to live at home.

★： I've thought about that. It's not my first choice, but that's probably what I'll end up doing.

Question: What does the woman advise Vince to do?

全文訳 ☆： こんにちは，ヴィンス。中に入って座って。これからかかる大学の費用のことを心配していると聞いたわ。

★： そうです，マークリーさん。うちの両親は僕を助ける余裕があまりないので。

☆： なるほど。多額のローンを組むよりは，最初の 2 年間はコミュニティーカレッジに通うことを考えてもいいわね。学費は安いし，自宅に住み続けられるでしょ。

★： 僕もそれは考えました。第 1 希望ではないですが，結局そうすることになると思います。

質問：女性はヴィンスに何をするよう助言しているか。

選択肢の訳 **1** 大学の費用のローンを組む。

2 コミュニティーカレッジに通う。

3 2 年間常勤で働く。

4 よその町の大学に通う。

解説 最初のやり取りから，女性は学費に関する助言をする立場の人で，男性は学生であろう。女性は you might want to consider a community college for your first two years の部分でコミュニティーカレッジに通うことを勧めていることから，**2** が正解。Instead of taking out a big loan と言ってローンを組むことは勧めていないので，**1** は不適。

No.7 – 解答 ③

スクリプト ☆： Are you OK, Matt? You keep sneezing and coughing.

★： I think my allergies are acting up.

☆： I used to have bad allergies, too. Every spring.

202

★： Did you have to take a lot of prescription medicine?

☆： Yes, several different types. Then I tried Dr. Gage, my naturopathic doctor.

★： And it was Dr. Gage who cured you?

☆： After using her herbal remedies for a few years, my symptoms gradually decreased, then disappeared.

★： That's amazing. Maybe I should schedule a consultation.

Question: What is the man considering doing?

全文訳 ☆： 大丈夫，マット？　ずっとくしゃみと咳をしているじゃない。

★： アレルギーが出てきたみたい。

☆： 私も以前ひどいアレルギーがあったの。毎年春にね。

★： 処方薬をたくさん飲まなければならなかった？

☆： ええ，何種類もね。それから自然療法の医師であるゲージ先生のところを試したの。

★： それでゲージ先生が君を治したの？

☆： 彼女の植物薬を何年か使ったら，症状がだんだん治まって，消えたわ。

★： それはすごい。僕も診察の予約を入れようかな。

質問：男性は何をしようと考えているか。

選択肢の訳 1　自分がかかっている医者から新しい処方箋をもらうこと。

2　もっと健康的な食事を取り始めること。

3　女性がかかっている医者に診てもらいに行くこと。

4　処方薬を飲むのを止めること。

解説 男性はアレルギーについて女性に相談している。女性のアレルギーを治した Dr. Gage のことを聞いた男性は，Maybe I should schedule a consultation. と言っている。「診察の予約を入れる」を「診てもらいに行く」と表した **3** が正解。

No.**8** – 解答　**4** ··

スクリプト ☆： Honey, what are you doing on the 17th?

★： This Saturday? Uh, I was thinking about going fishing with Ronan.

☆： Could you go on Sunday? There's an all-day teachers conference that I'd like to attend. I was hoping you could watch the kids.

★： OK. Maybe I'll take them to a movie, and then grab some dinner on our way home.

☆： I appreciate it, honey.

Question: What will the man do on the 17th?

全文訳 ☆： あなた，17 日の予定は？

★： 今週の土曜日？　あー，ローナンと釣りに行こうかと思ってたけど。

203

☆：日曜日にしてくれない？　終日の教師会議があって，出席したいの。子供たちを見ててくれたらと思ったんだけど。

★：分かった。映画にでも連れて行って，帰りに夕食を食べて帰ろうかな。

☆：助かるわ，あなた。

質問：男性は17日に何をするか。

選択肢の訳
1　ローナンと釣りに行く。
2　教師会議に出席する。
3　妻を映画に連れて行く。
4　子供たちの面倒を見る。

解説　冒頭で妻が夫に17日（土曜日）の予定を聞いているが，それは教師会議に出席したくて，子供を見てほしいからである。I was hoping you could watch the kids. のI was hoping you could *do* は控えめな依頼表現で，夫はOK.と承諾しているので，**4**が正解。**1**は当初の土曜日の予定で，**3**は映画に連れて行くのは妻ではなく子供たちである。

No.9 – 解答

スクリプト
★：It looks like more snow is forecast, Nadia. I guess I'll be clearing the driveway again.

☆：Maybe you should finally give in and hire that snow removal service we saw advertised.

★：I know, but I hate to spend the money. And shoveling isn't bad exercise.

☆：True, but you're not getting any younger. You don't want to strain your back again.

★：You've got a point. I'll call them for an estimate.

Question: What is the man considering doing?

全文訳
★：予報ではまた雪が降るみたいだね，ナディア。また屋敷内の車道を雪かきすることになるかな。

☆：もう諦めて，広告で見たあの除雪サービスを頼むべきじゃないかしら。

★：分かってるけど，お金を使うのが嫌なんだよ。それに雪かきは運動として悪くない。

☆：それはそうだけど，あなたは若くはならないのよ。また腰を痛めたくないでしょ。

★：君の言う通りだ。電話して見積をもらうよ。

質問：男性は何をしようと考えているか。

選択肢の訳
1　屋敷内の車道を除雪してもらうのにお金を払うこと。
2　新しい除雪用シャベルを探すこと。
3　もっと定期的に運動をし始めること。
4　医者に腰を診てもらうこと。

解説 話題は自宅の屋敷内の車道の除雪作業。driveway は一般車道から各家の車庫に通じる私設道のこと。夫は自分で除雪をしてきたが，妻が除雪サービスを頼むことを提案すると，夫は最初は「お金を使うのが嫌だ」と言ったものの，最終的には同意する。したがって，**1** が正解。

No.10 解答 ①

スクリプト ★： Did you see this promotion for cable TV? We can get 100 channels for the same price we're paying for 30 channels now.

☆： Don't you think we already spend enough time watching TV?

★： But we'd get more educational programs for the kids. And you'd like to have more movie channels, wouldn't you?

☆： OK, you win. But let's agree to at least talk about limiting how much we watch.

★： Fair enough.

Question: What does the couple decide to do?

全文訳 ★： このケーブルテレビのキャンペーン見た？ 今 30 チャンネルで払っているのと同じ金額で 100 チャンネル見られるよ。

☆： 今でもテレビを見ている時間は長いと思わない？

★： でも子供たちの教育番組が増えるよ。それに君だって映画チャンネルは多い方がいいだろ？

☆： 分かった，あなたの勝ちよ。でもせめてどれぐらい見るかを制限することについて話し合うことには同意してね。

★： いいよ。

質問：夫婦は何をすることに決めたか。

選択肢の訳 **1** チャンネル数を増やす。

2 映画チャンネルの支払いをやめる。

3 今のケーブルプランを続ける。

4 子供たちに教育的なテレビのみを見させる。

解説 話題は家庭のケーブルテレビ。夫はチャンネル数が増えるキャンペーンについて説明し，プランを変えることを提案している。妻が OK, you win. と言って夫に同意していることから，**1** が正解。

No.11 解答 ②

スクリプト ☆： How was the concert last night, Pierre?

★： Well, the band usually puts on a good performance, but I felt like they let down the audience a bit.

☆： How so? Didn't they play enough of their hit songs?

★： The music itself was fantastic. There was a good mix of hits from their old stuff and songs from their new album. It's just that our city was one of the last stops on the tour. They looked exhausted.

☆： I can imagine. Maybe they should've shortened their tour schedule.

Question: Why was the man disappointed?

全文訳 ☆： 昨晩のコンサートはどうだった，ピエール。

★： うん，あのバンド，いつもはいいパフォーマンスを見せるんだけど，少し観客をがっかりさせたように思えた。

☆： なんで？　ヒット曲を十分演奏しなかったの？

★： 音楽自体は素晴らしかったよ。古い作品からのヒット曲と新作アルバムからの曲をうまく組み合わせてた。ただ，うちの市はツアーの最終の方の公演地だったんだよね。すごく疲れているように見えた。

☆： 想像がつくわ。彼らはツアースケジュールを短くすべきだったのかも。

質問：男性はなぜがっかりしていたか。

選択肢の訳 **1**　バンドがあまりヒット曲を演奏しなかった。

2　バンドの演奏に元気がなかった。

3　バンドのツアースケジュールが変わった。

4　バンドが観客に対して無礼な態度だった。

解説 男性がバンドのコンサートにがっかりした様子は，男性の I felt like they let down the audience a bit の部分に表れている。その理由は，It's just that ... の部分から，ツアーの最終の方で疲れているように見えたから。これを正解の **2** では lack energy「エネルギーを欠く，元気がない」を使って表している。

No.12 解答 ①

スクリプト ☆： I don't know what's wrong with my dog these days. His behavior is getting worse.

★： What do you mean?

☆： Well, he barks for no reason, and he even ran out into the street yesterday. He's never done that before!

★： Why not take him to obedience classes?

☆： He's probably too old to learn anything now.

★： I wouldn't be so sure. I have a great book I used with my dog. It has tips for dealing with older dogs. I can lend it to you if you'd like.

☆： I suppose it couldn't hurt.

Question: What does the man imply?

全文訳 ☆： 最近，うちの犬がどうしちゃったのか分からないの。振る舞いがひどくなっていて。

★： どういうこと？

☆： そうね，理由なく吠えるし，昨日なんか道路に飛び出したわ。そんなこ

と今までしたことなかったのに！
★：訓練学校に入れてみたら？
☆：あの子は新しいことを覚えるには年を取り過ぎていると思うわ。
★：それはどうかな。僕の犬に使ったいい本があるよ。年を取った犬の扱い方のアドバイスが書いてある。よかったら貸してあげるけど。
☆：試してみてもいいかもね。

質問：男性は何をほのめかしているか。

選択肢の訳
1 女性は飼い犬の訓練をすべきだ。
2 女性は犬の訓練の本を買うべきだ。
3 女性の犬は健康上の問題があるかもしれない。
4 女性の犬は訓練するには年を取り過ぎている。

解説 女性は飼い犬の問題行動について男性に相談している。男性は犬を訓練学校に入れることや，年を取った犬の扱い方が書かれた本を読むよう勧めていることから，犬を訓練すべきだと思っている。よって，**1**が正解。**4**は男性ではなく女性の考えなので不適。男性の I wouldn't be so sure. は，遠回しに相手の意見に反対する表現。

スクリプト **Cochineals**

The idea of eating bugs is not socially accepted in many countries. It can therefore shock people to learn that some food products in their supermarkets contain a coloring made from insects. The insects, called cochineals, produce a substance known as carminic acid. To make the color, the insects are first harvested from cactus plants. The insects are then dried and processed to turn the carminic acid into carmine, a red dye that can be used as a food coloring.

Because of the quality dye that can be produced from cochineals, they were highly valued by ancient civilizations in the Americas. These societies used the dye to color clothing, food, and body paint. Today, it is used in some cosmetics as well as food. Some people, such as vegans and vegetarians, think that dyes made from plant sources like strawberries and beets should be used instead.

Questions
No.13 What is one thing we learn about carminic acid?
No.14 What do some people think about the dye made from cochineals?

全文訳　**コチニールカイガラムシ**

　虫を食べるという考えは，多くの国において社会的に受け入れられていない。そのため，スーパーマーケットの一部の食品に昆虫を原料とした着色料が含まれていることを知れば人々は驚くかもしれない。コチニールカイガラムシと呼ばれる昆虫は，カルミン酸として知られる物質を生成する。着色料を作るには，まずサボテンからその昆虫を採取する。次に，昆虫を乾燥させて加工し，カルミン酸をカルミンという食品着色料として使用できる赤色の染料に変える。

　コチニールカイガラムシは，良質の染料が得られるため，アメリカ大陸の古代文明で重宝された。これらの社会では，衣類や食べ物，ボディペイントを着色するのにその染料を使用した。今日では，食品だけでなく一部の化粧品にも使用されている。ビーガンやベジタリアンなど，代わりにイチゴやビーツなどの植物源を原料とした染料を使うべきだと考える人たちもいる。

No.13 解答

質問の訳　カルミン酸について分かることの1つは何か。

選択肢の訳
1　食べ物に苦い味を加える。
2　植物を乾燥させて作られる。
3　一部の植物に色を与える。
4　ある種の昆虫にある。

解説　タイトルが知らない語でも詳しく説明されるので落ち着いて聞こう。The insects, called cochineals の部分から，cochineal は昆虫だと分かる。そして続く produce a substance known as carminic acid から，この昆虫はカルミン酸を生成することが分かるので，**4**が正解。cochineals を「ある種の昆虫」と表している。

No.14 解答

質問の訳　一部の人々は，コチニールカイガラムシを原料とした染料についてどう思っているか。

選択肢の訳
1　ほかの選択肢に置き換えるべきだ。
2　植物に有害になり得る。
3　薬として使うべきだ。
4　あまりに貴重で化粧品に使えない。

解説　最後の方の Some people, ... が質問の some people と一致する。一部の人々はコチニールカイガラムシの代わりにイチゴやビーツなどの植物源を原料とした染料を使うべきだと思っている。正解は**1**で，dyes made from plant sources like strawberries and beets を other options と抽象的に表している。

B

スクリプト　**Icelandic Turf Houses**

For centuries, people in Iceland used turf — clumps of grass and dirt — to construct their houses. Turf was a durable material that could withstand the harsh climate and help keep people warm. Wood was in short supply and often needed to be imported, so it could not be replaced easily. For this reason, more-available materials such as turf and stones were used whenever possible. Turf not only provided insulation, it also protected Icelandic people from some natural disasters.

Turf houses were usually dug into the side of a hill. While they looked like individual buildings from the front, they were often joined together by a corridor at the back. This unusual feature allowed people to move from building to building without being exposed to the cold. Though almost no one lives in turf houses in Iceland today, many have been converted into museums and have become popular tourist attractions.

Questions

No.15 What was one reason Icelandic people built turf houses?

No.16 What does the speaker say about turf houses?

全文訳 **アイスランドの芝の家**

何世紀にもわたり，アイスランドの人々は，芝（草や土の塊）を使って家を建てていた。芝は，過酷な気候に耐えられ，また人々を暖かく保つのに役立つ，丈夫な素材だった。木材は不足しており，輸入しなければならないことが多かったため，簡単には代用できなかった。このため，できる限り芝や石などのより手に入りやすい素材が使われた。芝は断熱性を提供してくれるだけでなく，アイスランドの人々を自然災害から守ってもくれた。

芝の家は通常，丘の中腹に掘って造られた。正面から見ると個々の建物のように見えたが，多くの場合，奥では廊下でつながれていた。この珍しい特徴により，人々は寒さにさらされることなく建物から建物へ移動することができた。現在アイスランドでは芝の家に住む人はほとんどいないが，多くは博物館として改修され，人気の観光スポットになっている。

No.15 解答 ③

質問の訳 アイスランドの人々が芝の家を建てた理由の１つは何だったか。

選択肢の訳 1 木造の家よりも長持ちした。

2 石造りの家よりも建て直すのが容易だった。

3 環境にうまく適していた。

4 とても素早く建設できた。

解説 芝（turf）の利点を述べた Turf was a durable material that could withstand the harsh climate and help keep people warm. の部分から，芝は過酷な気候の中で人々を暖かく保つのに役立ったことが分か

る。これを「環境に適していた」と抽象的に表した **3** が正解。

No.16 解答

質問の訳　話し手は芝の家について何と言っているか。
選択肢の訳　1　今日ではもう存在しない。
　　　　　　2　多くの場合，互いにつながっていた。
　　　　　　3　丘の上でのみ建てることができた。
　　　　　　4　ほかの国々でも一般的だった。
解説　芝の家の構造などについて説明した後半で，they were often joined together by a corridor at the back と言っている。join ~ together は複数の物を1つに結合するという意味で，これを connect を使って表した **2** が正解。almost no one lives とあるが，芝の家自体は博物館として改修されるなどして残っているので，**1** は不適。

(スクリプト)　**The Breakdown of Wet Wipes**

　Wet wipes are causing problems in sewer tunnels around the world. In 2015, for example, workers in London had to clear an enormous 10-ton lump of fat from one sewer tunnel. Experts blame wet wipes that are being flushed down toilets for causing such problems. Although the wipes can pass through pipes in homes without any issues, they mix with grease in sewer tunnels to create serious blockages. Cleaning up these obstructions has been estimated to cost billions of dollars worldwide.

　As a result, new industry standards were set for labeling a product "flushable" based on how quickly it breaks down. Environmental groups, however, claim these standards are not useful because flushable wipes do not break down in sewer tunnels the way they do in laboratory tests. The environmental groups therefore created guidelines telling consumers which products do not create blockages.

Questions
No.17 What is one problem caused by wet wipes?
No.18 Why do environmental groups criticize the new industry standards?

全文訳　**ウェットティッシュの分解**

　ウェットティッシュは，世界各地の下水道トンネルで問題を引き起こしている。例えば，2015年，ロンドンの作業員たちは，ある下水道トンネルから10トンの巨大な脂の塊を除去しなければならなかった。専門家たちは，そのような問題を引き起こす原因は，トイレに流されているウェットティッシュにあると非難する。ウェットティッシュは家庭内の配管を問題なく通過できるが，下水道トンネル内で油脂と混ざり合い，深刻な詰まりを引き起こす。これらの障害物を除去するには，世界全体で数十億ドルもの費用がかかると推定されている。

これにより，製品の分解速度に基づいて「水に流せる」と表示する新しい業界規格が設定された。しかし，環境保護団体は，水に流せるウェットティッシュは，下水道トンネルでは実験室でのテストのように分解しないため，これらの規格は役に立たないと主張する。そこで，環境保護団体は，どの製品が詰まりを起こさないかを消費者に伝えるガイドラインを作成した。

No.17 解答　①

質問の訳　ウェットティッシュが引き起こす問題の1つは何か。

選択肢の訳
1　油脂と結合し下水道トンネルを詰まらせる。
2　下水道トンネルで働く人々を危険にさらす。
3　水に流される際に家庭の配管を詰まらせる。
4　安くリサイクルすることができない。

解説　まず，前半の部分から，トイレに流されるウェットティッシュが下水道トンネルで巨大な脂の塊を作るという問題点を理解しよう。続くAlthough the wipes can ... の部分がポイントで，they mix with grease in sewer tunnels to create serious blockages と 1 が一致する。Although A, B. の形では B に重要なことが述べられるので，Although が聞こえたら，間（コンマ）の後の内容をしっかりとつかもう。

No.18 解答　②

質問の訳　なぜ環境保護団体は新しい業界規格を批判しているのか。

選択肢の訳
1　実験室でのテストを利用して作られなかった。
2　実際の下水道トンネルの状況に基づいていない。
3　下水道トンネルへの損害が検討されなかった。
4　ガイドラインでは詰まりの問題が解決できない。

解説　however を含む文では重要なことが述べられる。Environmental groups, however, claim ... の部分によると，環境保護団体は，下水道トンネルでは，実験室テストのようにはいかないと主張。新しい業界規格は製品の分解速度に基づいていても，実際の下水道トンネルの状況には基づいていないという主旨から，2 が正解。

スクリプト　**Raising Angora Rabbits**

Angora rabbits are raised around the world for their wool because it is softer and much warmer than sheep wool. Due to the animals' small size and the need to constantly care for their coats, raising Angora rabbits for wool is best done on a small scale. More owners of small farms are becoming interested in raising the animals, as their wool is more profitable than sheep wool.

Removing the wool of some breeds of Angora rabbit requires cutting the wool once every few months. With other breeds, the wool can be easily removed by hand. The wool needs to be removed often because Angora rabbits clean themselves using their tongues, like cats. If they are not brushed regularly, they will swallow too much of their wool, which can cause death. Luckily, Angora rabbits can be easily trained to sit calmly while being brushed or having their wool cut.

Questions

No.19 What is one thing the speaker says about Angora rabbits?

No.20 What is one problem with wool from Angora rabbits?

全文訳　**アンゴラウサギの飼育**

　アンゴラウサギは，その毛が羊の毛よりも柔らかくはるかに暖かいことから，世界中で採毛を目的とした飼育が行われている。アンゴラウサギは体が小さく常に毛の手入れが必要なため，採毛を目的とした飼育は小規模で行うのが最適である。アンゴラウサギの毛は羊の毛よりも収益性が高いため，この動物の飼育に興味を持つ小規模牧場主たちが増えている。

　アンゴラウサギは品種によっては，採毛するのに数カ月に1度毛を刈り取る必要がある。ほかの品種では，簡単に手で毛を抜き取ることができる。アンゴラウサギは，猫のように舌を使って自分の体をきれいにするため，頻繁に毛を取る必要がある。定期的にブラッシングしないと，毛を飲み込み過ぎて死に至る可能性もある。幸い，アンゴラウサギは，ブラッシングをされたり，毛を刈り取られていたりする間，落ち着いて座るように訓練することが容易にできる。

No.**19** 解答 ②

質問の訳　話し手がアンゴラウサギについて言っていることの1つは何か。

選択肢の訳　**1**　牧場主たちはより大きなアンゴラウサギにより興味を持っている。
　　2　毛の手入れに多大な努力を要する。
　　3　アンゴラウサギを飼育するのはもはや収益性がない。
　　4　毛の品質はさまざまであり得る。

解説　アンゴラウサギの毛の特徴を説明した the need to constantly care for their coats の部分から，手入れが大変なことが分かるので，**2**が正解。coat は「(動物の)毛」という意味で，ここでは wool と同意。**3**は their wool is more profitable than sheep wool の部分と不一致。

No.**20** 解答 ③

質問の訳　アンゴラウサギの毛の問題の1つは何か。

選択肢の訳　**1**　アンゴラウサギがしばしば毛を噛んで台無しにする。
　　2　少なくとも1カ月に1回は刈り取らなければならない。
　　3　アンゴラウサギに害を及ぼす可能性がある。
　　4　アンゴラウサギは採毛されるのが好きではない。

解説　採毛について説明した後半部分からの出題。If they are ..., they will

swallow too much of their wool, which can cause death. の部分から，アンゴラウサギは毛を飲み込み過ぎると死ぬ可能性があることが分かる。これを「害を及ぼす」と表した3が正解。

E

(スクリプト) **Fireside Chats**

When Franklin D. Roosevelt became president of the United States in 1933, the country was suffering from an economic crisis. A quarter of the population was unemployed, people were hungry, and trust in the government was rapidly declining. Roosevelt decided to use a radio broadcast to help calm the growing feeling of panic. He wanted to talk directly to the American people and tell them that the government was addressing their concerns.

The speech was an immediate success. Roosevelt made similar broadcasts, known as fireside chats, throughout his presidency. The talks often mentioned respected figures like Abraham Lincoln and ended with the national anthem. However, it was Roosevelt's conversational, informal style that set his fireside chats apart from usual political speeches. People felt as if the president was in their homes, giving them updates on everything from World War II to farming.

Questions
No.21 Why did Franklin D. Roosevelt decide to make radio broadcasts?
No.22 How were the fireside chats different from regular political speeches?

(全文訳) **炉辺談話**

フランクリン・D・ルーズベルトが1933年にアメリカ合衆国の大統領に就任したとき，アメリカは経済危機に苦しんでいた。人口の4分の1が失業し，人々は飢え，政府への信頼は急速に低下していた。ルーズベルトは，高まるパニック感情を鎮める一助とするためラジオ放送を利用することにした。彼はアメリカ国民に直接語りかけ，政府が国民の懸念に対処していることを伝えたいと思ったのだ。

その演説は直ちに功を奏した。ルーズベルトは大統領在任中，炉辺談話として知られる同様の放送を行った。その談話ではしばしば，エイブラハム・リンカーンのような尊敬される人物の話を持ち出し，最後は国歌で終わった。しかし，ルーズベルトの炉辺談話を通常の政治演説と違うものにしたのは，会話調のカジュアルな彼の文体だった。国民はまるで大統領が自分たちの家にいて，第2次世界大戦から農業まであらゆる最新情報を伝えているかのように感じた。

No.21 解答

(質問の訳) フランクリン・D・ルーズベルトはなぜラジオ放送を行うことにしたか。
(選択肢の訳) 1 飢えた人々を助ける資金を集めるため。
2 政府に関する彼の懸念を共有するため。
3 国民にもっと熱心に働くよう促すため。

4 経済に関する国民の懸念に対処するため。

解説 ラジオ放送の目的は Roosevelt decided to use a radio broadcast to ... の部分で「高まるパニック感情を鎮める一助とするために」と述べられ，さらに「政府が国民の懸念に対処していることを伝えたいと思った」と続く。何に対するパニックや懸念（concerns = worries）かというと，前述の「経済危機」である。よって，**4** が正解。

No.22 解答 ①

質問の訳 炉辺談話は通常の政治演説とどう違ったか。

選択肢の訳
1 ルーズベルトはカジュアルな言葉を使った。
2 ルーズベルトは有名人にインタビューをした。
3 ルーズベルトは愛国的な音楽を演奏した。
4 ルーズベルトは国民の各家庭を訪ねた。

解説 However, it was Roosevelt's conversational, informal style that set his fireside chats apart from usual political speeches. の部分から，**1** が正解。it was ～ that ...「…したのは～だった」という強調構文の聞き取りがポイント。set A apart from B は「A を B から区別する」という意味で，質問では *be* different from を使って表されている。

F

スクリプト **Bajau Divers**

The Bajau people live on boats in the waters around Malaysia, Indonesia, and the Philippines, and spend most of their lives at sea. Some Bajau divers can fish beneath the ocean surface for up to 13 minutes without scuba equipment. Researchers found that Bajau people have larger-than-average spleens. The spleen is an organ that provides oxygen to the blood when the breath is held, so a larger spleen likely benefits the divers.

Bajau people with no diving experience also have larger spleens, so the researchers suspect the divers' abilities are partly genetic. In addition, DNA samples from Bajau people showed they commonly have genes that help more oxygen get to organs like the heart and lungs. The researchers want to learn more about how Bajau people have adapted to their environment. They hope that such knowledge will lead to better treatments for conditions such as heart disease.

Questions

No.23 What did researchers discover about the Bajau people?

No.24 What is one thing the researchers want to do?

全文訳 **バジャウ族のダイバー**

バジャウ族は，マレーシア，インドネシア，フィリピンの近海で船に乗って暮らしており，生活のほとんどを海で過ごしている。バジャウ族のダイバーたちの中には，ス

キューバの装備なしで，最大 13 分間，海面下で魚を捕ることができる人たちもいる。研究者たちは，バジャウ族の脾臓が平均よりも大きいことを発見した。脾臓は，息を止めたときに血液に酸素を供給する臓器であることから，大きい脾臓がおそらくダイバーたちにメリットをもたらしている。

　ダイビングの経験がないバジャウ族も脾臓が大きいため，研究者たちはダイバーたちの能力は遺伝的な部分があるのではないかと考えている。さらに，バジャウ族の DNA サンプルからは，彼らは通例，心臓や肺などの臓器により多くの酸素が行き渡るのを助ける遺伝子を持っていることが分かった。研究者たちは，バジャウ族がどのように環境に適応してきたかについてもっと知りたいと考えている。彼らは，そのような知識が心臓病などの病気のより良い治療につながることを期待している。

No.23 解答 ③

質問の訳 研究者たちはバジャウ族について何を発見したか。

選択肢の訳　1　もはや伝統的な釣り用具を使わない。
　　　　　　　　2　しばしば脾臓を摘出してもらう。
　　　　　　　　3　水中において身体的な強みがある。
　　　　　　　　4　陸上で息を止める練習をしている。

解説　研究者たちの発見は，Researchers found that ... larger-than-average spleens. の部分に手掛かりがある。この spleens を知らなくてもすぐに The spleen is an organ ... と説明が続くので，ここから臓器であることが理解できればよい。船上で暮らすバジャウ族は，脾臓が大きいために長い時間，海に潜っていられる。これを「身体的な強み」と表した **3** が正解。動詞 benefit「（人などの）利益になる」を **3** では名詞 advantage「有益な点，強み」で表している。

No.24 解答 ②

質問の訳 研究者たちがやりたいことの 1 つは何か。

選択肢の訳　1　バジャウ族が新しい生活様式に適応するのを助ける。
　　　　　　　　2　バジャウ族をより詳しく研究する。
　　　　　　　　3　その土地の環境を守るのを助ける。
　　　　　　　　4　世界各地のダイバーたちを研究する。

解説　研究者たちのやりたいことは，The researchers want to ... の部分から，**2** が正解。learn more about を study 〜 in more detail と言い換えている。

G

You have 10 seconds to read the situation and Question No. 25.

We have a few apartments. There's one in Wilson Heights, just a few minutes from the train station on foot. It's a studio apartment, so everything is in one room, but it's quite spacious. Right next door to that, in Downtown Hills, there's an older two-bedroom apartment available. Bronte Towers has a three-bedroom apartment available. It's right beside a bus stop, and a 25-minute ride to the station. Lastly, and just a short walk from the same bus stop, there's a spacious two-bedroom apartment for rent in Norton Villas.

Now mark your answer on your answer sheet.

全文訳

幾つかのアパートがあります。駅から徒歩でわずか数分のウィルソン・ハイツに1つ物件があります。ワンルームアパートなので，全てが一部屋にまとまっていますが，かなり広いです。そのすぐ隣のダウンタウン・ヒルズには，寝室が2つある古めの物件が空いています。ブロンテ・タワーズには，寝室が3つある物件が空いています。バス停のすぐそばで，駅までバスで25分です。最後に，同じバス停から歩いてすぐの所にあるノートン・ヴィラズには，寝室が2つある広々とした賃貸物件があります。

No.25 解答 ②

状況の訳　あなたは鉄道駅から歩いてすぐのアパートを希望している。寝室は最低2つ必要である。不動産業者があなたに次のように言う。

質問の訳　あなたはどの物件を見るべきか。

選択肢の訳
1　ウィルソン・ハイツの物件。
2　ダウンタウン・ヒルズの物件。
3　ブロンテ・タワーズの物件。
4　ノートン・ヴィラズの物件。

解説　状況から，駅から徒歩すぐである，寝室が最低2つ必要，という条件を押さえよう。ウィルソン・ハイツの物件は駅近だがワンルームなので寝室が最低2つ必要という条件に合わない。ダウンタウン・ヒルズの物件はその隣（＝駅近）で，寝室が2つあるのでこれが条件に合う。ブロンテ・タワーズとノートン・ヴィラズはいずれも駅近ではないので不適。

H

スクリプト

You have 10 seconds to read the situation and Question No. 26.

216

Well, from what you've told me, it sounds like it could be another kidney stone. You can't be too careful with this kind of thing. Ideally, I'd like you to come in for an examination first thing in the morning. If you can't come tomorrow, take one of the pills I gave you last time right away. If it is a kidney stone, that will help your body deal with it. If not, at least it will help relieve the pain until I can examine you.

Now mark your answer on your answer sheet.

全文訳

ええと，あなたが話してくれた内容からして，また腎臓結石の可能性があるように思えます。この類いのことには用心するに越したことはありません。理想的には，朝一番に検査しに来ていただきたいです。明日来られない場合，前回お渡しした薬を1錠，すぐに飲んでください。もし腎臓結石であれば，体がそれに対処するのを助けてくれるでしょう。そうでなくても，少なくとも，私があなたを診察できるまでの間，痛みを和らげる手助けとなるでしょう。

No.26 解答 ②

状況の訳 あなたは数日間，腹痛がある。向こう2日間は忙しい。医者に電話をすると，彼があなたに次のように言う。

質問の訳 あなたはまず何をすべきか。

選択肢の訳
1 追加の鎮痛剤を手に入れる。
2 以前にもらった薬を飲む。
3 後日もう一度医者に電話をする。
4 専門医に予約を取る。

解説 状況から，腹痛があること，向こう2日間は忙しいことを押さえる。医者の指示の中の take one of the pills I gave you last time right away から，**2** が正解。それぞれ pills を medicine，last time を earlier と表している。

スクリプト

You have 10 seconds to read the situation and Question No. 27.

I'm sorry, ExTravel hasn't notified us about the spa treatment offer. I'm sure your information is accurate, but we first need confirmation of the offer. The easiest solution would be for us to have a copy of your e-mail from ExTravel. We'll need a paper copy for our records, so please use the printer in our Business Center. After that, you'll be able to book your treatment, and we can follow up on the miscommunication between us and ExTravel. As you're a regular customer, I'll also try to get a room upgrade for you.

Now mark your answer on your answer sheet.

全文訳

　申し訳ありませんが，ExTravel からはスパトリートメントの割引について通知が来ておりません。お客さまの情報は正確だと思っておりますが，まずはその割引の確認が必要です。最も簡単な解決策は，私どもが ExTravel からの E メールのコピーをいただくことです。記録のために紙のコピーが必要になりますので，館内のビジネスセンターのプリンターをご利用ください。その後，お客さまはトリートメントの予約をしていただけますし，私どもは ExTravel との間の連絡ミスを詳しく調べることができます。また，お客さまは常連なので，お部屋のアップグレードができるか見てみます。

No.27 解答 ④

状況の訳　あなたはリゾートホテルにチェックインしている。ExTravel を通すとスパトリートメントが 20% 割引になるため，ExTravel を通してネットで予約をした。フロント係があなたに次のように言う。

質問の訳　あなたはまず何をすべきか。

選択肢の訳　**1**　スパで予約をする。
　　　2　確認のため ExTravel に連絡を取る。
　　　3　支配人に部屋のアップグレードを頼む。
　　　4　割引の情報を含んだ E メールを印刷する。

解説　状況から，ExTravel を通してホテルを予約したこと，スパトリートメントが割引になるはずであることを押さえる。冒頭から，ExTravel からホテルに通知が来ていない→スパトリートメントは割引にならないかも，という状況をくみ取ろう。The easiest solution would be for us to have a copy of your e-mail from ExTravel. とあり，次の文で館内のプリンターを利用するように言っていることから，**4** が正解。質問は「最初にすること」で，**1** は E メールを印刷した後の行動なので不適。

J

スクリプト

You have 10 seconds to read the situation and Question No. 28.

I'd like to cover a few points about food and drink. We do many outdoor activities, so students should bring a water bottle, as drinking water isn't available outside. Also, we prepare lunch on the premises and expect all children to eat school lunch unless they have special dietary requirements. We have many students, so we can't cover everyone's needs. All meals include meat, eggs, and cheese. A doctor's letter is required to opt out of school lunch, in which case you won't be charged for it. In such cases, students are required to bring a home-prepared lunch.

Now mark your answer on your answer sheet.

全文訳

食べ物と飲み物について要点を幾つか説明したいと思います。当校は屋外での活動が多いのですが，屋外には飲料水がないので，生徒たちは水筒を持参する必要があります。また，敷地内で昼食を用意しておりますので，特別な食事制限がない限り，生徒全員が学校給食を食べることが求められます。生徒数が多いので，全員のニーズに応えることはできません。全ての食事に肉，卵，チーズが含まれています。学校給食を取らない場合，医師の手紙が必要ですが，その場合，給食代は請求されません。この場合，生徒たちには家庭で用意されたお弁当を持参していただきます。

No.28 解答 ①

状況の訳 あなたは新しい学校に娘の入学手続きをしている。娘は乳製品にアレルギーがある。学校長があなたに次のように言う。

質問の訳 あなたは何をすべきか。

選択肢の訳
1 医師の手紙を入手する。
2 娘の要件をリスト化する。
3 学校の給食代を支払う。
4 特別な食事を申し込む。

解説 状況から，娘の学校の入学手続きをしていること，乳製品にアレルギーがあることを押さえる。All meals include meat, eggs, and cheese. から，学校の給食には乳製品（チーズ）が含まれる→給食を取らない，と判断する。続く A doctor's letter is required to opt out of school lunch から，**1** が正解。opt は「選ぶ」という意味の動詞で，opt out of school lunch は「給食を取らないことを選択する」という意味。

K

スクリプト

You have 10 seconds to read the situation and Question No. 29.

Thank you for calling Alexandra Park. Due to winter weather conditions, not all roads in the park are open. Taylor Road and Grand Point Road are closed due to heavy snowfall and will remain closed for at least two weeks. Bryant Pass Road is open, although snow chains are required on all vehicles due to its high elevation. Chains can be purchased at the Valley Garage in Campton City. There are no rental chains available within the park. Please be aware that studded tires are not allowed to be used in the park.

Now mark your answer on your answer sheet.

全文訳

アレクサンドラ公園にお電話いただきありがとうございます。冬の天候状況により，公園内の全ての道路が通行できるわけではありません。テイラー通りとグランド・ポイント通りは大雪のために閉鎖されており，少なくとも2週間は閉鎖されたままでしょう。

ブライアント・パス通りは通行できますが，標高が高いため，全ての車両にスノーチェーンが必要です。チェーンはキャンプトン市のバレー・ガレージで購入できます。公園内には利用可能なレンタル用のチェーンはありません。公園内ではスパイクタイヤの使用が禁止されていますのでご注意ください。

No.29 解答 ①

状況の訳 今は冬で，あなたは今週末に車でアレクサンドラ公園に行きたいと思っている。雪道で使えるタイヤを持っていない。公園の案内所に電話をすると，次のようなことを聞く。

質問の訳 あなたは何をすべきか。

選択肢の訳
1 タイヤ用のスノーチェーンを買う。
2 グランド・ポイント通りを行く。
3 タイヤをスパイクタイヤに変える。
4 アレクサンドラ公園でチェーンをレンタルする。

解説 状況の「雪道で使えるタイヤがない」から，スパイクタイヤ（滑り止めのために金属の鋲を埋め込んだタイヤ＝studded tires）もタイヤに付けるスノーチェーン（snow chains）もないと判断する。案内によると，車が通行できるのはブライアント・パス通りで，スノーチェーンが必要だと言い，買える場所を案内している。よって，**1**が正解。**3**は，スパイクタイヤでは公園内を走れないので不適。

220

| 二次試験・面接 | 問題カード Ａ 日程 | 問題編 p.152〜153 | ▶MP3 ▶アプリ ▶CD 4 37〜41 |

解答例 **One day, a man was arriving home after work.** It was late at night and he looked very tired, but his wife reminded him that he only had one more week before his retirement. The next week, the man's office held a retirement party for him. There was a banner in the office that wished him a happy retirement. The man was given some flowers and warm applause by the other staff members. He looked very happy. The following month, the man and his wife were gardening at home. The man was picking some vegetables, and his wife was watering the plants. They both looked satisfied and relaxed. Three months later, the man was at home watching TV with his wife. One of the staff members from his former workplace called him and asked if he could come back to work because sales had dropped lately.

解答例の訳 ある日，男性が仕事を終えて帰宅していました。夜遅く，とても疲れている様子でしたが，妻が定年まであと１週間しかないと夫に念を押しました。翌週，男性の職場は彼のために退職パーティーを開きました。オフィスには彼の幸せな退職を祝うバナーが掲げられました。男性はほかのスタッフから花束をもらい，温かい拍手を受けました。彼はとても幸せそうでした。翌月，男性と妻は，自宅でガーデニングをしていました。男性は野菜を収穫し，妻は植物に水をやっていました。２人とも満足そうでリラックスしている様子でした。３カ月後，男性は自宅で妻とテレビを見ていました。以前の職場のスタッフの１人が彼に電話をかけ，最近売り上げが落ちているので職場に復帰することができるか彼に尋ねました。

解説 解答に含めるべき点は以下の４つ。①男性が疲れた様子で帰宅，妻が「あと１週間しかない」と言っている，②翌週，職場のスタッフが男性の退職を祝っている，③翌月，夫婦がガーデニングをしている，④３カ月後，自宅で夫が電話に出ており，スタッフが「(職場に) 戻れますか」と言っている。カードの「これは間もなく退職する男性に関する話である」から，１コマ目の妻の発言は「退職まであと１週間よ」という意味である。４コマ目は，売り上げが急激に落ち込んでいるグラフがスタッフが男性の復職を願う理由と考えられる。「戻ってきてくれませんか」という「お願い」と捉えて asked him to come back to work と表してもよいだろう。staff は集合名詞なので一人一人を表す場合は one of the staff members などとする。

21年度第1回 面接

221

No. 1

解答例 I'd be thinking, "I feel a little bad that my former company isn't performing well, but I shouldn't be tempted to go back to work. Now it's time to enjoy the rest of my life with my wife."

解説 質問は「4番目の絵を見てください。もしあなたがこの男性なら，どのようなことを考えているでしょうか」。解答例は復職を拒否する立場で，「業績が悪いのは気の毒だが復職すべきではない」「妻と残りの人生を楽しむときだ」という内容。受諾する立場としては，「妻との時間を大切にしながらも非常勤で働くのは悪くない」などの考えがあり得るだろう。

No. 2

解答例 Yes. It's becoming less common for people to cook and eat at home nowadays. Many people work until late and end up eating fast food, so they aren't getting the vitamins necessary to stay healthy.

解説 質問は「今日の人々はバランスの良い食事を取ることの重要性を忘れてしまいましたか」。解答例はYesの立場で，家で料理をしなくなっているという根拠を述べた後，残業を理由にファストフードを食べて必要なビタミンを取っていないという説明を続けている。Noの立場では，健康志向の人や健康食品の増加を根拠に意見を述べることが可能。

No. 3

解答例 No. There are many active elderly people who can still work in Japan. Rather than retiring, they'll continue to earn a living for themselves. Also, they can share their knowledge with younger workers.

解説 質問は「今後，早期退職を選ぶ人々は増えるでしょうか」。解答例はNoの立場で，「日本ではまだ働ける元気な高齢者たちが多い」と述べた後，Also以下では「若い労働者たちと知識を共有できる」という高齢者が職場に残る利点を補足している。Yesの立場では理由として，割増退職金がもらえる，自由な時間を得られるなどを挙げることができるだろう。

No. 4

解答例 I think so. These days, people depend on the Internet for many things, such as shopping and banking. Because of this, people's personal information can be stolen by hackers. We should find better ways to protect important data.

解説 「サイバー犯罪は今日の社会でより大きな問題になっていますか」という質問。解答例のようにI (don't) think so. と始めてもよい。解答例はYesの立場で，「人々が多くのことをインターネットに依存しており，ハッカーに個人情報が盗まれる可能性がある」という意見。〈such as＋具体例〉や，因果関係を表すbecause of thisの使い方を確認しよう。

二次試験・面接 | **問題カード C 日程** | 問題編 p.154～155 | 🔊 ▶MP3 ▶アプリ ▶CD 4 42～45

解答例 **One day, a young woman was at an orientation for new employees.** She was talking excitedly with the other new employees during the orientation. She seemed interested in her new career and told them she wanted to work in the product development section. The personnel manager overheard her. A month later, the woman was in the manager's office. He told her that she would now be working in the sales section. The woman looked discouraged because she could not work in the product development section. The next week, the woman was working for the sales section. She was walking outside while talking on the phone and checking her schedule. She looked very busy and stressed. Six months later, the woman and the manager were talking about her evaluation sheet and her accomplishments at work. The manager seemed disappointed in her and said that she needed to do better.

解答例の訳 ある日，若い女性が新入社員向けオリエンテーションに出席していました。オリエンテーションの間，彼女はほかの新入社員たちと楽しそうに話していました。彼女は新しい仕事に興味があるようで，製品開発部門で働きたいと彼らに話しました。人事部長は彼女の話を小耳に挟みました。1カ月後，女性は人事部長のオフィスにいました。彼は彼女に，これから営業部門で働くことになると言いました。女性は製品開発部門で働けないので，落胆した様子でした。翌週，女性は営業部門で働いていました。彼女は電話で話し，予定を確認しながら，外を歩いていました。とても忙しそうで，ストレスを感じている様子でした。半年後，女性と部長は，女性の評価表と職場での成果について話していました。部長は彼女に失望している様子で，もっとがんばる必要があると言いました。

解説 解答に含めるべき点は以下の4つ。①女性が「製品開発部門で働きたい」と言い，人事部長がそれを聞いている，②1カ月後，部長が女性に「営業部門で働いてもらう」と通知している，③翌週，女性は忙しそうに通りを歩いている，④半年後，部長が「従業員評価」を見ながら女性に「もっとがんばる必要がある」と言っている。カードの下線入りの冒頭の1文から，1コマ目は新入社員向けオリエンテーションだと推測しよう。女性は製品開発部門で働きたかったが実際は営業部門の配属になったという流れがポイント。4コマ目の部長のせりふは，女性の評価が思わしくないことからくる発言だと考えられる。

21年度第1回　面接

223

No. 1

解答例 I'd be thinking that I should ask my manager to move me to the product development section. I want to be a good employee, and I'm sure I'll perform better by doing the job that suits me best.

解説 質問は「4番目の絵を見てください。もしあなたがこの若い女性なら，どのようなことを考えているでしょうか」。もともと製品開発部門で働くことが希望だったことから，解答例のように，製品開発部門で働きたい（＝異動したい）という主旨の考えが思い付きやすいだろう。

No. 2

解答例 No. Schools should focus on giving students the academic skills they need. Students can learn about working from their parents, or they can get a part-time job while in high school or university.

解説 質問は「学校は，生徒たちを将来のキャリアに備えさせる責任があると思いますか」。解答例は No の立場で，「（将来のキャリアではなく）必要な学力を与えることに重点を置くべき」という学校の役割についての意見を述べた後，将来のキャリアに備える別の方法を具体的に2つ述べている。Yes の立場では逆に，学力向上よりは，職業体験やインターンの機会の充実などキャリア教育に重点を置くべきという意見が考えられる。

No. 3

解答例 I don't think so. Many people today lead a more complex life than in the past, and their jobs or housework take up a lot of their time. So, it's difficult for them to find time to travel or do a hobby that reduces their stress.

解説 質問は「現代社会の人々は昔の人々よりもストレスに対処するのが上手ですか」。解答例は No の立場で，以前より生活が複雑になり，仕事や家事が忙しくて旅行や趣味の時間が取りにくい（＝ストレスにうまく対処できていない）という意見。今と昔を比較した質問なので，比較級を適切に使って答えたい。

No. 4

解答例 No. Many Japanese companies are already successful in other countries. They have excellent marketing departments to promote their products. The government should concentrate on improving people's lives in Japan.

解説 「政府は日本製品を海外で売り込むためにもっと努力すべきですか」という質問。解答例は No の立場で，「多くの日本企業はすでに海外で成功している」「（海外ではなく）日本の生活向上に集中すべき」という意見。already を用いた「すでに～（だから…する必要はない）」という述べ方は，should を含む質問に対する No の立場で使える便利な表現である。

2020-3

一次試験
筆記解答・解説　　p.226〜241

一次試験
リスニング解答・解説　p.242〜264

二次試験
面接解答・解説　　p.265〜268

解 答 一 覧

一次試験・筆記

1

(1)	1	(10)	2	(19)	1
(2)	3	(11)	4	(20)	3
(3)	4	(12)	1	(21)	1
(4)	2	(13)	3	(22)	1
(5)	3	(14)	3	(23)	4
(6)	2	(15)	1	(24)	1
(7)	4	(16)	3	(25)	2
(8)	1	(17)	2		
(9)	1	(18)	2		

2

(26)	1	(29)	3
(27)	3	(30)	2
(28)	3	(31)	4

3

(32)	4	(35)	4	(38)	2
(33)	2	(36)	3	(39)	4
(34)	3	(37)	1	(40)	1
				(41)	4

4　　解答例は本文参照

一次試験・リスニング

Part 1

No. 1	1	No. 5	2	No. 9	2
No. 2	4	No. 6	1	No.10	4
No. 3	4	No. 7	2	No.11	4
No. 4	2	No. 8	3	No.12	2

Part 2

No.13	3	No.17	3	No.21	1
No.14	1	No.18	1	No.22	4
No.15	2	No.19	3	No.23	3
No.16	4	No.20	2	No.24	2

Part 3

No.25	2	No.28	4
No.26	1	No.29	3
No.27	2		

一次試験・筆記 **1** 問題編 p.158～161

(1) ―解答 1 ･･･････････････････････････ 正答率 ★75%以上

訳 ミリアムは食事を作るときに健康的な材料を使おうとする。例えば，クッキーを作るのに，彼女はバターを使う代わりにオリーブオイルを使う。

解説 第2文のバターではなくオリーブオイルを使うという具体例から，健康的な材料（ingredients）を使うと分かる。それぞれ attribute「特質」，perimeter「外周」，surrounding「（複数形で）環境」の複数形。

(2) ―解答 3 ･･･

訳 取締役会のメンバーは，新しい CEO にいくら支払うかに関して意見の一致を見ることができなかった。提案された最初の額が高過ぎると感じる人もいた。

解説 reach (a) consensus on で「～に関する意見の一致を見る」というコロケーション。ratio「割合」，preview「下見」，simulation「模擬実験」

(3) ―解答 4 ･･･

訳 エレンのアパートは安かったが，すぐにそこに住むことに我慢できなくなった。エアコンがなく，屋根が雨漏りし，隣の部屋の赤ん坊がよく泣いたのだ。

解説 第2文の悪条件から，住むことが我慢できない（intolerable）状態になったと考えられる。in-（否定）＋tolerable「我慢できる」の構造。decent「適切な」，crucial「極めて重要な」，gracious「親切な」

(4) ―解答 2 ･･･

訳 深海は，温度が低く，気圧が高く，日光が当たらない，非常に住みにくい環境である。これにもかかわらず，多くの生物がそこでうまく生き延びている。

解説 inhospitable は「荒れ果てた，住みにくい」で，inhospitable environment は生存に適さないほどの過酷な環境を表す。quaint「古風な」，dignified「堂々とした」，confidential「（情報などが）秘密の」

(5) ―解答 3 ･･･

訳 スチュアートは祖母の肉体的弱さが心配になってきたため，彼女に老人ホームに入るよう勧めた。

解説 老人ホームに入るよう勧めたのは祖母の肉体的な弱さ（frailty）が心配になったからである。frailty は特に老齢者の衰弱を表す言葉として近年よく使われる。haze「もや，かすみ」，canal「運河」，statistic「統計値」

(6) ―解答 2 ･･･････････････････････････ 正答率 ★75%以上

訳 さまざまな生物を研究するため，科学者らはそれらを相違点と類似点に基づいて分類した。それぞれの種は特定のグループに分類される。

解説 空所後の them は various organisms を指す。第2文の place 〜 into a specific group と類義の classify「分類する」の過去分詞 classified が適切。それぞれ salute「あいさつする」，personify「人格化する」，extinguish「（火などを）消す」の過去分詞。

(7) ― 解答 ④

訳 A：ジェームズ，私たちの供給業者が今月支払いを受けていないと言ったよ。

B：うん，知ってる。経理部による見落としがあったんだ。供給業者に電話をして謝るよ。

解説 供給業者が支払いを受けていないのは経理部による見落とし（oversight）が原因と考えられる。underdog「勝ち目のない人，弱者」，overhead「諸経費」，upheaval「（思想・社会などの）大変動」

(8) ― 解答 ①

訳 男と彼の友人は地元の銀行を襲おうと共謀した。しかし，ほかの誰かが気付いて警察に通報したため，彼らは何もしないうちに捕まった。

解説 conspire to *do* で「〜しようと共謀する」。それぞれ inhale「吸い込む」，diminish「少なくする」，identify「同一物であると確認する」の過去形。

(9) ― 解答 ①

訳 ドミンゴの上司は彼に，彼の新しい工場の計画は実行可能ではないと言った。コストがかかり過ぎるし，完成までに時間がかかり過ぎる。

解説 第2文の悲観的な内容から，計画の実行は難しいと考えられる。正解の feasible「実行可能な」は possible より堅い語。fierce「どう猛な」，inventive「発明の，独創的な」，eventful「出来事の多い」

(10) ― 解答 ② 　　　　　　　　　　　　　　　正答率 ★75%以上

訳 新市長は，市に立ちはだかる問題の幾つかに取り組み始めることができる就任初日を楽しみにしていると述べた。

解説 目的語 problems に合う動詞は tackle「（困難な仕事に）取り組む」である。それぞれ insert「挿入する」，trigger「引き金を引く，引き起こす」，generate「（収益などを）生む，発生させる」の -ing 形。

(11) ― 解答 ④

訳 人が大きな手術を受けるとき，感染や神経損傷などの合併症が発生する可能性があるため，手術は通常，ほかに治療法の選択肢がない場合にのみ行われる。

解説 such as に続く infection「感染」や nerve damage「神経損傷」は合併症（complications）の具体例である。それぞれ denial「否認」，domain「領地，生息圏，ドメイン」，comparison「比較，比喩，例示」の複数形。

227

(12) – 解答 **1** ∙∙∙

訳 ヘンリエッタは非常に熱心な読書家である。彼女は本が大好きで，彼女にとって1週間に数冊を読み終えるのは珍しくない。

解説 第2文から，読書が好きな様子が分かるので，reader「読書家」を形容する語として passionate「熱心な」が適切。obscure「曖昧な」，uncomfortable「不快な」，feeble「弱い」

(13) – 解答 **3** ∙∙ 正答率 ★75%以上

訳 小道では，ハイカーはときどき野生動物に遭遇することがある。しかし，その動物に近づき過ぎたりえさを与えたりしないことが重要である。

解説 ハイキングで経験し得ることを想像すると，野生動物に遭遇する（encounter）ことである。scrap「解体する」，propel「前へ押し出す」，seal「封印する」

(14) – 解答 **3** ∙∙∙

訳 トッドは会社から解雇された後，新しい仕事を見つけるまでの数カ月間失業保険を受給した。

解説 following は after と同義。失業保険は会社を辞めた後に受給するものなので，dismissal「解雇」が適切。testimony「証拠，陳述書」，tremor「震動」，glossary「用語解説」

(15) – 解答 **1** ∙∙∙

訳 票の大部分が数えられた後，その候補者が勝てないのは明らかだった。彼は対立候補に選挙で敗北したことを認めることにした。

解説 concede は「（選挙・競技などで）（自分の）敗北［（相手の）勝利］を認める」という意味。opponent は競技相手や対立候補のこと。consolidate「強固にする，合併する」，foster「養育する，発展させる」，plaster「しっくいを塗る，こう薬を貼る」

(16) – 解答 **3** ∙∙∙

訳 ケリーは長いシャワーを浴びることで無意識のうちにホストファミリーの気分を害した。ホストファーザーが彼女に水をそんなにたくさん使うことに不満があると言うまで，彼女は気付かなかった。

解説 第2文の「～まで気付かなかった」という文脈から，無意識のうちに（unwittingly）ホストファミリーの気分を害したと考えられる。形容詞の unwitting は unknowing や unconscious と同義。sympathetically「同情して」，typically「典型的に」，diagonally「対角線上に」

(17) – 解答 **2** ∙∙∙

訳 その薬品の副作用の1つとして，鮮明な夢を見ることがある。服用者の約5%が睡眠中に強烈で現実かのような体験をしたと報告している。

解説 第2文の「睡眠中の強烈で現実かのような体験」と同義表現になるよう，「鮮明な（vivid）夢」とするのが適切。allied「同盟した」，stout「頑丈な，

でっぷりした」，fluent「流ちょうな」

(18) – 解答 **2** ••••••••••••••••••••••••••••••••••••••• 正答率 ★75%以上

訳　試合の前に，その少年はいつも有名サッカー選手に**サイン**を求める。彼は，選手たちが彼のノートにサインしてくれることを期待して，ロッカールームの入口近くで待つ。

解説　有名人からもらうものとして，autographs「サイン」が適切。「サインする」は第2文の sign *one's* name である。名詞「サイン」は sign ではないので注意。それぞれ telegraph「電信機」，editorial「社説」，exhibit「展示品」の複数形。

(19) – 解答 **1** •••

訳　多くの航空会社は，幼い子供が独りで飛行機に乗る場合，親または**保護者**の許可を得ていることを要請する。

解説　選択肢には「人」を表す語が並んでいる。a parent or guardian で「親または保護者」という成句。defendant「被告（人）」，servant「召使，使用人」，commuter「通勤［通学］者」

(20) – 解答 **3** ••••••••••••••••••••••••••••••••••••••• 正答率 ★75%以上

訳　その劇場へ来る人の多くは舞台が低過ぎて演者たちが見えないと不満を述べた。経営陣は舞台を1メートル**持ち上げる**ことを決定した。

解説　不評だった低い舞台を「高くする」と考えるのが自然。〈have＋O＋過去分詞〉「Oを〜させる」の構造で，elevate「（物を）上げる，持ち上げる」の過去分詞 elevated が適切。それぞれ snatch「ひったくる」，appreciate「感謝する，良さが分かる」，donate「寄付する」の過去分詞。

(21) – 解答 **1** •••

訳　古代では，地震は**神の**警告だと考える人もいた。彼らは，神が自分たちに行動を変えるよう言っているのだと信じていた。

解説　warning「警告」の詳細が第2文にある。God「神」とあることから，divine「神の」が適切。dutiful「本分を尽くす，忠実な」，sparse「まばらな，貧弱な」，lively「元気な」

(22) – 解答 **1** •••

訳　そのランナーは早くにほかのランナーから**抜け出して**レースをリードした。彼女が勝利のためにゴールしたとき，彼女と次のランナーとの間には大きな距離があった。

解説　break away「抜け出す」の過去形が適切。ランナーは2位と大差でゴールしたことから，away に「離」のイメージがあれば選べそうだ。cross the finish line は「ゴールラインを超える，ゴールする」。それぞれ hold down「〜を押し下げる」，bottom out「最低になる」，turn back「後戻りする」の過去形。

20年度第3回　筆記

229

(23) – 解答 **4** ･･

訳 会社のウェブサイトを更新するために雇われたウェブ開発者はひどい仕事をした。彼が引き起こしたあらゆる問題を解決するのに何カ月もかかった。

解説 目的語 problems に合う動詞は straighten out「～（問題など）を解決する」。-en は形容詞・名詞に付いて動詞を作る接尾辞。straight + -en「まっすぐにする＝正しい状態にする＝解決する」のイメージ。stumble on「～を偶然見つける」，trade in「～を下取りに出す」，rip off「～を剥ぎ取る」

(24) – 解答 **1** ･････････････････････････････ 正答率 ★75%以上

訳 マーシャは息子の様子を見に２階へ行き，彼が宿題をせずにテレビゲームをしているのを見つけてとても腹を立てた。

解説 check up on で「～（素行など）を調べる」，go check up on で「～の様子を見に行く」という意味だが，check で「息子を確認しに行く」というイメージが描けたら正解できそうだ。go through with「～をやり抜く」，get away with「～（軽い罰など）で済む」，fall back on「～を当てにする」

(25) – 解答 **2** ･･

訳 友だち同士の２人はひどいけんかをした後，１カ月間互いに口を利かなかった。しかし，最終的には２人は仲直りし，今では以前より増して多くの時間を一緒に過ごしている。

解説 後の now 以下の様子から，けんかの仲直りをした（made up）と考えられる。それぞれ keep away「近寄らない」，work up「徐々に進む，少しずつのぼる」，play out「尽きる」の過去形。

一次試験・筆記 2 | 問題編 p.162～165

全文訳 財布実験

　心理学者たちは正直さについてさまざまな説を立ててきた。最もよく知られているものの中に，それは誘惑に関係しているというものがある。しかし，最近この考え方は疑問視されている。人は，嘘をついたり，盗んだり，だましたりすることで望んだものが得られると信じているとしたら，そうする傾向にあることは論理的なことのように思えるが，ある興味深い実験によってこれが真実ではないかもしれないことが分かった。

　ある研究者チームが，人は何か価値のあるものを見つけたときにそれを返すよりは持っておく可能性が高いという理論を立て，これを検証するため，道で財布を見つけたふりをして，その財布を公共の場のいろいろな所に持っていった。それらの財布の中にはお金が入っているものもあれば，お金が入っていないものもあったが，全てに鍵が１

230

つとEメールアドレスが入っていた。それから研究者たちは，紛失した財布が見つかったと伝えるEメールが来るか待った。驚くことに，財布に多額のお金が入っていたときに最も多くの反応があった。しかも，金額がさらに増やされた場合にはもっと多くの財布が返ってきた。研究者たちは，これは多くの人がお金よりも正直であることを大事にしていることを示す証拠であると考えている。

　その後，研究者たちは，全ての財布に同額のお金を入れた追跡実験を実施した。しかし今回は，幾つかの財布には鍵，つまりなくした人だけに重要であろうものが入っており，入っていない財布もあった。鍵が入っている財布の返ってくる確率の方が著しく高かった。研究者たちは，このような結果となった最もあり得る理由として，人の正直さが他者をどれほど気にかけているかに強く影響を受けたことを示唆する。

> 〔語句〕 psychologist「心理学者」，theory「学説，理論」，question「疑問視する」，cheat「だます」，theorize「理論を立てる」，〈inform O that SV〉「Oに〜と知らせる」，value A over B「BよりAを重視する」，follow-up「（調査を）追跡して行う」，significantly「著しく」

(26) – 解答 **1**

解説 後の this idea に相当する内容が空所に入る。その「考え方」は While 以下で「人は望んだものを得るのに嘘をついたり，盗んだり，だましたりする」と説明されていることから，**1** を入れて「それ（＝正直さ）は誘惑に関係している」とすれば文脈に合う。

(27) – 解答 **3**　　正答率 ★75%以上

解説 まずは，実験はお金が入った財布は返ってこないという理論（仮説）を立てて行われたことを押さえる。しかし，Surprisingly とあり，実際は，多額のお金が入っていたときに最も多くの反応があったという意外な結果になった。空所後は「さらに多くのお金が入っていた場合はもっと多くの財布が返ってきた」という内容なので，追加を表す What is more「さらには，しかも」が適切。

(28) – 解答 **3**

解説 第3段落の実験では，全ての財布に同額のお金が入っていたが，鍵が入っている財布と入っていない財布があり，結果は鍵が入っている財布が高い確率で返ってきた。その鍵について「なくした人だけに重要」と表していることから，人の正直さが何の影響を受けたかを考えると，**3**「他者をどれほど気にかけているか」が適切。

全文訳 **変わった関係**

　クロサイは，かつてアフリカ大陸の大部分で歩き回っていた。しかし今日では，違法な狩りにより，クロサイは絶滅危惧種になっている。サイは，非常に嗅覚が優れている反面，視覚が大変弱いため，特に被害に遭いやすい。その結果，密猟者たちは風がクロサイの方向に彼らのにおいを運んでいない限りは，この動物に気付かれずに近づくこと

ができる。

どのようにしてサイがそのような状況を回避しているかを調査している行動科学の研究者たちは，アカハシウシツツキという鳥との変わった関係に気付いた。この鳥は，優れた視覚を持ち，近づく動物に脅威を感じるとシューシューという音を立てる。アカハシウシツツキは，サイの皮膚に住むダニとして知られる微小な生物によってサイに引き付けられており，この鳥はしばしばサイの背中の上に乗ってダニを探しつつサイをつつく。アカハシウシツツキが止まっているサイは，近づく脅威の存在にはるかに気付きやすいことが分かった。従って研究者たちは，鳥がサイに警告を与えていると考えている。これによって，サイがなぜアカハシウシツツキの存在を許容しているのかも説明できる可能性がある。

近年，ウシツツキが消えつつあり，これはサイにとって良くない知らせである。ウシツツキが食べるダニは牛にも生息しているが，農家は殺虫剤を使ってダニを殺してきた。多くのウシツツキがこれらの毒入りのダニを食べて死に，その結果，サイの生息地を含め，どんどん数が減っている。しかし，生態学者たちは，サイの個体群の保護のためにはウシツツキを再導入することが不可欠かもしれないと考えている。

[語句] rhinoceros「サイ」(rhino(s) は口語)，roam「歩き回る，うろつく」，vulnerable「弱い，被害に遭いやすい」，behavioral「行動に関する」，hiss「シューシューと音を立てる」，organism「(有機的) 生物」，tick「ダニ」，atop「～の上に」，peck at「(くちばしで)～をつつく」，perch「(鳥が) 止まる」，pesticide「殺虫剤」，reintroduce「再導入する」，vital「不可欠な」

(29) – 解答 ③　　正答率 ★75%以上

解説　空所前後はそれぞれ「クロサイは視覚が弱いために違法な狩りの被害に遭いやすい」，「密猟者はサイに気付かれずに近づける」という内容。つまり，サイは視覚が弱い（原因）⇒ 密猟者はサイに近づける（結果）の関係なので，Consequently「その結果」が適切。

(30) – 解答 ②　　正答率 ★75%以上

解説　第2段落はサイが密猟を回避する方法が説明されている。脅威を感じるとシューシューと音を立てるアカハシウシツツキが背中にいることで，サイも自分に近づく脅威の存在に気付きやすいという主旨から，**2**「鳥 (＝アカハシウシツツキ) がサイに警告を与えている」が適切。

(31) – 解答 ④　　正答率 ★75%以上

解説　空所後の which has ... から，空所にはサイにとって良くない知らせが入る。この後，ダニを殺すのに使われる殺虫剤が原因で多くのウシツツキが死んでいることが分かるので，**4**「ウシツツキが消えつつある」が適切。サイはウシツツキのおかげで脅威を回避していることから，ウシツツキが減ることはサイにとって良くない知らせなのである。

一次試験・筆記 **3** 問題編 p.166 ～ 172

全文訳 **シアトルの自転車シェアリング**

　シアトルは，環境に優しい都市であり，その住民たちは活動的なライフスタイルとアウトドア好きで知られている。そのため，シアトル初の自転車シェアリングサービスであるプロント・サイクル・シェアが失敗に終わったとき，多くの人が驚いた。使用されていないときに自転車を保管することができるドッキングステーションを軸にして計画されたプロントは，当初，企業スポンサーの援助を受けて非営利企業によって提供されていた。しかし，市民の反応は薄く，同市が介入してこのサービスを購入するのに至った。不満足な結果が続いた後，利用を促進するために同市はこのサービスのネットワークの拡張を発表したが，大幅な拡張はできなかった。結局，何年もの批判と財政問題ののち，プロントは 2017 年に廃止された。

　その数カ月後に導入されたスピンという新しい自転車シェアリングサービスの成功は，ただプロントの廃止について新たな疑問を提起しただけだった。雨の多い気候や急な坂道で知られるほかのアメリカの都市での自転車シェアリング企業の成功が実証されていることは，（プロントの廃止が）シアトルの気候や地形のせいではなかったことを意味した。それよりむしろ，プロントを批判する人は，ドッキングステーションの場所に関する深刻な問題を指摘した。スピンの自転車は，スマートフォンで開錠し，認可されたエリア内のどこでも置いていくことができ，またスピンが運営を開始したとき，プロントを利用することができなかったエリアの多くの利用者を獲得した。さらに，プロントのネットワークは，シアトルの既存の公共交通システムに無視されたエリアで適切にサービスを提供できていなかった。

　スピンが成功したとき，シアトルで同様のサービスが立ち上がり，同市が 2018 年に常設の自転車シェアリングプログラムを導入するのに至った。これは自転車を利用する人にとっては前向きな動きではあったが，事業を継続したいのであればプログラムに参加することを強制された企業からは否定的な反応を受けた。許可手数料や個別の自転車料金などの，これらの企業に課された義務的費用が高過ぎたのだ。スピンを含む 2 社がサービスを引き上げ，プログラム導入後すぐに同市を去り，同市の政策決定に再び注目を集めることとなった。

　語句 underwhelming「つまらない，がっかりさせる」，step in「介入する」，unsatisfactory「不満足な」，enlargement「拡張」，significantly「意味深く，有意に」，criticism「批判」，abandon「廃止する」，demise「廃止」，terrain「地形」，point the finger at「～を指摘する」，enroll「（人を）登録する，会員にする」，adequately「適切に」，mandatory「義務的な」，withdraw「取り消す，撤退する」，decision-making「意思決定，政策決定」，spotlight「(the spotlight で)(世間の) 注目」

233

(32) – 解答 **4**

問題文の訳　この文章によると，シアトル初の自転車シェアリングサービスについて何が言えるか。

選択肢の訳　**1**　市がこの会社への追加の資金提供を拒否し続けたことで同社は生き残れなくなった。

2　サービスが普及しなかったため，市は最終的に非営利企業にサービスを管理させることに決定した。

3　サービスは市民に人気があったものの，利益が低かったために市はほかのところからの資金調達を余儀なくされた。

4　運営していた会社がサービスを成功させられなかったとき，市はサービスを購入し拡張しようと試みた。

解説　第1段落第2文から，まずは，自転車シェアリングサービス（プロント）が失敗したことをつかもう。そして however を含む文から，市が介入してこのサービスを購入したこと，また the city announced an enlargement of the service's network から，市はサービスのネットワークの拡張を試みたことが読み取れる。よって，**4** が正解。

(33) – 解答 **2**

問題文の訳　プロント・サイクル・シェアの失敗の理由の1つとして挙げられていることは何か。

選択肢の訳　**1**　市の公共交通システムの改善により，人々が動き回るのに自転車を利用する必要性が少なくなった。

2　ネットワークのすき間［空白地域］が，一部の居住者にとって市内を楽に移動することを難しくさせた。

3　市の坂道や悪天候が多くの事故の原因とされたとき，自転車を利用する人がサービスの利用をやめた。

4　自転車の位置を追跡するのに使われるスマートフォンのソフトウエアの問題により，多くの自転車を利用する人がサービスを使わなくなった。

解説　第2段落の instead 以下に重要な情報がある。プロントの失敗の原因として，まずドッキングステーションの場所に関する深刻な問題がある。また Furthermore 以下では，公共交通機関がないエリアこそプロントが役立つにもかかわらず，ネットワークの不備で適切にサービスが提供できなかったことが読み取れる。これを正解の **2** では Gaps in its network「ネットワークのすき間［空白地域］」と表している。

(34) – 解答 **3**

問題文の訳　スピンが提供したサービスについて何が分かるか。

選択肢の訳　**1**　このサービスの自転車のタイプが，以前の自転車シェアリングサービスに比べると随分良かったものの，市民に人気がなかった。

2 このサービスは，市に自社の自転車シェアリングサービスを導入することを決定した有名企業と張り合えなかった。

3 市によって導入された新しいプログラムが原因で，サービスがあまりに高額になり，運営していた会社は経営を続けることができなくなった。

4 市民はサービスに好意的だったものの，それを運営していた会社はその会社が引き起こした環境的被害のことで市から批判された。

解説 第3段落はスピンの成功を受け，市が常設の自転車シェアリングプログラムを導入した話に展開される。第2文の主節（it received ...）から，否定的な内容が続く。第3文の the companies はプログラム参加を強いられた企業のことで，これらの企業に課された義務的費用がかかり過ぎたこと，スピンを含む2社が撤退したことが分かる。よって，**3**が正解。この**3**の文のように too ～ for A to *do*「あまりに～なのでAは…できない」のAが長い場合，for A が to 不定詞の後にくることがある。

全文訳 **南極大陸の野生生物**

　南極大陸は，ほとんどが氷で覆われた，広大でほぼ何もない大陸である。実際，その土地で常に凍っていないのは1%未満である。この大変小さな場所は，地上で子育てする種にとって最も利用しやすい環境を提供しているため，ユキドリなどの鳥類も含め，この地域の野生生物のほとんどにとってなくてはならないものである。南極には常在する人間はいないものの，調査基地，観光用宿舎や廃棄物集積場などの人間の存在の地物が近年ますます南極の自然環境を脅かしている。概して，人間の活動はこの不凍地域の80%に悪影響を及ぼしてきた。

　人間の活動がもたらした有害な結果の中に，在来の野生生物に対するかく乱と廃棄物と車両の排ガスによる汚染がある。大きな生態学的な懸案事項は，在来種を害する可能性がある外来の植物や昆虫種が意図されずに移入されることである。さらに，南極には比較的少ない種類の種しかいないため，在来種は非在来種に非常に取って代わられやすい。環境へのもう1つの脅威は石油探査である。南極条約体制によって現在では禁止されているが，この禁止は将来的に異議を唱えられそうである。石油業界における技術の進歩により厳しい環境での石油掘削がより経済的になり，石油会社は事業の拡張を推し進めている。例として，かつては石油を得ることが経済面で非現実的であった，気温が氷点下の地域であるアラスカのノーススロープでの掘削が現在進められている。

　南極条約体制は，南極大陸の55の場所を保護区域として指定しているが，これらは合わせても不凍地のほんの一部分にすぎない。そしてこの指定もあまり意味がないかもしれない。クイーンズランド大学の生物学者であるジャスティーン・ショウとその同僚たちによる研究は，南極で実施されている保護が，全世界における被害を受けやすい地域を保護する目的で計画されたプログラムを上位から下位の順で格付けしたランキングの下位25%にあることを示した。さらに同研究によって，55の保護区域全てが人間活

20年度第3回　筆記

235

動の場所の近くにあることも分かり、そしてそのうちの7つが生物学的侵入のリスクが高いと考えられている。ショウによると、南極大陸の生物多様性の保全は不可欠であるため、保護区域を設けるときに種の数が最も多い場所を優先すべきとのことだ。南極大陸が孤立した地域だからといってその生物多様性への深刻な脅威を被らないわけではないと今こそ気付くときである、とショウは警告する。

語句 vast「広大な」，permanently「永久に」，ice-free「氷結しない，不凍の」，indispensable「必須の」，presence「存在」，waste dump「廃棄物集積場」，consequence「結果」，disturbance「（環境の）かく乱」，counterpart「同等物」，exploration「探査」，drill「掘削する」，harsh「（気候が）厳しい」，sub-zero「氷点下の」，impractical「非現実的な，実現不可能な」，the Antarctic Treaty System「南極条約体制」，designate「指定する」，fraction「一部」，implement「実施する」，safeguard「保護する」，invasion「侵入」，conserve「保護［保全］する」，biodiversity「生物多様性」，prioritize「優先する」

(35) – 解答 ④

問題文の訳 南極の不凍地の重要性について何と述べられているか。

選択肢の訳
1 そこは、大陸内のもっと気温が低いほかの地域ほど多くの環境被害を被っていない。
2 そこは、人間が新種を持ち込む場所として、ほかの地域よりも大きな可能性を提供する。
3 そこには、人間の活動の高まりから逃れてきた大陸のほかの地域の動物が生息している。
4 子供を産むために陸にいる必要がある特定の種にとって最も行きやすい場所である。

解説 南極の不凍地について説明した第1段落の第3文の内容と4が一致する。本文の indispensable は「必須の、なくてはならない」という意味で、4 では need to を使って言い換えられている。また have their young on land を be on land to give birth to their young と表している。young は名詞で「（動物の）子」、give birth to は「～を産む」。

(36) – 解答 ③

問題文の訳 アラスカのノーススロープの例が示していることは、どのように

選択肢の訳
1 環境に悪影響を与える活動が生じても構わないように保護区域の指定が容易に解除され得るか。
2 南極条約体制のような協定が世界の資源豊かな地域に必要か。
3 掘削作業の革新によって厳しい気候の地域で石油を採取することの費用効率がより良くなったか。
4 外来種の移入が短期間でその土地の生態系を根本的に変え得るか。

解説 第2段落は環境への脅威として外来種の移入と石油探査が挙げられてお

り，手掛かりは後者にある。「石油業界における技術の進歩により厳しい環境での石油掘削が経済的になった」とあり，ノーススロープはその石油掘削が進められている例である。**3**が正解で，本文の Technological advances in ... が innovations in ... に対応している。

(37) – 解答

問題文の訳 ジャスティーン・ショウは南極の自然を保護するために何をするよう勧めているか。

選択肢の訳
1 保護区域を設ける際には，動植物の種類が最も多い地域を優先するべきである。
2 侵入種に脅かされている地域から多様性に欠けている地域に焦点を移すべきである。
3 人間活動がある場所に近い地域に生息する動物は氷で覆われた地域に移動させるべきだ。
4 南極の不凍地以外の場所にもっと多くの保護区域を指定すべきである。

解説 第3段落の According to Shaw, ... areas with the greatest number of species should be prioritized when establishing protected zones. 「ショウによると，保護区域を設けるときに種の数が最も多い場所を優先すべきだ」から，**1** が正解。prioritize は動詞で priority は名詞。人間活動の場所に近い保護区域のリスクは述べられているが，動物を氷で覆われた地域に移動させるべきといった記述はないので**3**は不適。

全文訳　ダーウィンの矛盾

およそ2世紀前，チャールズ・ダーウィンはビーグル号という船でインド洋を渡航した。温かく青い海は生命を育むのに非常に適した環境のように思えたが，ダーウィンは透明な海にたまにしかいない魚を見て，海洋生物が乏しいと気付いた。しかし，キーリング諸島として知られるサンゴ礁の群島に到着すると，彼はその周辺で豊富な海洋生物種を見つけた。いったい何がサンゴ礁の島を，ほぼ生命のない海洋砂漠に囲まれた肥沃なオアシスにしているのか，と彼は疑問に思った。

この謎は「ダーウィンの矛盾」として知られるようになり，長らく科学者たちの興味をかき立ててきた。ダーウィンの時代以来，彼らは，熱帯の海の透明度そのものがその生命の乏しさの理由だと考えてきた。それは海洋生態系の主要な栄養源である植物プランクトンとして知られる微生物によって曇っていないためである。しかし，キーリング諸島では，サンゴ礁やエビなどのその他海洋生物は植物プランクトンにありつける。植物プランクトンが必要とする栄養素である窒素やリンも，キーリング諸島周辺の海ではサンゴ礁やさまざまな海洋生物を維持するのに十分な高い水準で海に存在する。植物プランクトンの成長を支えている要因は，島効果（IME）として知られている。しかし当時の科学者たちを混乱させたのは，どうやって栄養素が周辺の海域に流出してしまうことなく，サンゴ礁の生態系内にとどまることができているのかということであった。

研究者たちは，ようやく全ての断片をつなぎ合わせて，IME の仕組みを解明した。それは海底の高い位置でのサンゴ礁の形成に始まる。サンゴ礁は日光を必要とするため，浅瀬でよく生育する。そして，サンゴ礁の生物多様性は，サンゴ礁が急勾配の場所よりも緩やかな斜面にある方が増す。これは，別の主要な IME 要因にとって緩やかな勾配が重要だからである。その要因は湧昇，つまり，深海からの栄養豊富な冷たい水が，栄養に乏しいが明るい上方の海域に上ってくることである。これは，サンゴ礁を養う植物プランクトンに食料を供給する。海綿動物として知られる海洋生物も，このプロセスの別の主要な部分を担っており，それはこれらがサンゴ礁と植物プランクトンの両方の老廃物を吸い込んで，その老廃物を食物連鎖のより上位の海洋生物が摂取できる物質に変え，その物質を食べられるよう付近の海域に放出するからである。これによって，サンゴ礁の生態系の閉じたループ内にエネルギーと栄養素をとどめる。サンゴ礁の生態系内の栄養素濃度は，陸上とサンゴ礁の両方で生息して死ぬ生物からの有機物によってさらに上がる。

熱帯のサンゴ礁は漁業にとって重要な資源であるが，同時に，海岸線への嵐や洪水の影響を和らげて沿岸部を守っている。気候変動によって地球の気温が上がり，世界各地で海流の動きが変えられるにつれ，サンゴ礁の生態系も大いに影響を受ける。未来の気象パターンが及ぼすサンゴ礁への悪影響を軽減できるよう，IME をより深く理解し保全する適切な対策を取ることがますます不可欠になるだろう。

語句 scarce「乏しい」, an abundance of「多数の〜，豊富な〜」, fertile「肥沃な」, amid「〜に囲まれた」, clarity「透明さ」, cloud「曇らせる，不透明にさせる」, phytoplankton「植物プランクトン」, sustain「維持する」, steep「急勾配の」, upwelling「湧き出ること，湧昇」, sponge「海綿動物」, suck in「〜を吸い込む」, convert A into B「A を B に変換する」, food chain「食物連鎖」, expel「放出する」, concentration「（溶液の）濃度」, enhance「高める」, buffer A from B「A を B から守る，かばう」, ocean current「海流」

(38) – 解答 ②

問題文の訳 「ダーウィンの矛盾」を最もうまく要約しているのは次の文のうちどれか。

選択肢の訳
1 あまり生命を育まないサンゴ礁は一般的に，多種多様な海洋生物が生息する海域に見られる。
2 周りの外洋に生命がないにもかかわらず，サンゴ礁は多くの海洋生物の個体群を育むことができる。
3 冷たい水の中で形成するサンゴ礁は，より温度が高い場所で成長するサンゴ礁よりも生命を育むことができる。
4 単独で生活する海洋生物はサンゴ礁近くに住むことを好む一方で，集団で見られる海洋生物は水が温かい海域を好む。

解説 Darwin's Paradox という言葉は第 2 段落に出てくるが，その内容は第 1 段落にある。対比を表す Although や Yet を手掛かりにどんな「矛

238

盾」かを読み取ろう。「ほぼ生命のない海洋に囲まれているにもかかわらず，サンゴ礁の群島には豊富な海洋生物種がいた」という主旨から，**2** が適切。

(39) －解答 ④

問題文の訳 科学者たちが島効果に混乱させられた理由は

選択肢の訳
1. 海洋生物は外洋にいる植物プランクトンを食べないが，サンゴ礁の群島近辺の海域では大量の植物プランクトンを食べるからである。
2. 小さいサンゴ礁の群島は，大きいサンゴ礁の群島よりもはるかにうまく植物プランクトンの喪失を防ぐことができるからである。
3. 小さい生物は十分な窒素やリンを得るが，大きい生物は十分な量の窒素やリンを得ることができないからである。
4. サンゴ礁の群島は，外洋で見られるよりも高い窒素やリンの水準を維持することができるように思えるからである。

解説 質問文の動詞 puzzle「混乱させる」が第 2 段落最終文に含まれている。この文の nutrients は nitrogen and phosphorus「窒素やリン」のこと。how 以下は科学者たちの疑問で，設問で問われているのは混乱の「理由」である点に注意。キーリング諸島ではサンゴ礁や海洋生物を維持するのに高水準の窒素やリンが存在するとあるが，これはサンゴ礁の群島と外洋（＝ **4** の open ocean）との比較である。よって，**4** が適切。

(40) －解答

問題文の訳 海綿動物は IME においてどんな役割を果たしているか。

選択肢の訳
1. 海綿動物は，特定の物質を食べられるような形に変えることで，生存に必要な物質を海洋生物に供給する。
2. 海綿動物は，海水に入る多くの日光を吸収するため，群島周辺の急勾配の場所により多くの栄養素を提供することができる。
3. 海綿動物が出す老廃物はサンゴ礁と植物プランクトン両方にとって重要な食料源である。
4. 海綿動物は，植物プランクトンを食べた後，自分を食べるより大きな海洋動物にその栄養素を受け渡す。

解説 sponges が登場する第 3 段落第 6 文（Sea creatures known ...）を参照。海綿動物の役割は as 以下にあり，その内容と **1** が一致する。本文の convert A into B「A を B に変換する」と **1** の change A into B が同義で，それぞれ A にあたる the products と certain materials は「海綿動物が吸い込んだサンゴ礁と植物プランクトンの老廃物」のこと。**4** は，海綿動物より大きな海洋動物（＝食物連鎖のより上位の海洋生物）は，海綿動物が食物プランクトンの老廃物をリサイクルして放出した物質を食べるのであって，海綿動物そのものを食べるわけではないので，that feed on them（＝ the sponges）が不適。

(41) – 解答 ④

問題文の訳 IME をより深く理解することはどう役に立つ可能性があるか。

選択肢の訳
1 科学者たちが，地球温暖化が沿岸部で発生する嵐や洪水のパターンにどう影響するかをより明確に理解するのに役立つ可能性がある。
2 科学者たちが，漁業がサンゴ礁周辺の生態系に及ぼした悪影響を軽減できる可能性がある。
3 地球の気温が上昇しているにもかかわらず，科学者たちが，どのように海流の温度が高くなるのを防ぐことができるかを理解するのに役立つ可能性がある。
4 科学者たちが，海流や気温の変化からサンゴ礁を守る方法を発見できる可能性がある。

解説 質問文の a better understanding と似た表現が第4段落の最終文にある。IME をより深く理解する目的は「未来の気象パターンが及ぼすサンゴ礁への悪影響を軽減できるようにする」ためである（〈so that S can〉「S が～できるように」）。weather patterns はその前の内容から，地球の気温や海流の動きのことと考えられるので，**4** が正解。「サンゴ礁への悪影響を軽減する」を **4** では「サンゴ礁を守る」と表している。

一次試験・筆記 **4** | 問題編 p.173

トピックの訳 賛成か反対か：今後もっと多くの人がベジタリアンになるべきである。

ポイントの訳 ・動物の権利　・コスト　・環境　・健康

解答例
　In my opinion, more people should become vegetarians in the future. They should do so for reasons such as animal rights and health.

　Becoming a vegetarian can play a big role in protecting the lives of animals. Factories that produce meat products often have bad conditions, and the animals kept there are treated poorly. If more people choose not to eat meat, then these factories will be forced to close down and fewer animals would be killed for food.

　A vegetarian lifestyle can also benefit our health. Meat products, especially fast food, contain high amounts of fat, which has been shown to cause heart disease and obesity. On the other hand, by eating more nutritious vegetables, people will get sick less often, resulting in improved health and welfare throughout society.

In conclusion, more people should become vegetarians to help protect the rights of animals and to improve their own health.

解説 序論：第1段落では，トピックに対する自分の意見を簡潔に書く。模範解答では，In my opinion「私の意見では」の後にトピックの表現をそのまま利用することで賛成の立場を明らかにしている。第2文では，ポイントの Animal rights と Health の観点を盛り込んで，「動物の権利や健康などの理由でそうする（＝ベジタリアンになる）べき」と述べている。

本論：本論では，序論で述べた主張の理由・根拠を2つの観点を使って順に詳しく説明する。解答例の第2段落は Animal rights の観点で，「肉製品を作る工場では動物がひどい扱いを受けている」という内容を述べた後，（ベジタリアンになれば）肉を食べない→工場が閉鎖→殺される動物が減る（＝動物の権利が守られる）という一連の流れを根拠にしている。第3段落は Health の観点で，also を用いることで第2段落とは別の理由であることを明確に伝えている。On the other hand「一方で」の前後で，肉製品が健康に及ぼす悪影響と，野菜を食べることのメリットが対照的に述べられている点を確認しよう。第2文の which は関係代名詞（非制限用法）で，先行詞は high amounts of fat「大量の脂肪」である。文は主語（名詞）ばかりで始めるのではなく，解答例の by eating more ... の by -ing「〜することで」や，in order to *do*「〜するために（は）」などの副詞句で文を始めるとバリエーション豊かな英文になる。

結論：最終段落では，トピックに対する意見を再び主張する。解答例は In conclusion「結論として」で始め，「動物の権利を保護する手助けをするため，健康を改善するために，もっと多くの人がベジタリアンになるべき」と2つの観点を再び盛り込んで1文でまとめている。このように，序論でトピックの表現をそのまま使った場合，結論では別の表現を使うようにしたい。結論の書き出しはほかに For these reasons「これらの理由で」などの表現がある。

そのほかの表現 cause, lead to, result in などの因果関係を示す（句）動詞は無生物主語の文で使われやすいため，積極的に使う練習をしておくとよい。さらに解答例の ..., resulting in 〜「…の結果〜になる」のような文のつなげ方ができるとレベルの高い英文になるだろう。ポイントの Environment「環境」の観点については，ベジタリアンになれば肉を食べない→家畜が不要になる→牧場を作るための森林伐採が減る→地球温暖化が軽減されるといった一連の流れを根拠にできるだろう。

| 一次試験・リスニング | **Part 1** | 問題編 p.174～175 | 🔊 | ▶MP3 ▶アプリ ▶CD 3 **28～41** |

No.1 – 解答 ①

スクリプト ☆： That was a great movie, Joe. Thanks for bringing me.

★： Glad you enjoyed it. Uh-oh, it's raining hard. You didn't bring an umbrella, did you?

☆： No. So much for walking to the restaurant! Isn't there a subway station two blocks away?

★： Yes, but we'll get soaking wet in this rain. Let's call a cab.

☆： We may have to wait a while for them to send one in this weather.

★： It's better than getting rained on.

☆： That's true.

Question: What will the couple do next?

全文訳 ☆： 素晴らしい映画だったわ，ジョー。連れてきてくれてありがとう。

★： 楽しんでくれてよかったよ。ああ，雨が激しく降っているね。君，傘を持ってこなかったよね？

☆： うん。レストランに歩いて行くのは諦めるしかないわね！　2ブロック向こうに地下鉄の駅があるんじゃなかった？

★： あるけど，この雨じゃびしょぬれになってしまうよ。タクシーを呼ぼう。

☆： この天気じゃ1台寄こすのにしばらく待たなければならないかもしれないわね。

★： 雨にぬれるよりはましだよ。

☆： それもそうね。

質問： 男女は次に何をするか。

選択肢の訳　1　電話でタクシーを呼ぶ。

2　レストランへ歩いて行く。

3　雨がやむのを待つ。

4　地下鉄に乗る。

解説 雨の中どうやってレストランへ行くかを話している。男性の Let's call a cab（= taxi）．という提案に対し，女性はしばらく待たなければならないと言って乗り気ではない様子だが，「雨にぬれるよりはましだ」という男性の意見を受け入れる。よって，**1** が適切。so much for は「～は諦めるしかない」という意味だが，すぐ後で地下鉄について言及していることから徒歩では行きたくないという意図をくみ取ろう。

No.2 – 解答 ④

スクリプト ★： My tooth is killing me!

☆： When did you last see a dentist, honey?

242

★： Maybe a few years ago. I never seem to have the time.

☆： And look where that's gotten you! Well, Dr. Prashad opens at 8:30, but she's always busy in the mornings, so you'd have to wait a while. Or you could take the afternoon off.

★： I have an important meeting after lunch, so that's out. I'll just have to go to the office late this morning.

Question: What will the man probably do?

全文訳 ★： 歯が痛くてたまらないよ！

☆： 最後に歯医者に行ったのはいつ，あなた？

★： 数年前かもしれない。そんな時間は全然ないようでね。

☆： それで今そんなことになっているんじゃない！　そうね，プラシャド先生の所が 8 時 30 分に開くけど，いつも午前中は忙しいから，しばらく待たなければならないわね。もしくは午後休むかね。

★： 昼食後に大事な会議があるから，それはないね。今日の午前中に遅れて出社するしかないね。

質問：男性はおそらく何をするか。

選択肢の訳 1　会議を取りやめる。

2　午後を休む。

3　痛みが和らぐかどうか待ってみる。

4　今日の午前中に歯医者へ行く。

解説 男性は午後会社を休んで（take the afternoon off）歯医者へ行くという女性の提案に「それはない」（that's out）と反対する。最後でも「今日の午前中に遅れて出社するしかない」と言っているので，**4** が正解。

No.**3**-解答 **4**

スクリプト ★： I can't believe this heat wave — over 35 degrees for 10 days straight.

☆： I think this must be a record. Global warming is really kicking in.

★： I wouldn't go that far. The world's climate has always gone through cycles.

☆： This is no cycle. Scientists say it's pollution, and it's getting worse.

★： They'll all be proven wrong in another 100 years.

☆： I hope you're right!

Question: What does the woman think?

全文訳 ★： 信じられない熱波だよ。10 日間連続で 35 度超えだ。

☆： これって新記録に違いないと思うわ。地球温暖化が本当に影響してきているわね。

★： そこまでは言わないけど。世界の気候はいつだって周期的に変動してい

20
年度第
3
回

リスニング

243

るんだ。

☆： これは周期なんかじゃないわ。科学者は汚染だって言ってるわ，そして
ますます悪くなってるとも。

★： 今後100年の間に彼らは全員間違っていたって証明されるさ。

☆： そうだといいけどね！

質問：女性はどう考えているか。

選択肢の訳　**1**　科学者はよく間違った予測をする。

　　　　　　2　汚染レベルは天候に影響を与えない。

　　　　　　3　高気温は全く心配するものではない。

　　　　　　4　熱波は地球温暖化と関係がある。

解説　男性が話題に出した熱波，高気温について，女性はGlobal warming
is really kicking in. と言っているので，**4**が正解。kick in は「影響
し出す，効き始める」といった意味。男女どちらの意見について問われ
るかは最後まで分からないため，それぞれの意見のポイントを押さえな
がら聞く必要がある。

No.4 －解答 ②

スクリプト　☆： Peter, some of the parents at the kids' playgroup are talking about
having another picnic.

★： Sounds like fun. Let me know when you've decided on a date.

☆： Actually, we were wondering if you could organize it.

★： That depends on when you have in mind. I'm away on business
for a week this month.

☆： Either Saturday the 14th or the 21st.

★： Hmm . . . The 14th should be OK. How does Fairfield Park
sound?

☆： Perfect. The kids love the jungle gym there.

Question: What does the woman ask the man to do?

全文訳　☆： ピーター，子供たちの遊び仲間の親たちの一部がまたピクニックをしよ
うって話してるの。

★： 楽しそうだね。日付が決まったら教えて。

☆： 実を言うと，あなたに仕切ってもらえないかって思ってて。

★： それはいつを考えているのかによるね。今月，出張で1週間いないんだ。

☆： 14日か21日の土曜日ね。

★： そうだな…。14日は大丈夫のはず。フェアフィールド公園はどう？

☆： ばっちりよ。子供たちはあそこのジャングルジムが大好きだもの。

質問：女性は男性に何をするよう頼んでいるか。

選択肢の訳　**1**　出張の日程を変更する。

　　　　　　2　遊び仲間のためにピクニックの手はずを整える。

244

3 ジャングルジムのある公園を見つける。

4 フェアフィールド公園への行き方を彼女に教える。

解説 話題は子供たちの遊び仲間のピクニックで，女性は we were wondering if you could organize it と言って，男性に仕切ってほしいとお願いしている。I was [We were] wondering if you could *do* は控えめにお願いする表現。正解は **2** で，会話中の organize を arrange に言い換えている。

No.5 －解答 ②

スクリプト ☆： We have so many things to throw away before we move!

★： Let's have another yard sale.

☆： We only made a little money with the last one. The newspaper ad was expensive, and the sale took up so much time.

★： Well, even a little extra cash would help.

☆： It's not worth it, considering all the other stuff we need to do before we move.

★： Yeah, I guess you're right. Let's just give what we don't need to charity.

Question: What do we learn about the woman?

全文訳 ☆： 引っ越す前に捨てなければならないものがたくさんあり過ぎるわ！

★： もう一度ヤードセールをしよう。

☆： 前回のでは少ししか稼げなかったわ。新聞の広告は高かったし，セールにはすごく時間がかかった。

★： でも，少しでもお金が入れば助かるだろう。

☆： やるだけ無駄よ。引っ越す前にしなければならないほかのこと全部を考えればね。

★： そうだね，君の言う通りかもね。とりあえず要らないものは慈善事業に寄付してしまおう。

質問：女性について何が分かるか。

選択肢の訳 **1** 彼女は自分たちの持ち物を慈善事業に寄付したくない。

2 彼女はもうヤードセールをしたくない。

3 彼女は引っ越しの日程を変更したい。

4 彼女は新聞に広告を出したい。

解説 最初のやりとりから，話題は引っ越しで，要らないものがたくさんあることをつかもう。もう一度ヤードセール（主にアメリカで，自宅の庭で不要品を売ること）をしようという男性の提案に対し，女性はヤードセールの欠点を述べて反対しているので，**2** が正解。新聞の広告については「高かった」と否定的な意見なので **4** は不適。

No.6 − 解答 ①

スクリプト ★： Hi, Peggy. What's the matter?

☆： I almost didn't make it to work today. My babysitter cancelled.

★： Again? Gosh, she doesn't sound very reliable.

☆： She's not, but I haven't found a new sitter yet. I had to leave the baby with a friend.

★： Hey, you know my sister Carol? She's great with kids, and she's looking for extra work. Shall I give you her number?

☆： Thanks. Let me just grab a pen and some paper.

Question: What does the man suggest to Peggy?

全文訳 ★： やあ，ペギー。どうしたの？

☆： 今日出社できないところだったの。ベビーシッターがキャンセルしちゃって。

★： また？ え，彼女，あまり信頼できる感じじゃないな。

☆： 信頼できないわ。でも新しいシッターをまだ見つけていないの。友人に赤ちゃんを預けてこなければいけなかったわ。

★： ねえ，僕の妹［姉］のキャロルを知ってるだろ？ 彼女は子供の扱いがうまいし，もっと仕事を増やそうと探しているんだ。彼女の電話番号を教えようか？

☆： ありがとう。ちょっとペンと紙を持ってくるわね。

質問：男性はペギーに何を提案しているか。

選択肢の訳　**1** 彼女が彼の妹［姉］に電話をすること。

2 彼女が友人に助けを求めること。

3 彼女が遅い時間帯に仕事を始めること。

4 彼女がキャロルの子供たちの面倒を見ること。

解説　話者は会社の同僚同士か親しい友人同士と見られ，話題は女性の信頼できないベビーシッター。代わりのベビーシッターが見つかっていないと言う女性に対し，男性は妹［姉］のキャロルのことを話す。男性の Shall I give you her number? から，**1** が正解。Shall I ～? という提案表現が質問の suggest「提案する」につながる点を確認しよう。

No.7 − 解答 ②

スクリプト ★： Ms. Hattori, have those textbooks we ordered arrived yet?

☆： No, they haven't. I called Mr. Abe, their sales rep, yesterday and he says his records show that they were shipped last Friday.

★： I see. Then could you please contact the delivery service and have them track the order?

☆： I did that right after I spoke with Mr. Abe. The delivery people said they'd check their records and get back to us ASAP.

246

★： Alright. Keep me informed. I really need those books.

Question: What is the status of the order?

全文訳 ★： ハットリさん，注文したあの教科書はもう届きましたか。

☆： いいえ，まだです。昨日，注文先の販売員のアベさんに電話したところ，記録では先週の金曜日に発送されたそうです。

★： なるほど。それなら，配送サービスに連絡して，注文の追跡をしてもらってくれますか。

☆： アベさんと話した直後にそうしました。配送の人は記録を確認して，できる限り早く折り返し連絡をすると言っていました。

★： 分かりました。状況を逐次教えてください。あの本が本当に必要なんです。

質問：注文状況はどうなっているか。

選択肢の訳 1　金曜日までに到着する。

2　調査中である。

3　製造業者に返送された。

4　まだ発送されていない。

解説 未到着の注文品について，配送の人が「記録を確認して，できる限り早く折り返し連絡をする」と言っていることから，**2** が適切。look into は「〜（問題）を調査する」。ASAP は as soon as possible の略で「エイエスエイピー」または「エイサップ」と読む。そのほか sales rep「販売員」（rep = representative），ad「広告」（= advertisement），「研究室」lab（= laboratory）のような略語も聞き取れるようにしておこう。they were shipped last Friday より，商品は発送済みなので **4** は不適。

No.**8** – 解答 ③

スクリプト ☆： What happened to Ray? I haven't seen him for a while.

★： He quit his teaching job and opened up a restaurant in San Francisco.

☆： You're kidding! What a switch! He's always been into teaching.

★： I know. It was all so sudden that I didn't even get the chance to say good-bye.

Question: What happened to Ray?

全文訳 ☆： レイはどうかしたの？　しばらく見てないけど。

★： 彼は教師の仕事を辞めて，サンフランシスコでレストランを始めたよ。

☆： 嘘でしょう！　なんて転換なの！　彼はいつも教えることに夢中だったのに。

★： だよね。とにかく突然のことで，お別れを言う機会すらなかったよ。

質問：レイに何があったか。

選択肢の訳 1　彼は今，教師として働いている。

2　彼はレストランの仕事を辞めた。

20年度第3回　リスニング

3 彼は新しいキャリアを始めた。

4 彼は学生に戻った。

解説 話題はレイという共通の知人の男性。レイについて説明した He quit his teaching job ...「教師の仕事を辞めてレストランを始めた」を，「新しいキャリアを始めた」と抽象的に表した **3** が正解。get a new job や change jobs は同業種での転職も含まれるが，今回のような異業種への転職は career が用いられやすい。

No.**9** – 解答 ②

スクリプト ★ : Hi, Charlene. How's life on the 10th floor? Have you settled into your new office yet?

☆ : Getting there. I still have some boxes to unpack, though.

★ : Too bad they moved your project team. It was more convenient having you on the 6th floor with us.

☆ : True, but the new space is much bigger and brighter. I know we have to meet with you guys regularly, but there are only a few floors between us.

★ : I guess it'll be good exercise if we use the stairs!

Question: What does the woman imply?

全文訳 ★ : やあ，シャーリーン。10 階の生活はどうだい？　新しいオフィスにはもう慣れた？

☆ : そろそろね。まだ荷ほどきしないといけない箱が幾つかあるけどね。

★ : 君のプロジェクトチームが移動して残念だよ。僕たちと 6 階にいてくれた方が便利だったのに。

☆ : そうね，でも新しいスペースはもっと広くて明るいわ。あなたたちと定期的に会わなければならないのは分かってるけど，数階しか離れていないわよ。

★ : 階段を使えばいい運動になりそうだね！

質問：女性は何をほのめかしているか。

選択肢の訳 **1** 彼女は間もなくもっと大きなプロジェクトに取り組み始める。

2 彼女は新しいオフィススペースの方が好きだ。

3 彼女は部下に会議を減らしてもらいたいと思っている。

4 彼女は新しいオフィスを探している。

解説 会社の同僚同士による会話と思われる。女性のチームが 6 階から 10 階に移動したことについて話している。男性は Too bad ... と言ってこの移動を残念がっている様子だが，女性は True, but ... と言って新しいオフィススペースの良い面を説明している。よって，**2** が正解。

No.**10** 解答 ④

スクリプト ☆ : What's up, Rick? You look frustrated.

248

★： I'm trying to put together my presentation for Friday's class.

☆： Right, you told me about that. Not going well?

★： Not really. I don't have much experience giving presentations, and the topic the instructor assigned is pretty dull.

☆： He doesn't let you choose your own topic?

★： After the first presentation, he does. I guess I'll just have to suffer through this one.

☆： Let me know if you want some help.

Question: What is one problem the man has?

全文訳 ☆： リック，どうしたの？　いらいらしているみたいね。

★： 金曜日の授業のプレゼンテーションをまとめようとしてるんだ。

☆： そうだったわ，そう言っていたわね。うまくいってないの？

★： あんまり。プレゼンテーションした経験があまりないし，講師が割り当てたテーマがすごくつまらないんだ。

☆： 講師は自分でテーマを選ばせてくれないの？

★： 初回のプレゼンテーションの後は選ばせてくれる。今回は何とか切り抜けるしかないかも。

☆： 手助けが必要なら言ってね。

質問：男性が抱えている問題の1つは何か。

選択肢の訳 **1** 授業の講師が彼を落第させそうである。

2 彼は期限に間に合わないことを心配している。

3 女性が彼と一緒に練習するのを断った。

4 彼はプレゼンテーションをするのに慣れていない。

解説 話題は男性の授業のプレゼンテーションで，男性の I don't have much experience giving presentations「プレゼンテーションした経験があまりない」を「プレゼンテーションをするのに慣れていない」と言い換えた **4** が正解。*be* used to -ing で「～するのに慣れている」。プレゼンテーションをまとめるのに苦労しているのであって，期限に間に合うかどうかは話していないので，**2** は不適。

No.11 解答 ④

スクリプト ☆： Romesh, I'd like a word with you about the new file clerk.

★： You mean Brent? He seems to work hard, and he's friendly enough, isn't he?

☆： Well, that may be, but I heard he was fired from his last position. Were his references checked thoroughly?

★： I assume so. It's standard procedure. Anyway, if his performance is adequate, let's leave well enough alone for now. We've got too much on our plates as is.

20年度第3回　リスニング

249

☆：I suppose you're right.

Question: What does the man imply?

全文訳 ☆：ロメシ，新しい文書係についてちょっと話があるんだけど。

★：ブレントのこと？　よく働いているようだし，十分に友好的だろ？

☆：ええ，そうかもしれない，でも前職をくびになったって聞いたわ。彼の身元保証はしっかり確認したのかしら。

★：そうだと思うよ。通常の手順だからね。いずれにせよ，彼の働きぶりが適切なら，現状でよしとしよう。今のままでもやるべきことはたくさんあるんだからね。

☆：あなたの言う通りかもね。

質問：男性は何をほのめかしているか。

選択肢の訳 **1** 女性は従業員をもっと雇うべきだ。

2 新しい文書係はくびになるかもしれない。

3 従業員を雇う手順が時代遅れである。

4 女性はブレントのことを心配し過ぎである。

解説 話題は新しい文書係のブレント。女性はブレントに不信感がある様子だが，男性は「よく働いている」「十分に友好的だ」などと肯定的な見方をしており，女性ほど心配していないことから，**4** が適切。reference は「身元保証，信用照会」という意味で，雇用の際に応募者の前職での実績や勤務状況に偽りがないかを前職の人に確認をする手順がある。

No.**12** 解答 ②

スクリプト ☆：I got some bad news about our car insurance.

★：Is the company raising the fee?

☆：Yeah, to $200 a month!

★：Wow! I knew we'd be penalized after my accident, but that's pretty steep.

☆：Yeah. I guess it will go back down eventually, but maybe we should consider switching companies.

★：I doubt it's worth it. We'd probably pay the same or even more. I'd get rid of the car if I didn't need it for work.

Question: What will the couple probably do?

全文訳 ☆：私たちの自動車保険について悪い知らせがあるの。

★：会社が料金を上げるのかい？

☆：そう，月額 200 ドルによ！

★：ええ！　僕の事故の後は不利になると分かっていたけど，結構高額になったね。

☆：そうなの。そのうちまた下がるだろうけど，保険会社を変えることを考えるべきかな。

250

★：その価値があるとは思えないよ。たぶん，同じ金額かそれ以上支払うことになるんじゃないかな。車が仕事に必要なかったら処分するのに。

質問：男女はおそらく何をするか。

選択肢の訳　1　車を売ろうと試みる。
　　　　　　2　今の保険会社にとどまる。
　　　　　　3　男性の事故を報告する。
　　　　　　4　保険契約を解約する。

解説　最初のやりとりから，話題は自動車保険料が値上げされること。女性の maybe we should consider switching companies の companies は保険会社のことで，男性はこの女性の提案を受けて I doubt it's worth it.「その価値があるとは思えない」と答える。つまり保険会社は変えない＝今の会社にとどまると考えられるので，**2** が正解。

A

 Argan Oil

Argan oil is often considered to be a wonder product, with cosmetics companies promoting its antiaging properties. It comes from the fruit of the argan tree, which grows in the dry landscape of Morocco, and is also used in food and medicine. Harvesting the fruit and producing the oil is a long, labor-intensive process that has traditionally been done by local women. However, trading the oil is often done by local men, with women earning little or no income.

NGOs have therefore helped establish workers' cooperatives that educate the women and help them trade and sell the oil in local markets. The cooperatives also help them negotiate with international customers. It is hoped that expanding production of argan oil will lift local women out of poverty and benefit the environment as more trees will need to be planted to produce the oil.

Questions

No.13 What is one thing we learn about the production of argan oil?

No.14 What have NGOs done for local women?

全文訳　**アルガンオイル**

アルガンオイルは，化粧品会社がその抗老化（アンチエイジング）性を宣伝しており，奇跡の製品と見なされることが多い。それはモロッコの乾燥した大地で育つアルガンの木の果実から採れるもので，食品や医薬品にも使用されている。果実の収穫とオイルの

生産は，伝統的に地元の女性によって行われてきた，長い時間と労力を要する作業である。しかし，オイルの取引は地元の男性によって行われることが多く，女性はほとんどあるいは全く収入を得ることがない。

　そこで NGO は，女性を教育し，女性が地元の市場でオイルを取引したり販売したりするのを支援する労働者協同組合の設立に一役買った。この協同組合は，女性が外国の顧客と交渉する手助けもしている。アルガンオイルの生産を拡大することで，地元の女性が貧困から抜け出すこと，またオイルを生産するためにより多くの木を植える必要があるため，環境のためになることが期待されている。

No.**13** 解答 ③

質問の訳 アルガンオイルの生産について分かることの 1 つは何か。

選択肢の訳　**1**　木々が枯れる原因となる。
　　　　　　2　乾燥地帯では不可能である。
　　　　　　3　かなりの努力を要する。
　　　　　　4　地元の環境を破壊する可能性がある。

解説　Harvesting the fruit and producing the oil is a long, labor-intensive process ... 「果実の収穫とオイルの生産は長い時間と労力を要する作業だ」の部分から，**3** が適切。labor-intensive は「労働集約的な，大きな労働力を要する」。選択肢の considerable「かなりの，相当な」は considerate「思いやりのある」と混同しやすいので注意。

No.**14** 解答 ①

質問の訳 NGO は地元の女性のために何をしたか。

選択肢の訳　**1**　女性が経営技術を得る支援をした。
　　　　　　2　女性に化粧品会社の仕事を見つけてあげた。
　　　　　　3　女性のために海外のメーカーを探してあげた。
　　　　　　4　女性の子供たちのために学校を設立した。

解説　NGO が女性のためにしたことは，後半の NGOs have therefore helped ... の部分にある。関係代名詞節を含む長い 1 文だが，耳に入った順に理解していこう。NGO が労働者協同組合設立を支援した→その組合は女性を教育して女性が地元の市場でオイルを取引したり販売したりできるよう支援した，という流れ。この取引，販売などを business skills「経営技術」と表現した **1** が正解。

B

スクリプト　**The Woman behind the Brooklyn Bridge**

　The Brooklyn Bridge in New York City is one of the great engineering achievements of the nineteenth century. It was designed by John Roebling, whose son Washington took over as the bridge's chief engineer after his father's death. It was built to connect the island of Manhattan with Brooklyn, nearly 2 kilometers away. While it was not the first suspension bridge, no other bridge of this kind had ever crossed such an enormous distance.

　Much of the bridge's construction was supervised by a woman, Emily Roebling. This was at a time when women were not allowed to vote. Emily was married to Washington, who became critically ill shortly after construction began. Emily delivered his daily instructions to the construction site, and over the next decade or so became highly knowledgeable about bridge specifications and construction materials. She subsequently oversaw the successful completion of the project.

Questions
No.15 What made the Brooklyn Bridge such an achievement at the time?
No.16 Why did Emily Roebling become involved in the bridge's construction?

　全文訳　**ブルックリン橋を陰で支えた女性**

　ニューヨーク市のブルックリン橋は，19世紀の偉大な工学的な功績の1つである。それはジョン・ローブリングによって設計され，彼の息子のワシントンが父親の死後に橋の技師長を引き継いだ。橋はマンハッタン島と2キロ近く離れたブルックリンを結ぶために建てられた。初の吊り橋ではなかったが，この種の橋でそれまでこれほど長い距離に架かるものはほかになかった。

　橋の建設の大部分は，エミリー・ローブリングという女性によって監督された。当時は，女性は投票することを認められない時代だった。エミリーはワシントンと結婚していたが，彼は建設が始まった直後に重病になった。エミリーは彼の毎日の指示を建設現場に届け，その後10年ほどの間に橋の仕様や建設資材に関する知識がかなり豊富になった。その後，彼女はプロジェクトの無事完了を見届けた。

No.15 解答 ②

　質問の訳　当時ブルックリン橋がそのような功績とされた理由は何か。
　選択肢の訳　**1**　2つの島を結ぶ初めての橋だった。
　　　　　　2　同種の橋では最も長いものだった。
　　　　　　3　女性によって設計された。
　　　　　　4　初の吊り橋だった。
　解説　While it was not ..., no other bridge of this kind had ever crossed such an enormous distance.「この種の橋でそれまでこれほど長い距離に架かるものはほかになかった」を「最も長い橋だった」と言い換えた**2**が正解。While A, B. の構造ではBに話者の言いたいことがくるため，Whileが聞こえたら短いポーズ（カンマ）の後の内容を集中して聞こう。

No.16 解答 ④

　質問の訳　なぜエミリー・ローブリングは橋の建設に携わったのか。

> 選択肢の訳　1　彼女は橋の建設に精通していた。
> 　　　　　　2　彼女はこの仕事に最も適任だった。
> 　　　　　　3　彼女は夫の父に指名された。
> 　　　　　　4　彼女は夫の代理を務めていた。
> 解説　父から橋の建設の技師長を受け継いだのはワシントンだが，Emily was married to Washington, ... の部分から，ワシントンが重病になったため，妻のエミリーがワシントンの代わりに建設現場を監督したことが分かる。**4**が正解で，her husband はワシントンのこと。

(スクリプト) **Space Rocks**

　One day, a Norwegian man called Jon Larsen noticed a tiny, shiny object on an outdoor table. Because it looked so unusual, he thought it might be a micrometeorite, a small piece of rock from space. After finding more, he asked scientists to analyze them. At the time, most micrometeorites had been found in remote areas such as Antarctica, so many scientists were doubtful about his discovery. One, however, took Larsen seriously. Together, they proved that these micrometeorites are always falling to Earth, and further research has shown that micrometeorites can be found all over the planet.

　Larsen's discovery is significant because micrometeorites can help us understand how our solar system was formed. Because of their great age, they provide hints about what materials were common when the sun was young. Larsen has shown that it is not always experts who help scientists learn new things about our universe.

Questions
No.17 What is one thing we learn about micrometeorites?
No.18 Why is Jon Larsen's discovery important?

全文訳　**隕石**

　ある日，ヨン・ラーセンというノルウェー人男性が，屋外のテーブルにとても小さくて，滑らかな物体があるのに気付いた。それはとても変わった見た目だったので，彼はそれを微小隕石，宇宙から落ちてきた小さな岩片かもしれないと思った。さらに幾つか見つけた後，彼は科学者にそれらを分析するよう依頼した。当時，ほとんどの微小隕石は南極などの遠隔地で発見されていたため，多くの科学者が彼の発見に懐疑的だった。しかし，ラーセンを真剣に受け止めた科学者が1人いた。彼らは協力して，これら微小隕石が常に地球に落下していることを証明し，さらなる研究によって，微小隕石が地球上のあらゆる所で見つかることを示した。

　微小隕石は私たちの太陽系がどのように形成されたかを理解するのに役立つため，ラーセンの発見は重要である。微小隕石は非常に古いため，太陽が若かったときにどのような物質が一般的だったかを知るヒントを提供してくれる。ラーセンは，科学者が私

たちの宇宙について新しいことを知る手助けをするのは必ずしも専門家ではないことを
示した。

No.17 解答 3

質問の訳 微小隕石について分かることの1つは何か。

選択肢の訳 1 もともと考えられていたほど一般的ではない。
2 寒い場所にしか見つからない。
3 地球上のどこにでも見つかる。
4 地球の石よりも硬い場合がある。

解説 微小隕石を発見したラーセンと科学者の研究について，further research has shown that micrometeorites can be found all over the planet と言っている。この all over the planet を anywhere on Earth と言い換えた **3** が正解。

No.18 解答 1

質問の訳 ヨン・ラーセンの発見はなぜ重要なのか。

選択肢の訳 1 私たちの太陽系に関する有益な情報を提供する。
2 新しい物質の発見につながった。
3 ほとんどの微小隕石が予測よりも古いことを示す。
4 太陽の年齢を証明するのに役立った。

解説 Larsen's discovery is significant because ... の because 以下にラーセンの発見が重要な（significant ≒ important）理由が続く。「微小隕石は太陽系がどのように形成されたかを理解するのに役立つ」を「太陽系に関する有益な情報を提供する」と抽象的に表した **1** が正解。

D

スクリプト **Vincenzo Peruggia and the Mona Lisa**

One day in 1911, an Italian man named Vincenzo Peruggia entered the Louvre Museum in Paris and stole the *Mona Lisa*, a painting by the Italian artist Leonardo da Vinci. Later, Peruggia tried to sell the painting to an art dealer in Italy, but the dealer reported him to the police. When Peruggia was arrested, he claimed he wanted to return the painting to its native country. Peruggia mistakenly believed the *Mona Lisa* had once been stolen from Italy.

While police were searching for the *Mona Lisa*, newspapers around the world reported the incident. It was the first time an art piece had received such worldwide media attention. Although it was a well-known painting before being stolen, many people believe it would not be as famous today had it not been for Peruggia.

Questions

No.19 Why did Vincenzo Peruggia say he took the *Mona Lisa*?

20年度第3回　リスニング

No.20 What do some people now believe about the theft?

全文訳　**ビンセンツォ・ペルージャとモナリザ**

　1911 年のある日，ビンセンツォ・ペルージャというイタリア人男性がパリのルーブル美術館に入り，イタリア人画家レオナルド・ダ・ヴィンチの絵画，モナリザを盗んだ。その後，ペルージャはその絵をイタリアの画商に売ろうとしたが，その商人は彼を警察に通報した。逮捕されたとき，ペルージャは絵を母国に返したかったと主張した。ペルージャは，モナリザはかつてイタリアから盗まれたのだと勘違いしていたのである。

　警察がモナリザを捜索している間，世界中の新聞がこの事件を報じた。1 点の美術品がこれほど世界的にメディアの注目を集めたのは初めてのことだった。モナリザは盗まれる前から有名な絵だったが，ペルージャがいなかったら今ほど有名になっていないだろう，と多くの人が信じている。

No.19 解答　③

質問の訳　ビンセンツォ・ペルージャはなぜモナリザを盗んだと言ったか。

選択肢の訳　**1**　彼はそれを盗むために画商に雇われた。
　　2　彼は美術館の警備が貧弱であることを示したかった。
　　3　彼はそれをイタリアに返却するべきだと思った。
　　4　彼はそれを偽造物だと信じていた。

解説　When Peruggia was arrested, he claimed he wanted to return the painting to its native country. の部分から，ペルージャが絵（モナリザ）を母国に返したいと思っていたことが分かる。これが絵を盗んだ理由だと判断して，**3** が正解。

No.20 解答　②

質問の訳　一部の人は今，この盗みについて何を信じているか。

選択肢の訳　**1**　イタリアの評判を傷つけた。
　　2　モナリザの名声レベルを上げた。
　　3　モナリザの価値を下げた。
　　4　イタリアの法律の改正につながった。

解説　Although it was ..., many people believe it would not be as famous today had it not been for Peruggia. に手掛かりがある。Although A, B. の B（話者の言いたいこと）の聞き取りがポイント。「ペルージャがいなかったら今ほど有名になっていないだろう」は「盗みがモナリザを有名にした」と言えるので，**2** が正解。believe 以下は仮定法過去と仮定法過去完了の混合で，had it not been for は「もし～がなかったら」。

E

スクリプト　**Helping Farmers**

　Modern farmers struggle with long working hours and often live in isolated areas. Though these problems are not unique to farming, it can be more difficult for farmers to take time off. Livestock and crops require daily attention, and even simple things, like forgetting to close a gate, can quickly lead to expensive losses. With so many serious issues to consider, simply asking a friend or neighbor to take over for a week or two is not usually possible.

This is where professional farm-sitters can help. With extensive experience and knowledge, professional farm-sitters can look after an entire operation. They can also enjoy the farming experience without having to own a farm. One big challenge, though, is that every farm operates differently. There are also difficult circumstances, like poor weather or disease outbreaks, that can be hard to handle. That is why good, experienced farm-sitters are in high demand.

Questions

No.21 What is one thing the speaker says about farming?

No.22 What is one problem that farm-sitters face?

全文訳 **農家を助ける**

　現代の農家は長時間労働に苦しんでおり，孤立した地域で暮らしているケースが多い。これらの問題は農業に限ったことではないが，農家にとっては休暇を取るのがより困難になり得る。家畜や農作物は毎日手入れが必要で，ゲートを閉め忘れるといった単純なことでさえ，即座に高額な損失につながる可能性がある。考慮すべき重要な問題が非常に多いため，単純に友人や隣人に１〜２週間の代行を頼むことは通常不可能である。

　これこそ，プロのファームシッターが助けになり得るところである。豊富な経験と知識を持つプロのファームシッターは，運営全体の面倒を見ることができる。また，彼らは農場を所有しなくても農業体験を楽しむことができる。とは言え，大きな課題の１つは，農場によって運営方法が異なることである。悪天候や病気の発生など，対処し難いだろう困難な状況もある。そういうわけで，経験豊富で優秀なファームシッターに大きな需要がある。

No.**21** 解答 **①**

質問の訳 話者が農業について言うことの１つは何か。

選択肢の訳　**1**　農家が休暇を取るのは困難になり得る。

　　　　　　2　政府の資金助成が削減されつつある。

　　　　　　3　耕種農業は利益が出なくなっている。

　　　　　　4　動物の飼育は作物の栽培よりも難しい。

解説　冒頭の Modern farmers struggle with ... から，農家の苦悩が話題である。続く Though these problems ..., it can be more difficult for farmers to take time off. の部分から，**1** が正解。difficult と take time off がそれぞれ hard，take vacations に言い換えられている。

257

No.22 解答 ④ ......

質問の訳 ファームシッターが直面している問題の1つは何か。

選択肢の訳 1 農場経営者からの信頼のなさ。
2 求職競争の激しさ。
3 農家に手順を変えるよう説得すること。
4 各農家の運営に慣れること。

解説 sitter はある人の代わりに世話をする人のことで，baby-sitter や pet-sitter のように使われる。幾つか述べられるファームシッターの課題のうち，One big challenge, though, is that every farm operates differently. に「課題は農場によって運営方法が異なること」とあり，これは「各農家の運営に慣れることが大変だ」と言えるので，**4** が正解。

F

スクリプト **Smart Streetlights**

Several cities in the United States are installing "smart" streetlights equipped with sensors and cameras that collect data on pedestrian traffic, automobile traffic, and air quality. This information is shared with smartphone applications so that people can track parking availability, traffic conditions, and air pollution. Companies are also developing streetlights that will be able to communicate with traffic signals to help police, firefighters, and ambulances reach their destinations faster.

Critics, however, worry that the gathering and sharing of all this data will put people's privacy at risk. They also argue that the costly technology is not a good use of limited city funds. In response, the developers say details like license plate numbers and people's faces will be deleted before the data is shared. They also say the streetlights will lower electricity use and, since they can be remotely controlled, will reduce maintenance costs as well.

Questions

No.23 What is one thing companies hope "smart" streetlights will do?

No.24 What is one concern that critics have?

全文訳 **スマート街路灯**

アメリカ合衆国の幾つかの都市では，歩行者の往来や自動車の交通量，大気の質に関するデータを収集するセンサーとカメラを備えた「スマート」街路灯を設置している。人々が駐車場の空き状況や交通状況，大気汚染を追跡できるように，この情報はスマートフォンのアプリで共有される。企業はまた，警察や消防士，救急車がより早く目的地に到着するのに役立つ，信号機と通信できる街路灯も開発している。

しかし，批評家たちは，このようなデータを収集して共有することで，人々のプライバシーが危険にさらされるのではないかと心配している。彼らはまた，高価な技術は限られた市の資金を有効活用していないと主張している。これに対して開発者は，ナンバー

プレートの番号や人々の顔などの詳細はデータが共有される前に消去されると述べる。彼らはまた，この街路灯は電力使用量を削減し，遠隔操作ができるため維持費も削減できると述べる。

No.23 解答 ③

質問の訳 企業が「スマート」街路灯がすることとして期待していることの1つは何か。

選択肢の訳
1 大気の質を改善する。
2 交通事故を減らす。
3 緊急サービスを助ける。
4 歩行者の安全を高める。

解説 "smart" streetlights の詳しい説明の中で，Companies are also developing streetlights that ... の部分から，この開発中の街路灯は警察や消防士，救急車がより早く目的地に到着するのに役立つことが分かる。警察，消防士，救急車を emergency services と表した **3** が正解。

No.24 解答 ②

質問の訳 批評家たちが抱いている懸念の1つは何か。

選択肢の訳
1 必要とされる技術がまだ十分に良くない。
2 この街路灯は人々の個人情報を記録する。
3 遠隔操作が要する電力があまりにも多い。
4 この街路灯は多くの都市に適していない。

解説 スマート街路灯に対する批判的視点として，Critics, however, worry that ... に「データを収集して共有することで，人々のプライバシーが危険にさらされるのではないか」という批評家たちの懸念が述べられており，この部分と **2** が一致する。put ～ at risk は「～を危険にさらす」。

20年度第3回 リスニング

259

一次試験・リスニング Part 3 問題編 p.178〜179　MP3　アプリ　CD 3 49〜54

G
スクリプト

You have 10 seconds to read the situation and Question No. 25.

This is John Goddard from the Languages Department of Larkspur University. I'm calling about scheduling a second interview for the Japanese Language Instructor position. We have your résumé and recent publications on file, but we're still waiting for a letter of recommendation from your former employer. Could you ask them about that? When you get it, please e-mail it to us. Once we have that, we can set up a time for your second interview. If you're offered the position, and you don't have resident status in Canada, we'll need copies of your passport and your work permit, too.

Now mark your answer on your answer sheet.

全訳

こちらはラークスパー大学言語学部のジョン・ゴダードです。日本語講師の職の二次面接のスケジューリングについて電話をしています。あなたの履歴書と最近の出版物は保管していますが，前職の雇用主からの推薦状をまだ待っています。それについて彼らに尋ねていただけますか。入手されたらそれを当大学にメールで送ってください。それをいただいたら，二次面接の時期が設定できます。もし採用が決定して，カナダの在住資格をお持ちでない場合は，パスポートと労働許可証のコピーも必要になります。

No.25 解答 ②

状況の訳　あなたはカナダの大学での教職の一次面接の後，次のような音声メッセージを受け取る。あなたはカナダの合法的居住者である。

質問の訳　あなたはまず何をすべきか。

選択肢の訳
1　パスポートのコピーを送る。
2　以前の雇用主に連絡を取る。
3　二次面接の予定を決める。
4　最近の出版物のコピーを送る。

解説　問題用紙の「状況」と冒頭の内容から，一次面接を通過して二次面接に進む段階にあることを理解しよう。前職の雇用主からの推薦状がまだ来ていないと言ったあと，Could you ask them about that? と依頼している。them は前職の雇用主で，that は推薦状を提出すること。よって，「あなた」がまずすることとして，**2**が適切。

260

スクリプト

You have 10 seconds to read the situation and Question No. 26.

SuperBuzz guarantees our prices are the best, in-store and online! Shop from Monday to Wednesday for big discounts on all computers and software. On Thursday and Friday, we're offering special discounts on computer accessories like scanners and printers. Over the weekend, save big on entertainment electronics like surround-sound speakers and high-resolution TVs. Also, be sure to check our advertisements in your local newspaper or our website for coupons with discounts on heaters, air conditioners, and vacuum cleaners. You can also download our smartphone application for huge savings this week on home entertainment systems.

Now mark your answer on your answer sheet.

全文訳

スーパーバズでは実店舗でもオンラインでも最良価格を保証します！ 月曜日から水曜日は，全てのコンピューターおよびソフトウエアを大幅に値引きします。木曜日と金曜日は，スキャナーやプリンターなどのコンピューター付属品の特別割引をします。週末は，サラウンドスピーカーや高解像度テレビなどの娯楽機器をお買い上げいただき大いに節約してください。また，暖房機やエアコン，掃除機の割引クーポンについては，地元紙の広告または当店のウェブサイトを確認してください。さらに当店のスマホアプリをダウンロードしていただくと，今週，家庭用娯楽システムが大変お得になります。

No.26 解答

状況の訳　あなたは次のようなスーパーバズ電気店の宣伝を聞く。あなたは自宅の仕事部屋用に新しいプリンターが必要で，最もお得なものを望んでいる。

質問の訳　あなたは何をすべきか。

選択肢の訳
1　木曜日か金曜日に購入する。
2　週末まで待つ。
3　店のスマホアプリをダウンロードする。
4　新聞のクーポンを持参する。

解説　状況から，家庭用プリンターを安く買いたいことを押さえる。まず月曜日から水曜日はプリンターと無関係なので聞き流す。次に木曜日と金曜日は，スキャナーやプリンターなどのコンピューター付属品が特別割引になると言っているので，**1**が正解。On Thursday and Friday のところで printer が安くなると理解して聞き進め，最後のスマホアプリは娯楽システムがお得になるものの話なので，**3**も不適だと確認し確定する。

I

[スクリプト]

You have 10 seconds to read the situation and Question No. 27.

Hi, honey. I just heard the forecast. They're predicting heavy snow and wind tonight. Your car's tires aren't suitable for that kind of weather. We should've put snow tires on last weekend. I called our usual shop and they're busy but said they can put on new tires tomorrow. I know canceling the conference isn't an option since you're the main presenter, so please take my four-wheel drive. I can manage without it while you're away. We should also eventually buy chains, since winter will just get worse from here. Take care!

Now mark your answer on your answer sheet.

[全文訳]

もしもし。今，天気予報を聞いたところだ。今夜は大雪と強風の予報が出ている。君の車のタイヤはそんな天候に適していない。先週末にスノータイヤを履かせるべきだったね。いつもの店に電話をしたら，忙しいけど明日，新しいタイヤを付けてくれると言ってた。君はメインの講演者だから会議をキャンセルするという選択肢がないことは分かっているから，僕の四輪駆動車に乗ってくれ。君がいない間僕はそれがなくても何とかやっていけるから。これから冬はさらにひどくなるから最終的にはチェーンも買った方がいいね。じゃあ気を付けてね！

No.27 解答 ②

[状況の訳] 今日，あなたは2日間の会議のため近隣の都市に車で行く必要がある。夫があなたの携帯電話に音声メッセージを残した。あなたは2時間以内に出発しなければならない。

[質問の訳] あなたは何をすべきか。

[選択肢の訳]
1 スノータイヤを履かせてもらう。
2 夫の車を借りる。
3 今夜チェーンを買う。
4 出席を取り消す。

[解説] 夫はメッセージの中で，今夜，大雪になること，「あなた」(妻) の車が適していないことを伝えた後，..., so please take my four-wheel drive と言う。この提案を受け入れると考えて，**2** が正解。スノータイヤの装着とチェーンの購入は，状況の「2時間以内に出発しなければならない」という条件に合わない。

J

[スクリプト]

You have 10 seconds to read the situation and Question No. 28.

I've been working on the timeline for establishing the Japan branch office. It needs to be up and running by April. It's October now, so moving there by the start of the year would be best, which means passing your current clients to coworkers so you can start building connections in Japan. However, that would leave us with nobody in your position here. That being the case, your priority right now should be selecting and training your replacement. Client introductions with your replacement will help ease him or her into taking over.

Now mark your answer on your answer sheet.

全文訳

私は日本支社設立のスケジュールを立てています。4月までに立ち上げて稼働していなければなりません。今,10月なので,年明けまでにそこへ移るのが最善でしょう。つまり,日本で人脈を築き始められるよう,今のあなたの顧客を同僚に引き継ぐということです。しかし,それだとここでのあなたの職位に誰もいなくなってしまいます。そういう事情から,現時点であなたが優先すべきことは,あなたの後任者を選んで育成することです。後任者と顧客を引き合わせることで後任者は安心して引き継げるでしょう。

No.28 解答

状況の訳 あなたは会社の新しい日本支社を率いることになっている。社長があなたに次のように言う。

質問の訳 あなたはまず何をすべきか。

選択肢の訳
1 同僚に今の自分の仕事を引き継ぐよう頼む。
2 日本での新顧客を探し始める。
3 会社を離れることを顧客に知らせる。
4 自分の職位にふさわしい人物を特定する。

解説 状況から「日本支社を率いる」という状況を把握する。社長は前半で幾つか指示を述べるが,まずすべきことは,However 以降の優先事項(your priority right now should be selecting and training your replacement)だと判断して,**4** が正解。replacement「後任者」を選択肢では「職位にふさわしい人物」と表している。

スクリプト

You have 10 seconds to read the situation and Question No. 29.

Good morning. Here's your ID badge and parking permit. Your boss, Ms. Rodriguez, is away on business and won't be available until tomorrow. So, you can give me the paperwork we asked you to fill out last week. If you have any questions about those forms, I can help with anything regarding your contract or health insurance. You can ask Stephanie in Accounting about anything related to pay, tax deductions, and so on. I need everything before you leave today, so prioritize that. After that, Julia can answer any questions about your office, but it should be ready for you.

Now mark your answer on your answer sheet.

全文訳

　おはようございます。こちらがあなたのIDバッジと駐車許可証です。あなたの上司であるロドリゲスさんは出張中で，明日まで不在です。ですから，先週記入するようあなたにお願いした書類を私に渡してください。それらの記入用紙について質問があれば，契約や健康保険については私がお手伝いできます。給料や課税控除などに関連することは経理部のステファニーに聞いてください。今日あなたが退社するまでに私は全ての書類が必要なので，それを優先してください。その後，ジュリアがあなたのオフィスに関する質問に答えられますが，それはもう準備ができているでしょう。

No.29 解答 ③

状況の訳　今日は新しい仕事の初日である。あなたは記入しなければならない納税申告書について質問がある。支店長があなたに次のように言う。

質問の訳　あなたはまず何をすべきか。

選択肢の訳　**1**　ロドリゲスさんに連絡を取る。
　　　　　　　2　支店長にIDを依頼する。
　　　　　　　3　ステファニーと話す。
　　　　　　　4　ジュリアに会ってオフィスをもらうことについて話す。

解説　状況と，異なる人物が含まれる選択肢を見て，「納税申告書の記入は誰が助けてくれるか」が聞き取りのポイントだと推測できるとよい。You can ask Stephanie ... related to pay, tax deductions から，tax forms についての質問はステファニーに聞けばよく，書類全部が今日中に必要でそれを prioritize するようにとも言っているので，**3** が正解。ただし，ここでは「まず何をすべきか」が問われているので，ほかに納税申告書を記入するために先にしなければならないことについてなど何か言わないか最後まで聞いてから判断するようにしよう。

二次試験・面接 | 問題カード **A** 日程 | 問題編 p.180 ～ 181 | ▶MP3 ▶アプリ ▶CD 4 46～50

解答例 **One day, a couple was working on their flower farm.** It was a big farm and there was a river nearby. However, the leaves of the flowers had been eaten by bugs. The couple looked shocked, and the husband said that they couldn't sell the damaged flowers. The next day, the couple was looking at their computer. They found an advertisement for ABC Bug Spray that said it could make flowers healthy. There was a picture of a farmer using the bug spray, and the husband looked interested. A month later, the couple was putting flowers onto their small truck. All of the flowers looked very healthy because the couple had bought the bug spray and used it to kill the bugs. The couple looked very happy. Six months later, the woman was at home reading a newspaper. An article said that chemicals were polluting local rivers.

解答例の訳 ある日，夫婦が自分たちの花畑で作業をしていました。それは大きな畑で，近くに川がありました。しかし，花の葉が虫に食べられていました。夫婦はショックを受けた様子で，夫は，傷んだ花を売ることはできないと言いました。翌日，夫婦はコンピューターを見ていました。彼らは，花を健康にすることができると書かれた ABC 虫よけスプレーの広告を見つけました。虫よけスプレーを使っている農夫の写真があり，夫は興味がある様子でした。1 カ月後，夫婦は自分たちの小さなトラックに花を載せていました。夫婦は虫よけスプレーを買い，それを使って虫を殺したため，花は全てとても健康そうに見えました。夫婦はとてもうれしそうな様子でした。半年後，女性は自宅にいて新聞を読んでいました。ある記事には，化学物質が地元の川を汚染していると書かれていました。

解説 解答に含めるべき点は以下の 4 つ。①夫婦が花畑で作業をしていて，夫が「これら（の花）は売れない」と言っている，②翌日，夫婦がパソコンで「ABC 虫よけスプレー　健康的な花のために！」という広告を見ている，③1 カ月後，夫婦は花をトラックに載せている，④半年後，妻が「化学物質が地元の川を汚染している」と書かれた新聞記事を読んでいる。3 コマ目に傷んだ葉に×が書かれた吹き出しがあることから，2 コマ目の後に夫婦が「ABC 虫よけスプレー」を購入し，花が健康になったという過程を補うことがポイント。4 コマ目で川の汚染の話が出てくるため，1 コマ目の描写で花畑近くの川に言及するとより良いだろう。

20年度第3回　面接

265

No. 1

解答例 I'd be thinking that we can't be sure it's our farm that has caused the problem. The chemicals could be from factories along the river, but maybe we should think about not using so much spray.

解説 質問は「4番目の絵を見てください。もしあなたがこの女性なら，どのようなことを考えているでしょうか」。解答例は「問題（＝川の汚染）が自分たちのせいか分からないが，虫よけスプレーをたくさん使わないようにすべきかもしれない」という考え。ほかには「スプレーとは別の花を健康にする方法を探すべきかもしれない」という意見も可能。

No. 2

解答例 I don't think so. Many people want to eat food that is very easy to prepare, like instant noodles. People know that such foods have many chemicals in them, but they care more about convenience than their health.

解説 質問は「人々は食べ物に使われている化学物質の量について心配し過ぎだと思いますか」。解答例は No の立場で，「人々は健康よりも化学物質を多く含む食品の利便性を重視している」という意見。Yes の立場では逆に，健康を気遣う人や環境保護に関心がある人が増えているためオーガニック食品が人気を高めているという点を根拠にできるだろう。

No. 3

解答例 No. The population in the country is declining year by year, so construction companies shouldn't build new houses and apartment buildings there. The land should be protected to make sure people have enough to eat.

解説 質問は「都市開発のために農地を利用するのは良い考えですか」。質問では Japan とは言っていないが，日本を基準に答えてよいだろう。解答例は No の立場で，shouldn't と should を用いて，「国の人口が減っているため農地に家やアパートを建てるべきではない」「人々を養えるように土地を保護するべき」という意見を述べている。

No. 4

解答例 Yes. There are many stories in the media about companies that treat their staff badly. For example, forcing them to work overtime. Showing how products are made can help consumers choose good companies.

解説 「企業は自社製品がどう作られているかを示すよう求められるべきですか」という質問。解答例は Yes の立場で，従業員がひどい扱いを受けているという内容に言及した後，For example を用いて残業の例を示し，「消費者が良い企業を選ぶのに役立つ」という製造過程を示す利点を述べている。

二次試験・面接 | 問題カード **B** 日程 | 問題編 p.182～183 | 🔊 | ▶MP3 ▶アプリ ▶CD 4 **51**～**54**

解答例 **One day, a couple was at their café.** Their café looked quite old and was empty except for two customers. The husband was talking to his wife at the counter and said that they should renovate their shop to attract more customers. His wife was thinking about it. That evening, the couple was at home watching TV with their pets. The woman was drinking tea, and while looking at her dog, she got an idea. A few months later, the couple had reopened their café as the ABC Animal Café. There were many customers in the café, including families. The couple was happy that they had attracted so many customers. The next week, somebody left some puppies in a box outside the shop and ran away. The husband found the puppies and looked shocked because it had happened again. His wife was looking at the puppies.

解答例の訳 ある日，夫婦が自分たちのカフェにいました。彼らのカフェはかなり古い様子で，2人の客以外は誰もいませんでした。夫はカウンターで妻と話しており，もっと多くの客を引き付けるために店を改装すべきだと言いました。妻はそれについて考えていました。その晩，夫婦は自宅にいてペットと一緒にテレビを見ていました。女性はお茶を飲んでおり，飼い犬を見ながらある考えが思い付きました。数カ月後，夫婦はABC動物カフェとしてカフェを再開していました。カフェには家族連れも含めてたくさんの客がいました。夫婦はこれほど多くの客を引き付けることができたことを喜んでいました。翌週，誰かが店の外に箱の中に入った数匹の子犬を残して逃げ去りました。夫はその子犬を見つけて，再び起こったためにショックを受けた様子でした。妻はその子犬を見ていました。

解説 解答に含めるべき点は，以下の4つ。①客が2人しかいないカフェで夫婦が働いている。夫が「店を改装すべきだ」と言っている，②その晩，夫婦はテレビを見ていて，妻は飼い犬を見て何かを思い付いた様子，③数カ月後，「ABC動物カフェ」という店名で，多くの客でにぎわっている，④翌週，店の外に子犬が捨てられており，夫が「まただ！」と言っている。1コマ目と3コマ目の違いに着目し，夫は客を増やすために改装すべきだと言っていることを理解しよう。また，3コマ目では店内に犬猫がいることから，There were many customers who enjoy interacting with animals in the café. などと描写してもよいだろう。

20年度第3回　面接

267

No. 1

解答例 I'd be thinking, "It's good that changing our café into an animal café has helped our business, but we can't take care of all of these dogs. We have to think of some way to save these poor animals."

解説 質問は「4番目の絵を見てください。もしあなたがこの女性なら，どのようなことを考えているでしょうか」。解答例は「店の営業的には良いが，可哀想な動物を救う方法を考えなければならない」という考え。We shouldn't have changed ...「変えるべきではなかった」などの後悔の気持ちや，We never imagined anyone would abandon animals like this.「このように動物を捨てる人がいるとは思わなかった」のような考えも可能。

No. 2

解答例 No. I think that some people just want to have a pet because they're cute. Maybe people should take courses to learn how much attention pets need, and then they can be allowed to have one.

解説 質問は「人々はペットを所有する責任を理解していると思いますか」。解答例は No の立場で，可愛いというだけでペットを飼う人に言及することで責任感が薄いことを示し，「ペットにどれだけ世話が必要かを学ぶ講座を受けたら飼う許可が得られるようにすべき」という具体策を提案。

No. 3

解答例 Yes. We often hear that the population in Japan is decreasing very quickly. The government says that it wants to help people start families, but people should be free to choose whether or not they want to do so.

解説 「社会は人々に子供を持つよう圧力をかけ過ぎていますか」という質問。解答例は Yes の立場で，政府の少子化対策に言及しつつも，but を用いて「人々は子供を持ちたいかどうかを自由に選べるべきだ」と述べている。No の立場としては逆に，少子化の問題点を挙げ，政府による対策の必要性を論じることができるだろう。

No. 4

解答例 Yes. Recently, many communities are having safety problems with wild animals. Hunting can help keep pets and farm animals safe from dangerous animals. Also, it can help to stop animals from eating crops.

解説 質問は「動物の狩猟は今日の社会で受け入れられますか」。解答例は Yes の立場で，野生動物に関する安全性の問題という観点を取り上げた上，狩猟の意義として，「ペットや家畜を危険な動物から守るのに役立つ」「動物が作物を食べるのを防ぐのに役立つ」と説明している。No の立場では，動物の権利や保護の視点で意見を述べることが可能であろう。

MEMO

英検受験の後は 旺文社の
英検® 一次試験 解答速報サービス

PC・スマホからカンタンに自動採点！

- ウェブから解答を入力するだけで，リーディング・リスニングを自動採点
- ライティング（英作文）は観点別の自己採点ができます

大問別の正答率も一瞬でわかる！

- 問題ごとの○×だけでなく，技能ごと・大問ごとの正答率も自動で計算されます

英検® 一次試験 解答速報サービス
https://eiken.obunsha.co.jp/sokuhou/

※本サービスは従来型の英検1級～5級に対応しています
※本サービスは予告なく変更，終了することがあります

旺文社の英検®合格ナビゲーター　https://eiken.obunsha.co.jp/

英検合格を目指す方には英検®合格ナビゲーターがオススメ！
英検試験情報や級別学習法，オススメの英検書を紹介しています。

［2023年度版 英検準1級 過去6回全問題集・別冊］　　　　　　　　　　　　　　S2n062